How to Make Your Money Last

TURN YOUR RETIREMENT SAVINGS INTO A STEADY PAYCHECK FOR LIFE

Jane Bryant Quinn

RODALE.

Portions of this book were previously published in *Making the Most of Your Money Now* (Simon & Schuster) and *How to Make Your Money Last* (Simon & Schuster).

© 2016 by Quinn Works and 1991, 1997, 2009 by Berrybrook Publishing, Inc.

Printed in the United States of America

Rodale Inc. makes every effort to use acid-free ∞, recycled paper ♻.

Library of Congress Cataloging-in-Publication Data

ISBN 978–1–62336–835–7   Direct Mail hardcover

2 4 6 8 10 9 7 5 3 1   Direct Mail hardcover

We inspire health, healing, happiness, and love in the world.
Starting with you.

To all my grandchildren—
the next generation coming up

Hallee, Elias, Dana, Jesse, Tyler,
Maisy, Hudson, Kai, Riley, and Juno

Contents

Introduction

I started this book because my head was popping with questions about the life phase we call "retirement." After decades of working, we're finally free—but free to do what? A whole generation is reinventing itself as it moves away from the role of earner toward the new status of "engaged and interested citizen, retired."

As we gradually find our footing, we're also trying to find a way of paying for it. None of us knows how many years we have ahead—20? 30? More? This year, my family celebrated my mother's 101st birthday. (She's sharp and happy, thank you for asking!)

Centenarians are rare but our lengthening life expectancies continue to surprise us all. On average, you'll reach your mid- to late-80s. The 90-plus population has tripled over the past three decades. We have every reason to worry that our money will run out before we do. Many of us are staying on the job well past traditional retirement age, not just because we like the work but because we need our salaries, too.

The way you look at your finances changes as you move from preretirement to your postretirement years. While you're still working, you focus on accumulating a satisfactory pile. You might have a dollar target in mind. More likely, you're saving whatever you can, aiming every year for "more." You're paying down debt (I hope) and focusing on investments that can make your money grow.

That flips when you enter retirement's door. Suddenly, you have to take the money you've saved and turn it into a reliable income for life. How large will that income be?

In a perfect world, you'll work on this question well before you leave your job. The answer will tell you when (and whether) you can afford to quit. In this imperfect world, however, you might be pushed into retirement unexpectedly. You'll need to figure out, pronto, how to manage with what you already have. Modest spenders can live on Social Security and, if they're lucky, a pension, dividends, and interest. You might pick up some extra income from a temporary or part-time job.

Often, however, that's not enough to pay the bills. You'll have to supplement your income with regular withdrawals from your savings and investments. These withdrawals amount to "homemade paychecks," landing in your bank account just the way your working paychecks did. If you're married, the paychecks have to cover the cost of two life spans as well as any emergency need for cash. What kind of standard of living can you afford? Will you have to keep working? And how do you stretch your savings to make the money last?

When I started asking those questions for myself, I looked around for information. There isn't much. I found books and websites on how to invest but practically nothing on how to prudently parcel your money out. If you take too little from savings, you're depriving yourself of some of the comforts that you worked for. If you take too much, you'll go broke.

I did find plenty of bad advice from financial firms and their salespeople (a.k.a. "advisers," "financial consultants," and brokerage firm "vice presidents"). I was shocked when I looked at the menu of so-called "safe" and "guaranteed" investments we're being offered. They're loaded with hidden costs and risks. Maybe the firms are unscrupulous, maybe just careless. Either way, people like us—with savings that we need to both hoard and spend—are walking around with targets on our backs. We're where the money is and, believe me, they're coming for it, or trying to.

Fortunately, important and objective research is currently being done on ways of creating reliable incomes for life. I've spoken to the key players and gathered their findings here. What surprised me—really surprised me—is how simple a retirement income plan can be. So simple that you can manage the investments and withdrawals yourself. If you'd rather not, I found several new sources of high-level help at rock-bottom costs. You don't have to pay big commissions and fees to get good advice.

I also learned a lot by talking with practically everyone I met about the retirement decisions they're making for themselves. Often, they were leaving money on the table because they hadn't heard about their alternatives. Social Security topped this list. I found people taking it at age 62—not because they had to but because it was there. They had no idea how much their monthly benefit would increase if they waited a few years to collect. If you're married and each of you has a Social Security account, you might be able to adjust your claiming dates to collect even more.

Then there's the question of what percentage of your retirement savings to put into stocks (or, rather, stock-owning mutual funds—the best bet for you and me). Some savers were so spooked by the near collapse of the financial system in 2007 and 2008 that they now invest only in bonds and insured certificates of deposit. But even if you can live on today's low fixed-interest rates, what will that income be worth in purchasing power as the years go by?

There's a lot of research linking the percentage you hold in stocks to the size of the sustainable income you can withdraw from your savings for life. Having read it, I've come to think of retirement as being split in half. For the first half—the near-term 10 years or so—holding safe or low-risk CDs or bond mutual funds makes a lot of sense. You need a reliable source of money in case stock prices decline. But to fund the second half of retirement—starting 10 or 12 years from now—you'll need to own investments that grow. American and international business, as a whole, has succeeded wonderfully over time (with occasional hiccups). We can share in that growth without breaking a sweat by buying and holding just two or three well-diversified stock-owning mutual funds. When you do this, you'll still be an "income investor." Future capital gains create spendable income just as interest and dividends do.

For prudent cash withdrawals from your retirement savings, the standard advice has been to take 4 percent of the total in the first year and add an increment for inflation in each subsequent year. But 4 percent is too much if you own only bonds and CDs. And it's perhaps too little when part of your money is invested for growth. You don't have to make a wild guess about how much of your savings you can afford to spend. There are recipes. Who knew?

While working on this book I changed my mind about a few things. For example, I developed a new respect for immediate-pay annuities that convert a lump sum of savings into an income for life. They offer a higher monthly income than you can prudently withdraw from investments that you manage yourself. (Don't confuse "immediate-pay" with the variable annuities that promise lifetime benefits. "Lifetime benefit" annuities are on my "no" list due to high costs and misleading sales. It's all explained in Chapter 6.)

Another example—I learned a new use for reverse mortgages. These loans against home equity are often a poor deal for people in later age, especially for those who have almost run out of cash. But if you take the loan earlier, in the form of a credit line, you can use it to increase the size of your monthly income. The credit line grows every year, which gives you a nice hedge against potential inflation.

A homemade paycheck isn't intended to cover everything. You need it only to fill the gap between your retirement expenses and your other sources of income, such as Social Security, pension, rents, part-time work, and whatever. Figuring out that gap is the entryway to retirement planning. Don't feel bad if you have to trim your expenses so as not to take too much from your savings every year. Almost everybody trims whether they confess it or not. Peace of mind is finding a way of life that works.

Every personal situation is a little different. Some people focus their plans on retiring at a certain age—anywhere from 45 to "never." Some get a buyout offer at 55 and wonder whether they can afford to take it. Some are pushed into retirement unexpectedly, through illness or job loss, and find that money is short. Some have retired already and need a clearer look (or a second opinion) on how to handle their money now. I've ranged over all the major financial questions I can think of, including health and life insurance. Inevitably, products and options will change in the future but, in my reporting, I sought general principles that will stand the test of time.

The biggest thing I learned, after digging into this subject for a couple of years, is the significance of our sense of self as we approach or enter this change of life. We need to find a new way of being—a fresh identity, different passions and pastimes, and a deeper involvement with family, community, and friends. We're not on the shelf (yet!). We have lots to contribute and the time to find our place. What gives us this freedom of mind and action is having an income that we're sure will last for life. This book was written to help you build it. After that, adventure calls.

Jane Bryant Quinn
New York City

1

The Joy and Challenge of Life After Work

Now that you can do whatever you want, what do you want to do?

Retirement challenges us like nothing else. We have to reinvent our lives. One day we're part of the vast American workforce—living by the clock, attacking new projects, and focusing our minds and skills. The next day we can sleep until noon if it pleases us. Then we bound out of bed, free at last, ready for coffee and lunch and . . . what?

Successful retirement—whenever it occurs—turns out to be work of another kind. The future is almost as blank a slate as it was when you were 18 and wondering what was going to happen to you. Fifty years later, you're fortified with knowledge and experience but with no place to take it. You might have a partner in life, children, grandchildren, status in your community, and a dog that loves you. Still, you have seven days a week and 52 weeks a year to fill. No sane human being can watch that much television or play that much golf. Maybe you'll be able to stay at work well past normal retirement age. Even so, you might shorten your hours. The last day of work can't be held off forever. You need an action plan to transition into this new phase of your life.

You also need a financial plan to make the most of the income and savings that you have available. That's what most of this book is about. "Money can't buy happiness," they say, but it sure can buy food, shelter, heat, phone service, streaming movies on TV, and gas for the car. A little extra buys plane tickets, ball games, concerts, and long-term peace of mind. It's hard to be happy if you're always worried about the bills. Learning how to stretch your available income and rightsize your life are the first steps toward retiring well. Even if retirement seems far away, steps you take now—to save and invest—can greatly improve your standard of living when your paycheck eventually stops.

But before I talk money, I'd like to talk about the nonfinancial challenges of life after full-time work. They're huge and, for most people, unexpected. We fling ourselves into leisure as if a grand vacation lay ahead. But permanent vacations can get pretty boring. When we were working, we had a sense of accomplishment and a place in the world, even if—at the end—we couldn't wait to quit. Now, having shut that door, we need another place. What are we retiring *to*?

Eventually, when you look back on your transition from work to retirement, you'll think of it as perhaps the most creative period of your life. Most of us still need an active sense of social worth. But instead of getting it from a workplace, ready-made, we have to make it ourselves. The challenge is to discover new interests, new places, and new friends. Your weeks should fill up again with projects, meetings, entertainments, and events—activities you chose yourself, to gladden your days and give purpose to your life. You'll probably take on these projects at a leisurely pace. I'm not suggesting that you'll want to be busy all the time. But neither will you want to look at a daily calendar that's blank.

It takes time to move from the worker role to the role of engaged, individual citizen. How long the transition takes will depend on your personal initiative and will. The faster you can bury the old "work-place you" and rise to a new "liberated you," the more content you're going to be.

Not everyone moves into retirement willingly. You might lose your job and spend some unhappy weeks or months rehashing that stressful time. Your health (or your spouse's health) might be dicey, which, for now, completely occupies your mind. The departure from work might have been so sudden that you had no time to prepare emotionally.

Widows, widowers, and the divorced face similar problems. They've been forcibly "retired" from married life and now face their own blank slate.

No matter how you get there, you (and your partner, if you have one) will have to figure out how to build another life. The questions will be the same for everyone.

Who are you, anyway?

For so much of our lives, we identify ourselves with our jobs. "I'm a lawyer." "I'm a teacher." "I'm an operations manager." "I work for IBM." Those who have young children might also say "I'm a mother" or "I'm a father." Our jobs and family responsibilities give us status and meaning. When we quit, or the children grow up, there's an instant loss of status that few of us are truly prepared for. We're in a new role—that of citizen-retiree. It's an empty vessel until we fill it up.

What are you going to do with the rest of your life?

A 3G retirement (golf, gossip, and grandchildren) isn't al-ways enough, cute as the grandchildren are. Most retirees today are vigorous, mentally alert, and eager to jump into something active and interesting. We have skills, smarts, and dreams. At work, we were accomplishing stuff, even if we got tired of it. As parents, we had the critical job of raising responsible adults. But what are we accomplishing now? Loss of meaning and purpose throws some retirees into depression, even those who thought they couldn't wait to start a leisured life. If you spend your hours in front of a TV set, you're likely to—quite literally—bore yourself to death. You'll need all your imagination and energy to discover a new role.

Where will you find friends?

When you worked, you made social contact simply by doing your job every day. You had people to chat with or complain about, customers to call on, and lunches with colleagues. When your job ends, however, your workaday friends are likely to fall away. You need to get out of the house and do things, not just for fun and intellectual interest but for the social companionship, too. Women are better at this than men but it can be a challenge for both.

THE FIVE STAGES OF RETIREMENT

The gerontology researcher Robert Atchley studied the transition from working life to leisure. Retirement, he says, is a process, not an event. Some people hustle through the stages. Others take months, even years, to reach serenity. The better you manage the first stage, the faster your progress is likely to be.

Stage 1: Preretirement. You gradually disengage from work. You're still doing your job but your imagination moves ahead. You talk with friends about their own plans for life after work and ask retired friends what they're up to now. You put together a budget to see if, and when, you can afford to leave your paycheck behind. If you're married, you have many talks with your spouse about how you each expect retirement to work—your hopes and fears, where you'll live, what you'll do with your time, whether you'll both retire at the same time and, if not, what the expectations will be. You think about what you might do next. If you hope for part-time work, now's the time to start making the contacts. There might be a project you can do for your current employer or others in your business. If you're being laid off, do your best to think about your next life, not your past one. You're not "unemployed" (bad place), you're "semiretired" (better place). Forward is your only choice.

Stage 2: The Honeymoon. You're free! No more deadlines or office stress. You'll do some of the things you've been meaning to get to— clean the closets, paint the porch, take a trip. If you already have a lot of interests, you might step up your engagement with them. If you've led a high-pressure work life, you might simply rest with your feet up, read, go fishing, take walks, or watch ball games. Assuming that your retirement was planned, you're happy, happy, happy with your decision. Your honeymoon can last for many months, provided that you're moving quickly toward your other interests. But it might last only a week or two if you have nothing to do and nowhere to go.

Stage 3: Disenchantment. Gradually, your days come to seem a little bit empty. You feel a loss of status, if you identified strongly with your job. To the younger, working world, you're obsolete. Even if you retired gladly, your new activities might not be as fulfilling as you'd hoped. You see fewer people and feel more isolated, especially if your spouse or partner is still working. You might notice that money is going out the door faster than you planned.

If you retired specifically to do something else, such as starting a business or taking up teaching, you might skip Stage 3 or pass through it pretty quickly. Ditto if you're an outgoing person who loves discovering new things. If not, disenchantment might catch you by surprise and slow down your adjustment. You're not so eager to get out of bed and can't figure out how to spend your afternoons.

You join a club or half try to volunteer for a local organization but it doesn't work out. If your health is poor you might come to feel that your life is effectively over. You're just taking up space. For some, Stage 3 might last a year or more while you obsess over what you "used to be."

Stage 4: Reorientation. It dawns on you how bored (and boring) you've become. Emotionally, you're finally ready to advance. Some retirees will go back to work. For the rest, it's like retiring all over again but with a more realistic eye. You take stock of your income and expenses and rightsize your life financially. You evaluate your experiments with new activities and start to engage more deeply with the one that interests you the most. One is all you need; others will come along. Your lingering work-life persona is finally being put to bed. You feel yourself growing into your new role.

Stage 5: Stability. You've got it together. You're finding new purpose and feeling productive again. You're happy (or at least satisfied) with your life and are living within your means. Along with new interests, you've discovered ordinary pleasures, such as browsing in a library or taking walks. Some retirees get to this stage pretty quickly—in fact, directly from the honeymoon. Others take years. You'll know you've arrived when all your thoughts are forward-looking and your days are full.

MAKE YOUR PLAN: IT'S LIBERATING!

The transition from work to "freedom" is harder than most of us realize until we get there. It starts with clearing the old stuff out of your head—your work, routines, and expectations of status. They get in the way of your life ahead. Post work, you can do anything that's within your budget and physical capabilities.

When your calendar is blank and you're wondering how to fill it, it seems natural to start a list.

You might begin by asking yourself what makes you happy— not only today but what made you happy in the past. It might be something you haven't done for 30 years. Never mind. Write it down. You're trying to capture anything—specific activities, experiences, relationships—that once put a smile on your face.

From there, branch out to everything you've ever thought of doing. No idea is trivial. Maybe you'd like to improve your tennis or golf. Read all of Charles Dickens. Research your family's roots. Get a puppy and train it. Learn woodworking. Take cooking classes. Take dance classes. Join a singing group (or start one). Join a weight-loss group or exercise class. Learn photography, including the art of editing photos digitally. Teach Sunday school. Take music lessons, maybe on an instrument you used to play before you got so busy. Join a bridge group. Join a chess club. Give parties. Learn another language. Walk a long mountain trail. Learn local history. Run for local office or join a political campaign team. Start a website to share your professional expertise. Join an investment club. Get more involved with your church or temple. Start a local newsletter. Coach sandlot baseball. Make pots. Paint (President George W. Bush started painting lessons when he left office). Volunteer for a worthy cause. Start (or join) a protest group. Tie flies for people who fish. Create gardens for yourself and your friends. Become a local tour guide or docent in a regional museum. Make beautiful holiday and birthday cards. Learn computer skills. Sign up for Skype or use the FaceTime app so you can talk to your children and grandchildren long distance, free. Run a charity fund drive. Make jewelry. Become a discount coupon maven. Join a yoga class. Sort the family photos and put them online. Attend local concerts and lectures. Write your autobiography. Have regular dinners with friends. Spend quality time with your spouse or children. Join AmeriCorps, for civic opportunities. Teach English as a second

language. Start a wine-tasting group. Try out for a local amateur theater production or offer to paint scenery. Find a bird-watching pal.
Travel—be it cruises, visits to children, group tours, or day trips to
interesting places near your home. Restore furniture or an old car.
Manage garage sales for neighbors. Etcetera, etcetera, and so forth,
as the king of Siam would say.

You might enjoy going back to school. Some retirees work toward
college or advanced degrees, others audit courses. A school near you
might offer extension courses to adults (check Road Scholar's Life-
long Learning Institute for opportunities). Free or low-fee college
courses are available online: Scroll through the offerings at edX.org,
Coursera.org, Udemy.com, and Udacity.com as well as the online
courses from Harvard, Dartmouth, Yale, Duke, the University of
California, Berkeley, and others (for a long list of what is available,
go to MOOC-list.com). Some courses are live; they require you to
be at your computer at certain hours and to complete assignments
(although not necessarily submit to tests). Others let you listen to
lectures whenever you want.

Finally, make a list of your skills. Are you good with your hands
or with computers? Do you know finance? Can you organize groups?
Create marketing campaigns? Work well with children? You have a
lot to offer your community that it can use. A focus on skills can help
direct you to volunteer groups that would be thrilled to have you.
Business people might join a local SCORE (Service Corps of Retired
Executives), an organization that helps small businesses get started
or expand. Financial people might assist a nonprofit with its books,
investments, and fund drives, or study to be a financial planner with
an emphasis on retirement prep. Those who drive a mean hammer
might volunteer with a local Habitat for Humanity. If you're good
with people, you might become a health or social service aide. A
skills list helps you assess job prospects, too.

You might not find your next life's work immediately—a delay that risks dumping you, grumpily, into the depressive Stage 3. But keep trying things out. One of them will click.

To get yourself moving, set up an engagement calendar—one of those month-at-a-glance hanging calendars or the calendar on your computer. Put something useful or interesting into your schedule every day. It might be work around the house (clean the closets, repair the screens), ordinary errands (shopping, doctor's appointments), community activities (club meetings, volunteer days), hobbies (consult your "makes me happy" list), or personal enrichment (reading, study). You might undertake weekly mini-explorations of nearby towns—to visit a new park, a small museum, a used-book store. It takes as little as one activity, plus normal chores, to structure your day. Something you have to do (or want to do) gets you up in the morning.

Regular activities also have the virtue of bringing you new friends as well as renewing relationships with friends who weren't also business colleagues. As often as possible, your calendar should include things you do with other people rather than things you do alone. If you like playing Scrabble or backgammon find a challenging partner rather than spend hours playing anonymously online. If you like to walk, find a walking partner. Cooks might find a cooking partner.

Have I mentioned exercise? One of the best things you can do for yourself is to join a gym, even if (like me) you've resisted exercise all your life. A vigorous workout greatly improves your general health, appearance, and well-being. It holds down doctor bills, takes off pounds, and keeps your joints and muscles moving. Studies show that if you lower your blood pressure and reduce "bad" cholesterol, you're less likely to suffer dementia in older age. Exercise classes are also great opportunities for socializing. Instead of grumbling about the office you can grumble about your abs.

If you're not yet online, a world awaits you. From your laptop or iPad, you can follow the news, communicate with family and friends, plan a trip, take a free online college course, research any subject that interests you, find answers to medical questions, follow your investments, shop, get book recommendations, nail the bargain plane tickets sold to people who can travel at the last moment, and find a vacation condo to rent for a month. For travel with a purpose, check the opportunities at RoadScholar.org (formerly Elderhostel). An Internet search for "senior travel" turns up organizations such as Senior Cycling and ElderTreks. These and similar groups offer adventurous trips in the United States and abroad—always with a good mattress and bathroom at the end of the day. We're past the age of going "scout."

THE WORLD OF THE SEMIRETIRED

For some, volunteering and leisure time interests aren't nearly enough. You spent your life working and miss the buzz. Doing part-time work or starting a home business is a terrific transition from full-time work to, eventually, full-time leisure. It's also the answer for people who need income to tide themselves over to their Social Security checks.

Some companies hire their own retirees for consulting or project work but don't limit yourself to the sort of thing you did before. People, organizational, communication, or management skills are transferable to many types of businesses. You could be a tour director or take seasonal work at a national park. The health professions are looking for recruits, especially people interested in working with the elderly. Local vocational schools offer short-term training for a wide variety of jobs. Online hiring halls such as Craigslist.com and SeniorJobBank.org list opportunities nearby.

If you're unfamiliar with the Web and social media, take a course. Employers nowadays expect to receive job applications by email. If they're interested, they'll turn to the Web to learn more about you. Older professionals and business people, in particular, should post their resumes and personal profiles on LinkedIn.com. The managers who do the hiring—almost certainly younger than you—will check LinkedIn just to see if you understand modern communications. If you're not on the Web you're invisible.

You might even start your own business. I can't find good numbers on how many retirees do so but a 2009 "recareering" study done by the Urban Institute for AARP gives you a hint. Of people in midlife who retired from their previous jobs and changed careers, about 31 percent say they went from working for other people to working for themselves.

Finding the right business idea takes time. Again, turn to lists. Write down lots of ideas, no matter how far-out they seem. Test them against your interests, abilities, and professional or social contacts, then winnow them down. A high percentage of retirement businesses take advantage of knowledge and connections that the retiree already has.

Many good books have been written about starting and running a small business. You might find a course for entrepreneurs at your local community college or the business school at a nearby university. There you'll learn not only from the teachers but from other business owners who are taking classes, too. Legal, sales tax, bookkeeping, and similar unfamiliar issues become manageable when you talk with people who have solved them.

One warning before you launch: Have a plan B. What will you do if the business doesn't work? You can probably afford to lose a small investment but don't endanger your home or wipe out your retirement savings. Always look ahead to what you'll be doing for the rest of your life.

RETIREMENT FOR TWO

Talk, talk, talk, talk, *talk* to each other. That's what every financial planner tells me that couples need to do when retirement first springs to mind. Single people need to think only about themselves when making plans. Couples, however, are making a dual decision. Are you both ready for retirement? If so, what next? If you both work and one of you isn't ready to quit, how will you handle the relationship? How will a homemaker feel when his or her partner is suddenly home all day?

Spouses or partners often assume that they both see retirement the same way and that's not necessarily so. When they start talking they might be surprised—pleasantly or otherwise—by what the other thinks. For example, a husband might expect his working wife to retire when he does, when in fact she's perfectly happy with her job. A wife at home might think her husband should work a few more years so they can accumulate more savings. Each spouse might have a different dream about where and how to live. One partner might have secretly run up debt that now has to be confessed.

These can be rough conversations if your differences are large. Somehow you need to get to the same page. The quality of your retirement will depend not only on finding new things to do but on developing new ways of living with each other.

Retirement gets simpler when both members of a working couple quit at the same time. You can travel when you want, make daytime social plans, share household chores and projects, or move somewhere else. A vibrant retirement life means keeping each other excited about what's happening every day.

If only one of you retires, however, you need to develop some ground rules. For example, the spouse or partner at home will typically take on more household chores. (When my late husband retired, our son took him into the laundry room and said, "Dad, this is a washing machine.") In return, the spouse at work should try to find more evening and weekend time for things you can do together. Most importantly, the spouse at home shouldn't pressure the working spouse to quit. If you pout long and hard enough, you might get your way but your spouse won't be a happy partner down the road. Why should a wife give up her work to husband-sit (or vice versa)?

As the retired spouse, you should make your own schedule, find your own friends, get your own life, even take your own trips. Eventually, your partner will be ready for leisure, too.

A full-time homemaker is in a different position. She (it's usually a she) has reinvented her life since the day she "retired" as an all-day parent. She might have gone to work full- or part-time or deeply involved herself as a volunteer. Her days have structure—shopping, cleaning, friends, hobbies, meetings, exercise, walking the dog. The last thing she needs is a crabby husband demanding to be entertained or ordering her around the way he ordered subordinates at work. On the other hand, she can't pretend that he isn't there. Talk, talk, talk about it. You're entering this new life together. A husband's free time, shared with his homemaker wife, can help her get out of a rut as well as set new directions for himself.

Not everyone can expect a bouncing, lively retirement life. Your health, or your spouse's or partner's health, might be poor. But even folks with limitations find positive ways to spend their time— connecting with friends, playing cards, learning things on the Internet, taking short day trips.

Whatever your situation, happiness lies in letting go of the past. All that matters now is who you are in the moment. Retirement is an adventure, demanding all of your creativity and force. So keep experimenting. No one but you can invent your new life.

2

Rightsize Your Life

You're never afraid to open your bank statement when you're living within your means.

You've cashed your last paycheck. The jig is up. Whatever assets you've earned or accumulated—Social Security, pension, savings, investments, home equity—are all you've got, now and forever. Can they support you comfortably for the next 25 or 30-plus years? If you think so, are you sure? If not, what are you going to do about it?

The questions are the same if you're still at work. You're covering your expenses now, but what will your budget look like when your work life ends, as eventually it will? Can you afford to retire soon or should you wait? It's time for a financial scan.

Before you start this exercise, take a deep breath. You'll be juggling your personal dreams and priorities as well as your budget. New questions will present themselves, perhaps forcing some changes you hadn't foreseen. If, on your first try, you can't bring your income and expenses into balance, put the numbers aside and tackle them again tomorrow or next week. You'll need time for the pieces to fall into place. And they will. Sooner or later, everyone figures out an acceptable way of living commensurate with income. You won't be turned out, fainting, into the street.

I wish there were some quick rules of thumb for making retirement money decisions. Good rules exist for the young and middle-aged: live on less than you earn, increase the amount of money you save every year, stay out of debt, use tax-favored retirement accounts, and invest for the long term. All the rest is ruffles.

When you leave the workforce, however, universal maxims go out the door. Every person and couple is unique. Your financial choices depend on such things as your health, your age when you left work, whether you're married or single, your spouse's or partner's age and health, whether you have a pension, how good your health insurance is, how much (or little) you've saved, how much planning you've done, whether your retirement was voluntary or forced, whether one of your kids (or a parent) needs financial help, how much debt you're carrying, how you feel about investment risk, whether you can (or want to) work part-time, and how easy (or hard) it is to match your spending to your means.

Managing your spending is key. Nothing matters more to the financial success of your retirement. The stock market isn't going to save you if you're burning through money. You can search for better investments later if you want. But first, pay attention to rightsizing your life.

Rightsizing means finding that happy place where the annual income you expect for the rest of your life matches (or exceeds) your annual cost of living. That's not always easy to do or, if you're a big spender, to accept. But once you've achieved that balance— emotionally as well as materially—you will find yourself at peace. You'll know that you can afford your life.

Some people save enough money, or have large enough pensions, so that their habits don't have to change very much after they retire. But let's face it, that's rare. Most retirees find that their income falls short so they need, at minimum, some nips and tucks. Making cuts is absolutely normal. Your friends are in the same boat even if it's not obvious.

Nipping and tucking might not make your priority list at first. You'd like to maintain your lifestyle, take more trips, and maybe fulfill a dream, such as buying a boat. We all want to live as richly as we can while we still have our health, even if we're dipping a little more into savings than is prudent.

That approach can work fine, for the first year or two, provided that you're spending discretionary money and have an actual plan to cut back—maybe sharply—in your later years. The plan is essential. Otherwise, you're just flying blind.

For a few, rightsizing means a substantial change in the way you live, such as selling your house right now and renting an apartment. That's a tough decision but the numbers don't lie. The sooner you reorganize your life and stop the leakage from your savings accounts, the faster you'll find your way to peace of mind. Life is full of pleasures that don't cost a lot and few pleasures are greater than feeling financially safe.

GETTING TO SAFETY IN FOUR AMAZINGLY LOGICAL STEPS

When preparing for retirement, we tend to focus on a number: "If I have $250,000 (or $100,000, or $70,000, or $1 million) in savings," we say, "I can afford to retire." The number is nice, especially if you reach it, but it's not the point—or not entirely the point. What matters is the amount of annual income that your savings can reasonably provide you with, for life. That dollar amount plus any guaranteed income such as Social Security defines your standard of living. Your task is to fit your spending to whatever money you have.

Assembling a budget will take a little time. You'll need to develop real numbers for your annual expenses, sound estimates of your expected income from savings, and a list—true to your feelings—of your priorities in life. You'll probably be making choices that you haven't faced before. "It was eye-opening," a friend said, who read this book in draft and worked through the planning process herself. "I was able to sit down with my husband and have an unemotional spending conversation based on actual fact."

Here are the four steps to creating a dependable retirement spending plan:

Step 1:   If you haven't retired yet, start by figuring out how much you're spending now (unless you have a black belt in budgeting, you probably don't know). Go back over your checkbooks, bank statements, and credit cards and add up what it cost you to live over the past 12 months. Then subtract the expenses connected with work. That includes such things as commuting costs, lunches, office clothing, take-home dinners because you didn't have time to cook, subscriptions to industry websites and publications, and dues to professional clubs. Subtract the amount you've been contributing to retirement plans, Social Security, and Medicare. Add to your budget whatever it will cost to buy Medicare or private health insurance. If you have credit card debt, add the cost of an accelerated repayment plan.

Those who have already retired should calculate what you're spending currently. You need to find out if it's more than you can afford over the number of years you are likely to live.

Step 2:   List the annual salary-type income you can expect (or are receiving) as a retiree. That includes such things as Social Security, pensions, income from an annuity you currently own, rental income, any royalties, trust income, and so on. Don't count any income from interest and dividends; it's covered under Step 3.

Step 3:   Add up the current value of all your financial assets—savings, retirement accounts, mutual funds, stocks, bonds.[1] Assume that you're going to spend 4 percent of the total on annual living expenses. For example, for every $100,000 you have in savings and investments, you can allocate $4,000 this year toward your bills. At this rate of withdrawal, plus an annual inflation adjustment, your savings could last at least 30 years. (I talk about the 4 percent assumption in Chapter 8. You might not decide on 4 percent, but for budgeting purposes it's a reasonable place to start.) This calculation assumes that interest and dividends are reinvested.

Step 4:   Add the 4 percent from your financial assets to your total salary-type income and subtract an estimate for income taxes. What remains is roughly the amount you can safely spend each year without running out of money. Don't worry about inflation at this point in your budget making. You're looking for a reasonable budget in this year's dollars.

Married couples should do this retirement calculation three ways—once for you as a couple, once for the wife if the husband dies, and once for the husband if the wife dies. After the first death,

---

1   Don't include the value of your home equity or the market value of any real estate investments. Unless you sell or take a reverse mortgage (Chapter 10), your real estate isn't available to pay your daily bills.

the survivor's guaranteed income will decline because he or she will lose one of their two Social Security checks (Chapter 3). The amount the survivor gets from a private pension might drop, too, depending on the choices you make when you leave the job (Chapter 5). There might be a life insurance payout. If so, add it to your financial assets and assume that you'll spend 4 percent of the proceeds.

If your income—as a single, a couple, or a widow or widower—exceeds your expenses, relax. You can spend more, give more to charity, or leave more to your kids. Move ahead to the chapters on ways of tapping your capital comfortably.

If there's a gap between your retirement income and expenses, don't worry. This is the puzzle that everyone eventually solves. The options are clear: Work longer (if you can) and put more money into your retirement fund. Or reduce your expenses to the level of income you have. That's it. You can use up your savings faster but then what happens? (You'd better have a great relationship with your kids.) You can try to raise the return on your investments by taking more market risk. But if your bets fail you'll be in even more trouble.

Even if you're fine as a couple, you should make budgetary changes if your projections show that one of you (typically the wife) would struggle if left alone. Perhaps more life insurance would fill the income gap. Or you could cut expenses now in order to build up more savings for the future. If the chief breadwinner—say, the husband—puts off retirement for a few years, he will not only receive a higher Social Security check, he'll leave his wife a higher survivor's benefit if he dies first.

Sometimes the gap between income and expenses is so large that nips and tucks won't do. If you can't (or don't want to) work longer, the best solution is usually to change the place you live. A house is a money pit, even if there's no mortgage. By slashing those costs and moving to a condo or rental apartment, you'll probably be able to keep up your spending on all the smaller things that give spice to life. If you're already a renter, look for a smaller apartment. You might also sell one of two cars, or sell both cars and rely on buses and taxis. A few adventurous people even go abroad to live.

If you're still deciding whether to retire, try living for a year on the amount of income you'll have when your paycheck stops. If you hate it, you might decide to stay on the job for the next couple of years and save money like mad.

If you have already retired and are spending more than 4 percent of your capital this year, that's a trumpet call. An alarm bell. An elbow in the ribs. The time has come for a serious look at your options.

Married couples—whatever their situation—need to make retirement and spending decisions together. That takes many conversations, not always easy ones. You might each be astonished to learn that you have different views on how and where to live and what you can or cannot do without. One or both of you might be blind to the budget because it challenges your hopes or makes you feel "poor" (even though you're not).

Again, it's time for lists. Each of you should write down the things that are most important to your personal happiness. For example, you might want to stay in your home, move to a condo but stay in your community, move to a warmer place, live near a golf course, live near the kids, keep your club memberships, keep a vacation house, take frequent trips, help your grandchildren, or whatever. Pin down their costs and set them against your expected retirement income. Working with real numbers helps partners face facts, set priorities, and negotiate compromises. Things lower on your lists might not make the cut.

Early on, you don't know how much you're actually going to spend for your retirement life. You have estimates but it takes daily living to prove them out. You might find yourself dipping into savings more than you intended, which means that your budget needs another scrub. Alternatively, you might spend less than you expected, suggesting that you can afford more recreation or a newer car. Keep reassessing the numbers, year by year. They'll tell you what to do.

SEVEN SPECIAL SITUATIONS

Seven items can't be shoehorned neatly into the budget process:

Real estate. There are various ways you can use your home equity to close a gap between your retirement income and expenses. You might take a reverse mortgage with a credit line (Chapter 10). You might sell the house, add the proceeds to your investments, and rent an apartment. You might sell, buy something cheaper, and put the remaining money into investments or cash reserves. Tapping home equity usually isn't part of the first budget conversation but swings into play if your current finances don't add up.

If you're holding real estate as an investment, for income or capital gains, consider how long you'll want to keep it. During your early retirement years, you'll still have the energy to be a landlord. If you have a vacation home, you might even decide to live there for a while and get renters for your larger home. But as time goes by, dealing with tenants and upkeep will get harder. Plan on selling the properties at some point and adding the proceeds to your savings and financial investments. (For real estate investing, see Chapter 9.)

Health care. People on Medicare spend, on average, about $2,000 a year for routine doctor and dental visits and commonplace prescription drugs, according to the Employee Benefit Research Institute. That amount doesn't vary much by age. Routine costs might be higher for people under 65 with high-deductible health insurance plans, and even higher if you have a chronic illness or depend on expensive drugs. But those are known costs. You can budget for them based on the expenses that you're incurring now. Health insurance premiums go into the budget, too. You don't have to worry (much) about paying for an ordinary illness or minor accident as long as your health coverage is good.

What you can't budget for are unexpected and serious illnesses that require long stints of home health care (mostly uninsured) or put you on a lifetime regiment of absurdly high-cost prescription drugs. For these costs, your current savings and investments become your medical reserve.

You can beef up your savings by deciding to spend a little less than 4 percent of your retirement nest egg. That creates a health-care cushion. But remember: In your older age, your discretionary spending will fall, giving you extra dollars to spend on health. For more on the cost of health insurance and choosing coverage, including long-term care insurance, see Chapter 4.

Debt. Debt is a killer for retirees. Americans 50 and older carry higher amounts of credit card debt than younger people do, according to a 2012 study of middle-income adults sponsored by AARP. About one-quarter traced their debt to unemployment. One-quarter borrowed to help relatives, such as unemployed children, grandchildren in college, and elderly parents. The rest of the debt arose from the normal run of emergencies, both household and medical.

If you're still working and in the retirement-planning stage, consider using your income to wipe out consumer debt rather than add more to savings. The return on investment by banishing debt equals the interest rate you pay. For example, cleaning up an 18 percent credit card gives you an 18 percent return on your money, guaranteed. By contrast, savings accounts are paying zip. You'll find consumer debt much tougher to repay once your paycheck stops.

If you've already retired, you might look for part-time work to help erase your debt, or tap your savings to double up on payments. Don't use your individual retirement account, however. That comes with a tax cost. If you're making payments to kids and grandkids, quit. Your priority now is protecting your own older age.

Mortgage debt is a different story. Only about half of older people now enter retirement with a paid-up home. If you're one of them, congratulations—a mortgage-free house confers real peace of mind. If you're part of the other half, however, don't tap into tax-deferred savings to pay off your loan. Treat your mortgage as one of the ordinary expenses that you budget for. If interest rates are low, you might even refinance into a 30-year loan to reduce the amount that you have to pay each month.

Caretaking. If you're working and your spouse falls seriously ill, your first impulse might be to quit and become a caregiver. But approach this decision carefully. It might make financial sense for you to keep your job and hire a home health aide to help your spouse during the day. Having a salary will provide you with extra income and perhaps extra savings from continuing contributions to a 401(k). You'll keep building your personal Social Security account. Finally, escaping from the house will ease the stress of being a caregiver, which is healthy for both of you.

As you look ahead, consider the likely progress of your spouse's disease. What will you need in the way of equipment? Should your home be modified and what will that cost? Should you move to a modern apartment without stairs? Is a nursing home in the cards and when might a transfer occur? If you have long-term care insurance, what will it cover and for how long (Chapter 4)?

Helping your children. In a perfect world, your money belongs to you alone. It doesn't belong to your kids. You raised them, educated them, and set them free to make their way in the world. Their standard of living lies in their own hands. Whatever money you've saved should go toward making your retirement as pleasant as you'd hoped. You're not obliged to send your grandchildren to college.

Now let's talk about real life. If one of your children stumbles—through job loss, illness, divorce—what are you going to do? Most parents don't say "Tough luck" and shut the door except in extreme cases (estrangement, persistent drug addiction, and so forth). You're probably going to help, even if reluctantly and even if your financial adviser says No. That might mean a tighter budget and a less care-free retirement than you'd hoped. Bring the child into your budget planning right away so that he or she understands how much you reasonably can afford to do and for how long. Take the same tack with a recent college graduate working hard in a low-paying job or trying to make it in the arts. You might volunteer some temporary help. As part of the deal, the child should have an active plan for be-coming independent, soon.

If your child is simply overspending and turning to your wal-let for help, "No" should come pretty easily. An able kid normally doesn't belong on your payroll. You might provide some stopgap help but you'll do the child a favor by insisting that he or she figure out an affordable life.

A special-needs child is another matter and beyond the scope of this book. For information on sources of help, turn to special-needs websites, your school district, your state's Medicaid program, and the federal Supplemental Security Income program. Nonprofit or-ganizations such as The Arc or the National PLAN Alliance can help with life insurance and special-needs trusts.

As for legacies, they're strictly optional. Some parents want to leave money to their kids and are willing to budget for it. Others plan to spend their hard-earned savings during their lifetimes. Either one of these perspectives works for me. Kids of well-to-do parents tend to expect a legacy. If you intend to spend it, or most of it, make that clear.

Special purchases. At some point within the next five years, you will probably need a new car. You might want to take one or two trips. Perhaps you intend to add a downstairs bedroom to your house to make it more convenient for your older age. The money you'll need for these kinds of expenditures should be set aside in a bank account, money market mutual fund, or short-term bond fund so it's there when you need it (Chapter 9). Your monthly budget is solely for everyday expenses. Your savings should cover large cash expenses that you can foresee.

An inheritance. How should you budget if you're expecting an inheritance? Best advice: Budget without it (yes, dear adult children, I'm talking to you!). Don't count on that money to bail you out. You can't be sure how much you'll get after your parents' health-care bills are paid or how long you'll have to wait for it (more people are living into their 90s; our family celebrated my mother's 101st this year). If your parent entered into a second marriage with someone younger, part of his or her money might be set aside, directly or in trust, for the new spouse's support. You might not inherit until after your stepparent dies. (Don't begrudge a stepparent who made your parent happy!) Base your retirement budget on your own resources. Any inheritance should be gravy.

WHAT IS YOUR HEDGE AGAINST THE RISK OF FUTURE INFLATION?

So far, you've figured out a spending plan that meets your needs today. But in most years prices are likely to go up. With as little as 2 percent inflation, you will need 22 percent more income, 10 years from now, to buy the same things you are buying now. With higher inflation you'll need even more. Where will that extra income come from?

Part of the inflation problem will take care of itself. As you get older, you will most likely spend less, in inflation-adjusted terms. A study by David Blanchett, head of Retirement Research at Morningstar Investment Management, found that retirees reduced their consumption by an average of 1 percent a year. Some of those are forced cuts, by people who retired on a small budget. But even people with substantial savings buy less. They don't need more household "stuff," they aren't as pressed to keep up with the Joneses as they were when they worked, and they have more time to bargain hunt. Your personal consumption costs might rise by less than the inflation rate. Inflation might even turn out to be lower than you feared—or higher.

Either way, you'll need to plan for at least some additional money each year. Where will it come from?

Your Social Security is adjusted annually for inflation. So are federal government pensions, veterans' benefits, and some state and local pensions. But those are the only increases that are automatic. You have to achieve every other "raise" yourself. In Chapter 6, you can read about creating your own private pension by using some of your savings to buy an inflation-adjusted annuity. Chapter 8 shows you how to plan your withdrawals from savings so you can raise your income every year by the inflation rate. Chapter 9 helps you diversify your investments for long-term growth. Chapter 10 suggests a way of using a reverse mortgage to increase your income every year. Figuring out how to handle potential inflation is a critical part of your retirement plan. If your income is fixed or dependent on low-rate savings, such as certificates of deposit, your standard of living will gradually drop.

IF YOU DON'T WANT TO DO THE MATH YOURSELF . . .

You can get a *very* rough cut at the maximum you can afford to spend from two online calculators: T. Rowe Price's Retirement Income Calculator and Fidelity Investments' Planning & Guidance Center. You enter your income and assets and get back a proposed monthly allowance that, theoretically, could last for life. The calculators give different results but they're in the same ballpark. (You have to register in order to use them but you don't have to become a customer.)

After that, you need to get serious. Many retirement planning questions have more than one answer. You need to test one set of possibilities against another to see how the alternatives play out. If you have only a couple of choices to make, you'll probably do fine on your own. But for complex and multiple choices, I don't recommend flying solo. God hasn't made enough erasers, yellow pads, hand calculators, or websites for you to work this out alone. If you make mistakes, you might endanger your standard of living in your older age.

Fortunately, God is making more fee-only Certified Financial Planners (CFPs) and I highly recommend that you seek their advice. At this stage of your life, it's the best investment you can make.

A CFP has taken and passed a set of rigorous exams on financial planning. *Fee-only* CFPs charge by the hour or at flat rates for specific services, all disclosed up front. They do not sell financial products or take sales commissions. There are no hidden costs. They'll give you specific advice that you can execute yourself. Or they'll manage your whole financial life, including investments, for an annual fee that's typically 1 percent or less.

Among other things, fee-only planners will project your income and expenses into the future, under various inflation assumptions; encourage you to develop realistic spending plans (read: budgets); evaluate the various types of pension plan distributions you're offered; discuss tax-friendly ways of rolling over money or company stock held in 401(k)s; explain the risks and types of various investments; help you allocate your assets among stocks, bonds, and cash; advise you on prudent ways of turning your savings into a lifetime income; and suggest ways of handling special responsibilities, such as a disabled child. Best of all, these planners will spark a long and careful discussion about your personal values and goals and how you hope to live during the retirement phase of life. That's what should drive the financial decisions you're going to make.

Be sure that your CFP is a real fee-*only* financial planner, not a financial salesperson in disguise! Salespeople often bill themselves as "fee-*based*" planners or advisers. They might charge a fee for what appears to be a fancy financial plan but is actually a sales document. Then they'll try to sell you financial products to complete the "plan"—typically, variable "living-benefit" annuities (high fees for you, high commissions for them), expensive mutual funds, or high-cost managed investment accounts. And they'll constantly try to resell—swapping you out of one annuity and into another to earn a new fee. I don't fault them; selling is their job. Your job is to avoid the biased advice that sales commissions generate. If annuities or mutual funds make sense, low-cost versions are available.

It might appear that fee-based salespeople—including stockbrokers, financial advisers, financial consultants, and commissioned CFPs—cost you less. There might be no fee up front or the fee might be waived if you buy annuities or other products. He or she might claim (falsely) that you're paying no fees (because "the insurance company" is paying). They might say they're "on salary," so get no special benefits from the products they sell.

Don't be fooled. These advisers always earn something extra by selling their firms' most profitable products, whether they're called "commissions" or not. You're probably paying more than you think and often for inferior advice. Financial salespeople don't have the expertise (or take the time) to help you master your budget, think through your personal goals, and help you match your goals to the money decisions you make. They keep their jobs only if they sell, sell, sell.

A fee-only planner, by contrast, will almost certainly save you money—first, because your life goals, your spending, and your savings will be aligned, and second, because you won't be led into buying expensive products that you might not understand.

Fee-only planners do have potential conflicts of interest. If they're managing your money for a percentage fee (say, 1 percent), they might be reluctant to recommend actions that remove large sums of money from your account. For example, they might advise you not to withdraw the cash needed to pay off your mortgage. But any temptations they have are far less consequential than the temptations facing commissioned salespeople. Besides, in my personal experience, fee-only planners *will* tell to you pay off the mortgage if it makes sense and you can afford it.

There's one limitation to be aware of. If immediate-pay income annuities are appropriate (Chapter 6), a fee-only planner might not be able to provide them because most of these products currently carry sales commissions. Some planners simply won't recommend them. The best planners will research the low-cost annuities on the market and, if prudent, refer you to an agent to handle the sale.

What if you've been working with a fee-based or commissioned adviser, paying the fees and sales commissions, and are happy with the results? The comfort factor is important so by all means stay there. An adviser who's also a Certified Financial Planner should be taking the time to discuss your personal goals as well as your investments. You're paying more than you have to for financial products and might not be getting the best advice. No matter, if you're gaining peace of mind.

But if you're uncertain about a product that the adviser recommends, want a second opinion, or don't yet have an adviser, jump to the fee-only planning world.

There's one group of commissioned advisers to treat with special caution: those who claim to be some sort of "senior specialist." There are more than 50 different "senior" designations—strings of impressive initials strung after the adviser's name. They purport to show that the adviser is "chartered" or "certified" or "accredited" for retirement planning due to some special course of study. Mostly, the designations are no more than marketing tools that the advisers paid for, with little or no serious study. They should actively repel you.[2]

Three designations, however, are based on a rigorous curriculum, according to retirement income expert Wade Pfau of the American College of Financial Services in Bryn Mawr, Pennsylvania. For income planning, you can feel comfortable if your adviser's business card says that he or she is a Certified Retirement Counselor (CRC), Retirement Income Certified Professional (RICP), or Retirement Management Analyst (RMA). You're also good with a Chartered Advisor for Senior Living (CASL), whose focus includes broader issues, such as health care and estate planning. But these credentials should be in addition to, not in place of, the Certified Financial Planner (CFP) designation. Fee-only planning is the foundation on which specialties can be built.

There are three networks of fee-only financial planners:

- *The Garrett Planning Network (GarrettPlanningNetwork.com).* Its members typically focus on people with average incomes and assets. They charge by the hour for planning and financial advice, although some of them manage money for a fee. They're especially helpful for single-purpose advice, such as saving for college or creating a retirement savings plan. Any planner who manages money should be a Registered Investment Adviser,[3] so ask about that.
- *The National Association of Personal Financial Advisors (napfa.org).* NAPFA planners tend to work with people who

---

2   Also be wary of advisers "accredited" by the U.S. Department of Veterans Affairs. The VA throws its vets to the wolves by approving practically anyone who asks, scamsters included.

3   Registered Investment Advisers (RIAs) are registered with the federal Securities and Exchange Commission or state securities office and are entitled to give individual investment advice.

have an above-average net worth. They'll help you develop a financial plan for your retirement if that's all you want. As Registered Investment Advisers, they also manage money for a fee. NAPFA planners focus on low-cost investing. The lower the cost, the higher your returns can be.

- *Financial Planning Association (plannersearch.org).* The FPA includes commissioned salespeople as well as fee-only planners. When you make a search, check the box that says "Fee Only." (Note that an adviser who works for a brokerage firm or insurance company is never a fee-only planner, even if he or she claims to be.)

At each of these websites, enter your zip code. A list will pop up showing the names of planners in your area. Add to your list any advisers that your friends recommend. Check them all online to learn something about their background and the kinds of services they offer. If they manage money, read the Investment Adviser Public Disclosure form (IAPD) that they file with the Securities and Exchange Commission at AdviserInfo.sec.gov. The IAPDs include Part 2 of their ADV ("adviser") form, which discloses, among other things, their educational background, fees, how much money they manage, their investment methods, whether they're truly fee-only (do they sell any financial products?), and any regulatory actions against them.

Once you've done your homework, call or email two or three of them and tell them who you are and a bit about what you need (retirement income planning? 401(k) advice? money management? tax planning? everything?). If it feels like a fit, make a personal appointment.

Napfa.org offers a useful, free "How To" guide called Pursuit of a Financial Advisor. There, you'll find a list of questions to ask at your first interview. That visit should be free. The planner should ask about you, your family, your goals, and your assets (don't hide anything; if you do, it will skew the advice you get). You want to hear about the planner's background, education, financial training and investment methods, the kind of expertise the office offers, how the planning process works, and whether he or she has other clients like you (teachers? civil servants? medical professionals? small business owners?). Ask how the planner is paid (Registered Investment Advisers have to give you the SEC-required ADV form, which discloses any commissions and fees). Get the phone numbers of clients you can call—and make the calls. You'll be surprised by what you can find out. It's also useful to visit at least two planners to get a feel for how different offices work.

One other source of help: big mutual fund groups that offer low-cost, fee-only financial planning and money management services. For more on these options, see page 261.

If the planner will manage your money or help you choose financial products, ask if he or she is a "fiduciary." That's the kind of adviser you want. By law, fiduciaries are duty bound to put your financial interests ahead of theirs. They should give you the best advice possible, without regard for the amount of money they can earn from your account. They'll give you a written list of fees. Fee-only planners are often Registered Investment Advisers and RIAs are always fiduciaries.

Salespeople who take sales commissions or whose firms take commissions usually are not fiduciaries. You might think of them as true investment advisers but, in fact, your relationship is strictly transactional. Their only obligation is to sell you investments that are "suitable" to someone in your circumstances. They can, and do, put their own interests first. For example, say that you want a blue-chip mutual fund. They might put you into one that pays to be on the firm's recommended list even though its cost is high and its performance mediocre. Always invest with a fiduciary.

In April of this year, the U.S. Department of Labor took a major pro-consumer step. It ruled that professionals who provide you with paid advice on managing your retirement plan must act as fiduciaries. The rule takes effect April 10, 2017. The financial firms have until

January 1, 2018, to fill in the details. Naturally, the industry immediately filed lawsuits, trying to kill or delay the change or make it difficult to enforce. Salespeople make their money by ignoring your "best interest."

Here's what you can do now to avoid being sold crappy products with high hidden costs: (1) When rolling a 401(k) into an Individual Retirement Account—or making any other investment—ask for written assurance that the adviser is a fiduciary. (2) Ask for a written list of fees (in dollars), percentage commissions (both upfront those paid in future years), and annual costs related to the investment. (3) If the answer to both requests is "no" (or a fudge), hang up the phone. That's not a real fiduciary. (4) Reject costly products, such as fixed-index annuities (see page 151). They're rarely in your "best interest," no matter who sells them. (5) Use the rules above when investing outside retirement plans, which are not yet covered by a mandatory fiduciary standard.

However you create your retirement spending plan—by yourself or with help—assume that you'll live a long and active life. Aim for a level of income that will last until you're 100, unless you have good reason to expect a shorter (or longer!) life span. If you're married, assume that your spouse or partner will be long-lived, too. That many years might seem impossible to plan for, but what if your money runs out when you're 85 and you're still taking yoga? Or, rather, *not* taking yoga because you can't afford it any more?

Stretching your money over 20- or 30-plus years isn't as hard as you think as long as you start out right. Over time, the number of your purchases will go down. You'll travel less and drive less. You might give up the house and move to an efficient apartment. You'll lose the urge to redecorate the living room. These natural changes will offset rises in consumer prices and medical costs. You can also get more from your assets than you probably think, which is what this book is about.

The great pleasure of rightsizing is that it takes you to a place you can comfortably afford. Never look back. Your life as an engaged and valued citizen is 100 percent ahead.

3

How to Double Your Social Security Income (Well, Almost)

Your payout could be worth as much as $1 million over your lifetime. Are you leaving some of that money on the table?

I love Social Security. It's America's finest retirement plan. Nothing else gives you the same combination of income for life, inflation protection, tax benefits, government-backed payment guarantees, and built-in spouse protection, with no annual investment fee and no market risk.

Every time I list those benefits, I say to myself, "Wow!"

Yet millions of retirees are letting part of their Social Security pensions go to waste. You might be losing hundreds of thousands of dollars, over your lifetime, because you filed for your benefits too soon or didn't check to see if you could coordinate claiming strategies with your spouse. If you're the primary breadwinner, the loss could be especially hard on your spouse if you die first (in most cases, it's wives who are left behind).

What surprises me, especially, is that so many people don't even know about their Social Security options or don't investigate what those options are worth. They take the money and run as soon as they're 62 or maybe 66, having no idea how much money they might be giving up.

The earlier you claim Social Security, the smaller your monthly checks will be. If you're married, filing early also lowers the income available to a dependent spouse. By filing just a few years later, you'll get a much larger lifetime check and your spouse will, too.

Some people have no real choice about when to claim their benefits. If your paycheck stops and you're short of money, you'll need your Social Security check—right now—to pay your bills. Your options are effectively closed. Sign up and be happy.

But before making this decision, ask yourself if there are other ways of getting by for three or four years more. It's not written in stone that you have to start your Social Security benefits when you leave your job. Maybe you can take part-time work. It might even pay to use some of your retirement savings to cover the bills for a while, so you can let your benefits grow.

If I can give you just one word of advice about when to sign up for Social Security, it would be *WAIT.* Here's the compelling arithmetic:

You can claim your retirement benefits as early as age 62. If you wait until your full Social Security retirement age, probably 66, your monthly check will be 33 percent higher. If you wait until 70, your check will be 76 percent higher, compared with what you'd have gotten at 62. Okay, that's not double the income, but it's pretty rich. You're credited with annual cost-of-living increases, too. If you're married and wait until 70 to claim your benefits, you're not only building a larger future income for yourself, you'll leave more income to a surviving, dependent spouse if you die first.[1]

There's an exception: Sometimes married couples can rack up a higher lifetime income if one spouse waits to claim benefits while

---

1   There are exceptions to the rule of "wait" for certain married people. See page 54.

the other spouse files early. This strategy comes into play when each of you has a Social Security record of your own. How well it works will depend on your health and the numbers (see page 54).

From Social Security's point of view, it doesn't matter when an individual worker retires. Your benefit is scheduled to last for your actuarial life expectancy, based on the month you put in your claim. If you start at 62, the payments are smaller because they're spread over a longer expected period. If you start at 70, the payments are higher because you have fewer remaining years. Almost certainly, you will die later, or sooner, than your "proper" date—*and you don't know which.*

Some people start at 62 even if they don't need the money because they'd really, really hate to feel like Social Security losers. If they put off collecting their benefits and died early, they'd feel rooked.

But excuse me—you will actually be dead and not feeling much of anything about your personal finances. Meanwhile, if you're married, your early retirement will have reduced the monthly Social Security income you left for a dependent spouse. Looked at that way, your beloved widow or widower is the person being rooked and you did the rooking.

Another temptation is to take the benefit at 65, the year you're eligible for Medicare. How shortsighted is that? If you wait just 12 more months, you can claim a full (and larger) retirement benefit with a better safety net for your spouse.

The danger today comes not from dying too soon but from living too long and running short of money—especially if your earnings have been above average. Life expectancy for people in the upper half of the income scale is several years longer than for those in the lower half. In fact, most of the gains in average longevity over the past century reflect the longer lives of educated people of means.

So if you're in good health, I beg you to gamble on a long life, not an early death. You'll probably be better off if you wait until 70 to collect your Social Security retirement benefits (or, at the very least, 66). If you have already filed for benefits, you can suspend them (see page 66), which starts your future benefit-building up again.

You'll think differently if you have a serious illness and don't expect to live to your normal life expectancy. If you're single, you'll want to file at 62 to get as much out of Social Security as you can. If you're married and the main breadwinner, however, you should still consider waiting until 66 or 70. By waiting, you're building a higher, inflation-protected survivor's benefit for the spouse you might leave behind.

A SCREED AGAINST "BREAK-EVEN AGE"

A common aid, when deciding when to claim benefits, is what's called a "break-even analysis." It tells you how many more years you have to live to make delaying benefits a better choice than claiming now.

As an example, say that you're single and could get $1,500 a month at 62 or $2,000 a month at 66. Your break-even age might be 78, meaning that if you live past 78, claiming at 66 will have been the better strategy. You'll have collected a higher-than-average amount of money over your lifetime. On the other hand, if you die before 78, claiming benefits early will have been the better choice. Generally speaking, your break-even age works out to be a little younger than your life expectancy because of the way the calculators work.

So now you know your break-even age. So what??? You cannot know how long you're actually going to live, which makes breakeven a pretty poor guide for making financial decisions. Maybe you'll last past the magic age and maybe not. You might be in poor health yourself, and not expecting a long life, but your spouse might live for another 30 years. By taking benefits at 62, you're reducing the check your dependent spouse will get for the rest of his or her life. (You won't hear your spouse grumble after you're gone, but your kids will.)

Another complaint about breakeven, if I haven't already complained enough: When you're 62, an age like 78 or 82 might seem impossibly far away. It's easy to think, *No way I'll live that long.* But guess what? You probably will, or your spouse will. If a married couple reaches 65, the chance that one of you will live until 90 is better than 40 percent. Even if both of you come from short-lived families, that doesn't mean you'll run true to type. So forget about trying to pick a "death age." Base your claiming decisions on your financial goals—giving a preference to *WAIT.*

The glory of Social Security lies in its value as longevity insurance. You'll keep getting inflation-adjusted monthly checks even if you live to 120. The larger your Social Security check when you first make a claim, the safer your older age will be.

SOCIAL SECURITY BASICS

Later in this chapter, I'll talk about ways of making the most of your Social Security claiming options. First, however, I have some under-brush to clear away. Surprisingly, for a social program that has pro-tected Americans for more than 70 years, Social Security's workings are not well known. Some retirees—especially married or divorced women—are losing money because of simple claiming mistakes. I can't cover every possible way of boosting your benefits (the Social Security handbook has 2,728 separate rules!). But here are the con-cepts and types of claims that you'll be working with:

Your primary insurance amount (PIA). This is the most important number in your Social Security record. It's the monthly benefit you'd receive if you retired at your full retirement age (66 in 2016; 67 starting in 2022). All the rest of your Social Security benefits, including those due your spouse, pivot around this central, primary dollar amount. Early retirement benefits are figured as a discount from your PIA.

If you're still working or haven't yet claimed your benefits, you have an estimated PIA. To learn the amount, call Social Security or check your Social Security Statement (see page 41). The estimated benefit assumes that you'll continue to earn money at your current rate. If your pay goes up, your estimated PIA at 66 will go up, too. The PIA can shrink if your pay goes down. If you retire earlier than 66, your PIA will be based on the highest 35 years of earnings you accumulated up to your early retirement date. If you keep working after starting benefits, Social Security will add those earnings to your record. Each year, your benefit will be recomputed, which could lead to a higher check.

Cost-of-Living Adjustment (COLA). When you're on Social Security, you get a cost-of-living increase every year (that is, every year when inflation is 0.1 percent or more). This is a rare and wonderful gift. Your purchasing power is protected no matter how high inflation flies. A few states offer COLAs or partial COLAs with their pensions. But most state and private pensions provide a fixed income that loses purchasing power every year.

Types of benefits. Best known is the *retirement benefit* that pays you a pension for life. *Spousal benefits* go to your husband or wife if they lack a sufficient Social Security account of their own. Ex-spouses can also make a claim on your account, provided that the marriage lasted at least 10 years. Four types of benefits are available to your family if you die: *survivor's benefits* for your spouse (and qualified ex-spouse); *mother's or father's benefits* for a spouse (or ex-spouse) who's taking care of your child who is under 16 or disabled (the disability has to have started before the child reached 22); benefits for your children if they're under 18 (or 19 and attending high school); and *parent's benefits* if you had been paying more than half the support for an aging parent. All these payments receive cost-of-living increases.

The earned-income test. You can collect a paycheck while receiving Social Security benefits. But if you're under full retirement age and earn more than a certain dollar amount in any year, your benefit will be temporarily suspended. The earnings limit applies to people filing for spousal or survivor's benefits, too.

If you're working and claim at 62, your benefit will be reduced by $1 for every $2 you earn over the limit. Starting in January of the year you reach full retirement age, you're docked $1 for every $3 you earn over the limit, up to your birthday month. Once you reach your birthday month, however, there's no more penalty for work. At that point, you can earn as much as you want and still receive your full Social Security benefits.

And here's a surprise—Social Security will gradually repay the money that was withheld during the years you made "too much." When you reach full retirement age, your benefit will be recalculated as if an earnings penalty had never been taken out—so your monthly check will rise, permanently. The money owed will be repaid over your expected lifetime.[2]

If you know that you'll earn more than the limit, tell Social Security in advance so that it can adjust your check. Alternatively, you can wait until you file your tax returns and let Social Security discover how much you earned. If it's over the limit, the government will calculate what the reduction should have been and stop sending you checks until it has recovered the amount owed.

Note that only your wages and earnings from self-employment count toward your earnings limit. You can receive any amount of interest, dividends, capital gains, rents, pensions, and other passive income and still get a full Social Security check. If you're married and your spouse is working, his or her earnings don't count, either. Social Security looks only at what you personally bring in.

The earnings limits for 2016 were $15,720, from ages 62 to 65, and $41,880 in the year you reach 66. To find the limit for 2017 and later, go to SocialSecurity.gov (or ssa.gov) and put "Earnings Test" into the Search box.

---

2   There's an exception for a surviving parent taking care of a young child, who takes a mother's or father's benefit and also earns a paycheck. Any money docked from this benefit, due to the earnings limit, is not returned.

The Government Worker Test. This test affects people with government pensions who also worked at least ten years in the private sector. All the Social Security rules theoretically apply to you. But your benefits will be reduced or offset by your government pension. For more on this, see page 71.

Your Social Security Statement. This statement shows your future, estimated Social Security payment at various ages as well as the benefits for your family. You can sign up for it online at ssa.gov/myaccount. If online registration fails, create an account in person by bringing identification to your local Social Security office. If you don't register online, Social Security will mail you a statement once every five years, starting at age 25. (Note that online registration always fails if you put a security freeze on your credit accounts.)

WHAT YOU NEED TO KNOW ABOUT RETIREMENT BENEFITS

Your retirement benefit is the monthly check you're entitled to receive, based on your personal earnings record. To qualify, you need at least 40 quarters of work in a job that's covered by Social Security. (A quarter is a three-month period; 40 of them add up to 10 years.) The dollar amount of your benefit is drawn from your highest 35 years of earnings, adjusted for rising wage levels. If you worked fewer than 35 years, you get a zero for each missing year. That pulls your benefits down.

The people least likely to have a Social Security record are those who spend most of their lives outside the workforce—often women who raise children. If you've reached your 50s and aren't sure if you're covered, call Social Security. You might find that you need just two or three more years of work to establish your own account. That's worth a job search right now. Once you're on Social Security's rolls, you also qualify for free hospital insurance under Medicare.

The magic number—your full retirement age. This is the age when you can claim your primary insurance amount (PIA). No discounts apply. How old you have to be depends on the year you were born. It's 66 if your birthday lies between January 2, 1943, and January 1, 1955. For people born later, full retirement age creeps up by two months every year. For example, if you were born in 1956, your full retirement age is 66 and four months. It reaches 67 for people born on January 2, 1960, or later.

Early retirement and its cost. You can retire as early as 62 but your benefits will be whacked. At 62, you'll get 25 percent less than the primary amount you'd have had if you'd waited until your full retirement age. If you retire at 64, your benefit will be discounted by 13.3 percent. These discounts affect your benefits for the rest of your life. For people born in 1960 or later, the penalty for early retirement is even more extreme. You'll lose 30 percent of your primary benefit if you retire at 62.

The government pays you to retire late. This is my favorite part of the Social Security law. You get a huge bonus if you start benefits later than your full retirement age. The bonus—called a "delayed retirement credit"—is worth two-thirds of your primary insurance amount for each month you delay your claim up to age 70. That's an 8 percent gain over each full year. If you retire at 70, the size of your monthly check will have increased by 32 percent, plus cost-of-living increases, compared with what you'd have been paid at 66.[3] If you're married and die first, your surviving spouse gets the benefit of that increase, too.

---

3   When your full retirement age reaches 67, you'll have fewer months to take advantage of the delayed retirement credits. Still, they'll be a terrific deal. For those born in 1960 or later, claiming at 70 will increase your benefit by 24 percent.

You can change your mind about taking retirement benefits. A decision to claim your check early doesn't have to be forever. If you regret taking benefits at 62 and have reached your full retirement age, you can tell Social Security that you want to put your checks on hold. Your account will be suspended and your future benefit will start to build up again, earning delayed retirement credits for the years after 66. See "The do-over" and "The voluntary suspension," page 66.

WHAT YOU NEED TO KNOW TO COLLECT SPOUSAL BENEFITS

As a spouse, you can claim benefits based on the earnings record of your husband or wife. You get up to half of the primary insurance amount that your mate would get at full retirement age. For example, if the husband gets $2,000 at age 66, the wife could get up to $1,000. To qualify as a spouse, you have to have been married for at least one year, although there are exceptions—for example, if you're the parent of your mate's biological child.

To receive the maximum, you have to claim benefits at your own full retirement age or later. If you claim earlier, your spousal benefit will be reduced. At 62, for example, a spouse gets 30 percent less than if he or she had filed at 66. Any reduction affects your future benefits permanently. (There may be instances, however, when it pays to file at 62—see pages 54 to 59.)

Two things must be true in order to receive a spousal benefit: (1) Your mate has to be at least 62 and have already claimed retirement benefits. If you decide as a couple that it's best to delay your mate's retirement claim, your spousal benefits will be delayed, too. (2) You generally cannot switch to the spousal benefit if you're already receiving Social Security based on your own earnings.

Same-sex married couples are entitled to spousal benefits on each other's account provided that the marriage has lasted at least one year. Previously, same-sex couples who married, then moved to states that didn't recognize their union, weren't entitled to spousal treatment. Now their unions are legal everywhere in the United States.[4] If you applied for spousal benefits and were denied, Social Security will provide back payments from the date of your application. Watch Social Security's website (ssa.gov) for guidance on how to proceed. Another good source is lambdalegal.org, an organization that fights for the civil rights of gay, lesbian, bisexual, and transgender people. Spousal benefits are also available to people in some legal civil unions or domestic partnerships.

Not every spouse gets a spousal benefit. It was designed for spouses, usually women, who didn't work long enough to have their own Social Security account or whose earnings were small. Spouses who worked during much of their marriage and built up a strong personal earning record receive retirement benefits based on their own accounts—higher than what they'd receive as "spouse."

Two-earner couples got a surprise in 2015, when Congress abruptly canceled two strategies that they were using to rake in double spousal benefits. You can still use one of those strategies if you were born in 1953 or earlier (see page 57). That's because Congress grandfathered those who were already eligible. Double benefits won't be available, however, to people born in 1954 or later.

Nevertheless, playing your cards right as a spouse can still make a big difference to the amount you receive as a couple over time. I've laid out the claiming rules, opposite. For clarity, I've generally written them from the point of view of a wife filing for benefits on her husband's account. (Social Security is too complicated for unisex writing.)

---

4   Veterans' benefits are beyond the scope of this book, as are state and railroad retirement plans. But "married" now means married, regardless of sex. Retirement plans through religious organizations should also recognize same-sex couples if they're subject to federal law regarding retirement benefits or employment discrimination based on sex.

All the benefits work the same way if the husband files on his wife's account or one of a same-sex married couple files on the other's account.

Rule 1:   For you to get a spousal benefit, your husband has to be receiving his own retirement benefit. If he delays his claim (which often makes financial sense) your spousal benefit will be delayed as well.

Rule 2:   For a full spousal benefit, you have to claim at your own full retirement age or later. Your husband's age doesn't matter. The size of your payment depends entirely on how old you are.

Rule 3:   If you claim early, your spousal benefit will be reduced.

Rule 4:   The size of your potential spousal benefit tops out at your own full retirement age—66 or 67. You get nothing extra by waiting one more year. Your benefit will not increase even if your spouse is earning delayed retirement credits. So spousal benefits should always be taken no later than full retirement age.

Big Rule 5:   You *cannot* receive a spousal benefit on your mate's account and, later, switch to a (higher) retirement benefit on your own account. Similarly, you cannot receive retirement benefits on your own account and later switch to the spousal benefit. That's because, when you put in a Social Security claim, you are "deemed" to be applying for both benefits at once. Social Security pays you the higher of the two. Sadly, few couples understand this, I've spoken with many women who thought they'd applied as spouses, at 62, only to learn that they had received their own retirement payments instead, and at a reduced amount. Had they known, they might have delayed their claim, in order to collect a higher retirement check in the future. By the time they discovered what happened, it was too late. Always ask the Social Security rep which of the benefits you'll receive.

Exception to Big Rule 5: You *can* receive both a spousal benefit and, later, your own retirement benefit if you were born in 1953 or earlier and file for the spousal benefit at your full retirement age. This strategy—called a "restricted application"—works well for couples who each have a substantial Social Security account of their own. See page 57 for details.

Rule 6: If you're married and each of you is 66, you can't both claim spousal benefits on the other's account. One of you has to file for retirement benefits while the other takes the spousal amount.

Rule 7: You can claim full spousal benefits when you're younger than 62 if your husband is on Social Security disability (ssa.gov/disability) or has retired and you're caring for his child who's under 16 or disabled. This check will stop once the youngest child reaches 16 (assuming no disability). When you reapply for spousal benefits, at 62 or later, the normal claiming rules apply. Your check won't be docked for the number of years you claimed benefits as the mother of a young or disabled child.

Rule 8: There are special cases where switching from retirement to spousal benefits is allowed. For example, say that you're single and started your retirement benefits at 62. Then you got married. After waiting a year, you can change to spousal benefits on your mate's account if he's receiving Social Security and that's a better deal.

Rule 9: You will be treated as a spouse even if you're legally separated. But the claiming rules are a little different for couples who aren't together. You won't be able to get spousal benefits on your estranged husband's account until he files for benefits of his own. By contrast, if you were divorced you could claim spousal benefits whether he retired or not (see page 60), provided that he's eligible for benefits and that the marriage lasted at least 10 years. If you've passed the 10-year mark, you should get on the horn to your lawyer and finalize the split. If not, drag out the proceedings until 10 years have passed.

WHAT YOU NEED TO KNOW TO COLLECT SURVIVOR'S BENEFITS

If your wife or husband dies, you're entitled to a survivor's benefit. The amount is based on the earnings record of the spouse you lost. If you've been receiving spousal benefits, Social Security will upgrade you to the survivor's benefit, which pays much more. If you've been receiving benefits based on your own earnings, you might—or might not—find that the survivor's benefit is the better deal.

Either way, however, your total Social Security income will decline. That's because when your spouse was alive you each received a check. When you're left alone, only one check will be coming in. For couples making a long-term financial plan, that's an important point to remember.

Same-sex married couples are also entitled to survivor's benefits. Before the Supreme Court's marriage ruling, survivors were denied benefits if they lived in a state that refused to recognize their union. At this writing, Social Security has not yet spoken on whether benefits will be paid retroactively. Survivors should apply and see what happens.

The claiming rules for any survivor are gruesomely complex, but here's a general overview.

Rule 1:   A surviving spouse can normally claim benefits starting at age 60 (50, if he or she is disabled). But by claiming before your full retirement age—say, 66—your check will be permanently reduced.[5]

Rule 2:   If you claim at 66 or older you can get up to 100 percent of your deceased spouse's benefit even if you retired early on your own earnings record. All that matters is your age when you make the claim for benefits as a survivor.

Rule 3:   You can take your own retirement benefit (based on your personal earnings record) or a survivor's benefit (based on your spouse's earnings) but not both at the same time. Which benefit to take and when depends on how the numbers work out. For example, you might file for the survivor's benefit, then switch to your own retirement benefit at 70, if that will maximize your income over your expected lifetime.

Rule 4:   You can claim full benefits at any age if you are caring for the worker's child who's under 16 or disabled. These are called "mother's" or "father's" benefits. If you earn a paycheck, however, your Social Security check might be reduced by the earnings limit as well as by the family maximum (see page 63). Mother's or father's benefits stop when the child is no longer eligible. You can apply for benefits again at 60 or older under the normal survivor rules.

---

5   For survivor's benefits, full retirement age will gradually rise to 67 for people born in 1962 and later.

Rule 5: To be eligible for survivor's benefits, you normally have to have been married for at least nine months. But there are exceptions—for example, if your spouse died in an accident or while serving in the military.

Rule 6: If your late spouse retired early or died before taking Social Security benefits, the rules are especially complex. Your benefit will be based on how long he or she worked and how old you are when you make the claim. Social Security will tell you what you're owed.

Rule 7: If you remarry at 60 or later, you have a choice. You can take spousal benefits on the account of your new spouse, or survivor's benefits on the account of your late spouse, whichever is higher. If you remarry before 60, however, you're not allowed to claim on your late spouse's account. If you have the bad luck to lose your second spouse, you can claim survivor's benefits on either of your late spouses' accounts, whichever is higher.

Rule 8: Survivor's benefits are also available to the young or disabled children of the worker who died and to his or her parents if the worker paid for at least half of their support.

Rule 9: Social Security pays a lump-sum death benefit of $255 to the surviving spouse. If there's no eligible spouse, the money goes to any child (or children) who were receiving benefits based on the worker's account or became eligible to receive benefits when the worker died (see page 62). If no children are eligible, payment is not made.

WHAT DIVORCED SPOUSES NEED TO KNOW

If you were married continuously[6] for at least 10 years and haven't remarried, you're eligible for spousal benefits and survivor's benefits based on your ex's earnings record. You get the same amount as you would if the divorce had never occurred. For general information, check the previous sections on spousal and survivor's benefits. A few of the claiming rules for divorced people are a little different, however. I've listed them here.

Big Rule 1:   No matter how mad you are at each other, try to let your marriage pass the 10-year mark if you're anywhere close. The right to claim on each other's accounts could be worth a lot of money to each of you in future years. If the final blowup came too soon, consider a legal or informal separation, saving the actual divorce until the marriage is 10 years old.

Rule 2:   You have to wait until 62 for spousal benefits even if you're caring for your ex's young child who's disabled or under 16. When you have an eligible child in care, you get the full benefit with no discount for filing early.

Rule 3:   You can claim a spousal benefit even if your ex has not filed for retirement benefits of his own under two conditions: Your ex is *eligible* to claim benefits now and you have been divorced for at least two years.

---

6   You can divorce and remarry the same person and still be married "continuously" unless the remarriage took place in the calendar year immediately following the divorce.

Rule 4:   If you've remarried, you can claim spousal benefits only on the record of your current spouse. If your new marriage also lasts at least 10 years and ends in divorce, you can claim on the record of either ex-spouse, depending on which benefit is higher.

Rule 5:   If your ex-spouse dies, you get a survivor's benefit if your marriage lasted at least 10 years and you have not remarried. If you did remarry, you can normally claim benefits only on the record of your new spouse, with one exception. If you remarry at 60 or later, you have a choice: Take spousal benefits on the account of your new mate (once the marriage has lasted for at least one year) or survivor's benefits on the account of your ex, whichever is higher.

Rule 6:   You don't have to be in contact with your ex in order to claim benefits on his or her account. But you do need your divorce decree, a document you should never throw away. If you can't find your copy, call your lawyer or go to the vital statistics office in the state or county where the divorce occurred.

Big Rule 7:   Payments to a divorced spouse (or two "exes" or even more!) *do not* reduce the benefits paid to the worker or his or her current spouse. You all can claim your full benefit based on the same account. The worker doesn't even have to know about it.

TIME TO DECIDE: WHAT DO YOU WANT FROM SOCIAL SECURITY THE MOST?

By now you know that Social Security isn't one-size-fits-all. You have choices, some of which will yield more retirement money than others. Which path you take will depend on your personal goals.

Here are the three main possibilities. Which one matters to you the most?

- Do you want immediate cash as soon as you're eligible? You'll get more spending money now but potentially less over your lifetime and a smaller benefit for a dependent, surviving spouse.
- Do you want to achieve the largest possible monthly benefit? You'll claim benefits at 70. If you're married, this strategy leaves the largest possible survivor's benefit to a dependent spouse. It might also maximize your income as a couple but not necessarily.
- Do you want the maximum benefits that you can expect as a couple over your probable lifetimes? In some cases, one of you should begin retirement benefits at 62 or 66, even though, for the early retiree, that means a smaller check (see page 54).

You might consider more than one of these goals when making your Social Security plan. Run the numbers to see how they each work out. The following sections make some suggestions for singles, couples, widows and widowers, the divorced, and families.

GETTING THE MOST FROM SOCIAL SECURITY WHEN YOU'RE SINGLE

For single people with no dependents, the Social Security claiming game depends entirely on your finances, your interests, and your health.

Begin benefits at 70 or shortly before if you're in good health and can afford to put off taking the money. Every year you delay retirement after your full retirement age, your benefit grows by a guaranteed 8 percent of your primary insurance amount plus the inflation rate—far better than you'd get from any commercial annuity. While you're waiting, you can fill the gap with earnings or withdrawals from a retirement account. At 70, your Social Security benefit tops out except for annual COLAs, so there's no point waiting any longer.

Begin benefits at 66 or 67 (if it's your full retirement age) to avoid taking a discount on your primary benefit. Another plus if you're still working: The earnings test doesn't apply. You can collect your whole paycheck and your full Social Security benefit, too.

Begin benefits shortly before your full retirement age if health concerns arise or you need the money. You'll get less than your full benefit but more than if you retired at 62. Still, the general advice applies. Don't claim early unless you have a very good reason for taking that route. You'll be short-changing yourself if you live a longer-than-average life.

Begin benefits at 62 if you're in poor health and believe that you'll die well before your average life expectancy (at 62, that's 82 for men and 84 for women; for the class of people with pensions, it's age 85 for men and 88 for women). This doubt should be based entirely on your personal medical condition. Don't say "My mom died at 71 so I probably will too." You cannot know. You might still be dancing at 92 and wishing you had a little more money to spend.

Choose 62, too, if that's truly the only way you can pay your bills. Your benefit will be cut by 25 to 30 percent compared with what you'd get at full retirement age. But if you need the money, well, you need the money.

But do you *really, really* need the money? It's not unusual for single people who work for middling wages (women, in particular) to file at 62 even though they're getting by on the salaries they earn. They're delighted to pull in a few hundred extra dollars a month and don't care that it's reduced by the earnings test. The money lost to the earnings test will come back, if you live long enough. But your monthly benefit check will be permanently reduced. Better to wait.

Finally, you'll choose 62 if your priority is to have more money now, period. Maybe you want to quit your job and write a novel or canoe the lakes of the Canadian northwest. Who am I to argue with that?

Special note for an older, single parent with a young child: Children can get benefits on a retired parent's Social Security record until they're 18 (or 19, if they're still in high school) provided that the parent has put in a retirement claim. You might want to claim early to provide the child with as many years of benefits as possible. Benefits are available for a natural child, adopted child, or stepchild.

GETTING THE MOST FROM SOCIAL SECURITY WHEN YOU'RE MARRIED

Some married couples draw all their benefits from a single earnings record, usually the husband's. That happens when the wife didn't stay in the workforce long enough to acquire a Social Security record of her own or has only a small one. Other couples have two good Social Security accounts to play around with—one for each partner. Either way, with proper timing you can add tens (or hundreds!) of thousands of dollars to your combined Social Security haul.

The Rules for Those Born in 1954 or Later[7]

Your best choices will depend on your ages, the life expectancies you assume, and how large a retirement account each of you has. Take the case of a wife with no Social Security account of her own (or only

---

7   My apologies for all this 1953, 1954 stuff. Congress created the complication. We have to live with it, like it or not!

a small one). She'll be eligible for reduced spousal benefits starting at age 62 or full spousal benefits at 66 (or 67). She can't get them, however, until her husband starts collecting on his own retirement account.

When should the husband claim? If he waits until 70 to retire, he will get a much larger check for life. During those years of waiting, however, no spousal benefit can be paid to his wife. That's money lost.

By contrast, if the husband files early (prior to full retirement age), his spouse can claim early benefits, too, but both checks will be reduced. Filing early also reduces the survivor's benefit available to the wife if he dies first.

In short, you're balancing extra spousal benefits during your early retirement years against a higher income during your later years (and a higher survivor's benefits for a dependent spouse). If your goal is to maximize your income as a one-earner couple, William Reichenstein, an investment professor at Baylor University in Waco, Texas, and head of research at SocialSecuritySolutions.com, suggests the following:

- If you're both the same age, your best bet is usually for the breadwinner—say, the husband—to file at full retirement age (66 or 67) and for the dependent wife to do the same. At that point, she'll get the full spousal benefit with no discount.
- If the husband is slightly older than the wife, he should file when she reaches full retirement age. For example, if he's two years older he'd claim benefits at 68 when she reached 66. Again, she'd get the full spousal benefit with no discount.
- If the husband is four or more years older, he should wait until 70, even if he has a shorter life expectancy. By claiming late, he will leave the highest possible survivor's benefit for his younger spouse. She would file for spousal benefits at her full retirement age—66 or 67.

- If the husband is a few years younger than his wife, he should consider claiming retirement benefits when she reaches full retirement age. By claiming early, he'll receive a lower check, but he lets her receive full spousal benefits as soon as possible. The tradeoff is that she'll get a lower survivor's benefit if he dies first.
- If the husband reaches full retirement age and is still at work, he should claim his retirement benefits right away. The earnings test no longer applies, so his salary won't be docked. To get the largest check, the wife should start her spousal benefits at full retirement age.

These rules are obviously very general and don't meet everybody's needs. Many of you will take benefits early because you need the money—clever strategies don't apply. But Reichenstein points you in a good direction if you can afford the wait. For more precision, I strongly recommend that you use one of the Social Security claiming services listed on pages 67 to 69. They look at your benefits and expected retirement date and show you what you and your spouse would get at different claiming ages. They're just as valuable for couples who will be claiming early as for those who will claim late.

Everything changes if you're a two-earner couple, each with a decent earnings record. Neither of you will get spousal benefits. Instead, you'll receive a retirement benefit—higher than the spousal allowance—based on your personal account. When to file will depend entirely on whether or for how long you'll want to wait in order to let your future benefits increase. For example, the husband might quit working but put off his retirement claim because, as a couple, they can live on the current earnings of the wife. Conversely, you might start benefits early because you've been eased out of your job.

If you both live long enough, you'll maximize your income, as a couple, by putting off claiming until age 70. But often that's not the best strategy. Try running the numbers using various life expectancies. It might be smarter for the lower-earning spouse to file for reduced retirement benefits at 62 while only the higher earner waits until 70.

But again, I recommend the claiming services on pages 67 to 69. You'll see real numbers rather than having to guess.

If You Were Born in 1953 or Earlier

You can still take advantage of a loophole that's now closed to everyone else. You, and you alone, can collect spousal benefits *and* your own retirement benefit, too. Ideal candidates for this double-dip opportunity are two-earner couples where each has a substantial Social Security account. You can proceed in one of two ways:

- The lower-earning spouse—say, the wife—claims reduced retirement benefits at 62. When the husband reaches 66 (currently, full retirement age), he puts in a "restricted application" for spousal benefits on the wife's account. He collects those benefits for the next four years. At 70, he switches to his own retirement account, which has been growing at the rate of 8 percent a year.
- Alternatively, the older of the couple—say, the husband—files for retirement benefits when the wife reaches full retirement age. That allows the wife to collect spousal benefits on the husband's account. When the wife reaches 70, she switches to her own higher retirement benefit.

  If the wife is the older of the couple, or the higher earner, just use this strategy in reverse.

Warning: You must make it absolutely clear to Social Security that you're filing for spousal benefits *only* and that you're qualified to do so. Ask for a "retricted application"—meaning that it's restricted to spousal benefits. You can claim it only if three things are true: (1) You are eligible for both a spousal benefit and your own retirement benefit. (2) You are claiming at your full retirement age—66 or 67 (or older). (3) You were born in 1953 or earlier (people born January 1, 1954, get to double dip, too). This benefit is no longer available to people born in 1954, on January 2, or later.

Restricted applications are still right and proper for people born in 1953 and earlier! Don't let Social Security tell you they can't be done!

Frustrating but true—some Social Security reps have never heard of a "restricted application" for spousal benefits. While writing this chapter, I exchanged half a dozen emails with a friend, aged 66, whose local office kept insisting, wrongly, that she'd have to take her personal retirement benefit because that was higher than her benefit as a spouse. If this happens to you, call Social Security at 800-772-1213 to make your restricted application claim. Even if the rep on the phone doesn't know what you're talking about, you can ask for a supervisor.

You'll have to be even more persistent, now that restricted applications are no longer available to everyone. A Social Security rep might say that that benefit has gone away. To prove that you're right, go to Social Security's website (ssa.gov). and enter "Recent Social Security Claiming Changes" into the Search box. The section called "Who will be affected" shows that the change starts with people born January 2, 1954.

You can apply for this restricted spousal benefit in person or online. On the application, look for the section called "When to Start Retirement Benefits." Find the question "If eligible for both retirement and spouse's benefit, delay receipt of retirement benefit: Yes or No." Answer "Yes." In the Comment field at the end of the online application, you might state that you're restricting the application to spousal benefits only.

If you file a restricted claim for spousal benefits and Social Security accidentally pays you your own retirement benefit instead, you have one year to fix the mistake. See "The do-over," page 66.

Some further comments:

- Restricted applications work even for spouses who are years apart in age. The older spouse claims benefits whenever it suits the couple's financial plan. The younger spouse claims the restricted spousal benefit at 66 and his or her own, higher retirement benefit at 70.
- The dollar value of this claiming strategy changes if the older spouse earned less money and has a smaller retirement benefit than the younger spouse. Spousal benefits for the younger and higher-earning spouse won't be as good. Still, it's money in the bank—worth using while the younger spouse waits until 70 to collect his or her own retirement benefit.
- Wipe out of your mind the loophole called file-and-suspend. It no longer exists. I mention it only to save those with long memories from hunting for it fruitlessly.

Are married women with paychecks being rooked? Many working wives strongly resent the spousal benefit. As they see it, the taxes they contribute to Social Security are "lost." They get spousal benefits whether they worked for pay or not.

In fact, you *always* get whatever benefit you earned. If it's smaller than the spousal benefit, your personal benefit will be topped up to the spousal level. So your taxes aren't lost. You are simply participating in a system that gives a minimum benefit to low-earning spouses (usually women) who might otherwise be super-poor poor in their old age. You're fortunate if you have a Social Security account of your own. In the vast majority of cases, the benefit you earn by working will be higher than the benefit you could claim as a spouse. So no, you're not being rooked.

GETTING THE MOST FROM SOCIAL SECURITY AS A WIDOW OR WIDOWER

If your spouse died young and you have a job, take a look at what you'd actually get by applying for survivor's benefits. The limit on earnings might reduce your potential benefit to zero. If you'll get at least something from the benefit, however, file for it. And file for children's benefits, if they're under 18 (or 19, if they're still in high school).

If an older spouse dies and you have been receiving spousal benefits on his or her account, you'll step up to a survivor's benefit—usually, 100 percent of what your late spouse was receiving.

A complication arises when you have a retirement benefit of your own based on your personal earnings. Your claiming decision will depend on which benefit or combination of benefits will eventually pay the most. If your own retirement benefit will be large, consider taking the survivor's benefit as early as age 60. Plan to switch to your own benefit at 70, when it has grown to the maximum amount. If your own retirement benefit will be small, however, play it the other way. Start your personal benefit as early as 62 and switch to your survivor's benefit at full retirement age (66 or 67). At that age, you're eligible for 100 percent of what your spouse was receiving when he or she died. If your deceased spouse took retirement benefits early, however, you might do better by switching to survivors' benefits before you reach full retirement age. A Social Security rep can tell you what the difference in dollar amounts would be.

GETTING THE MOST FROM SOCIAL SECURITY WHEN YOU'RE DIVORCED

The strategy for a divorced man or woman depends on two things: the size of your own Social Security earnings record, compared with that of your ex's, and how old you are when you make your claim. Here are your options:

If you have no retirement benefit of your own, you'll have to depend entirely on what you'll receive as an ex-spouse. If you file as early as 62, your check will be reduced by 30 to 35 percent. If you wait until your full retirement age, 66 or 67, you'll get the full spousal benefit—half of your ex's primary insurance amount. If your spouse is still working, his or her primary benefit is probably going up. So waiting to file will give you a higher future income, too.

If you have a small retirement benefit of your own, you'll probably do better by claiming as a spouse on your ex's account. Social Security will look at both benefits and give you the larger of the two. (Technically, you get your own benefit, which is then topped up to equal the spousal benefit.)

If you're still working, try to put off your claim until your full retirement age. At 66 (or 67), you can collect a full spousal or divorced-spouse benefit plus all your earnings, too. If you claim earlier, you might run into the earnings limit, which docks your check.

If you have a substantial earnings record based on your own years of work, you can live on your personal Social Security benefit and forget your ex. But that's not always the best idea. If you were born in 1953 or earlier, you're allowed to raise your total take by filing for spousal benefits at full retirement age (see page 57). At 70, you can switch to your personal benefit, which will have been enhanced by the annual 8 percent delayed retirement credit. Note that you can't use this strategy if you file earlier than full retirement age. Younger claimants are required to take their own retirement benefits if they're higher than what they'd get as a spouse. And because you filed early, those benefits will be reduced. (Unfortunately, this special benefit is not available to ex-spouses born in 1954 or later.)

If your ex dies and you haven't remarried, you're eligible for survivor's benefits. You get 100 percent of what your ex was getting if you've reached full retirement age when you make your claim. If you take the benefit earlier, it will be reduced.

But what if you also have a retirement benefit based on your personal earnings? You can't take both benefits at the same time. The answer might be to take them serially, one after the other. For example, say you're between 62 and 65 and had modest lifetime earnings. You might start with your own retirement benefit and claim your survivor's benefit at 66, assuming that it will be higher. Taking early retirement benefits does not reduce the amount of your future survivor's check. Alternatively, say that you have a substantial earnings record. You might claim as a survivor at 60 or older and switch to your own, higher benefit no later than 70. Check both approaches to see which best fits your personal income goals.

If you have remarried, you cannot claim on your ex's account, unless he has died and your remarriage occurred after age 60. If your new spouse dies, however, you have a choice between spousal benefits on your (living) ex's account or survivor's benefits on the account of the spouse who died. Compare them to see which pays more. If you divorce for the second time and each marriage lasted at least 10 years, you can take benefits on the account of either spouse, whichever is higher.

If your ex files for retirement benefits and then voluntarily suspends them, you will not be able to collect on his or her account. You'll have to wait until your spouse activates the benefits again (see page 66).

GETTING THE MOST FROM SOCIAL SECURITY AS A FAMILY

Your spouse, ex-spouse, children, and perhaps even your parents can get Social Security benefits on your record if you file for retirement benefits, die, or become disabled. Here are the rules:

Benefits for young, unmarried children. Children get their own Social Security benefits if they're under 18 (or 19 and attending high school). This rule casts a wide net. It covers natural and adopted children, stepchildren, children with a person the worker wasn't married to, and children in the care of an ex-spouse. It can even cover dependent grandchildren in certain circumstances. Benefits for children with serious disabilities continue after age 18 as long as the disability struck before they turned 22.

Mother's or father's benefits for a spouse of any age. These benefits go to a surviving spouse who is taking care of the deceased worker's child who is under 16 or disabled (the disability had to start before age 22). It can be a natural child, adopted child, or stepchild. The spouse must not have remarried. Spouses working for wages higher than the earnings limit will have their checks reduced (see page 39). Ex-spouses qualify only if they haven't remarried and are caring for the worker's natural or adopted child. In this case, stepchildren are not covered. An unmarried partner won't be covered (well, maybe in a common-law state if you meet the state's complex rules, but it's a long shot).

Survivor's benefits for a worker's dependent parents. This rule helps aging parents if a worker dies who had been paying more than half of the parent's support. The parent has to be at least 62 and not receiving a higher benefit based on his or her own Social Security earnings record.

The family maximum. Social Security sets a limit on how many dollars can be paid in family benefits. If the family goes over that limit, perhaps because there are several young children, spouse and dependent benefits are proportionately reduced.

Ways of Handling Family Benefits if You Have a Choice

Retirement timing. Normally, your family gains the most if you stay at work. But maybe you have plenty of savings for your older age and want to maximize the amounts that Social Security pays your young children—say, from a second marriage. By starting retirement benefits, your spouse and each child can make a claim on your account, subject to the family maximum. You might be especially concerned about the children if they're living with the other parent and you want to give them a financial boost.

Collecting a mother's or father's benefit on your deceased

spouse's or ex-spouse's account. If you have young children, go ahead and file, even if you're working and your wages are somewhat higher than the Social Security earnings limit. Every dollar you net today from your mother's or father's benefit is extra money in the bank. Claiming as a young parent will not reduce your future benefits if you apply for traditional spousal or survivor's benefits at an older age.

Collecting children's benefits. File immediately after the worker dies, retires, or becomes disabled. Children's benefits can be paid retroactively but only for up to 6 months (12 months if the worker is disabled).

RETIREMENT AND DISABILITY BENEFITS

Social Security benefits go to people who are qualified for coverage and are totally disabled (note that the bar for "total disability" is set high). You receive an amount, equal to your full retirement benefit, based on your personal earnings record (not on the record of your spouse). When you reach full retirement age, currently 66, your disability benefits turn into retirement benefits. The amount doesn't change, you simply get your money from a different program.

Once you're on Social Security disability, you might qualify for spousal benefits based on the earnings record of your current spouse or your ex (see pages 43 and 50). Check with Social Security to see what your options are at various ages. Often, the amounts are small, but better than nothing. (Note that taking disability generally prevents you from getting the spousal benefit.)

If you reach 66 and don't really need your retirement benefits, perhaps because you have a lot of savings or a high-earning spouse, you can ask to have the payments suspended. That allows your future retirement benefit to grow by a guaranteed 8 percent a year (plus inflation adjustments) until you reach 70. When you finally claim your check, it will be as much as 32 percent higher, just because you waited.

If you retire at, say, 62 due to poor health and have not applied for disability benefits, perhaps you should. At 62, your retirement check will be reduced. But if Social Security finds that you're totally disabled, and your disability started prior to the date you retired, your check will be increased to your full retirement amount. What's more, Social Security will refund the money you lost during the months that your benefit was reduced.

Social Security's disability insurance program runs by a fiendish number of rules that are beyond the scope of this book. For information, go to ssa.gov/disability. Once you're on the program, your spouse, ex-spouse, and children might qualify for benefits, too.

IF YOU FILE FOR BENEFITS LATE

If you file for benefits after your full retirement age, you can get paid for some of the months you missed. Social Security will backdate your application to the month you reached full retirement age or six months ago, whichever is smaller. This is true both for retirement benefits and spousal benefits. There is no backdating, however, if you file before your full retirement age.

CAN YOU DO BETTER BY TAKING SOCIAL SECURITY EARLY AND INVESTING THE MONEY?

Almost certainly not. It's tough to beat the guaranteed returns that Social Security offers to people who defer their benefit claims. Between ages 66 (or 67) and 70, your future check goes up by 8 percent of your primary insurance amount each year, plus an inflation increase. To beat that in the market, you'd need a remarkable four-year winning streak, timed exactly right.

Between ages 62 and 70, a single person would have to earn more than 7 percent a year, after investment expenses, assuming an average life span and inflation at 3 percent. A married couple would have to earn 9 percent or more to beat what Social Security offers for delaying their combined retirement and spousal benefits.[8]

If inflation exceeded 3 percent, your market returns would have to be even higher to stay ahead of the gains that Social Security pays. In a lower-inflation world, you could come out ahead with lower returns but it's hardly a slam dunk. You're always taking market risk.

OOPS, I CLAIMED BENEFITS EARLY AND REGRET IT— CAN I CHANGE MY MIND?

Yes, you can reconsider—and should. When you took early payments, you settled for less. There are two ways of building up your benefits again.

The do-over. If you change your mind within 12 months of starting retirement benefits, you can go back and start again. Tell Social Security that you want to withdraw your claim. You'll have to pay back the money you've already received. After that, it will be as if you never made the claim at all. You can retire at a future date as if for the first time.

You might want a do-over if you retired at 62 and then went back to work in a high-paying job. Or if you took spousal benefits early and realize that you don't need the income now. Or if you inherited money. Or if you've just read this chapter and discovered how much larger your check can be if you claim at a later age. Social Security lets you change your mind only once, so make it good. If you paid income taxes on the benefits you received and then gave back, you'll want to file an amended tax return.

The voluntary suspension. You're too late for a do-over if 12 months have passed. But if you have reached your full retirement age (66 or 67), you can tell Social Security that you want to suspend

---

8   Source: economist Russell F. Settle, cofounder of SocialSecurityChoices .com.

the benefits that you're currently receiving. That stops your monthly payments and no money has to be returned. From this point on, the benefit you'll claim in the future starts to grow again. Between ages 66 (or 67) and 70 you're eligible for delayed retirement credits, worth 8 percent a year.

Warning: When you voluntarily suspend retirement benefits, you're also stopping payments to anyone else with claims on your account. That means no spousal benefits, nothing for an ex-spouse, and nothing for any qualified children. Their claims can't be paid until you start your own benefits up again.

TOO MANY CHOICES! WHERE CAN I GET HELP?

Believe me, I understand. Merely researching all these possibilities drove me crazy for weeks.

The suggestions I've given should steer you in the right direction. But to illustrate, I mostly used fixed claiming ages (62, 66, and 70). It might be more advantageous for you to take benefits at 64 or 68. Your estimated PIA might be lower (or higher) when you actually put in your claim. For married couples, options vary depending on the spouses' relative ages and earnings. There are also tons of small, technical exceptions to the general rules. To get the very best advice on when to claim Social Security benefits, you need a customized report. Several websites can help you decide.

You might start with something simple and free. That would be AARP's Social Security Benefits Calculator, which you can find online. It estimates your retirement benefits based on the primary insurance amount shown in your Social Security record or—less accurately— your most recent salary plus an assumed, annual 2.5 percent raise. Unfortunately, this calculator lacks flexibility. It assumes that all married people want to maximize their monthly checks when your actual goal might be to maximize your lifetime benefits as a couple.

Another free site, AnalyzeNow.com, lets you include income

from pensions and savings when making your Social Security claiming decision. But it's strictly for do-it-yourselfers who know their way around Microsoft Excel. When you call up the site, click on "Computer Programs."

SocialSecurityChoices.com charges $39.99 for a personal report. It gives you an optimal claiming strategy based on three projected lifetimes: short, normal, and long. It also shows how much money you give up over your lifetime by claiming early. Married couples can look up any claiming age for each spouse to see what the dollar values are.

SocialSecuritySolutions.com offers four levels of service at different prices: $19.99 for a report showing your optimum claiming strategy based on the life expectancy you choose plus a strategy for longer and shorter life spans; $49.95 for an advanced report that lets you change assumptions, such as when you'll start retirement or spousal benefits; $124.95 for the advanced report plus access to an expert who will answer questions; and $149.95 if you want the company to help you file.

To get a customized report from the two sites above, you have to supply your estimated primary insurance amount (see page 38) and, if you're married, the estimated primary insurance amount for your spouse. To get these numbers, call Social Security at 800-772-1213 or find them online by creating a personal MySocialSecurity account at Social Security's website, ssa.gov. Social Security also has a Retirement Estimator, which guesses your future benefit based on your earnings record. I've found that estimate to be high compared with what Social Security says by phone.

One more site, called MaximizeMySocialSecurity.com, charges $40 for a report showing the best time to claim your benefits, plus $250 if you want an hour of one-on-one advice. It handles claiming strategies for children and the disabled as well as those planning to retire.

Maximize takes a different approach to the calculations. It adjusts Social Security's estimate of your primary insurance amount to account for likely inflation and wage growth in the future. This creates higher PIAs for people in their 40s and 50s and, often, lower ones for those in their 60s. It also requires people still working to enter their projected earnings plus all of their past, covered earnings, year by year. For past earnings, create a personal *my*SocialSecurity account online, at Social Security's website. From there, you can transfer your earnings record, automatically, into Maximize. People subject to the Windfall Elimination Provision have to enter their records, too. Like the other programs, Maximize lets you change your assumptions to test various retirement strategies. Founder and economist Laurence Kotlikoff recommends that you plan on living to 100, just to play it safe.

These programs won't all agree with one another because of the different calculation methods they use. I recommend that you work with at least two sites and compare results. The cost is small compared with the increased benefits you can potentially obtain. And you'll feel better knowing that you've had some expert advice. If you're several years away from retirement, plan on getting another report when you're at the brink. Things might have changed.

A special note for divorced spouses: You won't be able to get your ex's earnings record. But Social Security will tell you what your spousal benefit might be if you claim at various ages, so you can use programs other than MaximizeMySocialSecurity.com to help you plan. Unfortunately, you can't get information on your spousal benefit by phone. You have to go to a Social Security office with your divorce papers to prove that you're entitled to the information. The same is true if you're filing for survivor's benefits.

HOW SOCIAL SECURITY REPRESENTATIVES CAN HELP (OR NOT!)

Social Security representatives—in the office and on the phone—are a mixed bag. I have found them unfailingly polite. Many are very well informed. But many are not, and that's a problem for people trying to plan their future.

I strongly suggest that you speak with at least two representatives before making any decisions. If you've been to a local office, go back home and call Social Security's consumer line. If you've spoken with one rep by phone, call back and speak with another. If you get contradictory information, tell the second rep what the first one said and try to sort it out. You can ask for a supervisor at any time. You might even want to call a third time.

Sometimes you get a wrong answer because you haven't supplied enough information, so always prepare your questions carefully. If you're under full retirement age, ask what the effect of filing early has on your various benefits.

Questions involving filing for restricted spousal benefits are especially hairy. Ditto for widows, widowers, and the divorced who are trying to work out optimum claiming strategies. Even basic questions might be answered incorrectly. When I called with a personal question, for example, the rep on the phone kept insisting that my husband's full retirement age was 65 (that's a blast from the past). I asked her to check, and she came back with the right answer—66.

I don't mean to beat up on Social Security reps. They work hard and might answer dozens of questions a day. But as you've seen from this chapter, answers can be pretty complex. Reps need a lot of experience before they can be sure of their footing.

I should add that many financial planners and other advisers are almost entirely in the dark. They haven't paid much attention to claiming strategies for Social Security and might know little about the rules. Some of them subscribe to computer programs designed to help you optimize your Social Security checks. If they don't, or give you only generic answers, I suggest that you use one of the online services I list on pages 67 and 68 and take the results to your adviser.

Ultimately, the size of your Social Security benefit is entirely in your hands. A Social Security rep will *never* call up and say, "Hey, if you switch benefits you could be collecting $500 more." Or "Hey, why are you applying for retirement at 65 when you and your spouse have so many more options at 66?"

Your life, your retirement, your choice.

SOME SOCIAL SECURITY BENEFITS ARE LOPPED

Some people covered by Social Security will not get the full dollar benefit. Mostly, this means workers who also have government pensions. Here are the two lopping rules:

The Windfall Elimination Provision. This affects workers with two-stage careers. You earned a pension from a government agency or foreign employer that didn't withhold Social Security taxes and you also worked 40 quarters in private-sector Social Security jobs. Counting only your private-sector earnings, you look like a low-income worker with a short career. If true, that would entitle you to higher benefits than other workers get, relative to your earnings. But in fact, you were never a low-income worker. You simply spent 10 years in the private sector before or after a government career. Social Security reduces your benefit by up to half the amount your government pension pays.

The Government Pension Offset. This affects workers with government pensions whose spouses worked in a job that's covered by Social Security. You can file for spousal or survivor's benefits on your spouse's Social Security account, but your payment will be reduced by two-thirds of the amount of your government pension. This could eliminate your benefit completely.

DON'T FORGET MEDICARE!

Medicare starts at 65, even for people who wait until 66 or later to claim their Social Security benefits. Be sure you apply three months before your 65th birthday. Which plans to apply for depend on whether you're also in an employee or retiree group plan. Chapter 4 tells you how to decide.

GET TAX SMART ABOUT YOUR SOCIAL SECURITY INCOME

You get a big tax break on your Social Security income. For most beneficiaries, it's tax free. For the rest, half of it doesn't count when figuring what your tax will be.

Thanks to this special treatment, a dollar of Social Security income is worth much more after tax than a dollar of income withdrawn from an individual retirement account, because each IRA dollar is taxed in full.

At first blush, you might think it makes sense to take your Social Security benefits early to help pay your bills while you're letting your tax-deferred IRA grow. In fact, the opposite might be true. If your IRA is substantial, it's often better to draw on it for the first few years and let your tax-favored Social Security benefits grow.

The level of tax on your benefits depends on something called your "combined income." That's the modified adjusted gross income reported on your income tax return (including taxable withdrawals from retirement accounts[9]), plus any income from tax-exempt bonds, plus half—just half—of your Social Security benefit. The other half of your benefit isn't included in the combined income calculation at all.

Benefits are tax free for singles with combined incomes under $25,000 and married couples filing jointly with combined incomes under $32,000.

Up to half of Social Security benefits are taxable for singles with combined incomes between $25,000 and $34,000, and couples between $32,000 and $44,000.

---

9   But excluding withdrawals from tax-free Roth accounts.

Up to 85 percent of Social Security benefits are taxable for singles with combined incomes higher than $34,000 and couples higher than $44,000.

But remember, half of your Social Security benefits weren't counted when figuring how much "combined income" you're reporting. A married couple with no other source of income could have $64,000 in Social Security benefits before exceeding the tax-free threshold of $32,000.

In short, the tax break on Social Security income is much better than most people think.

WILL SOCIAL SECURITY GO BANKRUPT?

No.

If you're grabbing your Social Security checks at 62 because you think the system will fail, your political mind has taken over your rational, financial mind.

After the harsh stock market lessons of 2000 and 2008, Social Security won't be privatized, either. Beneficiaries don't want to deal with investment risk.

I was tempted to end the chapter there, but just in case the doomsters are still scaring you, I'll say a little more. The worst that can happen, if no changes are made to the program at all, is that benefits will drop by 25 percent around 2035 (which is probably past my sell-by date). At that level, current payroll taxes can fund Social Security indefinitely.

But benefits won't drop. There might be tweaks that reduce your benefits' future growth, especially if you're among those with higher incomes. But Social Security keeps millions of older people out of poverty and saves millions of adult children from having to support mom and dad. No president, no Senate, no Congress will let those voters down.

4

Getting the Most from Your Health Insurance—Before and After 65

Peace of mind is knowing that you can see a doctor when you're sick.

Employee coverage. Individual policies. Subsidized policies from the state and federal health insurance exchanges. Medicare, and, in the majority of states, expanded Medicaid. Equal rights for same-sex married couples. Most likely, you won't fall through the cracks in the medical system anymore. That's especially good news for people in their 50s and early 60s who retired early or work for companies or nonprofits that don't provide health insurance. Thanks to the Affordable Care Act (ACA) you cannot be refused a policy based on preexisting medical conditions. Importantly, there are also caps on the premiums you'll pay, relative to what the insurance companies charge younger people.

This new availability of individual health insurance is freeing employees from jobs they don't want. You don't have to keep working solely because you depend on your company's group plan. That gives you the option of transforming your life.

For most middle-class people, health insurance still isn't cheap, no matter which type of policy you have. How much it drains your budget depends on your age, situation, and coverage choice. Decision making is easier if you pass from a comprehensive employee plan directly to Medicare. It becomes more complicated if you're younger than Medicare age (65) and will have to spend a few years in the world of individual insurance. To get the most for your money it pays to know the rules.

A QUICK HEALTH INSURANCE PRIMER

Tourists (like us) in Insuranceville need to learn a few words so that we can speak with the natives. Here's the essential phrase book. With it, you'll be able to compare different policies' coverage and costs.

The *premium* is the amount you pay for the policy each month.

The *annual deductible* is the sum you have to pay out of pocket before the insurance company starts picking up bills. For example, if your deductible is $2,000, your first $2,000 in covered medical expenses are entirely yours to pay each year. The insurance starts paying as soon as your bills exceed that amount.

Your *co-payment* is the fixed amount you pay for each doctor visit. For example, it might be $15 for internists and $30 for specialists. Normally, it does not count toward the deductible. You pay it even when the deductible has already been met.

Coinsurance is the percentage you're required to pay toward certain bills after you've met the deductible. For example, you might owe 20 percent of the cost of a hospital visit or 50 percent of a doctor's bill.

Your *maximum out-of-pocket* is the most you're required to pay for the policy's covered medical services each year, no matter how sick you are. Once you've spent that amount—in deductibles, co-pays, and coinsurance—your policy should pick up 100 percent of your covered bills. The following year, the deductible and other kinds of cost sharing start all over again. (Your monthly premium payments aren't counted toward the maximum. Neither is the extra cost of using health providers out of your plan's network.)

Your *provider network* is the list of doctors, hospitals, imaging facilities, labs, and other professionals who participate in the plan and agree to accept its reimbursement rates. If you see a provider outside the network you will pay all or part of the bill, depending on the plan you have.

There are three general types of individual or employer plans: HMOs (health maintenance organizations), POSs (point of service plans), and PPOs (preferred provider organizations).

HMOs won't pay for doctors outside the network. Their premiums are generally lower because of their tight cost control. Usually, they require that you choose a primary doctor and get referrals from that doctor before you see a specialist. Sometimes you're allowed to see network specialists at will, although you'll probably need pre-authorization for expensive specialty care. These plans might also be called EPOs (exclusive provider organizations).

POS plans require you to pick a primary doctor within the network. That doctor can refer you to outside specialists, with the plan paying a smaller percentage of the bills.

PPOs, whose premiums are generally higher, let you see any provider in the network at will. Many plans let you choose outside docs but pay at a reduced rate and only for an amount the PPO considers "reasonable." All types of plans cover emergency services by doctors, clinics, and hospitals outside the network at in-network rates.

You run into *balance billing* if you belong to a PPO and take advantage of your option to see a doctor who doesn't participate in the plan. The PPO will pay a portion of the bill. But out-of-network doctors typically charge you more than network doctors do. You'll have to pay the balance, which can be much higher than you expect.

For example, say that your PPO sets $100 as a reasonable charge for a routine visit to the doctor. It covers 80 percent of the bill from a network doctor and 60 percent of the bill from a doctor outside the network. In network, your plan pays $80 and you pay $20. Out of network, the plan pays $60—but the doctor is free to charge you, say, $200. You'd wind up owing $140. The moral: Stick with network doctors. Balance billing can be horrendous for big-ticket procedures such as surgery. Out-of-network labs and imaging facilities might charge five to 10 times more than the PPO's schedule of reasonable costs.

Separate fees are being charged everywhere. This isn't a term of art, just a new way that doctors and hospitals are squeezing more money from patients. If your child breaks an arm and it's set at the emergency room, you might be charged extra for the sling. An ophthalmologist checking your eyes for glasses might add a separate "refraction fee" for testing your visual acuity. The hospital might escort you to a room to fill out forms, then charge a "room fee." Even though these are in-network providers, insurance typically won't pay. At every turn, the medical industry is fighting to keep its revenues up.

EMPLOYEE INSURANCE: COSTING MORE EVERY YEAR

The trends in employee coverage are not in your favor (no surprise there). Deductibles and co-pays are rising and your choice gets more limited year by year. Employers are experimenting with different ways of holding down their costs (although not necessarily your costs). If you haven't yet seen any of the new, alternative plans, you almost certainly will soon.

For now, PPOs are the plans most widely offered by corporations. They charge the highest premiums and give you the widest consumer choice. HMOs usually cost the least. POS plans fall into the mid-price range.

As a supplement to your insurance, your company might offer a *flexible-spending* plan. You deposit up to $2,500 by means of payroll deductions and use the money, tax free, to pay for qualified medical expenses. You can spend up to the limit even if you haven't yet put all the money in. Flex plans require you to submit proof that each expense meets the test. If there's still money left in the plan at the end of the year, you normally lose it. Some employers, however, let you carry over $500 or less to the following year.

High-deductible plans are the most popular of the new, cost-shifting alternatives. One-third of large companies are making this your only choice. Premiums are low but you pay a ton out of pocket if you have an accident or become seriously ill.

As with other plans, you pay all the medical bills yourself up to a specific annual deductible. That includes prescription drugs except those considered necessary for preventive care, which have to be provided free.

For 2016, the median deductible was around $1,500 for individual plans and $3,000 for families. Once you've met the deductible, you enter a cost-sharing zoning. You pay a percentage of each bill until you reach a maximum out-of-pocket amount. The 2016 maximum, including co-pays and coinsurance but not premiums, came to $6,550 for singles and $13,000 for families (a huge amount, which rises annually with inflation). Above the maximum, the insurance company pays all the remaining costs that year as long as you're using network providers. The following year, the deductibles, cost sharing, and maximums apply again.

High-deductible plans usually come with a *health savings account* (HSA). With this account, you can put away money through payroll deductions, tax free, to pay the portion of the medical bills that you're responsible for. If there's money left in the plan at year-end, it rolls forward to another year. You can even take it with you if you switch jobs or retire. Most large employers contribute something to their workers' HSAs but smaller ones generally do not. The maximum contribution allowed for 2015 was $3,350 for individuals and $6,750 for families (these amounts rise annually with inflation), plus an extra $1,000 for people 55 and older.

Cost-shifting plans get more inventive every year. They currently include: *fixed-contributions*—you get a fixed dollar amount to apply toward the cost of whichever plan on the company's menu you choose. That effectively raises the premium you have to pay for the more comprehensive plans. *Gated plans*—you pay less if you pass a health test or agree to take specific steps to control a health condition. *Unitized plans*—families pay per person rather than as a group, with costs based on each person's health and participation in wellness programs. That encourages you to use the lower-cost doctors and services in the network. *Reference-pricing*—your coverage pays a fixed amount for each medical service you use no matter what the doctor charges.

With all plans, you pay network health providers the fees negotiated by the insurance company. That's true even for the bills that fall within the plan's deductible, which you're paying out of pocket. Out-of-network providers will charge you their regular, higher fees.

Plans that shift costs to you are supposed to encourage you to shop for less-expensive care. That's possible in Massachusetts—the first state to require health-care providers to publish price lists. Some large employers require it, too. As an employee, you can go online, enter the medical service you need, and compare what various network doctors, imaging centers, and hospitals generally charge. If your doctor is charging more than others, ask for a discount.

More often, however, you can't find out, in advance, what medical services cost. Health providers don't reveal prices voluntarily. If your income is modest, you'll probably choose to save money by seeing the doctor less, which might be okay but might also endanger your health.

GETTING YOUR MONEY'S WORTH FROM AN EMPLOYER PLAN

Light users of medical care should look at low-premium policies. Heavy users should consider higher-premium policies with lower out-of-pocket maximums, because they reduce the number of expensive surprises. Some other tips:

- Use the doctors in your network. It's the fastest, easiest way to save money. If that means changing doctors, so be it. Medical care is increasingly data driven rather than based on docs' knowing your history over time, so any good doctor will do. Like it or not, that's modern medical life.

- Submit all your qualified bills to the plan, including those that you're required to pay out of pocket. That's the way the insurance company keeps track of whether you've met the deductible. Usually your health provider will submit these bills for you, but check.

- Use your company's flexible spending plan to get tax-free dollars for medical bills! Deposit roughly the amount of money you spend out of pocket in an ordinary year.

- High-deductible plans work well for people in good health (and who stay that way!). Your premiums are lower and you don't face a lot of medical bills. Your costs will jump, however, if an illness or accident lays you low, because of the high deductibles. If you find that you'll need expensive treatments in the future, you might switch to an HMO or PPO, if your company provides one, during the annual open enrollment period.

- If your high-deductible plan comes with a health savings account, deposit as much as you can afford. You can use that money tax free to pay for qualified out-of-pocket medical expenses. If you're healthy and don't draw much from this account, it can grow to a substantial amount over many years.

- Check your medical bills. Odds are there's a mistake and—I promise—it won't be in your favor. Overbilling hurts more than ever, now that you're shouldering a higher percentage of the cost. Don't settle for the opaque bills that hospitals send out. Ask for an itemized statement. You might find duplicate charges or services that weren't performed. Doctors use codes to identify each treatment; you can use the Internet to find out what they mean and whether they're correct. Services such as the Alliance of Claims Assistance Professionals or Medical Billing Advocates of America can help you find someone to check the bills and solve any problems. They cost a minimum of around $50 to $75 an hour, rising to $100 or more. So they're best used when you have the complex, multiple bills that accompany a major illness.
- Don't skimp on preventive services. Under the Affordable Care Act, most of them have to be cost free, even under high-deductible plans. This includes colonoscopies, mammograms, cancer screening, and immunizations, among many others. Certain prescription drugs are also on the "preventive" list. *One warning:* Your "free" screening might come with an unexpected hospital or anesthesiologist's bill. To me, that's bait and switch. It shouldn't be allowed. For the list of free services, go to HealthCare.gov and type "Preventive Care" into the Search box.
- To cut your costs for maintenance drugs, use your plan's mail-order services. For some pills, however, it's cheaper to pay out of pocket. Many chain drugstores charge just $4 for a 30-day supply and $10 for a three-month supply. To find them, type "$4 a month for prescriptions" into a search engine.
- Discuss price with your doctors. They should be using only labs and other services that are within your network. Even in network, some labs are less expensive than others. Use any

tools your employer offers that help you compare costs, then tell your doctor what you've found. Some docs will give you a discount if you're paying out of pocket, especially if you'll pay cash.

- Stay out of your hospital's expensive emergency room if at all possible. Look for local, stand-alone urgent care centers that are on your plan if your health issue isn't life threatening. Okay for a broken finger; not okay for chest pains. Walk-in clinics at chain stores such as CVS, Publix, Target, Walgreens, and Walmart are good for minor ailments and flu shots. They're staffed by nurses and accept most major health insurance policies.

- Learn how to take care of your illnesses yourself and follow your doctor's directions to the letter. Of the people readmitted to the hospital soon after being discharged, a large percentage didn't follow doctor's orders.

- Know the rules on emergency coverage. Under the ACA, plans have to cover you at in-network rates if you're taken to an out-of-network hospital. Before you take a trip, find out your plan's procedure for getting permission to see an out-of-town doctor at in-network rates.

- When you go to a hospital for surgery, the hospital might call in an assistant surgeon or consultant who is not on your health plan. You unknowingly gave "permission" when you signed the admission forms. You might get a huge, unexpected bill that your health plan usually won't pay. This can happen even at hospitals that are on your plan and sometimes at the instigation of your in-network doctors. Some emergency room docs and consultants might be out of network, too. To me, this practice amounts to theft—docs stripping you of money when you're anesthetized and can't complain. You might try to defend yourself by telling your own doctor not to allow it and writing "no out-of-network providers accepted" on the hospital admission form but I can't guarantee that will work. A nasty business. Totally unfair. A few states have made it illegal for health professionals at an in-network facility to charge you out-of-network rates. It should be illegal everywhere.

- Private health insurance normally doesn't cover you when you travel abroad. Instead, consider a short-term medical travel policy. It should pay most of the cost of emergency care, after deductibles and co-pays, as well as medical evacuation. Travel policies exclude normal treatment for a preexisting condition but will protect you if the condition suddenly becomes acute.

- If you lose your job and with it your health insurance, sign up immediately for COBRA. Your company will send you a letter explaining how to do it. COBRA keeps you on your company's plan, at your expense, while you shop the ACA Marketplace for something cheaper. Never leave a gap in your coverage. Just a few unlucky days without health insurance could cost you your life savings.

- Lose weight. Quit smoking. Drink less. Eat right. Wear seat belts. Exercise. There is no doctor bill so cheap as the one that you don't incur in the first place.

Employee Benefits for Nontraditional Couples

The constitutional right to marry, established by the Supreme Court in 2015, is a godsend for same-sex spouses who were previously barred from employee health plans. But what's following the court decision is not all good news. Health benefits for domestic partners who choose not to marry might be wiped out. The rules and practices of employer plans are evolving. For the latest news, keep checking the website of Lambda Legal (lambdalegal.org), which fights for the civil rights of gay, lesbian, bisexual, and transgender communities. As of this writing, here's the state of play:

- *Married same-sex couples:* The majority of employee health plans already extended benefits to same-sex spouses, even before the Supreme Court ruled. A minority barred them, especially in states that didn't recognize their unions. The right-to-marriage decision doesn't specifically require private companies to open up their health plans to same-sex spouses. But if they don't, they'll be vulnerable to lawsuits based on sex discrimination. The upshot: a big win for same-sex spouses seeking affordable health insurance.

- *Unmarried same-sex couples in registered domestic partnerships or civil unions:* About one-third of civilian workers have access to employee health benefits if they register in their states as domestic partners, according to the federal government's National Compensation Survey. In general, companies offered this option only because gay couples couldn't marry. Now that they can, a number of employee plans are dropping partnership benefits and covering only spouses. Effectively, they're forcing their employees to the altar, whether they want to marry or not. More enlightened companies are keeping their benefits for domestic partners, on the ground that it's none of their business how employees choose to structure their intimate relationships. With any luck, that's the future.

- *Unmarried opposite-sex couples in registered domestic partnerships or civil unions:* About one-quarter of civilian workers have access to benefits for a committed partner of the opposite sex. They, too, risk losing health benefits if their employer decides to cover only married couples. But employers who set up this benefit for couples of the opposite sex are probably more committed to accepting nontraditional relationships, hence are less likely to drop them.

- *Transgender couples:* They have the same right to marry and the same right to enter into a domestic partnership as any other couple. They qualify as a spouse or partner under whatever health plan their company offers.

- *Couples who switch to individual insurance from an employer plan:* Same-sex spouses must be accepted on individual policies, under the Affordable Care Act. Many ACA plans also accept domestic partnerships, regardless of sex.

THE AFFORDABLE CARE ACT: A SAFETY NET THAT REWRITES YOUR CHOICES IN MIDLIFE

Before I get into the workings of the Affordable Care Act, let me tell you a story.

I've been a freelance writer for most of my working life. It almost didn't happen, solely because of my obsession about staying medically secure.

Back when I had a corporate editing job, the *Washington Post* asked me to turn in my gray flannel suit and start an independent column on personal finance. I didn't worry about the financial risk of working for myself (my corporate job didn't pay me much anyway), but I was terrified at the thought of losing the group health insurance that my family depended on. After much back and forth, the *Post* agreed to put me on its own group plan even though I wouldn't be an employee. So I gambled and took the offer. Writing that column changed my life.

That's one of the reasons I feel strongly about the ACA. You're not nailed to a job anymore to ensure yourself decent health insurance. You can make life and career choices without regard to where or whether you choose to work. Over time, that will bring a tremendous change to the texture of American life.

Under the ACA, insurance companies have to sell comprehensive, individual policies to people under 65 regardless of health. They can't cancel your coverage, raise its price because you get sick, or sell policies that are essentially meaningless. If your income lies in the low or middle range you can get subsidies to help pay the premiums (see page 90).

With these guarantees, you can rewrite the second chapter of your life. For example, you can retire early and be assured of health care even if your employer doesn't have a retiree plan. You can leave a big company and work for (or start) a small business that doesn't offer benefits. You might join a small nonprofit or quit your job and become a volunteer. If one spouse retires early, the other one doesn't have to keep working just to hold on to the family's coverage. You can create a retirement budget without worrying that a single illness will blow it up. If you're laid off, you don't have to pray that you'll qualify for private insurance or, if not, that your body (and life) will hold up until you reach Medicare age.

You're still faced with high out-of-pocket costs in the form of deductibles and coinsurance. I don't want to kid you about the expense of American medical care. But at least you'll be covered for catastrophic costs.

You can buy individual policies in one of two ways. The first way is to use the ACA Marketplace online. There, competing health insurance companies post the policies they have for sale, along with their prices and the medical networks they use. You can choose a policy yourself or ask an insurance agent for help. You *must* purchase through the online Marketplace to qualify for government-subsidized premiums (see page 90). Alternatively, you can skip the Marketplace and go directly to a health insurance agent. That might be a better route if you earn too much to qualify for subsidies. All new policies, regardless of how you buy them, are subject to the new consumer-protection rules.

The ACA requires individuals to have health insurance or else pay a fine. That might stick in your craw but why would you even want to go bare? Your reward is that if you become seriously ill you won't be a financial burden on your family, the medical system, or the taxpayer. Bankruptcies due entirely to unpayable medical bills should become a thing of the deplorable past. The requirement to buy insurance also brings healthy, younger people into the system, which is what makes it possible for insurance companies to hold down premium costs for people in midlife.

Before the ACA took effect, people in their early 60s paid four to six times more for health insurance than people in their early 20s, assuming that they could get individual coverage at all, according to the Henry J. Kaiser Family Foundation, which studies health-care policy. Now those in their early 60s pay no more than three times more than young people do. In your early 50s, it's about twice more. In a handful of states, applicants of all ages pay the same.

You still might decide to stick with your job, purely for the group health insurance, even if you'd rather not. Anyone can buy coverage on the ACA Marketplace but you generally can't get subsidies if you're eligible for an employee group plan. An unsubsidized ACA plan will probably cost more than the employee plan does. You might also have to accept higher deductibles and coinsurance.

On the other hand, your income might drop if you resigned from your company in order to do something different with your life. At that point, a subsidized ACA policy might cost less than you're paying for employee coverage now.

How Much Will It Cost If You Ignore the Law and Don't Buy Health Insurance?

The annual fine, for 2016 and beyond, is the higher of the following amounts: 2.5 percent of your family's taxable income; or $695 for each adult plus $347.50 for each child, with a family cap of $2,085. And, um, yes . . . there's something else. If (when!) you get sick, the uninsured medical bills will knock your budget out of the park. Count on it.

Navigating the Health-Care Marketplace

To find an individual policy, start with HealthCare.gov and click on "Get Coverage" then click on "See Plans & Prices." You'll be asked a couple of questions and then directed to your state's Marketplace (also known as an "exchange"). There, each plan shows you what it covers and what it costs. It's generally easy to sign up online.

The ACA mandates four types of plans for individuals—Bronze, Silver, Gold, and Platinum. They all cover the same essential health benefits. But they vary in the way they price specific medical services, the drugs they cover, the doctors and hospitals in their networks, the size of your premium, and the amounts you pay out of pocket. There might be more than one policy under each heading—for example, an insurer might offer Silver and SilverPrime. The premiums on Marketplace plans vary from county to county within your state.

How to Pick a Plan

Bronze plans generally carry the lowest premiums. They also charge you the highest annual deductibles (typically, $5,000 to $6,000 for individuals) and other out-of-pocket costs. Nevertheless, Bronze might be the plan to buy if you rarely see the inside of a doctor's office. High deductibles don't matter when you have hardly any bills to pay. If your health suddenly changes, you'll pay the Bronze policy's maximum out-of-pocket in the current year. At the end of the year, you can switch to a plan that pays more of your costs.

As you go up the "metals" ladder, plans charge higher premiums and reduce your deductibles and out-of-pocket costs. The deductibles on Silver plans commonly run in the $2,000 to $3,000 range (but can be higher). They tend to pay more of your expenses, compared with Bronze plans. You might choose a Silver if you see doctors often but, to your knowledge, have nothing major coming up.

The second-cheapest Silver plan is the benchmark policy used to calculate any tax subsidy that you might be owed.

Be sure to check what's offered by all the insurance companies on your local Marketplace. One company's Silver plan might cost you less than another company's Bronze plan. If your income is especially low a "modified" Silver plan is usually the best buy of all (see page 93).

Gold plans cost more and pay even more of each bill. In many (not all) plans, the annual deductible is $1,000 or less. You'd go Gold if you have a chronic illness that requires lots of drugs and doctor visits or if you have surgery coming up.

Platinum, the plan with the highest premium, requires you to pay the least in deductibles and other cost sharing. Many companies don't offer Platinum. If it's available, you might choose it in a year that you have expensive surgery coming up, then switch to a plan with lower premiums in the following year.

Each plan puts up a standardized summary of its costs and coverage on the Marketplace website so that you can make comparisons. Be sure to click through the details. It's boring but there's money to be saved. For example, one plan might count the cost of expensive drugs toward your deductible while another plan might not, making the second plan more expensive than it looks. The plans might also charge different levels of coinsurance for different services. Coinsurance can be a killer if your bills are high.

Preventive procedures such as regular checkups, adult immunization, colonoscopies, and cholesterol or breast cancer screenings are exempt from the deductible. You're covered for these procedures right away, at no extra cost. You can find the full list at HealthCare.gov. Take a look and be sure to take advantage of as many of them them as you can.

All of the Marketplace plans will cost less, maybe quite a bit less, if you qualify for tax credits to help pay the premiums.

The Joy of Subsidies If You're Eligible

Depending on the size of your income, you might be entitled to a subsidy. It's paid in the form of an income tax credit that reduces the cost of your health insurance premiums. You're eligible if your income ranges between 100 percent and 400 percent of the federal poverty level, based on your family size. The subsidy shrinks as your income goes up and eventually phases out. In 2016, individuals got the credit with incomes between $11,770 and as much as $47,080. The range for two-person households was $15,930 to $63,720. Larger families have higher maximums. These income limits rise with inflation every year.

If you qualify for a tax subsidy there's a ceiling on what you can be charged in premiums. People at the poverty level pay no more than 2 percent of their income. At the upper end, people at three to four times the poverty level pay no more than 9.5 percent of their income. Your ceiling payment plus the subsidy buys the second-cheapest Silver plan in your area. If the second-cheapest Silver plan costs less than 9.5 percent of your income, no subsidy is given.

If you do get a subsidy, you can apply it to a higher-priced Silver plan or to a Gold or Platinum plan, but you'll have to pay the additional premium cost yourself. You can also apply your subsidy to a Bronze plan, to reduce its up-front cost. But remember that with Bronze you're trading lower premiums for much higher cost sharing.

The Premium Subsidy Is Run Through the Income Tax System, and Here's How It Works

When you apply for a policy in the ACA Marketplace, you're asked to estimate your income for the year. The website calculates the subsidy based on your estimate. That money can be paid directly to the insurance plan you choose. The plan will bill you monthly for the remaining premium amount.

When you file your tax return, the IRS will look at your actual income compared with your estimate. If your income turns out to be higher than you expected, you'll have to pay some or all of the subsidy back. There's an extra line on your tax return to report what you owe. If your income turns out to be lower than your estimate, you deserve a higher subsidy than you received. The IRS will pay you the extra money in the form of a refund or a reduced tax payment. (If you're really punctilious, you can report changes in your expected income during the year and your subsidy will be adjusted automatically, up or down.)

You'll pay the lowest possible insurance premium, up front, if you assign the entire subsidy to the insurance plan right away. However, this raises the risk that you might have to pay some of the money back. You might consider asking that only half or three-quarters of the subsidy be paid to the insurance company. You can claim any remaining subsidy in cash when you file your return.

Assets such as home equity and the money in retirement plans aren't counted when figuring the subsidy—only the modified adjusted gross income that you report on your tax return. If you're retired comfortably with a home, some cash, a nest egg in a tax-deferred retirement account, and a middle income, you'll probably be eligible for help.

Warning: **You could lose your subsidy in a year that your income jumps!** For example, you might earn a capital gain by selling stocks, bonds, mutual funds, or any other securities. You might sell some real estate or take money out of an individual retirement account. That additional income could make you too "rich" for a tax credit that year. If the gains don't repeat in the following year your income will decline and you'll find yourself back in tax-credit territory. (Inheritances don't count as income, although earnings from the inheritance do.)

If your income is too high for subsidies, you can still buy on the ACA Marketplace. Or call a health insurance agent to see if you can find better or cheaper coverage somewhere else.

Special Alert for people whose regular income is nearing the upper limit for tax subsidies. It will cost you a fortune if it rises above the line! As long as you qualify for the tax-credit, the ACA caps your premium payments at 9.5 percent of income. But if your income rises even one dollar above the line, you're not protected anymore. You'll have to pay the policy's full market price, which could reach 16 percent of your income or more. A two-person policy priced at $5,000 with the tax credit could cost $15,000 if you can't claim the credit anymore.

Sooooo—if you think you might pop above the line, try a little jujitsu with your cash flow. You might take a smaller amount out of your individual retirement account, reduce your freelance work, send bills for consulting jobs at the end of the year so you'll be paid in January instead of December, pay tax-deductible bills in December, take investment losses to offset your gains, or cut down on the number of days you work in your business. If you have your own business, consider reducing your income by making the maximum contribution to a simplified employee pension (see page 163; contributing to an individual retirement account won't work). You might also put off taking Social Security until you're at least 66 (that's a good idea anyway—see Chapter 3).

To find out how much more it will cost you if you exceed the income limit, go to the Health Insurance Marketplace Calculator at the Kaiser Family Foundation (KFF.org) and enter different levels of income. You'll see immediately how your premiums and credits will rise and fall. Losing the protection of the income ceiling hammers older people, in particular, because in most states they can be charged so much more than the young.

If you can't afford a normal Marketplace policy, there's an escape hatch. It's called a "catastrophic policy." You can buy it if the cheapest policy on the ACA Marketplace costs more than 8 percent of your income. You still have to pay the maximum out-of-pocket that the law allows and are not entitled to tax credits. But premiums are relatively low and you're covered for serious accidents or illness. You get preventive care plus three primary-care visits to the doctor at no extra cost. These policies can also be sold to anyone under 30, regardless of income.

Buyers with low incomes get an even bigger break. If your income falls between the poverty level and 250 percent of the poverty level you're eligible for reduced cost sharing through a "modified" Silver plan. Cost-sharing subsidies can reduce your annual deductible to as little as $100 to $500. They reduce co-pays and coinsurance, too. You might have to hunt for these plans but be sure to do so if you think you're eligible.

If "hardship" renders you absolutely unable to pay, you can be exempted from having to buy a health insurance policy. To find out if you qualify, go to HealthCare.gov and type "Hardship Exemptions" in the Search box. You're off the payment hook but that's not good news. You're still uninsured.

Getting Your Money's Worth from an ACA Policy

- If you're a heavy user of medical care, add up the competing policies' annual premiums and maximum out-of-pocket costs. That's the amount you'll probably pay each year, so investigate the cheapest policy first. *Important note:* The "maximum out-of-pocket" refers only to bills you receive from providers in your plan's network. If you're treated by out-of-network providers, even inadvertently, your annual costs will rise above the so-called maximum.

- If you're a light user of medical care, add the premium and the annual deductible. That's your minimum probable cost.

- Plan designs vary widely, which is why you have to read each policy's coverage disclosures. Some plans might charge you no more than a co-pay for routine doctor visits even if you haven't met your deductible. That would be a good choice for light users of medical care. Other plans might make you pay out of pocket for expensive drugs in addition to the deductible. That can be a killer.

- Check each plan's medical network to see which doctors and hospitals participate. Somewhere on the summary of benefits there's a link to its list. You want to see your area's top hospitals there. Ideally, you also want to find your own favorite doctors. If not, however, there are many, many good doctors. Picking new ones is often worth it when it means saving money on premiums and cost sharing. Double-check with the doctors, including the ones you're seeing now. The lists on the website aren't always accurate.

- If you take prescription drugs, check each plan's summary for the level of cost sharing. Some plans don't pay until you've met the deductible and then charge you 20 or 30 percent of the price. If you use a lot of drugs, that's going to be expensive. Other plans handle prescription drugs separately from the deductible. You might pay $10 per prescription for generic drugs, $35 for preferred brand-name drugs, $70 for nonpreferred drugs, and a percentage payment for specialty drugs. The summary gives you a link to the plan's formulary, which lists the drugs it currently covers. All the plans cover routine drugs or a reasonable substitute but vary in their choice of expensive drugs. Your doctor can appeal in special cases.

- If you're a snowbird with houses in two states, you have to buy the policy in your primary state of residence. Make sure that it uses a national provider network or maintains cooperative ties with plans that will cover you in the second location.

- Don't smoke. Smokers are charged up to 50 percent more.

- If you're working and your company health plan doesn't offer benefits to your spouse, he or she can buy a policy on the Marketplace and receive tax credits, if eligible. If your company does offer spousal benefits but you can't afford them, your spouse can still buy on the Marketplace but tax credits aren't allowed. That's a huge flaw in the program. It especially hurts lower-income workers who can't afford their employer's family policy. If an ACA-improvement law is ever passed, a fix should be at the top of the list.

- If you're working and have a comprehensive employee plan, you can't drop it and use tax subsidies to buy something cheaper on the Marketplace. ACA policies are for people who don't have access to other forms of good and subsidized coverage. Two exceptions: You can buy an ACA plan, with subsidies if your employee plan is so poor that it doesn't offer you much or if your company charges you more than 9.5 percent of your income for individual coverage.

- If you're 65 and eligible for a company retiree plan that covers a younger spouse, your buying decision depends in part on how the plan blends with Medicare. It might pay for you to go on Medicare while your spouse gets an ACA policy. Or it might pay to keep the retiree plan. For more on this, see pages 105 and 106.

- If you're in a retiree plan and under 65, you can switch to a Marketplace policy if the tax credits or coverage make it a better deal. You have to wait for the open enrollment period to make the change.

- All individual policies have to cover the same essential medical services that the Marketplace plans do. Tax credits, however, are available only if you buy through the Marketplace rather than from an insurance company directly.

- To claim tax credits, you have to file a tax return. The credits are refundable if you don't earn enough money to owe taxes in the year the credits were received. That means that the government will send you a check for what the subsidy was worth.

- You get no premium subsidy, even if you're within the income range, if the size of your expected subsidy is higher than the cost of the Silver benchmark plan in your area.

- If you don't qualify for subsidies, you can still buy on the Marketplace. You might also use its plans as price and coverage benchmarks for judging any health insurance plan offered outside the Marketplace.

- You can buy a plan or change plans during the open enrollment period, which runs from November 15 to February 15. These dates apply both to Marketplace plans and the plans you buy directly through insurance agents. If you wind up with no plan because you missed the deadline, you'll be uninsured for the year and will owe a tax penalty. You can buy or change a plan at any time, however, if there's a change in your status. That would include divorcing, losing job-based coverage, or moving out of your current coverage area.

- If you move to a new area, coordinating coverage can be tricky. Apply for a new plan in advance so that it will take effect as soon as you arrive. If you wait until moving day or later, the new plan might not cover you for two to six weeks. During that time, you should still be on your old policy's books. It will insure you for emergency room treatment at in-network rates but higher out-of-network rates will apply to doctor and hospital bills. Talk to your current insurer about the best way to make the changeover. Ideally, your new policy will start on the day the old one stops.

- Shop for a plan every year, don't just renew the plan you have. Prices, premiums, and services are changing all the time. The odds are high that a switch will save you money.

- Married same-sex couples can obtain family policies under federal rules. At this writing, the situation is mixed for those in registered civil unions or domestic partnerships. Some insurance companies provide you with family policies, others don't. The Plan Finder at Finder.HealthCare.gov has a same-sex filter that directs you to plans that will cover your partner.

- Some health insurance plans include dental coverage. More often, it's available on the Marketplace as a separate purchase.

- You can get help! The ACA provides for local "assisters" or "navigators" who will help you in person or by phone. At HealthCare.gov, click on "Individuals and Families" then "Get Answers" and go to the "Find Local Help" button for the names of the organizations in the 34 states it serves. The 16 states (and the District of Columbia) that run their own Marketplace sites have lists of their own. If you're not on the Web, local health services have the navigators' phone numbers. Health insurance agents can help you, too. For the names of some local agents, go to the website of the National Association of Health Underwriters at nahu.org.

- For online answers to dozens of detailed questions about the ACA and who's eligible for subsidies, go to the excellent site run by the Kaiser Family Foundation at KFF.org. Search for "Frequently Asked Questions about Health Reform." You can also get answers at HealthCare.gov by clicking on "Glossary" at the bottom of the page or entering a keyword into "Search."

At 65, you fall into the arms of Medicare, which takes care of you for the rest of your life. Whew.

THE FUNDAMENTALS OF MEDICARE

Medicare offers something for everyone at 65. You qualify if you've met the work requirements for Social Security (40 quarters of coverage) or your spouse or registered domestic partner qualifies and you're on his or her account. You also have to be a citizen or permanent resident. To be sure that you don't miss out on any reimbursements, start the sign-up process three months before your 65th birthday.

Medicare comes in four parts. Which parts to take and when depend on whether you have other health insurance, such as an employee or retiree group plan, and what kind of coverage is available to a spouse under 65. This guide should help you decide. But first, a quick zip through Medicare's details.

Part A covers hospitalizations, short stays in a skilled nursing facility, hospice, and a limited amount of home care (but not long-term custodial care). It doesn't cost you anything in premiums—you've already paid for it in payroll taxes. You do pay deductibles and other forms of cost sharing. At 65, sign up for Part A even if you're still working and have an employee group plan (or are covered by a spouse's group plan). For you, Part A will serve as a backup. Any qualified bills not covered by your private plan are automatically submitted to Medicare, which pays them up to the Medicare-approved amounts. One exception: Employees should not sign up for Part A if they're enrolled in a high-deductible plan that includes a tax-favored health savings account (see page 78). You can't contribute to an HSA if you're enrolled in Medicare.

Part B, also known as Traditional or Original Medicare, covers your doctor bills, lab tests, outpatient care, medical equipment, emergency services, certain preventive services, and many other medical needs, such as drugs administered in your doctor's office. You can see any doctor you want as long as he or she accepts Medicare, as most do. You pay a premium that rises with inflation every year. You also pay a deductible and, normally, 20 percent of any covered service. You owe no percentage payments, however, for lab tests and preventive services. Prescription drugs aren't included in Part B.

Part C, also known as Medicare Advantage, is the name applied to Medicare plans run by private insurance companies. These plans provide the same services that are covered under Parts A and B. In fact, you have to sign up for A and B before you can enroll in a Part C plan. Advantage plans usually include prescription drugs plus some extra benefits such as free gyms, exercise classes, and vision care. In return, you generally have to stick with the doctors and hospitals in your insurer's network. There might be an option to go out of network. If you use it, however, you'll pay a higher percentage of the cost. Premiums and co-pays vary greatly among Advantage plans. Some cost less than you'd pay for Traditional Medicare plus a Medicare supplemental policy and a prescription drug plan (see page 100). Others cost more, depending on the services you use. By law, there's a cap on your out-of-pocket costs ($6,700 in 2016), as long as you stick with network providers. Many Advantage plans cap your costs at $3,500 or less.

Part D is for prescription drugs. These insurance plans are all privately run. Each insurer covers a slightly different list of drugs, so check for the ones you use before signing up. They also charge different premiums and apply widely different co-pays, deductibles, and coinsurance. You pay the least out of pocket for generic drugs. Co-pays rise for preferred brand names and rise again for brand names that are "nonpreferred." For expensive specialty drugs, you'll pay a percentage of the cost. The plan might not cover your specialty drug at all unless your doctor appeals. Buy Part D even if you currently take no or few drugs, choosing the cheapest one in your area. It's insurance against the risk that you'll suddenly need medications that could cost $2,000 or $3,000 a month or more. If you're in a Part C plan, it will include prescription drugs.

Medicare supplemental insurance plans, known as Medigap plans, are also sold by private insurance companies. They pick up many of the bills that Traditional Medicare excludes, including deductibles, co-pays, and the 20 percent coinsurance that you have to pay for most doctors' bills. There are 10 standard plans[1] identified by letters. All the plans under a particular letter—say, all the A plans—offer the same mix of benefits no matter which insurance company you buy from. That makes it easy to compare costs. You cannot be turned down for Medigap if you apply within six months after turning 65 or enrolling in Part B. After that, some companies might reject you for health reasons. You don't need Medigap if you enroll in a Part C plan, which usually includes some form of supplemental coverage. Some people skip Medigap entirely on a bet that the gaps in Medicare won't cost them much.

Where to Get Information on the Plans

It's all on the Web.

- For details on Parts A and B, go to Medicare.gov and click on "What Medicare Covers." Using the Search box, you can find and download the booklet "Medicare & You." If you're on Medicare already you'll be mailed this booklet every year. Or call for it at 800-633-4227.

- For information on all the Part C and D plans in your area, go to Medicare.gov and click on "Find health & drug plans." Each insurance company puts up a standardized page of coverage and costs, plus links to a list of the doctors, hospitals, and other providers in its network. That makes it possible to compare. Part C Medicare Advantage plans, in particular, vary widely in the amounts they charge for premiums and co-pays. Run cost comparisons before signing up. Once you're in an Advantage plan, inertia will probably keep you there.

---

1   Massachusetts, Minnesota, and Wisconsin have their own standard plans.

- Run cost comparisons for your Part D drug plan, too. There is almost certainly a drug plan in your area that costs less than the one you're using now. As an experiment, go to Medicare's plan finder and follow the prompts. You'll get to a page where you can enter all the drugs (with dosages) that you take regularly. You can also enter local pharmacies. Once the plan finder has this information, it will show you the drug plan or plans that you can buy at the lowest cost. Save all this information and shop again next year during the annual enrollment period. Again, you will probably find something cheaper because plans change. Make a switch every year if that's what the numbers tell you. Those who don't switch are probably throwing money away.

- For information on the standard Medigap plans, go to Medicare.gov and type "Medigap Plans" into the Search box. If you enter your zip code, the website will give you the range of premiums being charged in your area. Another click shows you the names of the companies selling the plans. To sift for the lowest-cost policy, you have to click on each company's website and find its free price quotes. The time you spend is worth it. Right now, I'm looking at standard A policies for my zip code. I could pay anywhere from $97 to $297 for exactly the same benefits. Hmmm, which should I choose?

- If you're not on the Web, you can use health insurance agents to help you find Part C and D plans.

Don't Miss the Enrollment Dates! That Will Cost You More

First-timers should be enrolled in Medicare Parts A and B by the month they turn 65. To remind you, Medicare will send you a letter three months before the deadline. It will contain a user name and password, directing you to MyMedicare.gov. You can sign up online, by phone, or by personal visit to the Medicare office. There's a three-month grace period for sign-ups after 65 but if you start late your coverage will be delayed. The same deadline applies to the Part D drug plans.

If you miss the grace period for Parts B and D, you can sign up during the next general enrollment period, from January 1 to March 31 for coverage starting July 1. But it costs you money. There's an increase in your lifetime premium for every month you dragged your feet. What's more, you'll have no medical insurance during the time you weren't enrolled.

Once you've enrolled in Part B you can choose to take these services through a Part C Medicare Advantage plan. If your Part C plan covers prescription drugs, you don't need Part D.

If you qualify for Medicare, you're entitled to Part A automatically. There are no late penalties for missing the sign-up deadline. Your Medicare card will come in the mail if you sign up for Social Security retirement benefits prior to age 65. If you haven't started benefits yet, you'll have to get in touch with Medicare yourself. You'll need the card to show the doctor and hospital you're insured and for which parts.

If you don't have enough working credits to qualify for Medicare automatically and don't qualify on the record of your spouse, you can buy into Part A. In this case, you do have to sign up by 65. Otherwise, late penalties apply.

If you're already enrolled in Medicare, you can change plans once a year during the open enrollment period that runs from October 15 to December 7. Your new plan will start covering you on January 1.

If you are still working, at 65, at a large or mid-size company, your employee group health plan covers your bills for hospitalization, medical care, and prescription drugs. Nevertheless, sign up for Medicare Part A. It doesn't cost you anything and might get you double coverage for some hospital expenses (see below). You can skip the B and D plans for now; they cost money and your company already pays these bills. When you retire and lose your employee coverage, you can move to a Medicare B or D plan at no extra cost, regardless of your age. Be sure to sign up within eight months of leaving your job. Otherwise, penalties apply.

If you're 65 and working for a small company (fewer than 20 employees), your employee group plan will probably turn into a modest Medicare supplement plan. You'll have to enroll, right away, in Medicare Parts A, B, and D. Your employer should tell you what your options are.

Normally, you have to pay a higher premium if you sign up for Parts B and D after 65. There's no penalty, however, when you're coming directly out of an employer- or union-sponsored plan. The plan will give you a letter proving that you had what's called "creditable coverage." You'll have to take it to a Medicare office, in person, and sometimes the approval process can take months. So start your application right away.

How to Get Double Insurance Coverage if You Work Past 65

If you're 65 or older, working for a large or mid-size company, and have an employee group health plan, you're potentially doubly insured. You can have Medicare and your group plan, too.

Sorry, you can't get both plans to pay the same bills (dream on). But if you sign up for Medicare Part A, it can pick up some of the costs that your employer plan excluded. Here's how that works:

All your medical bills go to your employee group plan first, which pays them up to the limit of the policy. The group plan is your "primary payer." Any costs that your plan fails to cover are forwarded automatically to Medicare, which becomes your "secondary payer." Medicare pays any qualified bills after applying its own coverage rules, deductibles, and coinsurance.

Double insurance works in reverse if you work for a very small company (fewer than 20 employees). In that case, Medicare is your primary payer. That's where your hospital bills go first. Your group plan, if there is one, becomes the secondary payer for any qualified costs that Medicare excluded. The plans for a few mid-size companies follow this pattern too.

There are different rules for matching Medicare with other types of health insurance, such as multi-employer plans, veterans' plans, and plans for government employees.

When you first sign up for Medicare, you'll be asked whether you have any other health coverage as a worker, retiree, or spouse. It's important to list which is primary and which is secondary. Your employer plan, hospital, doctors, and Medicare all need that information so that your bills will go to the right place and in the right order. For information on which plan is the primary payer ask the director of your company's plan. You can also search for "Your Guide to Who Pays First" at Medicare.gov, or call Medicare's Coordination of Benefits Contractor at 800-999-1118.

So far, I've been talking about double coverage only for Medicare Part A, which comes at no extra cost. Doctor and lab bills, however, fall under Part B. If you want Medicare as your primary or secondary payer for those services, you have to pay the Part B premiums. Usually, that's not worth the cost, as long as you're in an employee plan.

Your Money-Saver's Guide to Getting the Most Out of Medicare

- *If you have no other health plan,* sign up for Medicare Parts A and B at 65. Traditional Medicare lets you choose your doctors, hospitals, and other providers. Add Part D for drugs and, perhaps, a Medigap plan. A Part C Medicare Advantage plan usually includes both prescription drugs and supplemental coverage, and might cost you less. To get an Advantage plan's full benefit, stay within its network of providers.

- *If you're still working and covered by an employee group plan,* sign up for Part A at 65 but consider delaying enrollment in Parts B and D. Your private plan should cover most of your medical and prescription drug bills. When you leave the group plan you can sign up for the rest of Medicare at no extra cost.

- *If you're working but don't like your employee group plan,* you can drop out and take Medicare instead. Note, however, that Traditional Medicare has no ceiling on out-of-pocket spending while employer plans do.

- *If you're still working at 65 and contributing to a health savings account,* you can't have the HSA and Medicare, too. You might find it cheaper to avoid Medicare for now and stick with your employee plan—especially if the employer also contributes to the account. Money in your HSA accumulates tax free if used for medical expenses. *Warning*: If you sign up for *any* Social Security benefits, you'll be enrolled automatically in Medicare Part A. In that case, you'll be allowed to keep and use the HSA money you already have but you won't be able to add any more to the account. You *can* make contributions, however, if your spouse goes on Medicare.

- *If you're covered by a retiree group plan,* find out how it meshes with Medicare. There's no standard approach. Some of the larger plans pay full benefits, so you'd keep it and sign up only for Medicare Part A. Others, especially smaller plans, function mainly as Medigap insurance for retirees 65 and up. They'll pay only the bills that aren't eligible for Medicare reimbursement, so you'd sign up promptly for Parts A, B, and D. Alternatively, consider a Medicare Advantage plan, if it's cheaper than all your other premiums combined. But note: Once you leave the private retiree plan you can't get it back.

- *If you're 65 and covered as a spouse on a worker's group plan,* sign up for Medicare Part A. Whether to buy Parts B and D depends on the premium the worker pays to keep you in the company plan. Sometimes it's cheaper for the worker to switch to individual coverage in the company plan while you sign up for Medicare.

- *If you're younger than 65, covered under your spouse's employee plan, and your spouse retires,* you cannot go on Medicare yet. To get those benefits, you have to be 65 yourself. While you're waiting, you generally have three choices: (1) If there's a company retiree plan that pays full benefits and your spouse keeps it, you should be covered too. (2) If there's no retiree plan and your spouse goes on Medicare, you can buy a private individual policy. Shop the ACA Marketplace or call a health insurance agent. (3) You can take the COBRA option offered by the employee plan. It lets you extend your group health benefits for up to 18 months, at your expense. Consider using COBRA if you're within a few months of reaching 65. Otherwise, you'll probably find a cheaper plan in the individual market.

- *If you're older than your spouse and haven't worked long enough to qualify for Medicare,* you can enroll at 65, provided that your spouse is at least 62 and Medicare-qualified.

- *If you're a same-sex couple and married,* you qualify for spousal benefits under employee plans. You also qualify for Medicare as a spouse if you haven't worked the 40 quarters needed to claim benefits on your own. To meet Medicare requirements, you have to have been married for at least one year.

- *If you're in a legal civil union or domestic partnership,* some employee plans offer you the same benefits as a spouse. Medicare also provides benefits if you've been legally partnered for at least a year.

- *If you signed up for a Part C Medicare Advantage plan and the plan drops your doctor or eliminates a local group of specialists,* you can probably keep them by switching to Part B (Traditional Medicare) during the annual open enrollment period (October 15 to December 7). Buy a Part D drug plan and, perhaps, a Medigap plan at the same time. Alternatively, think carefully about how important those particular doctors are. The Advantage plan will have many good doctors, too, and might cost you less.

- *If you're in a Medicare Advantage plan and the plan denies coverage for drugs or medical services that your doctor authorizes,* appeal, appeal, appeal! The Centers for Medicare and Medicaid Services, which oversees these privately run Advantage plans, has found many of them denying legitimate claims, delaying appropriate treatments, and wrongly limiting medical services and prescription medications. Fines have been paid by some of the industry's biggest names. This is an ongoing problem with Medicare Advantage, so beware. Exercise your right to appeal the plan's decisions. If the problems persist, switch to another plan or to Traditional Medicare during the next open enrollment season.

- *If a hospital keeps you overnight on "observation" status but doesn't admit you,* it's potentially putting your Medicare coverage for skilled nursing home care at risk. Medicare helps pay for skilled care only if you first spend three days as a hospital inpatient. If one of those days was listed as observational, you won't qualify. Any time that skilled care appears to be in your future, you or your representative should insist that the hospital formally admit you. Note that Medicare does not pay for long-term custodial care.

- *If you're a snowbird with homes in two states,* register for Medicare in your official state of residence. You'll need a plan that covers you in both places. That probably means choosing Traditional Medicare plus a Part D drug plan rather than a Medicare Advantage plan.

- *If you're planning to move and are in a Medicare Advantage plan,* switch to Traditional Medicare in the year before you go. Your current Advantage plan won't cover providers at your new address or will cover them only at out-of-network rates. Traditional Medicare keeps you covered everywhere. Once you've made the move, you can decide whether to switch to one of the local Advantage plans.

- *If you haven't worked long enough to qualify for Medicare,* and don't qualify as a spouse or divorced spouse, you can buy Parts A and B (they come together). The premiums are high but aid is available for people with low incomes. Sign up at 65 to avoid paying late penalties. Alternatively, look for a policy on the ACA Marketplace. You might be eligible for premium subsidies if your income is modest. (People eligible for Medicare can't shop on the Marketplace.)

- *If you're receiving Social Security disability payments,* you can get Medicare earlier than 65. The rules are complicated. Call to find out where you stand.

- *If you're in a Part D drug plan,* shop for a new plan at every open enrollment time. These plans raise and lower their prices for drugs all the time. You might save a lot of money by switching to a new plan. *Warning:* Premiums are fixed for the year but drug prices can rise midyear.

- *If you're shopping for Medigap,* consider buying the best plan you can afford right now. It might be impossible to upgrade at a later date if your health goes bad.

- *Make use of every free preventive service you're offered.* You can find the full list at Medicare.gov. Look for "Your Guide to Medicare's Preventive Services."

- *You say you don't care how much your doctor charges?* Some doctors with wealthy patients opt out of Medicare. You have to pay the full bill yourself. Most likely, these doctors will use anesthesiologists and other professionals who also opted out. Are these better doctors? Neither you nor I have any idea. I do know that millions of people get great care from docs who take Medicare, as all of mine do.

How to Pay Your Medicare Premiums

Part A costs nothing if you qualify for coverage. Premiums for parts B, C, and D can be deducted automatically from your Social Security retirement check, if you're receiving it, or from your monthly annuity if you're a civil service retiree.

If you've put off taking retirement benefits you can have the premiums taken automatically from your checking or savings account. Alternatively, Medicare will send you a monthly bill, payable by check or credit card. Be sure to pay on time! If you don't, you'll risk losing medical coverage temporarily.

On-time payment gets even more critical if you filed for retirement benefits at 66 and suspended them in order to earn the 8 percent delayed retirement credit that Social Security offers between ages 66 and 70 (see page 42). If you skip a premium, Medicare will take it out of your suspended benefits. Technically, you have now waived the suspension. That means you're no longer eligible for the annual 8 percent increase—*and no one will tell you.* Social Security won't restart your retirement checks unless you specifically ask for them. So you'll arrive at age 70 having lost out on four years of retirement payments and with nothing to show for it. That's what I call harsh.

SHOULD YOU BUY LONG-TERM CARE INSURANCE?

Long-term care (LTC) insurance helps pay the bills—at home or in a nursing home—if you become unable to care for yourself. Married couples in particular should consider it. The policy protects the standard of living of the healthy spouse if the other spouse falls permanently ill. A year of care can cost $85,000 or more.

But can you afford a policy? The answer is probably yes if your company offers it as a group-health perk. Group LTC plans usually take all comers if you sign up during the hiring process. If you wait more than 30 days you'll be accepted only if you pass a health exam.

Spouses always have to pass an exam if the plan offers them coverage, too. You can probably take the policy with you when you leave the job at no increase in price, but check.

Policies are much more expensive outside of the workplace—so much so that they're principally bought by people with upper-middle incomes and above-average assets. Individual policies always require a health exam. The older you get, the higher the risk that you or your spouse won't pass. Couples can buy a shared policy that costs less than two separate policies. Policies for women are usually far more expensive than policies for men of the same age.

Premiums depend on your age when you enter the plan. The older you are when you sign up, the higher your cost will be. In theory, your premiums are supposed to stay level for life. In practice, most insurers raise them from time to time, sometimes by 10 or 20 percent. At this writing, I know of only three companies, Mass-Mutual, New York Life, and Northwestern Mutual, that have never raised prices on existing policyholders.

U.S. tax policy might help you pay. You can tax-deduct medical expenses that exceed 10 percent of your adjusted gross income.[2] Qualifying expenses include the premiums for LTC insurance.

As a rule of thumb, you shouldn't spend more than 5 percent of your retirement income on LTC premiums. You can lower your annual expense by choosing a policy that covers you for three years rather than five years or more. (The majority of nursing home stays don't exceed three years.) Inflation adjustments can be cut, especially in your older age. You might set the waiting period at six months or more before the policy clicks in. To cut costs even further, you might insure only 50 or 75 percent of the expected cost of care, intending to make up the difference from personal savings.

Be sure to give yourself lapse protection. Loss of memory is a

---

2   7.5 percent through 2016 for taxpayers 65 and older.

leading reason for needing nursing home care and one of the things you might forget is to pay your LTC insurance bill. Two solutions: Arrange to have the premiums paid automatically from your checking account or ask the insurance company to notify someone if your policy is being canceled for nonpayment. You're allowed a grace period for reinstatement.

There's one more option for long-term care coverage: Move to a continuing care retirement community that includes nursing home benefits as part of the entrance fee (see page 277).

If you're single, you might skip long-term care insurance and put your money into additional savings. If you ever need care, and own a home, you can sell it and use the proceeds toward the nursing-home bill. For care at home, you can tap your home equity with a reverse mortgage (see page 282).

Single or married, those without LTC insurance have to depend on their savings and, perhaps, help from their families if they need care. But there's also a safety net called Medicaid, a program run by the states with joint state and federal funding. It covers nursing home expenses for people who run out of money. A few states provide modest payments for home care, too.

Singles are generally expected to liquidate their assets to pay their nursing home bills. If the money runs out, Medicaid steps in. Your house and furnishings can be preserved, however, if one of your children lived with you and took care of you.

If you're married and only one of you is sick, a certain amount of income and assets are set aside for the healthy spouse. State rules vary but in general the spouse at home can keep his or her own income and retirement account, the house and furnishings, a car, and a modest amount of other assets. For middle-income couples, that just about covers everything; Medicaid will foot most or all of the nursing home bill. The at-home spouse will be expected to contribute, however, if you have more assets than the Medicaid rules allow. That's why you buy long-term care insurance.

Special note to late-marrying couples: Long-term care might become a mare's nest when an older couple marries and they have children with a former or deceased spouse. Their respective children expect to inherit from their parents. If one of you enters a nursing home, the spouse at home might have some financial responsibility—and, trust me, his or her kids won't like it. You're spending *their* money on a second spouse. You can't get rid of this obligation by writing a prenuptial agreement. So . . . yet another reason for insurance.

DON'T SKIMP

Health insurance is one of the most important items in your budget. The older you get, the higher your medical costs are likely to be. Under 65, your access to coverage is now protected, even if you have a preexisting condition. From 65 up, Medicare takes a load off your mind. Still, rising coinsurance costs give all of us an incentive to shop around. We're not used to asking doctors about prices, but we're going to learn.

5

Pensions Are for Stre-e-e-etching

A new look at the comfort of a guaranteed income for life.

Traditional pensions—a monthly check for life—don't get much respect in the private sector. Not many companies offer them today. Employees with access to pensions tend to take their money in a lump sum, if given the choice, rather than sign up for a fixed and regular income. Those who do take fixed incomes, however, get a lot of comfort from their choice.

In government, traditional pensions are generally beloved. Federal pensions rise with inflation every year and are super safe (U.S. senators and representatives are in this plan!). Almost all state and local government pensions are safe as well. True, a few of these plans have clipped benefits a bit—by raising the amount you're required to contribute, paring annual inflation increases, changing the way pension benefits are calculated, or cutting future payments to new hires. But current and near-retirees from state and local government jobs can generally count on getting the checks they've been promised or are receiving now. Only in the very worst municipal bankruptcy case would pensions for current retirees be reduced.[1]

Whatever your plan, you have some critical choices to make when you retire. Your decisions will deeply affect your security in your older age.

CHOOSING YOUR PENSION BENEFITS: WHAT SUITS YOU BEST?

Most private pension plans and some government plans offer you two ways of taking benefits.

1. You can sign up for guaranteed monthly payments for life. The checks will keep coming even if you pass 100 or 115. If you're married, you can also cover the lifetime of your spouse. Your main enemy is inflation. If the pension is paid in fixed dollar amounts, it will lose purchasing power every year. On the other hand, you'll generally spend less as you age and won't have to worry that the money might run out.

2. You can take the value of your pension in the form of a lump sum, roll it into an individual retirement account, invest it in mutual funds, and withdraw a preplanned amount from your IRA every year. Your enemy is investment risk. In a poorly managed IRA, the money might run out before you do. On the other hand, if you manage these investments well you'll achieve a reliable income, keep up with inflation, and even leave something for your heirs. (Chapter 8 shows you how to do this.)

----

1   At this writing, there are only two cases—in Central Falls, Rhode Island, and in Detroit. But others could follow.

Which approach you choose will depend a lot on your temperament as well as your age and financial circumstances. What will make you the happiest? What will make you feel safe? Here's a guide to making this important decision.

Consider taking the regular monthly pension if:

- *you have no appetite for investing.* If you took the lump sum and managed it yourself, you'd keep the money in bond funds and bank accounts with little or no diversification into stocks. Low-interest investments will not yield anywhere close to the same income for life that you'd get from a pension. If you put your money into the hands of an investment adviser it might turn out well but, then again, it might not. It all depends on the adviser you choose. If you don't know much about the markets, you won't be able to tell whether you're getting the right investments for someone of your age and circumstances.

- *you want a guaranteed monthly income and have at least a modest amount of other savings.* Between your pension and Social Security, you can cover your regular bills. Social Security also provides inflation protection. Your savings give you flexibility and money for emergencies.

- *your pension is adjusted for inflation every year.* Nothing is safer than a guaranteed lifetime income that rises with the cost of living. This kind of pension is a gift that keeps on giving.

- *you're of traditional retirement age—say, 65 or older.* Fixed pensions aren't for people retiring at 60 or younger. There's too much uncertainty ahead.

- *you want to protect your spouse.* A pension can guarantee a monthly income for your spouse for life. By contrast, an income based on market investments might run down, especially if your spouse doesn't know much about money management. Even if your own health is poor, which might tempt you to take the lump sum, consider your spouse's health before making your decision. Pensions help protect a widow or widower who is long-lived.

- *your spouse has a 401(k) or similar plan at work.* Your spouse's plan could be the money that you invest for growth, while your own plan provides a fixed income for life.
- *you're in good health and your family is long-lived.* If you (or your spouse) live well into your 90s, the chances are good that the pension will pay you more, over your lifetime, than outside investments will. That is, unless you're very lucky with your investments.
- *you're a spender who will blow through a lump sum pretty fast.* A fixed pension protects you from yourself.
- *you want some quick money*—maybe to repay debts or to buy an RV for retirement travel—but otherwise would prefer a steady income. If your company allows it, consider taking a small portion of your pension in cash and the rest in monthly checks for the rest of your life. If the company doesn't offer this option, however, find the RV money somewhere else.
- *you've compared the fixed pension with what you could get from an insurance company's immediate-pay annuity, which also pays an income for life* (see page 129). Some companies subsidize their pensions by keeping costs low. That makes them a best buy. Others will buy you an insurance company annuity, in which case you might do better by taking the lump sum and buying the annuity yourself. To find out which is better, go to ImmediateAnnuities.com. Enter the dollar amount of the proposed lump sum into the site's calculator. You'll see instantly how much monthly income various types of annuities would pay, including annuities that also cover

your spouse. If your pension pays more than you could get from a top-rated insurance company,[2] stick with the pension. Make the same comparison if you already get a pension and the company offers to buy you out with a lump sum.

- *you want a regular lifetime income and an adviser tells you that you can get more per month by cashing in your pension and buying a "variable" annuity.* You can't. Variable annuities charge higher fees (including a fat commission for the "adviser") and their returns aren't guaranteed. If you add a guaranteed lifetime payout, they charge even more (see page 137). Keep your pension. You'll be tens of thousands of dollars ahead.

Consider taking the lump sum if:

- *you're a terrific investor or your money is in the hands of a good investment adviser.* You're reasonably certain that you can get more from the lump sum than the pension would pay. You also have a clear-cut spending plan that controls the amount you'll withdraw from your savings every month. You're sure you won't blow through the money in your early retirement years. For help shaping a withdrawal plan, see Chapter 8.
- *you want financial flexibility.* When you invest a lump sum you can vary your withdrawals—say, taking more before you apply for Social Security and less afterward.
- *you'll roll the lump sum directly into an individual retirement account, for investment, rather than spending it.* That preserves your savings and your tax deferral. If you put the money into your bank account and start spending it, you'll pay income taxes immediately plus a 10 percent penalty if you're under 59½.

---

2 For the top ratings, see page 129.

- *you have other sources of income that can support you for the next few years*—say, a spouse's earnings or other savings and investments. You'll roll your lump sum into an IRA, diversify your investments, and let the money accumulate. You don't have to touch it until you reach 70½, when mandatory IRA withdrawals start.

- *you have little or no savings.* You'll live on your Social Security benefit. The lump sum will provide you with cash to cover health shocks or other emergencies.

- *you're rich enough not to need a pension.* You can roll the lump sum into an IRA and leave the money to your kids. Consider switching to a Roth IRA. You'd pay taxes on the lump sum but your kids could enjoy the future earnings tax free. (For more on retirement accounts, see Chapter 7.)

- *you live with a dependent partner, not a spouse.* Pension plans accept same-sex spouses as income beneficiaries but many don't accept those in domestic partnerships or civil unions. Rolling a lump sum into an individual retirement account can benefit you both. You might choose the traditional pension, however, if your partner has sufficient assets of his or her own, for self-support.

- *your health is so poor that you don't expect to live to your full life expectancy.* You can tap a lump sum for larger payments than you'd get from a pension because the money doesn't have to cover a long life span. (If you're married, however, consider your spouse's life span before making this decision.)

- *the lump sum would buy you an insurance company annuity that pays more than your pension will.*

- *you doubt that the company you work for is financially sound.* Most private pensions are insured by the Pension Benefit Guaranty Corporation. If your plan fails, the PBGC will pick up the payments but not necessarily in full (see page 122). Prudence suggests that you take the lump sum.

- *your spouse agrees.* The pension laws are written to protect dependent spouses, usually women. You cannot take a lump sum unless your spouse consents, in a notarized statement filed with the plan. Memo to spouses: Don't give consent lightly. Once the money leaves the pension plan and goes into an individual retirement account, the IRA holder could name anyone as beneficiary. Spouses lose their legal protection except in cases of divorce.

ARE YOU MARRIED? PROTECT YOUR SPOUSE!

There are two ways of taking a pension: a larger monthly payment that lasts for your lifetime and then stops (a *single-life pension*) or smaller payments that last for the lifetimes of you and your spouse (a *joint-and-survivor pension*). By federal law, the default choice for federal and private pensions is joint-and-survivor. If you die, your spouse (including a same-sex spouse) is entitled to a benefit worth at least 50 percent of the amount you received, for life. Many companies give you the option of leaving your spouse 75 percent of your pension amount or even 100 percent. (Some plans contain "pop-ups" that raise your payment if your spouse dies first.)

Couples should take great care when making this decision. The most common pension regret that I hear from married retirees is that they took the single-life option (with the spouse's consent) and wish they hadn't. You might be attracted to the larger monthly payment because money is tight. But if it's tight now, what will happen to the survivor if the pension holder dies and that source of income ends? What if the death occurs in an accident, two weeks after retirement? If your spouse depends on your income, it's better for the two of you to reduce spending now, as a couple, than to live higher on the hog and leave the survivor broke. In some plans, taking a single-life pension will also cut your spouse out of retiree health benefits if you die first.

The single-life choice might work fine if your spouse has a sufficient pension or assets of his or her own, or if your spouse is so ill that he or she is likely to die before you do. Otherwise, don't disinherit your spouse. Take the full 100 percent joint-and-survivor payments if they're offered. At the very least, take the version that leaves your spouse with 50 percent of what you received as a couple and ensure that there are plenty of other assets for his or her support. Remember that, at your death, a spouse will lose one of the two Social Security checks you collect as married retirees. You don't (or shouldn't!) want your spouse to lose your pension income, too. Think duty as well as love.

Spouse Alert #1! Many state and local government pension plans do not cover spouses automatically. The retiree will receive a single-life pension unless he or she specifically chooses joint-and-survivor. As a spouse, you might not even be aware that a choice is possible. Your beloved retiree might choose the single-life check thoughtlessly—to provide a larger income, not specifically to cut you out. But the result is the same. Surprise, honey, when I die you're broke!

Spouse Alert #2! Some state and local plans haven't recognized same-sex spouses. Now the law requires them to, but you might have to fight for it.

Spouse Alert #3! If you'll need the pension, be sure to preserve your right to receive it. Private plans that provide lifetime payments generally have to offer you a "preretirement survivor's annuity." It's a form of life insurance. The annuity guarantees that if your spouse dies before his or her pension starts, you'll get at least half of what the lifetime monthly benefit would have been if he or she had retired early. You pay for this insurance in the form of a small reduction in the future pension check if your spouse lives.

As a spouse, you can waive this right to a preretirement annuity. If you do and the worker lives to retire, you'll have a slightly larger pension income, as a couple. If your spouse dies before retirement, however, your future pension vanishes. A surviving spouse gets nothing.

I once got a sad letter from a widow. She had waived her preretirement benefit thinking that it covered only the years before her husband retired—and indeed, the company's form letter was none too clear on this point. When he died unexpectedly, she was horrified to learn that she had lost his postretirement pension, too. Don't waive the preretirement benefit if you'll need your spouse's pension to live on. If you've already waived it and change your mind, it can be reinstated provided that your spouse is still alive.

SAY NO, LOUDLY, TO PENSION MAX

A financial adviser or insurance agent might present you with what sounds like a fabulous idea—"pension maximization," or "pension max" for short. At retirement, you take the larger, single-life monthly payments and use some of the money to buy an insurance policy on your life. If you die first, your spouse can use the insurance proceeds to buy a lifetime annuity equal to what the pension paid. If your spouse dies first, you'll live on the higher payments for the rest of your life. Ta-da!

As you've probably guessed, there's a worm in this apple. Several worms, as a matter of fact. To begin, the fancy, computerized, pension max presentations are often misleading. After paying for the insurance policy, you might have less to live on—after tax—than if you had taken the joint-and-survivor annuity (most of these presentations don't show after-tax results). To make the plan appear to work, the insurance agent might lowball the size of the policy you need or the size of the premium you have to pay. If you die, your spouse might not be able to buy an annuity that replaces your pension in full. What's more, the market will have changed, perhaps raising the annuity's cost. If your spouse skips the annuity and invests the life insurance proceeds in mutual funds, there's no guarantee that he or she will manage it well or that it will last for life.

This scheme might work if your spouse is ill and you expect to outlive him or her. But if you're so sure, why buy the insurance at all? It also will work if you both live a long time so that, by the time you die, the proceeds of the insurance should readily cover the annuity your survivor needs. But what if you die sooner than you both expected? What if you reach a point where you can't afford the insurance anymore?

My bottom line: If you're of traditional retirement age and want your surviving spouse to have a known income for life, do *not* gamble on pension max. Take the 100 percent joint-and-survivor deal. Retirees in their 50s might cover a spouse with a 50 percent joint-and-survivor pension and buy low-cost 30-year term insurance (not expensive cash-value life insurance) to provide the income the spouse would lose if you died first. For more on life insurance, see Chapter 11 and refer to the appendix.

HOW SAFE IS YOUR PENSION IF THE PLAN FAILS? IT DEPENDS

Most private pensions are backstopped by the federal Pension Benefit Guaranty Corporation (details at PBGC.gov; click on "For Workers & Retirees"). Part or all of your pension will be paid from this fund if your plan fails. Some nonprofits also belong to the PBGC (ask your employer about it).

A minority of private companies transfer workers' pensions to an insurance company. At that point, you'd lose PBGC protection. If the insurance company fails, your annuity would be backed by your state's insurance guaranty association. State protection is more limited than the coverage that the PBGC provides (find your state's details at nolhga.org), but it would be surprising for a major insurer to go broke.

Many nonprofits create what's known as "church plans" and do not belong to the PBGC. These could include such employers as religious institutions, schools, and hospitals, including very large ones. If your church plan fails, part or all of your pension vanishes.

There's no backup insurance for federal, state, and local pension plans other than law and politics. So far, that combination has proved pretty powerful.

And, of course, there's no backup for lump sums invested in stocks and bonds.

DO YOU ENVY PEOPLE WITH PENSIONS?

Younger people aren't much interested in traditional plans. They want retirement accounts where they can invest their saving for (of course!) stupendous growth. But perspectives change as the years go by. If you won't get a pension and the thought of a guaranteed income lights you up, you can buy a pension in the form of a lifetime annuity—as you'll see in the chapter coming up.

6

Should You Buy Yourself a Pension?

Lifetime annuities, the Rodney Dangerfield of investments, don't get no respect—except from me.

When you retire, peace of mind means fresh money landing in your bank account every month. That's how you lived when you had paychecks coming in. Losing that paycheck is startling no matter how much money you've saved. The wife of a major multimillionaire told me a couple of years ago that she worried about how they'd pay their bills when her husband retired and his professional income stopped. (Maybe she was a bigger spender than I'd thought.)

Most of us don't have major millions to rely on, so creating a reliable lifetime income becomes a challenge. There's Social Security—guaranteed and inflation indexed but probably not enough to live on. You can make regular withdrawals from your savings and investments (see Chapter 8), with potential for growth but at the risk of running out.

There are also lifetime pensions—an object of envy for people who don't have them. Corporate pensions are nice even though their fixed payments gradually lose value to inflation. Government pensions that rise with the inflation rate are even better.

The funny thing is that you can buy yourself a simple fixed or inflation-indexed pension in the form of a commercial, immediate-pay annuity. It gives you a guaranteed income for life. Yet buying one is probably the last thing on your list.

Why do retirees turn their backs on lifetime annuities? And can I change your mind? Annuities aren't for everyone, but for the right person they are the answer to a prayer.

Annuities are created by insurance companies and sold through insurance agents, banks, brokerage firms, and financial advisers. They come in many different types.

Some are complex annuities that combine investment products with a lifetime income. These I do not—repeat, *not*—recommend (see page 137). Instead, consider the simple, low-cost annuities that are designed purely as pension substitutes.

Simple annuities are easy to understand. You put up a sum of money in return for a monthly lifetime income. The size of your payment depends on your age and the current level of interest rates.[1] At this writing, for example, a 65-year-old man might put up $100,000 in return for $540 a month for the rest of his life. The older you are when you buy the annuity, the higher the payment. A 70-year-old man might get $620 a month. Payments to women are lower than payments to men of the same age because, on average, they live longer. The monthly income from their investments has to be stretched over a longer period.

The insurance industry calls this group of simple products SPIAs—single premium immediate annuities. You can choose fixed or rising monthly payments or payments linked to the inflation rate.

---

1   All prices in this chapter are based on the level of interest rates in mid-2016. At higher interest rates, monthly payments would be higher, too.

The annuity can cover your own life or the life of yourself and a spouse or partner. You might choose to annuitize part of your savings and invest the rest.

ANNUITIES AND THE "SUCKER FACTOR"

What bothers people about annuities is what I call the "sucker factor." If you put up $100,000 and die next year, you'll feel (from the grave) that you were a sucker. That's because the remaining money stays with the insurance company, in its reserves. It's used to help pay the annuity holders who lived longer than you did.

But it's this very sucker factor that makes immediate-pay annuities so attractive. Because some people will indeed die early, the insurer can afford to pay everyone more per month than they could prudently draw out of their personal investments. That's true whether you die early or late.

For example, take that 65-year-old man who has $100,000 in savings. An immediate annuity would pay him $540 a month. Now say that he skips the annuity and invests in stock and bond mutual funds instead. A prudent withdrawal rate would be 4 percent plus an increase for inflation in every future year. That means he starts with only $333 a month—$207 less. His investments should last for 30 years but he might never catch up with the income he could have had from the annuity. He'll do better than the annuity if stock prices hit a fantastic run, but he can't count on that in advance. In the meantime, his investments need constant managing (the worry factor) and they're not guaranteed.

Now let's say that our man dies after just a few years. So what? The annuity served his purpose. It paid him more than he'd have gotten from his investment plan, helped pay the monthly expenses not covered by Social Security, and insured him in case he lived "too long." Among the people most likely to live longer than average are those with a good education, some retirement savings salted away, and a history of good health insurance, which probably describes you.

If the sucker factor still drives you nuts, there's a way to make yourself feel a little better. You can buy an annuity with payments "certain" to last for 10 or 15 years, even if you die earlier. That ensures that you (or, rather, your heirs) will get at least some of your money back. For example, say that you buy a lifetime annuity with 10 years certain and die after seven years. For the following three years, your monthly check will be paid to your beneficiary. You could also buy a cash refund option that guarantees a return of all the money you put in.

Every benefit has a price, of course. In return for the certainty of 10 or 15 annual payments, you have to accept a lower monthly check. Even so, that check might be larger than the amount you could prudently take from a mutual fund account invested in stocks and bonds. That's especially true if you keep most of your savings in bonds or certificates of deposit.

Another rap against annuities is that you lose control of your money. But you shouldn't even consider annuitizing all the savings you have. Retirees need ready cash to cover health shocks and other emergencies, as well as gifts and pleasure spending. You should also keep some funds invested in stocks, whose long-term growth will provide a cushion for your older age (see Chapter 9). Ideally, you'd buy an annuity that, together with your Social Security and other reliable income, covered all (or most) of your basic bills. The rest of your money would remain under your control.

Finally, there's the legacy question. You can't pass the remaining value of an immediate-pay annuity to your heirs. But realistically, what are your plans for the money you've saved? Will you use it chiefly for your own support with the remainder going to the kids? Fine. The money you put into the annuity gives you a higher guaranteed income while you live. The rest of your money can be invested more aggressively to provide a fund for the family you'll leave behind.

You are *not* a candidate for annuities if you're living on Social Security (and perhaps a fixed pension) with only a small amount of ready savings. Those savings should be kept on hand for surprise expenses. You also wouldn't annuitize if your health is poor or if you're so rich you can't run out of money.

However, if you're living on interest, dividends, and Social Security and feel pinched, your life might improve if you took some money out of bonds and used it to buy an immediate-pay annuity instead. You haven't reduced your capital, you've simply shifted that capital into a higher-paying investment. Suddenly, you'll have more cash in your pocket. You can take a cruise or go out to dinner without feeling that you've overspent.

You're an Ideal Candidate for an Immediate-Pay Annuity If:

- you're in good health, have a reasonable amount of savings but don't feel safe financially.
- you're temperamentally unable to invest a large portion of your assets in stocks so you keep most of your money in bonds.
- you like receiving regular income.
- you want investments that pay without your having to work at it.
- having a sufficient retirement income takes priority over leaving a large legacy.

If this describes you, immediate-pay annuities are a good choice.

When you're shopping for any annuity, by the way, check the insurance company's safety-and-soundness ratings. Tip-top scores aren't essential. Insurance companies rarely go out of business. Even if they got into trouble, they'd normally sell their book of annuities to another company. If the annuity you're looking at meets your goals and the company is well diversified among many lines of business (*not* just annuities), it's fine to accept a rating that's a couple of notches down the scale. Top-rated companies generally pay you a little less income per month than lower-rated companies do.

But don't go too far down the quality ladder. Insurance expert Joseph Belth, who blogs at josephmbelth.com, proposes the following cutoffs:

- *For "extremely conservative" investors who still want the highest scores:* AAA or AA+ from Fitch Ratings and Standard & Poor's; A++ from A.M. Best; and Aaa or Aa1 from Moody's.
- *For "conservative" investors:* no lower than AA or AA− from Fitch and Standard & Poor's; A+ or A from A.M. Best; and Aa2 or Aa3 from Moody's.

WHAT KIND OF INCOME DO YOU WANT FOR LIFE?

Annuities, as pension substitutes, pay lifetime incomes in various ways. Here are your choices.

Immediate-pay fixed annuities.[2] These annuities are the simplest of the lot. You put up some money and in return get a fixed monthly income for life. It's just like having a paycheck. Immediate-pay fixed annuities cost the least of all the types of annuities available and, at the start, pay you the most per month. As a sample strategy, you might put half your savings in annuities and half in stock-owning mutual funds. At first, you'd spend the annuity money and barely

---

2   The insurance industry, which loves to confuse you, sells another type of annuity it calls "fixed," or "fixed income," or "fixed indexed" (see page 151). It's complicated, way more expensive than immediate-pay fixed annuities, and pays agents much higher commissions. It's not a true pension substitute. Stay away.

touch the stocks, leaving them alone to grow. As the years passed and your annuity payments lost purchasing power, you'd start dipping into your growth investments to help support your lifestyle.

Immediate-pay fixed annuities are also easy to shop for. Just go to ImmediateAnnuities.com and enter the lump sum you want to commit. You'll get a list showing the various types of payment methods available. You might cover your life alone or the lifetimes of you and your spouse, with or without something left to a beneficiary if you die early. Click the box next to three types of payment schedules that interest you. You'll get a free report showing the top 10 or 12 annuities in each of the categories and how much they'll pay each month. No salesperson will call. If you want help, call the Immediate Annuities.com founder and agent, Hersh Stern, at 800-872-6684. You can buy through Stern or use the list as a benchmark when talking to your own insurance agent or financial planner.

After you've checked this website, go to two other sites that might give you a better quote: TIAA-CREF.org and Vanguard.com.[3]

Choose the insurance company that makes the best offer, consistent with the safety-and-soundness rating you want. Depending on your age, the highest-paying insurer might give you anywhere from 4 percent to 20 percent more than the lowest payer.

If you have been saving money in a tax-deferred variable annuity (see page 138) and want to convert it to an immediate-pay fixed annuity, find out what your current insurance company will offer you per month. Compare that price quote with the payments available through the sites above and choose the best one. If you decide to switch companies, your new insurer will handle the paperwork.

---

3   At Vanguard.com, click on "See fixed income annuities through Vanguard." Vanguard customers can get a quote online immediately. If you're not an existing customer, call 800-357-4720.

Immediate-pay variable annuities.[4] With these annuities, you are casting your lot with the future growth of the economy. The money is invested in a mix of U.S. and international stock and bond funds (also known as "subaccounts"). Every month, you receive a certain percentage of the portfolio's value, after fees. For example, you might ask for payments at the rate of 4 percent a year. You'll get a higher dollar amount if the markets rise and a lower dollar amount if they fall. You'll like this product if you can handle variations in your "pension" payment and believe, as I do, that the stock market—hence, your annuity income—will outpace inflation in the years ahead.

If you go this route, you have two choices to make.

First, how do you want your annuity invested? You get to choose the mutual funds from a list the insurance company offers. The higher the percentage you steer into stocks, the greater the variability of your monthly payments but also the better your chance of increasing your income over time. If you prefer to put more into bonds, your income will be steadier but isn't likely to rise very much.

Second—and this is more complicated—what interest rate do you want to assume your mix of investments will pay? This is called your AIR (assumed interest rate). It's important because it affects the dollar amount by which your monthly income will rise or fall. For example, say that you choose a 4 percent AIR because you expect that your investments will earn at least that much over time. For the amount of your monthly payment to rise, your investments have to earn more than 4 percent, after fees. If your investments decline, your payment drops by the market percentage plus 4 percent more. After each decline, the market will have to regain the amount you

---

4   Very different from tax-deferred variable annuities and less expensive— see page 138.

lost, plus more than 4 percent (after fees), before your payout will exceed its previous high.

The AIR you choose affects your chance of getting a higher income in your older age. If you start with a high AIR (a high monthly payment), you'll probably get lower dollar payments in the annuity's later years. You're effectively using up your expected investment gains in advance. Conversely, if you choose a low AIR, you'll start with a smaller payment but should enjoy gains in your later years. The agent who sells the annuity will probably guide you toward a mid-range AIR. No matter which rate you choose, your monthly payments—large or small—will last for life.

Inflation-adjusted immediate annuities. With these products, the payment you receive rises every year by the prior year's inflation rate so you preserve your purchasing power (with a year's lag). The first monthly payment is low compared with your other annuity choices. That's because this annuity is priced to cover expected inflation plus a comfortable safety margin for the insurance company. The upside is that you're not taking any inflation or investment risk. This annuity will serve you particularly well if you're a younger retiree and the economy—some years in the future—is hit with inflation that's unexpectedly high. For older retirees, immediate-pay fixed annuities might be a better choice. They provide higher payments at the start and you have fewer years to worry about inflation. In recent years, you've barely had to worry about inflation at all.

At this writing, I know of only two companies that offer inflation-adjusted annuities—American General Life Insurance and Principal Life Insurance. You might get a better quote by buying them through the low-cost Vanguard mutual fund group (see footnote on page 130).

Fixed-increase annuities. Like inflation-adjusted annuities, these products raise your monthly payment every year. But you pick the percentage increase you want—anywhere from 1 percent to 5 percent or so, depending on the company. The higher the fixed increase you want, the lower your initial monthly income will be.

Deferred-income annuities, also known as longevity insurance. These annuities are an interesting choice, especially for people who want to invest money now while being sure of having a future income that will last for life. You buy the annuity today but receive no income until a certain number of years have passed. When that time comes, you'll start receiving regular monthly payments for life.

You might buy a deferred-income annuity for one of several reasons: as a backup to protect against the risk of outliving your savings; to provide income after you leave a post-retirement part-time job; or to provide your spouse with a guaranteed income if you die first and don't have enough life insurance.

Deferred-income annuities cost much less up front (meaning that they pay more per $1,000 invested) than immediate-pay annuities do. For example, say that a 65-year-old woman puts up $50,000 at age 65. If she started withdrawals right away and chose fixed payments, she'd get $250 a month, at recent interest rates. If she started at 75, she'd get $550. If she waited until 80, she could receive $930.

Depending on the insurance company, you can elect fixed payments, fixed-increase payments, or inflation-adjusted payments. For an extra fee, most of these products let you add money at a later time. Some provide cash in an emergency or let you change the date when you expect to start taking income. You might want a benefit payable to heirs if you die before the annuity payments start. Buying any of these perks, however, reduces your future monthly income.

Warning! If you buy with IRA money, the annuity's value usually counts toward the size of your required withdrawals at age 70½—see page 190. Exception: You can buy a "qualified" longevity annuity for up to $125,000 that's not subject to the withdrawal rules.

Fixed-term annuities. These are the opposite of deferred-income annuities. You buy a fixed income, payable immediately and lasting for a certain number of years. At the end of the period, your income stops. These could be useful bridge products—say, for people who need income but don't want to sell their stocks right now or who have an illiquid investment that can't be cashed out right away. You might also use them to provide some income while waiting until you're 70 to claim Social Security.

Charitable gift annuities. Charitable gifts are beyond the scope of this book. But they're certainly another way of providing yourself with a lifetime income. You give a lump sum to a charity that guarantees you a fixed monthly payment. Your gift also generates tax deductions and avoids the capital gains tax if you donate appreciated securities. At your death, the charity takes any money remaining. There are other types of gift annuities, too. Ask the nonprofits you're interested in for details.

IF AN IMMEDIATE ANNUITY SOUNDS GOOD, WHEN SHOULD YOU BUY IT?

Annuity companies usually say, "Buy sooner rather than later." That sounds pretty good if you're keeping a lot of money in safe, low-interest bank accounts. Immediate annuities will pay you much more per month than you're earning now. You're losing potential income every year you wait.

Nevertheless, financial planners generally advise you to put off the annuity decision. The older you are when you buy, the higher the monthly payment. But that's not the main reason for delay. By waiting, you allow for surprises in your life that might change your mind. For example, your health might take a turn for the worse, you might inherit money, or you might have to use a chunk of cash to help one of your children. The delay preserves your options.

How long should you wait? Your window for buying immediate-pay fixed annuities and inflation-adjusted annuities is age 70 to 80, most of the experts say. By then you should have a good fix on how your retirement plans are working out and how long your other investments are likely to last. If you're leaning toward an immediate-pay variable annuity linked to stocks, however, you might start as early as 65. You could also stagger your purchase: start with the variable or inflation-adjusted version and add a fixed-payment annuity later.

If your health is poor, you can get a health-impaired immediate annuity. It pays a higher income per month than you'd normally get. You might be interested as early as age 60 or even 55 if you feel that you need the income guarantee.

DON'T GIVE IN TO TEMPTATION! PROTECT YOUR SPOUSE!

An annuity that covers two lives pays less per month than an annuity that covers only one. For example, take a 75-year-old couple with $100,000 to spend on income protection. If they choose to cover the lifetime of only the husband, they'll get $730 a month. If they cover both lives, they'll get $575. The younger the spouse the lower the joint monthly payment.

Differences this large tempt a surprising number of couples to gamble on taking the higher check today. They'll think about the future tomorrow. The future, unfortunately, usually arrives in the form of an obit for the husband and much reduced circumstances for the wife. So please. It's cruel and unusual punishment to knowingly slash the future income of a dependent spouse, even if the spouse agrees.

There are a few circumstances when you might want to cover only a single life. For example, maybe your spouse or partner has enough assets to be self-supporting. Maybe he or she is ill and likely to die first (although you can't be sure). Maybe you have life insurance that you think will protect your spouse or partner if you're the first to die (but will it, really? Check "pension maximization" on page 121). Or maybe the spouse is so young that adding her to the annuity (in this case, it's usually a "her") would slash monthly payments by 30 to 50 percent (younger spouses definitely need life insurance protection).

If your spouse or partner is roughly your age, however, and his or her lifetime financial protection isn't guaranteed, choose a joint-and-survivor annuity that covers you both.

For more information, refer to the appendix.

WHERE TO GET HELP WITH AN ANNUITY PURCHASE

You can buy the simplest annuities with a phone call (see Vanguard .com, TIAA-CREF.org, and ImmediateAnnuities.com). But they're generally not a do-it-yourself investment. This chapter should help you decide whether you want to consider annuities and, if so, what kind. But it's helpful to have an adviser—*not a salesperson*—explain these products and help you decide whether they fit your needs.

Ideally, you'd work with a fee-only financial planner (see page 27) who helps you explore your personal retirement goals. He or she should be familiar with the best ways of matching simple, immediate-pay annuities with your other investments to produce a livable income. Unfortunately, many good planners ignore even low-cost annuities. That's because sales commissions are built into the invisible cost structure and fee-only firms don't take commissions. But these firms are starting to pay more attention as the benefits of immediate-pay annuities become clear. Up-to-date fee-only planners should research the low-cost annuities on the market and refer you to someone who can handle the sale. They also might work through Hueler Income Solutions, an online service that offers annuities at the same low prices that institutions get.

If you work with a planner, broker, adviser, or agent who takes commissions, however, you will *not* be steered toward a simple low-cost annuity. They'll have something else in mind.

THE SEXY, CONFUSING, HIGH-COMMISSION ANNUITIES THAT FINANCIAL ADVISERS LOVE TO SELL

Now we've arrived at a special class of annuities that combine investing with promises of a secure retirement income. They're sold—*insistently* sold—by financial advisers who earn sales commissions. If you even breathe the words "income investment" you'll find it hard to escape the room until you've signed up.

These wonders are called *variable annuities with living-benefit guarantees*. They're sold as a combo "safe" stock market investment with a guaranteed income on the side. Their value, as future income, can rise with the stock market but never fall. Wow. All gain, no loss. Super-high fees but, heck, you wouldn't begrudge them to an adviser who brings you such a fantastic opportunity (would you?).

Unfortunately, it's much harder than you think to turn living-benefit annuities into stories of success. Investors buy them in the hope of earning a better retirement income than a plain-vanilla annuity would provide. But the high fees are likely to drain that hope away.

Advance warning, when you read about living-benefit annuities: They're complicated! The people who buy them rarely understand how they work. Some of the salespeople might not know much, either, except that the product pays high commissions (in the range of 5 to 7 percent plus perks such as luxury cruises, iPads, and diamond rings). Occasionally, living-benefit annuities become a good deal although you can't predict those times in advance. For success you need low fees (rare today, except from groups like Vanguard and TIAA-CREF) and exceptionally strong stock markets (average gains aren't enough). If your adviser suggests that you buy one of these annuities, work your way through this section before saying yes. Your best answer is more likely no.

A Sort-of-Simple Explanation

The best way to explain[5] these annuities is to say that they come in two parts—an investment fund (which can be sold separately) plus a living-benefit rider. It's generally a deferred investment; you plan to make use of it 10 or more years from now. Here's how it works.

Part 1 of the contract: a variable annuity (VA). This is a pure investment. You put your annuity money into a mix of stock and bond mutual funds (called "subaccounts" in annuity-speak). The insurance company gives you a list to choose from. Any gains accumulate tax-deferred. There's a surrender charge if you cancel the annuity within a certain number of years (usually seven to 10, but it could be longer).[6] When you withdraw the earnings, they're taxed at ordinary income rates.

The risk, of course, is that your investment fund will do poorly. It might not provide as much future retirement income as you had hoped. This leads me to . . .

Part 2 of the contract: a guaranteed living-benefit rider. Insurance companies solved the investment risk by adding a second part to the variable-annuity contract—a minimum lifetime income guarantee. You'll receive that income no matter how well or poorly your investments perform. If they do poorly or provide only mediocre returns, the annuity will pay the promised amount, starting in the year you choose to retire. If they do well, you'll get more than the contract

---

5 I've streamlined the example so that your eyes won't glaze over. Each insurance company has its own quirky rules.

6 Many insurers sell VAs with short or zero surrender charges, but those products pay lower commissions so salespeople have less incentive to tell you about them.

guarantees. Naturally, buyers assume that their future income will increase because they invest at least some of their annuity in stocks. Anyway, that's what the salesperson's presentation will show. But the odds are that you'll earn only the promised minimum amount. The explanation lies in the size of the annual fees and the way the contract works.

How Parts 1 and 2 of the contract work together: Your living-benefit annuity has two values—an *investment value* and a *benefit base* or *income base* (different companies use different names).

The *investment value* reflects the gain or loss in the mutual funds you choose for the variable annuity, minus the annuity's costs. If you put in $100,000 and the net market increase, after costs, is 8 percent, your investment value rises to $108,000. If the net decline is 8 percent, the investment value drops to $92,000. You can always withdraw the annuity's investment value in cash (although there are usually penalties for early withdrawals).

The *benefit base* is your original investment plus a guaranteed annual percentage increase. A typical minimum increase today is 5 percent.[7] If you invest $100,000, the benefit base will rise to at least $105,000 in the first year, $110,250 in the second year, and so on. It keeps on rising by 5 percent even if your investments do poorly. After 10 years, you're going to feel pretty good. Your $100,000 is now worth $163,000—and it happened automatically.

There's a hitch, of course. This is the insurance industry, not a public charity. You appear to have $163,000 (in this example) but you *cannot* withdraw that money in a lump sum. An annuity's benefit base is not real cash (alas), it's just a number spewed out by a

---

7   I'm using 5 percent for all my examples in this section. Be aware that the contract's guaranteed payment might be higher or lower than 5 percent of the benefit base.

computer. To collect on that paper gain you have to "annuitize"—that is, turn the gain into monthly payments for life. You might or might not get full value of that $163,000, depending on how long you live and what the spouse benefits are.

So far, I've been talking about the minimum income that the annuity provides. In a strong stock market, your benefit base can grow by more than the increase that is guaranteed. That's one of the things that sells consumers on the product. If the value of your investment fund rises by more than, say, 5 percent, *after costs*, the increase is added to your base (a "reset"). That puts your future guaranteed lifetime payments on a permanently higher level.

As an example, take the $100,000 annuity mentioned above. In the second year, your guaranteed benefit base rises by 5 percent to $110,250. Let's say that the net value of your investments does much better, rising to $120,000. That higher number becomes your new benefit base. In the third year, your guaranteed increase will be figured as 5 percent of $120,000. Good news. You're ahead.

The story isn't nearly as pretty, however, when the stock market falls. To show the effect, let's assume that your $100,000 investment declines in the second year to a value of $90,000. Your guaranteed benefit base will still rise by 5 percent of your original investment. On paper, you now have $110,250, which is nice. For you to earn higher future monthly payments, however, the value of your investment—again, after costs—has to make up the $10,000 loss, *plus* 5 percent, *plus* something more. The longer it takes for your investment to recover, the further it will fall behind the guaranteed 5 percent increases in the benefit base. You might never qualify for an income higher than the minimum guarantee.

Now the Really Bad News: Costs

High annual fees make it especially hard for you to earn more than the minimum guarantee. A low-cost company such as Vanguard charges perhaps 1.75 of your investment account for a variable annuity with a living-benefit rider, which gives you a fighting chance. But most commercial insurance companies charge 3.5 percent or more for the total package—the annuity, the income rider, the mutual funds, a death benefit (contained in most contracts), and overhead. That's $3,500 a year for every $100,000 you invest. Fees rise even higher if you want payments made to a beneficiary if you die first. These crazy expenses come out of your contract's investment value. And remember: You've already paid a sales commission of 5 to 7 percent.

So let's look at the real annuity math. Say that you're paying 3.5 percent in fees and your contract's benefit base is rising by 5 percent a year. Your investment value will have to rise by 8.5 percent just to keep you even, and more than 8.5 percent before your future payment will rise above the minimum. That requires strong, steady stock market returns, especially when the contract starts, or some lucky big years that cause your benefit base to reset at a higher level. You might have earned a reset if you happened to buy the annuity near the bottom of the market in 2009 or 2010 but not in most other years.

What if the value of your investments rises but only by a modest amount? Any rise less than 8.5 percent leaves your investment values behind the increase in the benefit base. You might think that your mutual funds are doing well but they're not doing well enough to qualify you for an income higher than the guarantee.

What if the stock market declines in value? You might land in a hole that you can't dig out of. At that point, your investments will have to rise by enough to regain your market loss *and* cover your annual expenses *and* exceed the increase in your benefit base before you'll get anything more than the guaranteed minimum payment.

Most annuity sellers make this investment goal even tougher to reach by requiring you to hold at least 30 to 40 percent of your investments in bonds. So you don't get the full value of a strong stock market year.

Bottom line: You have to get really, really lucky in the market to fulfill your hopes of a payment higher than the minimum guarantee. The contract is stacked against you because of the fees.

How Is Your Living Benefit Paid?

There are two types of guaranteed income riders—a *guaranteed minimum income benefit (GMIB)* and a *guaranteed lifetime withdrawal benefit (GLWB)*. An insurance company will offer one or the other, never both. The chief difference between them lies in the choices you're offered when you start relying on the income guarantee.

To show you how each of them works, let's say that you start with $100,000 and, 10 years later, your benefit base has risen to $160,000.

If you have a guaranteed minimum income benefit (GMIB), the only way to use that $160,000 is to turn it into a lifetime annuity. It can cover your life alone or, if you die, the life of a beneficiary such as a spouse. The annuity usually comes with "10 years certain," meaning that at least 10 years of payments are guaranteed even if you don't live that long. These lifetime annuities are *not* competitively priced. Their fixed payouts, based on then-current interest rates, will be lower than those available on the open market. But you're locked in.

If you put off collecting the income for a few extra years your future payments will rise in two ways. First, the benefit base will continue to increase by 5 percent a year (in this example), giving you a larger pool of money to draw from. Second, the older you are when you start the annuity payments, the higher the monthly amount you'll receive. If your spouse wasn't on the contract he or she can usually be added when the lifetime payments start.

If you have a guaranteed lifetime withdrawal benefit (GLWB), you'll use that $160,000 by taking fixed withdrawals for the rest of your life (and your spouse's life, if the contract already covers both of you—a spouse or other beneficiary can't be added at this point). The withdrawals are set at, say, 5 percent of your benefit base when the income starts. In my example, that's $8,000 a year. If you put off taking the income, your $160,000 benefit base will continue to increase—again giving you a larger pool of money to draw from. You might also get a higher percentage withdrawal for waiting past age 65 or 70. With some GLWBs, payments increase if you enter a nursing home. In neither case can you take the benefit base in a lump sum. It is paid only in monthly amounts.

IF YOU'RE MARRIED, WILL YOUR SPOUSE GET LIFETIME BENEFITS, TOO?

It's hard to believe, but the majority of the "living-benefit" contracts sold so far cover only the buyer (usually the man), not the spouse. If the man dies first, the income ends. The couple might not even realize what they've done because these contracts are so opaque. There's a "death benefit," which you might assume continues the payments to the spouse. But it's more like an insurance payout. It doesn't come close to replacing the income a surviving spouse could lose.

If you've already bought such an annuity, it's too late to extend it to your spouse. But you can switch into a better annuity (in a tax-free exchange) or buy more life insurance so your survivor won't go broke.

Warning! Many salespeople—brokers and financial planners—don't know how spousal benefits work in these kinds of annuities. They'll say, "Yes, this covers your spouse," thinking only of the death benefit. But you have to ask, specifically, "Is my spouse entitled to the same guaranteed income I'll be getting if I die first?" To be on the safe side, ask to be shown the section of the contract that makes that exact promise. Only GMIB contracts allow your spouse to be added after you die.

YOUR LIVING BENEFITS ARE ALWAYS PAID FROM YOUR OWN MONEY FIRST!

Many buyers of living-benefit annuities don't understand where the money comes from to pay the lifetime income they receive. You're told that your benefit base is increasing by, say, a guaranteed 5 percent a year. That sounds as if you're earning 5 percent on your investment. The salesperson might even encourage you to believe that. But it's not true! Not even close.

The monthly payments you receive from the insurance company, for all or most of your life, will come entirely out of your annuity's investment account. That's your own money. It's made up of the original sum you put up plus any interest or dividend income, adjusted by gains and losses, and minus fees. In other words, *you're paying yourself.* And by the way, you're continuing to pay the contract's high annual fees. You start getting paid with the insurer's money only if you live long enough for your own money to be exhausted.

Strategically, you'd like to start receiving payments from the insurance company's money as soon as possible. You can make this happen by exercising a right included in the contract. You're allowed to make withdrawals from your investment account every year, up to a fixed percentage amount. In the example I've been using, you could take out 5 percent. Presumably, you'd put it into other investments, such as mutual funds. The faster you work your annuity's investment account down to zero, the sooner the company will have to start using its own resources to make your guaranteed income payments.

For more on this game plan, see page 145.

If You Already Own a Variable Annuity with a Living Benefit How Do You Get the Most Value from It?

Your best option for income will depend on how well the investments inside your annuity are doing. Have you had good luck or bad luck?

The good luck case: Your investments are worth as much as your guaranteed benefit base or close to it. You have two choices:

- Leave the annuity alone and let the rising value of your investments increase your guaranteed future monthly payments. This is the outcome you hoped for when you first invested.
- Withdraw the money to make other investments. You can roll the proceeds into a new or existing individual retirement account. Or you might switch to a different, lower-cost annuity in a tax-free exchange.

The bad luck case: Your investments haven't done well enough. They've fallen way behind the value of the annuity's benefit base and will probably never catch up. Remember that your benefit base rises smoothly at, say, 5 percent a year. Meanwhile, your investment account is at the mercy of up-and-down markets and is chopped every year by fees. What's your next move? Again, you have two choices:

- Do nothing. Your benefit base will continue to grow by 5 percent. At some point in the future, you can turn that higher amount into a monthly income for life. You will gradually be getting your own money back. You might or might not retrieve all your money by the time you die.
- Make the smart choice, which I'm guessing will apply to most of the readers of this section. Start taking your guaranteed minimum withdrawals right away (say, 5 percent a year). Take the money even if you're still working and don't need it. Every withdrawal reduces the size of your investment account. Your goal is to strip out your cash while you're still alive and invest it somewhere else. Meanwhile, your benefit base will continue to increase. Once you've emptied your investment account, you can tell the insurance

company to start paying the monthly income you were guaranteed. You will then be enjoying your own money (which you've withdrawn) and the insurance company's money, too. You'll finally be profiting from the protection you paid for.

What to do with the withdrawals you make from your investment account will depend on your circumstances. If you own the living-benefit annuity in an individual retirement account, you can roll the money directly into your IRA and reinvest it. If you own the annuity outside an IRA, you can switch the proceeds into a different (and lower-cost) annuity tax free, in what's called a 1035 exchange. Depending on your age, you might choose an immediate-pay annuity or Vanguard's low-cost variable annuity with guaranteed withdrawal benefits. Finally, you can take the money and use it for current expenses. In that case, however, you'd owe income taxes on any gain (see page 155).

Five caveats: (1) You might have to hold the annuity for a certain number of years or else pay a penalty. Wait until the penalty period expires before starting withdrawals. Even with these contracts, however, you can usually get at least some money out penalty free. (2) Don't withdraw more than the guaranteed amount. If you take even $1 over, you'll probably lose your right to an income for life. Your company's customer service rep can tell you what the amount should be. (3) A few contracts cancel your lifetime income if you take *any* withdrawals over the first ten years. Stay away from them. (4) Your contract might promise a higher guaranteed payment once you reach a certain age—say, 60 or 65. If you're close to that age wait until you pass it before starting withdrawals. (5) If the guaranteed payout rate is lower than the long-term bond rate (not the case today), your contract is less valuable. It will be hard to reduce your investment account to zero. In this case, it might pay to let the investment account grow for a few years more to see if its value exceeds the benefit base.

Are You Still Unsure About How to Get the Most Value Out of Your Existing Living-Benefit Annuity?

No surprise there. In this section, I've passed on advice from the best annuity experts I know. Still, the living-benefit options are confusing.[8] How much are you really paying in fees? When is the best time to start withdrawing benefits? If you die first, what does your spouse or partner actually get? Should you switch to an annuity with lower costs? Are there angles to your contract that, if used, will yield a higher payment? How much can you withdraw without losing your income guarantee or reducing it sharply? If your insurance company offers to give you cash in return for surrendering a future benefit (see page 150), should you accept?

For answers to these and any other questions you have about your existing annuities, I recommend a service called Annuity Review, run by Mark Cortazzo at the MACRO Consulting Group, Parsippany, New Jersey (AnnuityReview.com). Cortazzo is a financial planner and annuity expert. For $299, his team will analyze up to two variable annuities with living benefits. He'll advise on the investments you've chosen, check the spouse protection (if any), and tell you how to make the most of your guaranteed withdrawals. If you're already working with an adviser you might use this service as a second opinion.

More Things You Need to Know About Variable Annuities with Living-Benefit Riders

1. You buy these annuities not because you're thrilled by their minimum income guarantee. Instead, you're hoping to exceed

---

8   This book's biggest understatement.

that minimum, thanks to the stock market's expected, long-term gains. To have even a shot at success, however, you have to put at least 90 percent of your investment into stock-owning mutual funds, says annuity expert Moshe Milevsky of York University in Toronto. Yet most insurance companies currently limit your stock holdings to about 60 or 70 percent of your investment, with the rest in bonds. In other words, they're protecting themselves by programming you to fail. Annuities invested in a moderate mix of stocks and bonds will never—repeat, never—yield enough to increase your future retirement income. You will get only the annuity's minimum guarantee.

2. Your insurance company probably has the right to increase the internal cost of your existing annuity, up to certain caps. That reduces any chance you have of earning a future income higher than the guarantee. The caps are disclosed in the prospectus on page one zillion and three.

3. In general, don't add more money to the annuity if your investment value is below the benefit base. Doing so helps the insurance company, not you. The more money you have in the annuity, the less likely the company will ever be forced to use its own funds for your lifetime payments.

4. Variable annuities with income riders often include a death benefit, payable to your spouse or another beneficiary. If you make withdrawals from your investment account the death benefit usually declines by the same amount.

5. If you buy a variable annuity with a living-benefit rider and you're married, be sure the rider covers your spouse as *primary beneficiary*. If it doesn't, and you die first, your spouse or partner will receive what's left of the money in the investment account (if any) or perhaps a death benefit, but no lifetime income payments. Many salespeople don't point this out, especially if you're buying the annuity with funds from your individual retirement account. The IRA might name your spouse or partner

as beneficiary but that's not enough. He or she has to be on the rider, too.

6. Don't hold an annuity inside a self-directed IRA at a brokerage firm. For convenience, the broker will usually name the IRA as the annuity's beneficiary. If you die, your spouse will get the proceeds of the IRA but won't qualify for continuing annuity income. Hold variable annuities with a living benefit outside your self-directed IRA.

7. The guaranteed minimum income drops a bit for living-benefit riders that cover two people instead of one. If the single life rate is 5 percent, that for a couple might be 4.5 percent. Covering a dependent partner or spouse is the right thing to do, of course, regardless of the extra cost.

8. Some variable annuities let you change your mind. You can drop the living-benefit rider and stop paying the fees, or withdraw your cash anytime without penalty.

9. Annuities can be cash cows for financial advisers who choose to put their own interests ahead of yours. They'll watch to see when your annuity can be exchanged without penalty. Then they'll tell you that a better one has come along and encourage you to switch. If you do, the adviser earns a new commission, you start a new penalty period, and you might have lost some valuable benefits by giving the old investment up. On the other hand, a proposed switch to a low-cost annuity, such as those sold by Vanguard or TIAA-CREF, can make a lot of sense.

10. The mutual funds you buy inside annuities generally yield less than the same funds bought independently of annuities. That's because of the tax treatment as well as the annuities' fees. Outside the annuity, you pay the low capital gains tax on your shares' increase in value; inside it, you pay at the ordinary income rate when your gains are withdrawn. Over all but the very longest holding periods (15 to 20 years), you'll net more from direct mutual fund investments than you will from buying the

same funds inside a variable annuity, after taxes and fees.[9] You also pay lower investment charges and no sales commission if you buy the funds from a no-load mutual fund group.

11. Don't buy a living-benefit annuity unless you intend to annuitize—that is, turn its future value into an income for life. Most likely, that will become your best option, and at the minimum income level the insurer guaranteed. As an alternative, consider a deferred-income annuity (see page 133). It costs less and will probably give you a better return.

Special Note to People Who Bought a Living-Benefit Rider Before the 2008 Financial Collapse

You're in luck. In the early '00s, insurance companies competed to offer ever-richer benefits without charging you as much as they really cost. Guaranteed lifetime accumulations and payments ran to 6 or 7 percent.

Now many insurers are suffering seller's remorse. Those guarantees are too rich compared with what the companies can earn from interest rates today. Some of them are asking you to give up your high future benefits. In return, they'll add money to your investment account. They might also try to get you to cancel a lucrative death benefit that would go to your spouse or another beneficiary.

If you still want the lifetime income, throw the offer away. The "free" cash doesn't begin to cover the value of the big payouts you'd lose. You might take it, however, if you're seriously ill, with a shortened life span, and the annuity's income rider doesn't cover the lifetime of your spouse.

---

9   The break-even period is shorter if you're in the top federal and state income tax brackets or if you buy from a low-cost provider such as Vanguard or TIAA-CREF.

In some cases, the insurance company forces you to make a change. For example, you might be required to shift the investments in your annuity toward more bonds and away from stocks. If you don't, you'll lose your high lifetime income guarantee. The lower allocation to stocks makes it less likely that your guaranteed income will rise in the future—just what the insurer wants. To me, that's dirty pool. You've lost a benefit you have been paying for. If you're facing this demand, shift your investments as required but don't sit on them. Instead, start taking your annual guaranteed payouts immediately (see page 145). Right now. That's the best way of getting value for your money.

The Mystery Investment: A "Fixed-Index" Annuity with a Living Benefit

This is another one of those deals that give you the hope of gain with the promise of no loss. It's known as a "fixed annuity," "indexed annuity," "equity-indexed annuity," or "fixed-index annuity" (FIA). Regrettably, it is not truly fixed and not truly indexed. The various names give salespeople options when they pitch it. You want growth? They say "equity index." You want safety? They say "fixed."

A fixed-index annuity has nothing to do with the simple, fixed immediate-pay annuities I wrote about on page 129. These confusions of nomenclature are what make it so dangerous for the average person to stray into what amounts to the financial industry's worst neighborhood.

Three things make fixed-index annuities mysterious: (1) The insurance company won't disclose what you're paying for the underlying investments. (2) The company can control the size of your gain (if any) by changing the way it computes your potential profits as you go along. That's like betting on a horse after the race is over. (3) These products appear to be linked entirely to stocks but they're not. They're constructed to yield bondlike returns. Odds are, you won't get anything more out of them than their fixed-income guarantees.

In design, fixed-index annuities resemble the living-benefit annuities discussed above. When bought as a pension substitute, they come in two parts—an investment fund plus a guaranteed living-benefit rider. The guarantee pays, even if your investment does poorly. If it does especially well your future income might exceed the guarantee. What's different about this annuity is the restricted way that the insurance company figures your potential investment gains.

Another Sort-of-Simple Explanation

The FIA comes in two parts and here's how they work:

Part 1 of the contract: the investment. This is a pure tax-deferred investment. You sign up for a specific term, ranging from seven to 15 years, with a penalty for early withdrawals. Your gain, if any, depends partly on how well the stock market does over the period, as measured by Standard & Poor's 500 stock market index, not counting dividends. (That's a loss right there. A substantial part of the S&P's long-term returns—two to three percentage points a year—comes from reinvested dividends.)

The rest of your potential profit depends on how much of the S&P's gain the insurance company decides to give you. Typically, you get a percentage of any increase—say, 50 or 75 percent. There might also be a percentage cap on how much your account can rise in a single year. Caps are currently running between three and six percentage points. For example, say that the S&P rose by a lovely 16 percent this year. On paper, you're entitled to 75 percent of that increase, which seems to give you 12 percent. But if your account has a 6 percent cap, that's all you'll get. If you started the year at $1,000, you'll start the next year at $1,060. With a 3 percent cap, you'd start the next year at $1,030. Stocks went way up but your FIA account didn't. Some FIAs claim "no caps," but—trust me—they get the same fees and profits from another corner of your investment.

There are other ways of calculating a FIA's annual gain. For example, instead of looking at the market's rise from January through December, your annuity might give you an average of the year's monthly gains. That could work out to less than the 12-month gain or it could be more. You cannot know in advance and certainly cannot figure out the math. Some FIAs offer a first-year "signing bonus" but you pay for it in the form of lower credited investment returns.

If the stock market falls you'll be credited with zero interest for the year. That's the "no loss" clause. Your investment value will not decline. As you've seen, however, you pay for this clause by giving up part of any market gain—maybe a substantial part.

Warning! The insurance company can change the amount you're allowed to earn on your account. Usually, it makes these changes once a year. It might decide to lower (or raise) the amount of the stock market's gain it will credit you with or set the cap on your gain at a lower (or higher) level. These changes reduce the insurance company's risk by reducing your chance of gaining more than the company planned for. So you're not really "in the market" or linked to stocks, you just think you are.

There's a minimum investment guarantee. At the very least, you might get back the money you put in (or, more likely, 87.5 percent of the money you put in) plus annual interest at 1 percent. You can withdraw up to 10 percent of your investment every year without paying a surrender charge. For larger withdrawals, the surrender charge is stiff.

One more problem: You don't know what you're paying for the fixed-indexed annuity itself. It's not transparent. The sales materials (or "adviser"/salesperson) might say "no annual fees, no investment charges" but that's not true. The costs and (typically high) commissions are built into the product and come out of your investment return.

You can renew this annuity when its term is up. The costs and options you're offered on renewal might not be as good as those you started with.

Part 2 of the contract: the guaranteed lifetime withdrawal benefit (GLWB). This works just like the GLWB I discussed on page 142. You're assigned a "benefit base" (or similar name) that rises by a fixed amount each year—say, 5 percent. If the investment value of your annuity rises significantly, your future lifetime income could exceed the 5 percent guarantee. If not, you'll get the minimum 5 percent that the contract calls for. Always remember—you are *not* earning 5 percent on your investment. When your annuity payments start, you're receiving your own money back in annual 5 percent increments (see page 144).

The price of the GLWB rider is disclosed when you buy. With some GLWBs, payments can rise if you enter a nursing home.

Occasionally, you'll find a fixed-index annuity with a high lifetime income guarantee such as 6 percent. In return, you agree to be locked into the investment for 10 years or more or else pay a surrender charge. You will almost certainly not earn more than the guarantee. You'd buy the product only for the income, not for the dream of a higher investment return. And again: For many, many years, the insurer will be paying you with your own money.

Another warning: FIA advertising has been rife with misleading claims. They're so often missold that they've earned their own warning—an Investor Alert—at finra.org, the organization that oversees securities firms. Thanks to new regulations, the industry is moving toward cleaning up its act. But bad sales are still being made, especially to older people. A FIA might lock up your money for the next 10 years—painful, if you're in your 70s and need access to cash.

Stay out of expensive investments that tout "no loss, all gain." It's a snakepit down there.

What Happens When You Reach 70½?

If your guaranteed living-benefit rider is inside a traditional IRA there could be a problem. You'll have to start making minimum annual withdrawals at age 70½ and they might be higher than the GLWB or GMIB allows. GLWBs generally let you take the higher amount without breaking your lifetime income guarantee, but check. If you have a GMIB, however, it might not offer you that option.

You can avoid having to calculate a withdrawal amount if you turn the investment into an immediate-pay lifetime annuity. Age 70½ is a little young for that but you might have no choice. The annuity forces your hand.

You don't face a minimum withdrawal risk if you put the annuity into a Roth IRA, but the other drawbacks apply.

HOW ARE ANNUITY WITHDRAWALS TAXED?

When you're buying a pension in the form of a commercial lifetime annuity, taxes matter. Here are the rules, in brief:

- The income from investments left inside a variable annuity accumulates tax deferred. You can change the investments from one of the annuity's mutual funds to another with no tax consequences.
- You can switch from one variable annuity to another with no tax consequences through what's called a 1035 exchange. The agent will handle the transfer for you.
- For "qualified annuities"—purchased with funds from a retirement account and rolled into an IRA (see Chapter 7): All

the income you withdraw from a traditional IRA is taxed at ordinary income rates. Income from a Roth IRA can pass untaxed (see page 167).

- For "nonqualified annuities"—purchased with savings you keep outside a retirement account: Any earnings on your annuity investments are taxed as ordinary income, not as capital gains, regardless of the source. If you take a lump sum, the earnings are taxed all at once. If you take monthly benefits from an immediate-pay annuity, a deferred-income annuity, or a variable annuity, your income is partly tax free (because it's a return of your original investment) and partly taxable (due to the earnings on your annuity investments). The same is true if you annuitize a guaranteed minimum income benefit (GMIB—see page 142).

  If you're taking minimum annual withdrawals from a GMIB without annuitizing or from a guaranteed lifetime withdrawal benefit (GLWB), they'll be taxed entirely as income until you've received an amount equal to all the earnings on your investment. After that, the withdrawals are considered a tax-free return of your original capital. If you have a GLWB and live long enough to use up your investment earnings plus your principal, your income becomes taxable again. That's because you're finally being paid entirely by the insurance company rather than from your own money.

- If your investments lose money and your account is smaller than the amount you originally put into the annuity, all your withdrawals are considered a tax-free return of principal.

- When you die your estate will potentially owe income taxes on the value of tax-deferred annuities that can be left to heirs. They're also subject to estate taxes if you're in that bracket.

- You owe income taxes on any investment gains if you give the annuity to a charity.

- You can switch money from a 401(k) or similar tax-deferred retirement plan into a qualified annuity tax free.
- Income from annuities is not counted when figuring what tax, if any, you owe on your Social Security benefits.
- Money withdrawn from a tax-deferred plan, prior to age 59½, is subject to a 10 percent tax penalty on the earnings, unless the money is withdrawn at a level of payments expected to last for your lifetime.

SUMMING UP

Should you consider an immediate-pay or deferred-income annuity?

▶ No—if you are living on Social Security plus modest savings. You need your savings at hand for flexibility.

▶ No—if you're living on Social Security plus an inflation-adjusted pension with savings on the side. You already have enough steady income to last for life. Your inflation adjustment is your longevity insurance.

▶ No—if you have so much money that you'll never run out (lucky duck).

▶ No—if you have a substantial amount of investments, are tapping no more than 2 or 3 percent of the total every year, and are living comfortably on the money. You already have enough income to last for life.

▶ Maybe—if you have a substantial amount of financial assets but need to withdraw more than 4 percent plus inflation adjustments to pay your bills. You have little or no margin for error if you hope to make your money last for life. Annuitizing part of your savings raises the amount of income you can depend on. Ideally, the annuity payments plus Social Security would cover your bare-minimum expenses. That frees you to invest the rest of your money in well-diversified stock-owning mutual funds for growth.

▶ Yes—if you have substantial savings and are trying to live only on interest and dividends because you're afraid of touching the principal. Shifting some of your principal into an annuity will increase your standard of living and give you a lifetime income guarantee that you don't have today.

▶ Yes—if your diversified investments include a large commitment to bonds or bond mutual funds. You might put part of your bond allotment into annuities to get a higher income from the "safe" part of your portfolio. With your income secured, you might be more willing to put most of the rest of your investments into stocks for long-term growth.

▶ Yes—if you're so afraid of stocks that you're keeping all of your money in the bank or bond funds. Switch to some form of immediate-pay or deferred-pay annuity for a higher income.

▶ Yes—use a deferred-income annuity if you want to guarantee yourself an income starting in 10 or 15 years. Buying now costs you less and gives your investments more time to grow.

Should you consider a variable annuity with a living-benefit rider?

▶ Maybe—if you want the income guarantee *and* can find an annuity that lets you invest 90 percent of your money in stocks *and* doesn't charge more than 3 percent in total fees, including all the mutual fund fees. That's a needle in a haystack these days.

▶ No—if you're forced to keep more than 10 percent of your annuity investments in bonds. You'd be paying a high price for a lifetime income that will probably never exceed the guarantee. Assuming that you plan to hold the annuity for 10 years or more before making withdrawals, consider a deferred-income annuity instead.

▶ No—if you're in your 70s or older. Your money will be locked up for seven to 10 years. The only product even to consider is one with no penalty for early withdrawals.

▸ No—if you can afford it only by buying it through a tradi-tional individual retirement account.

▸ Yes—if the slim chance of an upside makes you so happy that you don't mind winding up with only the guaranteed mini-mum income. Maybe you'll be one of the charmed ones who do better than the guarantee by lucking into some strong bull markets during the annuity's early years. If not, you fully un-derstand that the only way to get value from the guarantee is by annuitizing or taking fixed withdrawals for life and then living a long life.

Should you consider a fixed-index annuity with lifetime monthly payouts?

▸ Maybe—if you're looking at the rare annuity that guarantees a higher lifetime payout rate (say, 6 percent) than you'd get from other types of annuities *and* a fixed lifetime income is all you want from the investment.

▸ No—if you're buying because you expect a stock-linked in-vestment return that's higher than the guarantee. Odds are you won't get it.

Fundamentally, annuities are not an investment even if they're tricked out to look like one. They're a risk-management tool. They insure you against the risk of living beyond the amount of money you have in savings and investments. But if you're allergic to annu-ities and want to create a lifetime income directly from your savings and investments, flip to Chapter 8.

7

Powering Your Retirement Savings Plans

If you haven't saved pots of money, don't waste time kicking yourself. It's never too late to give your future a boost.

When retirees are asked if there's anything they'd have done differently in their lives financially, the number one answer is (drumroll...) save more money. Younger, we tend to behave as if the retirement fairy will magically carry us through. That's everyone's plan A. By midlife, with faith in magic dimmed, we move to plan B, otherwise known as "I'll work till I drop." But you can't count on keeping your health or your job from now to the horizon. You also need plan C.

Plan C—to make up for lost time—is to "power save." If you're working, squeeze your paycheck like a sponge in order to put more money away. If you're no longer working full-time, find part-time work and save every dime.

If you're living entirely on your savings, go to plan D. Trim your budget and manage withdrawals and taxes so that your money will last a few extra years. Check the tax-saving rules later in this chapter.

Central to all these solutions is the nation's greatest gift to savers, the tax-favored retirement plan. With these plans, the earnings on your savings build up tax deferred (sometimes tax free). They come in many types, for employees and the self-employed. With employee plans, contributions are deducted from your paycheck automatically—a splendid and reliable way to save. Cash unseen is cash unspent. Your company might even match a percentage of the money you put in, a freebie no employee should miss. Contributions to plans for the self-employed can be automated, too. Typically, your money is invested in mutual funds.

Tax-favored retirement plans are solely for people with paychecks. You have to fund them with earnings, not with unearned income such as Social Security, pension, interest, dividends, or rent. The higher your unearned income, the more of an earned paycheck you might be able to put away.

Some people think it's no longer worth contributing to a plan when they're close to retirement age. Why put in money just to take it out a couple of years later? Two reasons. First, those might be your highest earning years so the tax benefits are the greatest. Second, you *won't* be taking out all of the money right away. You might live for another 30 years or more. That's a barrelful of time for your pre-retirement contributions to grow tax deferred. So please. Take these tax breaks while you're still working and can get them.

THERE'S A TAX UMBRELLA FOR EVERYONE

Tax-favored savings plans pop up everywhere in the working world. Which ones you can use depend on your employment status. Here are your choices:

If you work for a company with a retirement plan, you can have a percentage of every paycheck put away. On average, workers in their mid-50s to mid-60s are contributing 8.7 percent of the money they earn, according to a 2015 study by Vanguard called "How America

Saves." At 65 and up, they're saving 10.2 percent. Stretch savers do even better. The maximum contribution allowed in 2016 is $18,000 plus another $6,000 if you're 50 or older.[1]

Realistically, that's too high an annual goal for many workers. But you can probably raise the amount that you're contributing now. Ask your employer to deposit another 2 or 3 percent of your pay into the plan. Odds are, you won't even miss the money after a couple of months have passed. Vanguard reports that women, well aware of their longevity, save a larger percentage of their pay than men at the same income level.

The type of plan that you have available depends on where you work. Businesses generally offer 401(k)s.[2] Public school teachers, university employees, and employees of certain other tax-exempt institutions get 403(b)s. Certain state and local governments provide 457s. These plans differ slightly in their withdrawal rules and often in the range of investments available. But they all defer the tax on your earnings.

Some companies let you put more than the dollar limit into your 401(k). You get no tax deduction for the excess but the investment earnings build up tax deferred. When you leave the company, you can roll the money into an individual retirement account (IRA).

If you're a middle-income employee and participate in a company plan such as a 401(k), you're allowed to fund a personal IRA on the side. You could start the IRA and tax-deduct your full contribution if your modified adjusted gross income doesn't exceed $61,000 in 2016. There's a partial deduction for employees with incomes up to $71,000. For marrieds filing jointly, the limits are $98,000 for the

---

1　These numbers rise with inflation every year unless inflation is very low. Contribution limits for the year immediately ahead are usually issued by the IRS around mid-October. You can find them at IRS.gov.

2　These plans are all named after sections in the Internal Revenue Code.

full deduction and up to $118,000 for the partial. If you are married to someone with a workplace plan and have no plan of your own, the income caps for tax-deductible IRA contributions are even higher.

If you work for a company and have freelance income on the side, you can start an IRA for that separate income regardless of the size of your regular paycheck. If your outside earnings are substantial, consider a SEP-IRA rather than a regular IRA or a solo 401(k)—see below.

If you have no employee plan, invest in an individual retirement account. The basic IRA is stingier than the 401(k) but for the average earner it works just fine. You can contribute up to $5,500 in 2016, or up to $6,500 if you are 50 or older. If you're married and your spouse has no earnings, you can put away up to the same amounts in a spousal IRA in his or her name. That provides as much as $13,000 in savings per couple.

Note: You can't put anything more into an IRA than you actually earn. If your part-time job pays, say, $4,500, that's your maximum contribution.

The savings options brighten if you're self-employed and earn a substantial income. You might start a SEP-IRA (simplified employee pension, handled like an IRA) with a maximum contribution of up to $53,000 in 2016. If you work with your spouse you can each fund an account. Any other employees have to be included in the plan, on the same terms and at your expense, if they worked for you in at least three of the past five years.

Even better, consider a solo 401(k) if you have no employees except possibly a spouse. There you can contribute as much as $53,000 plus $5,500 if you're 50 and older, plus a second account for your spouse.

Annual contributions are not required with either of these plans. You can put in zero if your business had a bad year.

Where to find individual plans: IRAs, SEP-IRAs, and solo 401(k)s can be had from mutual fund groups, stockbrokers, financial advisers, banks, and insurance companies. I vote for the plans offered by no-load (no sales charge) mutual fund groups, such as Vanguard, Fidelity, and T. Rowe Price, or full-service discount brokers, such as Charles Schwab and TD Ameritrade. They'll charge you lower fees for services and investment products than if you go through advisers who earn sales commissions. The lower your costs the higher your long-term returns.

Funding an individual IRA takes discipline. There's no employer to do it for you by sluicing the money out of your paycheck and into your IRA account. The best way to protect yourself against your desire to spend is to set up your own automatic savings plan. Make the IRA contributions through your online bank account, on whatever schedule suits your paycheck. Or authorize your IRA trustee to take the monthly amounts out of your checking account.

Spouse Alert! If your spouse dies while holding an employee 401(k) or similar plan, you inherit the money automatically. That is, unless you specifically signed one of the plan's consent forms allowing the money to be left to someone else. Some solo 401(k) plans also include spouse protection, but check.

No spouse protection is built into IRAs or SEP-IRAs in most states. The owner of the account can normally leave it to anyone he or she wants, inside or outside the family. To be on the safe side, ask your mate to get a copy of the IRA beneficiary form that he or she signed, to see where the money will go. Sometimes spouses are cut out of their inheritances by accident (see page 193).

Spouses have a half interest in an IRA that's a marital asset if you live in one of the community property states.[3] But if your mate put someone else's name on the beneficiary form you will have to

---

3   Alaska, Arizona, California, Idaho, Louisiana, Nevada, New Mexico, Texas, Washington State, and Wisconsin. The half-interest retained by the worker can be left to anyone.

fight for the money. The plan trustee has to follow the beneficiary form unless ordered otherwise by a court. If, say, a husband left the whole IRA to his children from a previous marriage and the money was paid out, you'd have to sue the children. You can agree to have your share of the IRA go to someone else but it has to be in writing, notarized, and filed with the plan trustee.

RETIREMENT PLANS AND TAXES: PICK YOUR POISON

Retirement savings plans come in two versions: traditional plans and Roths. They're differently taxed. Which is the better bet depends on how you see your retirement income playing out.

Traditional Plans

Traditional IRAs, 401(k)s, and similar plans make up the bulk of retirement accounts. Contributions are deductible on your tax return. The money you put away grows tax deferred. When you start drawing it out, it's taxed at your ordinary income rate. That's the whole deal. No taxes now but definitely taxes later.

These accounts are intended, specifically, to help you retire. You'll generally pay a 10 percent penalty, in addition to income taxes, if you withdraw money before you reach age 59½. The penalty is waived in certain circumstances such as disability.

You're not required to take withdrawals until age 70½. After that, the tax man cometh. You have to start taking out money, in an increasing percentage, every year. The amounts are dictated by the IRS and depend on your age (and the age of your spouse, if he or she is sole beneficiary of the account and at least 10 years younger than you are). Generally, the minimum required withdrawal starts at a little less than 4 percent.

Your plan's trustee will tell you how much you have to take. If you're holding more than one 401(k) you have to draw the proper percentage from each one individually. If you have more than one traditional IRA, however, you can take the total required withdrawal from just one of the accounts or from any combination of them. You can do the same if you have more than one 403(b). But you have to keep the types separate. You can't count a withdrawal from a 403(b) toward the amount you have to take from your traditional IRA.

Be sure to get the numbers right. The IRS squashes people who don't make their withdrawals on time. As a fine, it takes 50 percent of the money you should have taken from your plan but didn't. To make it easier to keep track, consolidate your retirement accounts. Your 401(k), 403(b), and 457 can all be rolled into a single IRA.

Naturally, there are tiny differences among these plans. (What's a tax code for if not to complicate things?) Here are three: (1) If you hold a 401(k) or 403(b) and leave your job at age 55 or older you can make penalty-free withdrawals as long as you stay in the plan. You don't have to wait until age 59½. (2) If you hold a 457 plan and have left your job, there's no early withdrawal penalty at any age. (3) If you hold a traditional IRA and are under 59½ you can take out money penalty-free by using a loophole called rule 72t.

Rule 72t is a godsend for people who need money early but perhaps for only a few years. No early withdrawal penalty is due provided that the amount you take would result in "substantially equal"[4] payments over your lifetime (or the joint lifetimes of you and the IRA's beneficiary). What's especially valuable is that you don't have

---

4 There's more than one way of calculating "substantially equal" payments and the method chosen makes a huge difference to the amount you can take each month. The IRS's free Publication 590-B, "Distributions from Individual Retirement Arrangements (IRAs)," leads you through the numbers for one of the methods, although, if it were me, I'd throw in the towel and ask an accountant or planner. Even the IRS threw in the towel. Pub 590-B advises that you see a professional if you want to consider the two other methods.

to make these withdrawals permanent. You can stop or reduce them if they've been running for at least five years or when you reach 59½, whichever is longer. That lets you use IRA funds for short-term needs—for example, to pay your bills while you're looking for a new job or until Social Security starts—without depleting the entire account.

Note that you're avoiding only the 10 percent early withdrawal penalty. Any money you take out of a traditional IRA, at any time, remains taxable at your ordinary income rate. Your heirs will be taxed on withdrawals, too, but won't owe the 10 percent penalty.

Roth IRA Plans

Roths have a different story to tell. There's no tax deduction for the money you put in. All the earnings, however, grow tax free. In fact, they can grow tax free for the rest of your life. You're never required to take money out. Heirs who inherit Roths can take advantage of its tax-free accumulations, too.

Another plus is that you can withdraw your own contribution at any time and at any age without penalty, so you always have ready access to your savings. If, say, you put $5,000 into a Roth today and suddenly find that you need the money, you can take it right out again, no muss, no fuss.[5]

You can take out the earnings on your Roth investment tax free provided that you've passed 59½ and have held the Roth for at least five years. It takes only one small investment to start the five-year

---

5   You will get a 1099-R from your IRA trustee, which might make you fear that you're being taxed. You aren't, but you have to report it properly on your tax return. The 1099-R shows code J for an early withdrawal. You show the withdrawal on line 15a of your 1040. On line b, which asks how much tax you owe on that money, put down zero. Fill out IRS Form 8606 for nondeductible IRAs and file it with your return.

clock. From that point on, you're covered for all additions to the account as well as for any new Roths you establish.

You can find Roth versions of IRAs and solo 401(k)s. Many companies offer Roth 401(k)s to their employees. Unfortunately, they're not yet common in 403(b)s, 457s, and similar plans, which generally are slower to adapt.

Any employee can contribute to the Roth version of a company retirement plan.

By contrast there are income limits on who's allowed to start an individual Roth IRA, but they're so generous that most people qualify. In 2016, singles can contribute the full amount to the Roth if their modified adjusted gross income doesn't exceed $117,000 and a partial amount on incomes up to $132,000. For married couples filing jointly, the income limits were $184,000 for the full contribution and up to $194,000 for the partial.

If you're an employee who earns more than the limits, there's a backdoor way to set up an individual Roth IRA. You can start a traditional IRA, which will be nondeductible because of your high earnings level, then transfer that money immediately into a Roth. There are no income limits on transfers. (Some taxes will be due, however, if you have owned a traditional IRA for a while.)

Should you take the traditional IRA or the Roth if you have a choice?

Consider the Roth for several reasons. You always have cost-free access to your own contributions if you need them. Tax-free income feels like a triumph when you retire. Withdrawals from a Roth don't count toward your "combined income" (see page 72) when you're figuring whether your Social Security checks are taxable (withdrawals from regular IRAs do count). There are no age requirements for withdrawals. You can leave the money to heirs tax free.

On the other hand, consider a traditional plan if you're in a high tax bracket and expect to be in a lower bracket when you retire. It's advantageous to take the deduction while your earnings are still high.

Should you mix it up?

If your employer offers both a traditional plan and a Roth you can, if you want, allocate part of your contribution to each. The traditional plan gives you a tax deduction now, the Roth gives you tax-free income in the future. If your employer matches the money you put up, the match will always go into a traditional plan, so you might wind up with both types, like it or not.

If you're offered only a traditional plan, you might put in at least enough money to cover the full employer match. For the rest of your contribution, consider starting a Roth IRA outside the plan. Once you've put your annual maximum into the Roth, you can return to your employer plan in order to save even more.

If your employer doesn't offer a match, set aside enough of your paycheck to join the plan—perhaps 3 percent. After that, consider an independent Roth. This approach makes sense only if you *will* fund the Roth! If you find that you're slacking on your contributions, forget the Roth and increase the amounts you're putting into the company plan. There's nothing like automatic payroll deductions to build up a retirement account.

If you're still on the company payroll past 70½, you can keep making contributions to your 401(k). No withdrawals are required until you leave the job. You can also contribute to Roth IRAs as long as you have earnings.

With traditional IRAs, by contrast, 70½ is the witching age. Contributions stop and withdrawals start. The same is true for holders of 457 plans except that you might be allowed to contribute extra money in the three years before normal retirement age. If you're self-employed and have a solo 401(k) you can keep making contributions as long as you have earnings, but withdrawals have to start at 70½.

INVESTING YOUR RETIREMENT PLAN

I'll reserve most of my comments on investment strategies for Chapter 9. Here I'll just outline the choices you're likely to have to make when managing your retirement plan.

- Employer 401(k) plans provide you with a menu of mutual funds to choose from—usually 20 or more. You're expected to diversify your contribution among the various investment types—large stocks, small stocks, international stocks, bonds, and so on. Often, employers provide online tools to help you decide what percentage of your money to keep in each type of fund. For more on this decision—called "asset allocation"—see page 213. Keep it simple. Two to four funds will usually do.

- Most of the mutual funds in retirement plans are "managed funds," meaning that they're run by investment professionals. These managers try to pick the stocks and bonds that will beat the market. Good luck with that. They generally miss (see page 239).

- If you're lucky, your company's menu will include "index funds." These funds, essentially run by computer, invest in the market as a whole. Years and years of studies show that the returns from index funds beat a large majority of the funds run by professional managers. They're also lower cost. You can read more about index funds on page 235. A sound 401(k) buy would be a set of three core index funds that cover all the main markets: U.S. stocks, international stocks, and high-quality U.S. bonds.

- You might also be offered managed funds invested in particular sectors of the stock market, such as health care, real estate, or technology. But you don't need to buy these sectors separately. Your index fund owns them all.

- A few plans offer emerging markets funds covering companies in Southeast Asia, Latin America, Eastern Europe, and Africa. They might be of interest if they're not also covered by your plan's broad international fund.

- Special sectors on the fixed-income side might include a short-term bond fund (see page 247), a high-yield bond fund, which invests in the bonds of lower-quality companies (see page 253), and a stable-value fund, backed by insurance companies and paying a fixed rate of interest.

- By all means, consider target-date mutual funds if your plan offers them. It's one-stop shopping. Target-date funds contain both stocks and bonds in a mix determined by professionals to be appropriate for your age. As the years go by, your fund gradually shifts away from stocks and toward fixed-income investments. For more on target-date funds and how to use them, see page 257.

- For those who want professionally managed portfolios (other than target-date funds), a few employee plans offer personal advisory services. At a cost of perhaps 0.25 to 0.5 percentage points a year, managers will choose funds for you and change them as needed. To be worth their fee, these managers should take all your financial assets into consideration, not just the money in your 401(k). In general, they're for people with a high net worth who might otherwise choose a personal financial adviser.

- If your plan offers stock in your company, avoid buying anything more than a small amount of it—say, 5 percent of your investments or less. Both your job *and* your retirement savings shouldn't ride on just one company's success. If your company uses stock to match your contribution, you don't have to keep it. Exchange it for mutual funds. It's not disloyal. Your employer won't care.

- Your plan might also provide a brokerage house window. That lets you put part or all of your 401(k) into the hands of a stockbroker or financial adviser to be managed independently. Your "reward" will be higher costs and probably poorer results than if you had stuck with index funds or target-date funds. (That's an editorial comment.)

- A handful of plans let you put part of your money into a deferred-income annuity that eventually will provide you with an income for life. For more on deferred-income annuities, also known as longevity annuities, see page 133.

- The splendid Thrift Savings Plan (TSP) for federal government workers offers target-date funds invested only in index funds. The mix includes government bonds, corporate bonds, large-company stocks, medium and small company stocks, and international stocks. Participants can also invest in these funds separately if they want a different mix from the ones that the target-date funds supply. The Thrift Savings Plan is the simplest, finest, and lowest cost retirement plan on the planet.

- Some public school teachers and state and local employees with 403(b) and 457 plans can choose from a mix of mutual funds. Others aren't so lucky. The majority of these plans restrict your investments to tax-deferred annuities. There are fixed annuities with an interest rate that appears attractive but might drop to a below-market rate in the future. Also variable annuities that let you put your money into stock funds, bond funds, and short-term money market instruments.

  In general, these 403(b) and 457 annuities are lousy deals. They're larded with fees that chop your investment returns. There's usually a penalty if you switch your money to another type of investment before five or more years have passed. You might be drawn into these investments because you're approached by a colleague who sells them on commission. Trust me, your colleague is doing you no favors. Before you sign up, ask your employer for a list of your investment choices. Choose mutual funds (preferably index funds) if they're available. If not, go for the lowest-cost annuity on the list and petition your employer to do better by you.

- Many college and university employees are offered excellent 403(b)s. They're often invested with TIAA-CREF, a low-cost investment company that provides a sensible mix of mutual funds and inexpensive annuities. Almost without exception, the university-based economists, professors, and financial researchers I speak with are invested entirely in index funds, usually with TIAA-CREF (some have switched to Vanguard).

- Many 401(k) and 403(b) plans carry high fees. If your plan falls into that category and there's no employee match, you might consider saving in a low-cost Roth IRA outside the plan, provided that you're within the income limits (see page 168). To find out how your plan's fees and options stand up to the competition, check the 401(k) Ratings Directory at BrightScope.com.

- If your spouse also has retirement accounts, don't invest as if you live on different planets. Assuming that you'll go off together into the sunset, your plans should complement each other. For example, say that you like the idea of holding 60 percent in stocks and 40 percent in bonds for a couple your age. That's the way you allocate your own 401(k). But, unknown to you, your spouse's plan might be 100 percent in stocks—perhaps because he or she hasn't looked at it for many years. As a couple, you're farther out on an investment limb than you'd like. On a rainy Sunday, fire up your laptops (or pull out your printed plan documents), reevaluate each plan's investment options, and work out a combined asset allocation that makes sense to you both.

- If you have an independent IRA, a financial adviser might suggest that you invest all or part of it in a variable annuity (see page 137). The pitch: The gains from the mutual funds in your annuity will accumulate tax deferred. But the gains in your IRA are already tax deferred. All the annuities do is add costs.

USING A SELF-DIRECTED IRA

A self-directed IRA opens you to a wider range of investments than are offered by mutual fund groups. A plan at a brokerage firm, for example, lets you buy almost any of the firm's products—not only individual stocks but also the various structured notes, annuities, partnerships, and other exotics on offer, usually at high cost. Awful stuff. Personally, I wouldn't touch 'em.

If you want to buy gold, you have to open an IRA with a trustee willing to handle that type of investment. Your trustee can purchase gold, silver, or platinum bullion coins and bars (but not numismatic coins). All transactions have to be entirely independent of you, your relatives, or any businesses you own. For example, you can't sell to the IRA coins you already possess. You can't hold the coins in your personal safe-deposit box; they have to be kept in an approved depository at the IRA's expense. If you violate the rules and the IRS finds out, your tax shelter will blow up. The entire sum in the IRA could become taxable in the current year plus a 10 percent penalty if you're under 59½.

Self-directed IRAs can also be used for holding business interests, such as shares in a movie deal, private equity, and startups. The trustees who manage these kinds of investments often double as the agents selling the deals. They earn fees from them, which the IRA pays. Buyer beware.

IRAs are not allowed to purchase collectibles, such as gems, antiques, rare books, or art. Nor is an IRA allowed to hold life insurance.

Real Estate and the Self-Directed IRA

You can use IRA money to invest in rental real estate and other properties. But why would you want to? The rules make it costly to hold real estate in an IRA, especially when compared with buying real estate stocks.

For example, you need a trustee willing to oversee the IRA and a manager to handle the property for you. It has to be purchased with IRA funds. Mortgage lenders don't like IRA real estate so it's probably going to be a cash transaction. All rental income goes back to the IRA and the IRA pays all the expenses. The account will have to hold some cash in case your property doesn't throw off enough rent to cover the monthly bills. It also needs cash for unexpected expenses such as repair costs if a tenant damages the place. If you still have earnings, you can provide some ready money by making annual contributions into the IRA. When you're not working, you have to be prepared to transfer money into your real estate IRA from another IRA if cash runs short. You can't get a home equity loan on the IRA's property. If you do find a mortgage, the part of the profits financed by the loan becomes unrelated taxable business income, with the tax paid from the IRA every year. An IRA can't deduct capital losses or the property's expenses, including depreciation. Any profit is fully taxable. You can't take advantage of the low tax on capital gains.

It's essential that you and your close relatives not be connected with the property in any way. The IRA can't buy it from you, rent it to you, or let you use it rent free. You can't manage the property or put sweat equity into it—all work has to be done by outside contractors. You can't collect the rents yourself or even change a lightbulb or repair the steps. If you do, you can be nuked by the IRS. Where there's personal involvement, a traditional IRA collapses and its entire value becomes taxable. If you're using a Roth IRA, no taxes will be due but you'll lose the tax shelter on all future gains.

Real estate is especially risky for people with traditional IRAs who reach 70½. At that point, you have to start taking your required minimum withdrawal and real estate isn't liquid. If you don't have enough money in other IRA accounts to make the full withdrawal and can't sell the property in time, your required withdrawal might fall short. That triggers a 50 percent penalty on the amount you failed to take. The IRS doesn't accept a letter saying, "Gosh, I couldn't sell the house." You should have thought of that.

Given the complications and expenses, especially the management expense, it's much smarter to hold real estate outside an IRA. That reduces your costs, provides tax deductions, lets you put in sweat equity, and reduces your taxes when you sell. If you ignore all this excellent advice (!), buy your real estate with an IRA set up exclusively for that purpose. If for any reason you make a mistake that causes the real estate IRA to become taxable, the savings in your other IRAs will remain safe and tax deferred.

WHAT TO DO WITH YOUR EMPLOYEE PLAN WHEN YOU LEAVE YOUR JOB

When you leave a job, your number one objective, financially, is to preserve the tax umbrella over your retirement savings. There are six ways to do this:

1. If you take a new job with an employer who also offers a 401(k), you can move your money into the new employer's plan. Your old mutual funds will be closed out. You'll choose new ones, and the entire transfer will be tax free. This choice is a good one, because it consolidates your retirement savings in a single account. But the transfer can be slow.

2. If you want, you can generally stay with the old 401(k), even after you retire, as long as you have at least $5,000 in the plan. There are pluses and minuses to this choice for retirees. *The pluses:* Your money might be managed at a lower cost than you'd pay elsewhere. You're familiar with the mutual funds. If you're between 55 and 59½ you can generally make withdrawals without penalty. You're in a safe investment world where the financial wolves can't get you. *The minuses:* There might be limits on how and when you can take the money out. Some plans charge higher fees than you'd pay at a no-load mutual fund. You might lose track of the old 401(k) or pay no attention to what's happening to the investments there. If you die and your heir is someone other than your spouse the heir could lose tax advantages that would have been available if the money had been rolled into an IRA (see page 183).

3. Most commonly, people leaving an employee retirement plan transfer the money, tax free, into an IRA known as a "rollover IRA." There's no dollar limit on the amount you can roll. For this new investment, you have several options:

You might choose the IRA offered by the investment company that already administers your plan. That's an especially attractive choice if your plan is being managed by a no-load mutual fund group such as Vanguard or Fidelity, a discount broker such as Charles Schwab, or a low-cost firm that specializes in retirement plans. You can keep the mutual funds you have or choose new ones.

Alternatively, you might roll your 401(k) money into an IRA offered by a different investment firm from the one that your company is using now. The best choices would be the low-cost providers mentioned above. Make the change, for sure, if your current 401(k) is with a firm whose advisers charge sales commissions, even if you're not using those advisers. Such firms often put high-cost mutual funds into their IRAs. Switch, too, if you're in a 403(b) or 457 plan whose only investment option is a fixed or variable annuity. The change will cut your costs.

Beware, beware the friendly "advisers" who call, mail, and even visit you at your desk at work. They're usually selling terrible stuff that will make them rich while drenching your retirement dreams. Run away if they mention variable annuities, nontraded real estate investment trusts, energy partnerships, or private placements (see page 265). These high-cost, high-commission investments should be off the table when IRA salespeople have to become fiduciaries on January 1, 2017 (see page 32). But don't count on it. Keep your B.S. sniffer on.

4. If you have multiple retirement plans, roll them together into a single IRA. Separately, they're a pain to keep track of and probably add to your costs. Traditional retirement plans are rolled into traditional IRAs. Roth plans are rolled into Roth IRAs. You can switch a traditional IRA into a Roth but will have to pay taxes on the amount of money moved (see page 180).

If you put extra money into your 401(k), above the official dollar ceiling, that part wasn't tax deductible. When you leave the plan, you can roll the entire amount into a traditional IRA. When you make withdrawals, however, you will have to adjust for the portion of the IRA on which you have already paid the tax (such fun!). Alternatively, you can roll the pre-tax portion of your IRA into the plan of a new company you join or into your own self-employment plan. The remaining portion can then be switched into a Roth IRA, tax free. Always file Form 8606 with your tax return when making nondeductible contributions, so the government can keep track of what's taxable in your IRA and what isn't.

5. With some 401(k)s, you can ask the plan to send you installment payments for a fixed number of years. The plan might also offer a lifetime annuity from a particular insurance company (see Chapter 6). Before saying yes to an annuity, check Immediate Annuities.com to see if there's a different insurer that will pay

you more per month. If you previously allocated some of your 401(k) money to deferred-income annuities, that contract will remain in force.

6. If you want to buy individual stocks (I hope you don't—see page 244—but just in case) roll your retirement plan into a self-directed IRA with a discount or full-service brokerage firm or financial adviser.

   Note: When you move money from one plan to another, the check should go directly from your old plan to your new one without passing through your hands. The trustee of your new plan will tell you how to do it. If the check goes to you, it's counted as a taxable withdrawal. To avoid paying taxes you have to deposit it into your personal bank account, write a new check, and send it to the new plan within 60 days. Don't try it. Too much can go wrong.

Important tax-saving note for people who own company stock in their retirement plans: If the stock has risen substantially in value, you'll save taxes if you *don't* roll over this portion of your 401(k) into an IRA. Instead, ask the plan to distribute the shares directly to a brokerage account (say, at a discount brokerage firm, including the firms attached to mutual fund groups such as Fidelity and Vanguard). If you don't do that, you'll owe ordinary income taxes (plus a 10 percent penalty if you're under 59½) only on the value of the stock when it first went into your plan. For example, if you hold the stock at an average price of $10 and it's now worth $30, your ordinary tax rate applies only to the $10. When you sell it, the remaining $20 will be taxed at the low capital gains rate. This tax saving is especially valuable if you're in a high bracket and the gain is large. If you'd rolled that stock into an IRA, you'd have owed ordinary income taxes on the entire amount when you took the money out.

There are lots of complications to this tax-smart transaction. Talk to an accountant before making a decision.

SHOULD YOU SWITCH MONEY FROM A TRADITIONAL IRA INTO A TAX-FREE ROTH IRA?

You can roll any amount of money from a traditional IRA, 401(k), or similar plan into a tax-free Roth IRA regardless of how much income you earn. There's a cost to this transfer, however—perhaps a big one. You pay current income taxes on the money you move even though you don't withdraw any of the cash. Sometimes the tax is worth paying, sometimes not.

You might want to switch to the Roth if: (1) You don't expect to need the money until your later age, if ever. (2) You plan to leave most or all of the Roth to your heirs and want them to receive it tax free. (3) You expect to be in the same (or a higher) tax bracket when you retire, although you can't know for sure. (4) You're young enough so that the future growth in your investments could more than offset the cost of paying the current tax. (5) You can pay the taxes due from outside funds without having to take money out of your tax-sheltered retirement account.

You might not want to switch to the Roth if: (1) You'll have to use funds from the IRA to pay the tax. That greatly reduces the amount of money left to grow tax deferred. (2) You expect to drop to a lower tax bracket when you retire. (3) The Medicare tax on the transfer (see page 181) would bump you into a higher bracket. (4) You're 65-plus and expect to withdraw a substantial amount of your IRA during your retirement.

In short, Roth conversions are great for people who don't need the money and want to pass most of it to heirs tax free. For the average person, however, the size of the current tax might overwhelm any likely benefit from future tax-free growth.

If you decide to convert, call up the firm where you keep your traditional IRA and tell it to make the change. Presto, it's now a Roth. If you want to convert only part of your savings, the firm will roll that portion into a separate Roth account. The best way to proceed is to convert just enough money each year so that the extra income you have to report doesn't push you into a higher bracket.

Check all the costs of conversion, not just the income tax cost! An unpleasant surprise lies in wait for people on Medicare who switch a large amount of traditional IRA money into a Roth. That's because the amount of your transfer is added to your taxable income for the year. If it bumps up your income by too much you'll have to pay a higher premium for Medicare Part B (the medical plan) and Part D (the drug plan). In 2016, you owe a higher premium if you are single with a modified gross income above $85,000, or married filing jointly with an income above $170,000. If your regular income for the year is, say, $50,000 and you convert $120,000 into a Roth, you put yourself into higher-premium territory.

When figuring whether you owe this higher premium, the government looks at the most recent tax return available. That generally means that in 2016 your premium is based on the income you reported in 2014. If you're married filing jointly and your spouse is on Medicare, he or she will pay the higher premium, too. Once you've completed the Roth conversion and your income drops back, your Medicare premium will return to its normal, lower level. (You can apply for relief from the premium increase if your income has declined for certain specific reasons, including losing a job or losing your spouse.)

Next there's the potential higher tax for people on Social Security. The Roth conversion might raise your reported income by enough to increase the tax you owe on your Social Security benefits (see page 72).

Finally, if the sum you convert to a Roth is large enough, it might also lift you into the select group that pays a 3.8 percent tax on unearned income. You're caught if your income for the year exceeds

$200,000 for singles and $250,000 for married couples filing jointly. Unearned income includes interest, dividends, capital gains, rent, and so on.

There are plenty of calculators on the Web that purport to show you whether it's worth converting to a Roth but none of the ones I've looked at include the potentially higher Medicare and Social Security costs or the tax on unearned income. So don't make a move without talking to a tax accountant. Roth conversions aren't a game for amateurs.

WHEN YOU'RE TAKING MONEY FROM SAVINGS TO PAY YOUR BILLS, WHICH TYPE OF ACCOUNT SHOULD YOU TAP FIRST?

Retirees have many possible sources of income: Social Security, taxable savings and investment accounts, tax-deferred retirement accounts such as traditional IRAs, and Roth IRAs that grow tax free. The more tax-efficiently you use your money, the longer your nest egg will last. Here are some general rules on which accounts to tap first:

- Normally, spend taxable savings before dipping into a traditional IRA or similar account. "Taxable savings" means money that's not held in a tax-deferred or tax-free retirement account.
- There are a couple of times when you should tap a traditional IRA first, before using taxable savings. For example: (1) You're in a low tax bracket and your heirs are in a high one. The IRA money is worth more if you take it now. (2) You want to shrink your IRA so that, when you reach 70½, the required withdrawals won't be as large. That might save you from paying a higher tax on your Social Security benefits when IRA withdrawals start (see page 71).
- If you're in the low, 15-percent tax bracket, you might decide to withdraw extra money from your IRA, even if you don't

need it now. Take it from the stock funds you own and rein-vest it in stock funds in your taxable account. From this point on, you'll get the low capital gains rate on their increase in value.

- Spend taxable and tax-deferred savings if that helps you put off taking Social Security until you reach 70, if you're single, or perhaps 66 to 70 if you're married. At older ages, you will get the highest possible individual or family benefits for life (see pages 42 and 54). If you take benefits earlier you will get less.

- Normally, tap a traditional IRA before tapping a Roth. The longer the Roth can grow tax free the better. But tap the Roth first if you're in a particularly high tax bracket and expect your bracket to drop in future years.

- If you have both a taxable and a tax-deferred account for long-term investments, stuff the taxable account with stocks. That way, any profits will be taxed at the low rate for capital gains. All your taxable bonds, such as Treasury funds, go into the tax-deferred account. Interest income is taxed at ordinary income rates no matter where the bonds are held.

DID YOU INHERIT AN IRA? HERE'S HOW TO STRETCH ITS FABULOUS TAX SHELTER OVER YOUR ENTIRE LIFETIME

The tax breaks in an IRA don't have to end when the owner dies. If you inherit an IRA most or all of the money you receive can continue to grow tax deferred or tax free. To get these lifetime tax breaks, how-ever, you have to play your cards right.

You've played your cards wrong if, dazzled by the inheritance, you cash out of the IRA and pop the proceeds into your bank or investment account. Any money you remove from a traditional IRA becomes current income. You'll have to report it and pay the taxes all at once. Most likely it will push you into a higher bracket, which can eat up your inheritance fast. Generally, no taxes are due if you cash out of an inherited Roth IRA, but you lose the right to let the money grow tax free in future years.

You will probably want to take at least some of your inheritance for current use. But anything you intend to save or invest should stay cradled in its tax shelter. Here's how to handle an IRA you inherit, be it a traditional IRA or a Roth.

If you inherit an IRA from your spouse, you have four choices:

1. Treat the IRA as your own, telling the trustee to change the name on the account. You'd do this if you're happy with the cost and services of the current IRA plan. You don't have to keep the same investments. You can look over the menu of mutual funds the plan offers and make different choices.
2. Roll the money into a new IRA in your name, income tax free. You'd do this if you're not happy with the current plan and want to switch. For example, you might want to leave the brokerage firm that your spouse used and reinvest with a no-load mutual fund group. The new firm will help you with the transfer.
3. Roll the money into an IRA you hold already. You'd do this to consolidate your accounts. Traditional IRAs can be rolled into other traditional IRAs tax free. Roths can be rolled into Roths.
4. There's a special option for spouses who inherit a traditional IRA when they are under 59½. Normally, people that young cannot make withdrawals without paying a 10 percent tax penalty. But if you need money now, you can avoid the penalty by retitling the account as an "Inherited IRA." An "Inherited IRA" is a legal term of art. Instead of putting only your own name on the account, you retitle it using both your name and the name of the spouse you inherited from. For a rundown of all the rules, see page 186. *Please note:* If you make this choice you should retitle the IRA again when you reach 59½, putting it into your name alone. That

gives you the option of stopping withdrawals and waiting until you're 70½ to start again. Holding the IRA in your own name also gives your beneficiaries maximum flexibility for timing their own withdrawals from what remains of the IRA, if you die.

What if you're under 59½ and you inherit a Roth IRA? Don't bother retitling it as an inherited IRA. You can draw out your spouse's contributions at any time and at any age without penalty. That will probably be enough to satisfy your immediate need for cash. There's a penalty only if you withdraw the earnings on the contributions if you're under 59½ and your spouse held the IRA for fewer than five years.

Spouses who inherit an IRA should name new beneficiaries right away. For example, you might name your kids. Once their names are on the account, they'll be able to continue using the IRA tax shelter at your death. If you die before naming new beneficiaries the money will usually go into your estate, to be paid out (*and taxed!*) right away. Always use the IRA's official beneficiary form. That's the only way of passing the tax shelter to your heirs (see page 188).

Note that spouses enjoy a considerable advantage over non-spouses, when inheriting an IRA. It's one of the financial plusses of marriage for same-sex couples who have substantial assets in retirement plans.

If you inherit an IRA from someone other than a spouse — for example, from your parent or life partner:

You're not allowed to roll the money into an IRA of your own. Instead, you have two choices:

1. Take your full inheritance out of the IRA right away. That might make sense if the amount is small and you need the cash. If it's a traditional IRA, you'll pay income taxes on the money in the

current year. Nonspouse beneficiaries *do not* pay penalties for withdrawals made when they're younger than 59½. If you inherit a Roth IRA and cash it in, no taxes are due.

2. Retitle the account as an Inherited IRA—a legal entity that keeps the tax shelter going. That's a terrific option, especially for IRAs of any size. Once established, the Inherited IRA lets your investments continue to grow, tax free or tax deferred. Each year, you'll be required to withdraw at least a minimum amount based on your life expectancy. In midlife, however, the minimums are small. At 40, you'd have to withdraw only about 1/44th of the amount. The next year, 1/43rd of the amount, and so on. Potentially, the shelter can last as long as you live. If you die, your heirs can put any remaining money into an Inherited IRA of their own. *To reach this happy result, however, you have to get the paperwork right!* One small slip and the shelter will collapse, forcing you to take the money (and pay any taxes) all at once. Check out the rules, below.

The All-important Rules on Creating Inherited IRAs

The retitling rules for Inherited IRAs are very specific. You have to put your name on the account *as beneficiary* and the name of the account's original owner. It's helpful to include the date the original owner died. That's true both for a traditional IRA and a Roth.

Here's an example of how the rules work if you inherit money from someone other than your spouse:

Emily Jones dies, leaving her IRA to her son, Riley. The account should be retitled "Emily Jones IRA (deceased February 2, 2016) for the benefit of Riley Jones beneficiary." If Emily has another son, Justin, and leaves half the IRA to each of them, Riley would title his half as shown above. Justin would title his half "Emily Jones IRA (deceased February 2,

2016) for the benefit of Justin Jones beneficiary." The wording can change a little bit but the same essential facts must be there.

If you're inheriting from your spouse, you'd set up an Inherited IRA only if you're younger than 59½ and want to start drawing out money right away. Here's how the rules would apply to you:

Matthew Smith leaves his wife, Amanda, a traditional IRA worth $150,000. The account should be retitled, "Matthew Smith IRA (deceased January 5, 2016) for the benefit of Amanda Smith, beneficiary." That allows her to make early withdrawals without paying the 10 percent tax penalty. If Amanda's financial adviser makes a mistake, however, and retitles it just plain "Amanda Smith," it becomes her personal IRA. In that case, she won't be able to avoid the penalty until she passes 59½. Mistakes are not unusual, so keep an eye on this.

What if you're the second-generation beneficiary of an Inherited IRA? You, too, can keep the tax shelter going. All you have to do is retain the name of the original owner when you retitle. For example:

Riley Jones, son of Emily, dies. Emily had left him her personal IRA, which he converted into an Inherited IRA. He made six years' worth of withdrawals before his death. Riley's daughter, Rebecca (Emily's granddaughter), inherits. She's allowed to convert the account into an Inherited IRA of her own. The proper new title would be "Emily Jones IRA (deceased February 2, 2016) for the benefit of Rebecca Jones, beneficiary." Rebecca can't restart the clock by taking withdrawals based on her own life expectancy. However, she can complete the withdrawals that her father, Riley, was entitled to over his lifetime. The assets in that single IRA account could eventually be stretched over 80 tax-free years or more.[6]

Important: You're not limited to the minimum withdrawal from an IRA. You're allowed to take any larger amount you want, in any year. Choosing the minimum, however, preserves more of the money for your own older age.

If you inherit money from a 401(k), 403(b), or similar employee plan:

The tax rules are the same as if you inherited an IRA. Spouses can roll the money into an IRA in their own names or into an Inherited IRA. Nonspouse beneficiaries have to choose the Inherited IRA if they want to preserve the tax shelter.

IF YOU'RE THE PERSON WHO STARTED THE IRA, HOW CAN YOU HELP PRESERVE THE ACCOUNT FOR YOUR HEIRS WHEN YOU DIE?

Three tips:

1. Name one or more beneficiaries for every IRA account you own, using the account's official beneficiary form. If your spouse is the beneficiary, he or she can turn the money into a personal IRA. If you name someone other than a spouse, specify percentages— for example, "one-third to each of my three children." At your death, the children can ask the IRA trustee to split the account

---

6   A proposal in Congress would require nonspouse beneficiaries to withdraw Inherited IRA money over just five years. If passed, it would presumably grandfather heirs who are using the stretched-out withdrawal rules allowed today.

into three pieces so each of them can set up an Inherited IRA of his or her own. If more children are possible, you might say "to all my children, in equal amounts."

Make sure that the beneficiary form jibes with the provisions of your will. If there's a difference between the two, the people named on the beneficiary form will get the money (see page 193)

Don't leave the beneficiary form blank! If you do, your heirs, including your spouse, will lose their chance to roll their inheritance into IRAs of their own. Instead, the money will probably be paid into your estate. From there, it's distributed as cash. Money from traditional IRAs is taxed as income to the beneficiaries, in the current year. Money from a Roth is not taxed but the beneficiaries will lose the option of letting part or all of their inheritance accumulate tax free.

2. File copies of the IRA beneficiary form with your plan trustee, your lawyer, your financial adviser, and in a place in your home where your heirs will find it. Tell the heirs about the Inherited IRA option and what it can do for them. You might even leave a letter with a copy of your will. There's no guarantee that your beneficiaries will know about Inherited IRAs. Their own financial advisers might not know, either.

3. You can name a trust as beneficiary of your IRA but do it only if you have a very good reason. Trusts are complicated and expensive. You'll need an experienced estate-planning attorney to avoid wrong-footing the many IRS rules. One mistake and the IRA's tax shelter could blow up.

    Trusts are worth their cost if you're leaving the IRA to young children who aren't capable of handling money. Or you want the income from the money to go to your second spouse, with the principal going to children from your former marriage when the second spouse dies. Or your beneficiaries are spendthrifts or have drug problems. For a simple inheritance, however, leave the trust out of it.

IS MY IRA SAFE?

Yes. By law, your investments are kept in a separate trust, not mixed with the assets of the investment company. If the company goes broke, your accounts are protected.

DEFEND YOURSELF FROM FINANCIAL "ADVISERS"!

I'd guess that the majority of advisers—brokers, planners, mutual fund call centers, insurance agents—know almost nothing about the rules for Inherited IRAs. They might tell you to roll the money into an IRA of your own, which you can't do if you're not the IRA owner's spouse. They might say there's nothing to do except take the money and pay the tax, which you now know is wrong. They might "help" you by putting the money directly into your own name, making it taxable immediately or costing you the tax-free gains provided by a Roth. If you make a mistake based on bad advice, tough luck. It can almost never be undone. For more details on inheriting IRAs, I recommend two books, both by retirement plan experts: *The Retirement Savings Time Bomb . . . and How to Defuse It* by Ed Slott and *Retire Secure!: A Guide to Getting the Most Out of What You've Got* by James Lange. You need to know the rules yourself to be sure that your adviser does the right thing.

AFTER THAT MAGIC AGE . . .

You can't hang on to a traditional retirement plan forever. When you reach age 70½, you have to start taking required minimum distributions (RMDs) every year.

The IRS sets the withdrawal rates. They're intended to empty all your plans over your lifetime or the joint lifetimes of you and your spouse if your spouse is your beneficiary and he or she is more than 10 years younger. For your official federal life expectancy, see the

IRS's Uniform Lifetime Table. You can find it on the Web or in the IRS's free Publication 590-B, "Distributions from Individual Retirement Arrangements" (IRAs)[7]—a guide to how these plans are taxed.

How do you figure your withdrawals? It's easy—and I say this as one who's allergic to arithmetic. The steps are:

1. What was the value of your IRA last December 31? Look at the December 31 value before you turned 70½ if this is your first withdrawal. Count the value of any annuities you bought with IRA funds (except qualified longevity annuities—see page 133).

2. What is your life expectancy according to the Uniform Lifetime Table? Use this table if you're unmarried or if your spouse is your beneficiary and is no more than 10 years younger than you are. If your spouse is more than 10 years younger, use the Joint Life Table.

3. Divide the value of the IRA by your life expectancy. That gives you the minimum withdrawal for the current year.

4. Do this for each traditional IRA and SEP-IRA you have. Add up the results. That's the amount that must be withdrawn. You can take it from one IRA or from several as long as the total dollar amount is met.

5. Go through these same steps for every 403(b) you own. Again, you can take the annual payment from any of your 403(b)s as long as you withdraw the required total amount.

6. If you own more than one type of plan—say an IRA, a 401(k), a 403(b)—you have to withdraw from them separately. Money taken from an IRA can't satisfy the amount you're supposed to

---

7 Publication 590-A covers putting money into retirement accounts. Publication 590-B covers taking it out. These withdrawal rules apply to money held in all employer-sponsored plans and all IRA-based plans except Roth IRAs.

take from your employee account. You can get rid of all these separate calculations by consolidating your retirement accounts into a single IRA.

7. If you're holding more than one 401(k), you have to take the required minimum from each of them separately. Again, consider rolling your 401(k) into an IRA. Keep in mind, 401(k)s don't necessarily offer good inheritance options.

If you can't or don't want to figure out the proper withdrawals yourself, the trustee for your retirement plan will usually help. It will calculate the payment and move the money to any account you name. You'll also find calculators on the Web. Or ask an accountant or qualified financial planner.

It's critical that you take at least the minimum required amount each year. If you withdraw too little you'll be socked with a 50 percent penalty on the sum that you should have taken but didn't (unless you can convince the IRS that you were all thumbs with the life-expectancy tables). Don't wait until the very end of the year for the withdrawal. If there's some sort of delay at the financial institution that's holding your money, you might miss the deadline.

What if you're still working at 70½? You can continue to contribute to your employer sponsored plan. No Federal law requires you to start withdrawals at 70½ (although your company might require it). Normally, withdrawals begin after you retire. There's an exception for people who own more than 5 percent of the company, including owners of solo 401(k)s. They have to start withdrawals at 70½ even though they're still on the job.

Traditional IRAs work a little differently. Once you reach 70½, you can't make contributions, even though you're still earning a paycheck, and must take annual withdrawals. There are no such restrictions on Roth IRAs. You can continue to make contributions past 70½ and never have to take withdrawals if you don't want to.

MAKE SURE THAT THE RIGHT PERSON GETS YOUR MONEY!

When you set up an IRA, the paperwork includes a beneficiary form. Don't fail to fill it out. The form normally dictates who gets the money left in the IRA when you die. It trumps what it says in your will or your prenuptial agreement, and can even preempt a divorce agreement. It ignores what you've promised or what's fair. In most states, the person or persons named on the IRA beneficiary form inherit the money, period.

Say, for example, that you divorce and remarry. The divorce agreement stipulates that your ex has no claim on your IRA. Your will leaves the money to your second spouse. But you forget to take your ex off the IRA beneficiary form. Too bad for the new spouse. In most states, your ex inherits the lot. I've read of cases where the money went to a sibling or a parent instead of to a spouse or child simply because the IRA owner neglected to change a form that he or she created years ago.

There are two exceptions to this rule. The first is for community property states, where a spouse has a half interest in a plan that's a marital asset (see page 164, footnote). The second exception applies to a handful of states that remove the name of an ex-spouse after the divorce. But state law can be tricky so don't count on it. Fix the beneficiary form yourself.

To change your IRA beneficiary, ask the IRA trustee for a new form. You should name primary and secondary beneficiaries in case the primary beneficiary dies before you can change the form (for example, if you and your spouse die in the same accident). It's important to check the wording with the lawyer who drew up your will to be sure that you get the result you want. For example, when leaving an IRA to a child you should probably add the words "per stirpes." That lets your child's children (your grandchildren) inherit if the child dies before you do. Specify "stepchildren" if you want them to inherit, too. Once you've filled in the form, get it witnessed properly and send it back. Do this any time your life circumstances change—for example, if you marry, divorce, or have a child. I know that paperwork is boring and you probably assume that you have plenty of time. But—not to be morbid—you have no idea how much time you have. Now is always the best time to set things right.

8

The Speed Limit on Retirement Spending: Still 4 Percent?

When to step on the gas, when to tap the brakes.

We've reached a central question in retirement planning: How much cash can you take from your nest egg every year without running the risk of eventually going broke? We're talking about your financial nest egg, also known as your "portfolio"—stocks, bonds, mutual funds, certificates of deposit, and so on. The next chapter talks about how to invest these savings for the best results. This one helps you budget by showing how much you can afford to spend. The spending rate is your speed limit. It helps ensure that your money will last as long as you do.

Spending rules are important even when you don't follow them to the letter. They save you from accidentally using up too much of your money when you first retire.

Some retirees manage their spending so well that they don't have to touch their basic savings. Their IRAs remain mostly intact until they're required to start making withdrawals at age 70½.

Most of us, however, will depend partly on our savings to pay our monthly bills. It's critical to know how much we can afford to take.

Here's the classic answer to the question: You can take 4 percent of your total financial savings in the first year you retire (or the first year that you start drawing on the money). In each following year, take the same amount plus an increase for inflation. If your investments are well diversified, you can start with 4.5 percent.

That's been the gold standard in financial planning ever since it was developed 25 years ago. It would have carried you through the worst periods the U.S. economy has endured, measured from the mid-1920s. If you stick to those withdrawal rates and are properly invested, your money should last at least 30 years. For any period better than "the worst," your money will last longer than 30 years. You'll have more to spend in your later years and can leave a legacy as well.

The 4 percent rule is based on the historical performance of U.S. stocks and bonds. But what if the next 30 years take a different course? That's a question I've asked myself as my husband and I plan for the day when we won't have paychecks anymore. The projected Quinn budget works on a roughly 4.5 percent initial withdrawal plus inflation adjustments, but we're prepared to be flexible. We want to spend enough to be able to enjoy ourselves yet not so much that we start to worry. Leaving money for our kids is on our minds, but primarily we'd like to maintain the style of living that we worked for. Those are pretty common goals. You're probably in a similar emotional place.

There's also the question of being "properly invested." The research on 4 percent (and other withdrawal rates) assumes that you're keeping half your money broadly invested in blue-chip stocks and the rest in intermediate-term government bonds.[1] That assumption

---

1   Whenever I use the generic terms "stocks" or "bonds" I *always* mean stock or bond mutual funds or exchange-traded funds. *Never* individual stocks or bonds. See page 244 for the reasons why.

might stop you cold. Many retirees wouldn't dream of holding 50 percent of their savings in stocks. You might be able to follow the 4 percent rule while holding just 30 percent in stocks but that's a close call. If you don't trust stocks at all, your safe, initial withdrawal rate goes down to about 2.5 percent.

So it's more than a question of whether a 4 percent withdrawal rate works. The question is whether it works for *you*. If not, what are your alternatives?

Before we go further, let me explain how the 4 percent rule came to be.

UNPACKING THE FAMOUS 4 PERCENT (OR 4.5 PERCENT) RULE

The 4 percent rule arose from research done by financial planner Bill Bengen of El Cajon, California, in 1993. His clients wanted to know how much they could safely withdraw from their nest eggs each year without the risk of running out of cash. He tested various spending rates against historical investment returns, using 30-year periods that overlapped.[2] Here's what he came up with:

1. It's generally safe to spend 4 percent of your nest egg in the first year you retire. Withdraw the money at the start of the year, put it in your bank account or money market mutual fund, and use it to pay your bills. In the second year, withdraw the same amount plus an increase to cover the inflation rate. In the third year, do the same. Proceed this way, year after year.

    As an example, assume that you start with $100,000 at a

---

2   "Overlapping" means that every January 1 he started a new 30-year period. The first period ran from 1926 to 1956; the second from 1927 to 1957; the third from 1928 to 1958, and so on.

time when inflation is running at 3 percent. In year one of re-tirement, you'd take out $4,000 (your 4 percent). In year two, you'd increase your withdrawal to $4,120—last year's $4,000 plus $120 (that's a 3 percent increase for inflation). In year three, you'd take $4,244—last year's $4,120 plus $124 for inflation. And so on and so on. After inflation, you will have roughly the same amount of money to spend every year. In the rare case of deflation (last seen from 1930 to 1933), you'd lower your with-drawal by the deflation rate.

2. Bengen's basic studies assume that half your money is invested in Standard & Poor's 500 index of leading U.S. companies and the other half in an index of intermediate-term U.S. Treasury bonds (maturing in four to ten years). You can't buy these in-dexes directly but you can come very close to their performance by holding low-cost stock and bond index mutual funds (see pages 235 and 251).

3. Bengen found that you could hold as little as 30 percent in stocks and still succeed—just barely—with a 4 percent cash withdrawal rate (plus inflation increases) over 30 years. The rest of your money would go into intermediate-term bonds. Below 30 percent, you wouldn't make it through a worst-case economic scenario.

    You could also succeed—just barely—if you held 100 per-cent in stocks, but it would be too wild a ride for retirees. The optimum appears to be 50 percent in stocks. Those interested in building more wealth could go up to 75 percent, provided that they could live with wider swings in stock market prices.

4. Bengen used his annual withdrawals to *rebalance* his portfolios every year. Rebalancing means that you bring your allocation to stocks and bonds back to its original starting point. For exam-ple, say that your investment plan calls for you to hold 50 per-cent of your money in stocks and 50 percent in bonds. Over the year, stock prices rise so that you're now 55 percent in stocks.

You'd take most of your annual withdrawal from the stock account (and perhaps some from the bond account) to bring your allocation back to 50/50. For more on rebalancing, see page 208. The division you choose between stocks and bonds is known as an asset allocation. Bengen assumed that you'd stick with the same allocation for life.

5. All withdrawals go into a cash account that you can draw on to pay your current bills.

6. Historically, it hasn't mattered how well or badly stocks or bonds performed during a given year or handful of years. Eventually, one period's losses were restored by another period's gains. Bengen called 4 percent (plus annual additions for inflation) the **SAFEMAX**. That withdrawal rate carried retirees successfully through the 1929 stock market crash, the Great Depression of the 1930s, and the Stagflation that began in 1973. The initial pot of money always lasted for at least 30 years. In 97 percent of the 30-year periods, the money lasted for much longer than 30 years—an important point for retired people with a younger spouse. It's also important information for retirees who want to spend more than 4 percent.

7. Bengen assumed that you are a buy-and-hold investor. If you try to time the market by buying and selling when you think stock prices are low or high, you're on your own. You will almost certainly earn less than the market averages, over time. No spending rule will work.

8. In 1998, Bengen updated his research to add smaller-company stocks to the investment mix. The new allocation still put 50 percent of the retirement portfolio into intermediate-term Treasury bonds. On the stock side, he put 23 percent into Standard & Poor's 500-stock index and 27 percent into an index of smaller stocks. Historically, smaller-stock indexes swing more widely in price than the S&P but they have also delivered stronger long-term growth. With this simple diversification, Bengen's

SAFEMAX rose to 4.5 percent[3] the first year, plus annual inflation increases. The money still lasted for 30 years or more.

The 4.5 rule worked for people holding anywhere from 45 to 65 percent in stocks. Below or above those percentages, they wouldn't have made it through every historical 30-year period. With too little in stocks, you don't get enough growth to deal with unexpected inflation. With too much in stocks, you're hit so hard when the market falls that your withdrawals eat up your nest egg before it has a chance to recover.

Bengen let the small-stock index stand in for other types of diversification, such as international stocks and real estate investment trusts. If they were included in the mix, it's possible that his suggested safe withdrawal rate would rise a little higher.

9. Bengen made no adjustment for taxes because everyone's tax situation is different. He assumed that you held the money in a tax-deferred retirement account. So your 4 or 4.5 percent withdrawal isn't spendable income. You have to reduce it by the amount of income tax you pay.

10. The withdrawal rule is applied only to the value of your stocks, bonds, mutual funds, certificates of deposit, and similar financial investments. That's the pot of money that you're trying to stretch over 30 years. Don't count any nonfinancial assets, such as home equity or investment real estate. If you need to tap real estate equity, there are other ways (see Chapter 10).

11. The 4 or 4.5 percent rules assume that you want a steady annual inflation-adjusted income that you can budget for. You don't want an income that rises or falls depending on market performance.

---

3   For Bengen's data, see his book *Conserving Client Portfolios During Retirement*, published by the FPA Press.

12. It's too early to know if the 4 or 4.5 percent rules will work for those who retired in 2000, the year when the tech-stock bubble burst. Over the following 15 years, these retirees endured a second stock market crash, when the financial system almost came apart, and years of low interest rates on bonds and bank accounts. Nevertheless, Bengen says that the rules are working so far for buy-and-hold investors who stayed the course. The markets' recoveries made up for their previous losses (markets have always recovered, eventually).

SEVEN QUESTIONS ABOUT "SAFE" WITHDRAWAL RATES

Should the withdrawal rule be raised to 5.5 percent?

If you're flexible about your spending, you can start cash withdrawals at 5.5 percent of your nest egg plus an annual inflation increase. This rule is based on research by financial planner Jonathan Guyton of Cornerstone Wealth Advisors in Edina, Minnesota (cornerstonewealthadvisors.com). Bengen settled on 4 percent because it carried retirees successfully through the three worst 30-year periods for investment growth that the U.S. economy has ever known (those starting in 1929, 1937, and 1973). But all the rest of the periods showed decent and sometimes outstanding growth. So why plan for the worst? Guyton asks. The odds strongly favor something better. Starting at 5.5 percent provides you with a higher income, a more comfortable life, and, he says, a 99 percent probability that your money will last for 30 years or more. His only caveat: You have to be willing and able to cut your spending a bit if the markets turn bad for several years. For example, you might stop taking inflation increases until stocks recover or lower your annual draw by 10 percent.

The 5.5 percent rule nicely coincides with what your gut

would tell you anyway: Relax when things are going well; tighten up when they're not.

Should the withdrawal rule be lowered to 3 percent?

Historically, the 4 percent rule has carried retirees through previous periods of low interest rates not unlike those we've seen in recent years. It also succeeded when stock valuations were high (high valuations run before a market fall, eventually). But we haven't yet been through a period like the recent one, with low interest rates and high market valuations running hand in hand. Many forecasters think that this combination foretells subnormal stock and bond returns over the next few years. For this reason, Wade Pfau, a professor of retirement income at the American College of Financial Services in Bryn Mawr, Pennsylvania (retirementresearcher.com), thinks it's more realistic to start your cash withdrawals at 3 percent if you intend to spend at a steady, inflation-adjusted rate. If, after several years have passed, the markets have performed better than expected, you can start spending more.

Should your withdrawal rate depend on the state of the stock market when you retire?

This approach requires some technical knowledge. It also enters the dark realm of market forecasting. Michael Kitces, director of wealth management of the Pinnacle Advisory Group in Columbia, Maryland (kitces.com), bases his safe cash withdrawal rate on the P/E10. That's the ratio of current stock prices to the earnings of the 500 companies in Standard & Poor's stock index, adjusted for inflation and averaged over the past 10 years.

Fortunately, you don't have to figure this out yourself.

You can find the P/E10 just by entering "Shiller PE Ratio"[4] in your search engine. If the ratio lies above 20, the market is considered overvalued, implying lower, long-term returns ahead. In that case, your initial withdrawal rate shouldn't exceed the classic 4 or 4.5 percent, Kitces says. Between P/E10s of 12 and 20, where the market is "fairly valued," you might start withdrawals at 5 percent plus annual inflation increases. Below 12, the market is undervalued, suggesting higher returns ahead. With that prospect, your withdrawal rate could start at 5.5 percent.

But remember: We're talking forecasting, which is a black art. The future is always, *always* unknowable.

Can you withdraw the interest and dividends that your investments earn?

Yes, but don't treat them as extras. They have to be counted toward your 4 or 4.5 percent withdrawal. With mutual funds, you can take interest and dividends as quarterly payments. An easier way is to have them reinvested in your funds automatically and take your withdrawal all at once at the end of the year. Either approach works. What does not work is taking your 4 or 4.5 percent *plus* the dividends.

Is the "safe" 4 percent withdrawal rate too safe?

Probably yes. In 97 percent of the periods Bengen studied, retirees wound up—30 years later—with at least the same amount of money they had when they started and usually

---

4   This ratio was developed by Nobel Prize–winning economist Robert J. Shiller of Yale University. It's also known as the Cyclically Adjusted Price Earnings Ratio, or CAPE. It does not try to call market tops and bottoms. Over- or undervaluation often persists for many years.

much more. If you follow that course, you'll favor your heirs over your personal standard of living. Why do that? Take out more. Live it up!

The problem, of course, is that you never know. That's why planners (and financial writers!) generally advise you to start with 4 or 4.5 percent, take your annual inflation raises, and see where you stand after 10 years or so. You can increase your draw if the markets have risen. Warier advisers tell you to start with 3 percent. Or start with 5.5 percent if the extra is discretionary money that you can do without.

What about taking 6 or 6.5 percent?

Normally, withdrawals this high could leave you broke after 15 years or so. But you can safely jack up your spending by adding a reverse mortgage in the form of a credit line (see pages 285 and 291). The credit line supplements the income you're taking from your nest egg.

What about planning for fewer than 30 years?

If you're older than 70 or in poor health, you might decide that your money will have to last for only 20 years. A withdrawal rate of 5 percent plus annual inflation adjustments should get you through. You could even start with 6 percent if you're able to reduce your spending in a bad market year. For a 15-year retirement, you might start with 6 percent (7 percent, if you're able to cut back).

Don't take this decision lightly. We're living to much older ages than any of us expected, even with chronic illnesses. If you're married, be sure to take your spouse's possible lifetime into consideration as well as your own. Guys sometimes run on their own clocks, forgetting that their wives, especially younger wives, will survive them by a decade or two.

Research suggests that if you establish a short payout

period—say, 20 or 15 years—at a high annual withdrawal rate, you should reduce your stock allocation to perhaps 30 percent with the rest in short- or intermediate-term U.S. Treasury bonds. You need the extra protection in case the stock market takes a deep dive when withdrawals start. Treasuries usually go up in price when stocks go down.

BUT, BUT, BUT REAL PEOPLE DON'T LIVE BY RULES

So true! It's unlikely that your own savings, investments, and spending needs fall into the simple patterns used to develop the safe withdrawal rules. Nevertheless, there are plenty of lessons to be learned from the research.

To use the classic withdrawal rules safely you can't be allergic to stocks. If you keep all your money in certificates of deposit, bonds, or bond mutual funds, and draw 4 percent (plus annual increases for inflation), your nest egg might last for just 18 years in a low-interest-rate world. In an average interest-rate scenario, your money could last 25 years. But the odds increase that something will go wrong, including unexpected expenses. You have no cushion and no chance of drawing a higher income in future years. If you feel comfortable only with a pure fixed-income portfolio, you should drop your initial withdrawal rate to 2.5 percent, Pfau says. But remember: Over the next 30 years, the value of America's corporations and their stock prices are going to grow—providing investors with more financial flexibility in their later lives.

You can't use any old stock or bond investment and expect the 4 or 4.5 percent withdrawal rules to work. The research is very specifically based on the long-term price performance of major U.S. stocks and intermediate-term U.S. Treasury bonds. Your own investments have to come very close to matching those averages for your withdrawals to last for life. There's only one way of ensuring this happy result: Put your money into low-cost stock and bond index mutual funds. Index funds track the market, so your returns should match the returns that the research projects. By "low cost" I mean annual fees of 0.3 percent a year or less.

If you buy other types of investments, such as individual stocks, high-cost mutual funds, or high-yield bond funds, there's no guarantee that your long-term gains will equal those of the market every year. Perhaps you'll get lucky and do even better. In the real world, however, there's plenty of evidence that you will probably fall behind. If you don't keep up with the market, withdrawal rates starting at 4 or 4.5 percent could deplete your money faster than you planned for.

Life runs more smoothly if you simplify. You probably approached retirement with a mixed bag of investments: a handful of individual stocks, a concentration of stock in the company you used to work for, assorted mutual funds, municipal bonds, high-yield bond funds, certificates of deposit, and who knows what. It's not at all clear that you're well diversified. Nor is it clear how to draw out your 4 or 4.5 percent. Which stock should you sell? Which mutual fund do you want to keep? What's the best way to rebalance?

Decisions come easier and are more likely to succeed when you consolidate your investments into the smallest possible number of stock and bond mutual funds (see Chapter 9). This arrangement lets you take your withdrawals out of "stocks" or "bonds" generically without having to pick particular stocks or bonds to sell. Simplifying your investments also makes them easier to manage, especially for novice investors and even experienced investors in their older age.

Life also runs more smoothly if you maintain a two-year cash reserve. The cash reserve should be high enough to assure that your daily bills will be paid over the next two years. If there's a storm in the stock market or bond market, you can skip your withdrawal that year and use your reserve to cover your expenses. You don't have to return to your withdrawal plan until prices turn back up. This approach helps you avoid having to sell assets at a loss. For more on working with a cash reserve, see page 228.

You have to know what your savings and investments are currently worth in order to turn them into an orderly income for life. If you're simply tapping your nest egg for whatever amounts of money you need, you're flying blind. You don't know whether you're taking 2 percent or 8 percent so you can't make a solid estimate of how long your money might last. When planning your retirement budget, make a list of your financial holdings, inside and outside any retirement accounts, and establish their current value. Revalue your nest egg annually to help you decide which funds to tap for your annual withdrawal.

You need the safest possible investments in the bond portion of your nest egg. When the stock market falls, you might need to take annual withdrawals from bonds while you wait for stock prices to recover. That means holding the types of bonds that tend to rise in value or at least hold pretty steady when stocks decline.

Historically, the best choice has been intermediate-term Treasury bonds. You'll find them in government bond mutual funds with "durations" of about five or six years (see page 248). After a short hiccup, these funds performed wonderfully during the stock market dives of 2000–2003 and 2008–2009—going up in price when stocks collapsed. Short-term bond funds worked well, too. By contrast, risky, high-yield (junk) bond funds plunged right along with stocks. As a safety net, they failed.

None of the withdrawal-rate researchers tested high-quality[5]

---

5   Both individual bonds and bond funds carry safety ratings. Those for investment-grade bonds and bond funds range from a high of AAA, Aaa, or A++ to a low of A, B++, or A1, depending on the designations used by the rater.

tax-deferred municipal bonds to see if they could be substituted for intermediate-term governments. But they might work, for a portion of your money. If you'll be depending on munis for your annual withdrawal whenever stock prices fall, you should buy mutual funds, not individual bonds. Funds are your best guarantee of ready access to cash. (For more on individual bonds, see page 255.)

High-quality corporate bonds haven't been tested, either. They'd work better than junk bonds but not as well as Treasuries. A mix of Treasuries with a small percentage of corporates in a general, high-quality bond mutual fund should meet the 4 percent test.

Rebalancing is important but not to the decimal point. To rebalance a portfolio means to bring it back to a predetermined asset allocation—say, 50 percent in stocks and 50 percent in bonds (see page 198). Some investors choose to rebalance to a lower stock allocation as they get older. That's comforting but not optimal—see page 217.

All the withdrawal-rate research assumes that you rebalance once a year. That's convenient for keeping track of your withdrawal plan but not critical. Your plan won't fail if, in a given year, you're off by 5 or 10 percentage points or so. There's a lot of give in the numbers because of the unpredictable way that markets behave. You could work your way back to an ideal balance over two or three years. Many 401(k) plans offer free automatic rebalancing if you sign up for it.

There are two reasons to rebalance:

- Rebalancing makes it more likely that you'll be able to make your planned, annual withdrawals from savings over 20 or 30 years. Note that this strategy does not produce the highest long-term investment returns. That's because stock markets usually go up. By selling when stocks rise and reinvesting the money in bonds, you are taking away from very investments that will gain the most. If you don't rebalance, however, your portfolio will eventually contain too much in stocks. When the market falls, it might because imprudent to take money out.

- Rebalancing limits your investment risk. As an example, say that stocks rise to 60 percent of your portfolio and you don't rebalance. If the market suddenly falls, you'll take a larger percentage loss than if you'd rebalanced and were holding only 50 percent in stocks. When the market improves, of course, the 60 percent stock portfolio will recover faster. But rebalancers generally don't care about that. Their interest lies in limiting loss so they can rely on their withdrawal plan each year.

Rebalancing matters the most during a plunge in prices for stocks. For example, say that you've taken your withdrawal for the year and stock prices are still going down. The percentage you own in stocks is below your target amount. You're afraid that prices will fall even further. What to do?

The right answer is to hold your nose, shut your eyes, and rebalance. Sell more bond shares and use the money to buy stocks at lower prices. When the market goes back up, you'll have more shares at work to capture the gains. Do the same thing if bond prices fall: Rebalance by selling stock shares and reinvesting in bonds. Don't wait for the end of the year if prices are falling fast.

But will you do it? Or will you find it too scary to buy stocks (or bonds) when they're down and you don't know where the bottom is? Small errors of rebalancing won't hurt your plan. But failing to take advantage of deep drops in price will make it harder for you to stretch your money over your life span.

At the very least, don't sell in a panic. Hang on to the stocks and bonds you have and reconsider your withdrawal rate once the scare has passed. Then promise yourself to make annual rebalancing a habit. The more you do it, the easier it gets. For tax management when you're rebalancing, see page 219.

How secure you feel about your withdrawal plan will depend on what happens to stocks in the first few years after you retire. That's the most critical period. If the stock market falls, your annual cash withdrawals will keep depleting your nest egg while you wait for the market to recover. You might even have the bad luck to suffer through two steep declines within just a few years (I'm thinking 2000 and 2008). The 4 or 4.5 percent rule should still work but only if you have the fortitude not to sell. Investors who dumped stocks after the 2008 financial collapse and failed to buy back in 2009 when stocks started up again missed the huge price recovery that would have put their retirement back on track.

Conversely, you might enjoy a long, strong stock market rise during your early retirement years with only brief declines (an example would be 1983 to 2000). In this case, your nest egg should grow fat enough that you won't have to worry if stocks weaken 15 or 20 years from now. It will be easy to stay the course.

Which type of market comes your way depends entirely on luck. You can weather either sequence of returns, financially, provided that you can endure emotionally. The withdrawal rules suit investors who buy, rebalance, and hold.

You won't have to worry about what happens to stocks right after you retire if you maintain a safety net. Your safety net is your two-year cash reserve plus a holding of short-term bond funds. With these in place, you won't have to withdraw any money from your stock funds until prices go back up. For more on this strategy, see page 257.

The withdrawal rules help you provide for a younger spouse. In almost all of the 4 and 4.5 percent withdrawal scenarios, the money lasts longer—sometimes much longer—than 30 years. You'll also be able to leave a legacy for your children or a charity if that's one of your goals.

When you have a much younger spouse, consider holding at least 50 percent in stocks and perhaps up to 60 percent. You'll need the money to last for your spouse's lifetime as well as your own. As long as you have a two-year cash reserve, you can skip withdrawals in years that stocks decline.

Always evaluate your stock, bond, and cash portfolio as a whole. You might rush to sell stocks if the market drops 30 percent. But if you have only half your money in stocks, and if the bond market rises (as Treasury funds usually do when stocks decline), your total portfolio might be down only 10 percent or so. That should be something you can live with. The reason you own both stocks and bonds is to keep the dollar value of your combined investments from dropping too far.

You could raise the amount you're taking out of your nest egg if your investments have done well for many years. Everyone makes midcourse corrections. You might reset your withdrawals at a moderately higher rate now that you have less time ahead, or take a lump sum for a special purpose.

Consider starting with a higher withdrawal rate if you unexpectedly lost your job at age 60 or so. A higher withdrawal could help you defer your Social Security benefits until you reach full retirement age (see page 42). At that point, you'll get a larger check. Once Social Security starts, you could reduce your withdrawals from savings by the same dollar amount.

You might want to lower your take if you plan to reduce your stockholdings as you age. Bengen's original rule called for a 50/50 division between stocks and bonds, lasting through the entire 30-year period. But he found (no surprise!) that a 50 percent allocation to stocks frightened many of his older clients. He began to advise that retirees start with 50 percent in stocks and reduce that amount by one percentage point a year. The less you hold in stocks, however, the less your opportunity for long-term growth and the harder it becomes to make your savings last for 30 years. If you follow this strategy, consider starting your withdrawals at 4 percent or less.

You can skip the annual withdrawal if you already have more than enough money in cash reserves to get through a couple of years. New retirees sometimes overestimate what they're likely to spend. Once you get settled, you might find that you don't need quite as much as you originally thought. Some of you will leave the extra money in your nest egg to grow. Others will start spending a little more, for fun (that would probably be me . . .).

You might not have to touch your nest egg during your early retirement years. Some retirees can live comfortably on Social Security, pension, and income from other sources, such as rental real estate or a part-time job. You might add interest and dividends, which probably amount to 2 percent or less of your investments' total value. You'd tap your savings only for splurges, such as vacations, gifts, moving expenses, or unexpected health-care costs. If you start making regular withdrawals at some point in the future, you'll have a shorter remaining life span and, presumably, a larger nest egg. You could start spending 5.5 or even 6 percent, plus inflation increases, and still feel pretty sure that your savings will last for life.

You might never need your nest egg, thanks to your moderate spending or other sources of income. In this case, you're managing the money entirely for your children. To build up their inheritance, you might put 90 percent in stocks. Money that you're required to take out of an IRA or other tax-deferred retirement accounts, after age 70½, can be reinvested, for the kids, in a taxable account.

You'll have to adjust your thinking when you reach 70½, if you have a tax-deferred retirement account. At that age, you have to start taking required minimum distributions (RMDs) every year. The distribution rate is designed to use up the money over your expected life span, not to preserve it beyond your life span. Your first RMD generally comes to 3.7 percent of the assets in these accounts. You can take more, of course, but if you can manage on 3.7 percent, that's all to the good. The required percentage withdrawal rises a little every year. At 80, it's 5.4 percent. You'll be taking more money, in dollar terms, if the market goes up, and perhaps less if the market goes down.

Whether this jibes with your 4 or 4.5 percent withdrawal plan, plus inflation adjustments, will depend on how much or how little your investments have grown over the years. If your RMD comes to more than your withdrawal plan called for in the current year, reinvest the unneeded money in a bank account or mutual fund. For more on RMDs, see page 190.

Be sure to take income taxes into consideration when creating your retirement spending plan. You might feel rich because you have $1 million in your individual retirement account. But after state and federal taxes, a 4 percent withdrawal ($40,000) might be worth $24,000 or less. Match your standard of living to your annual income *after tax*.

YOUR ASSET-ALLOCATION DECISION IN A NUTSHELL

There's a tight link between a safe withdrawal rate and the amount of money you decide to allocate to stocks or bonds. I've mentioned it, here and there, as I reported on the new retirement-income research. Here, I've pulled it all together into a single section to help you make your own asset-allocation decision.

Your first consideration should be your cash reserve. How much money do you need to set aside to be sure that your bills are paid for the next two years (or the next three years if you're a natural worrier)?

Next, decide what percentage of your remaining money you want to keep in stock-owning mutual funds. A typical range would be somewhere between 40 and 65 percent, although that can be stretched to as low as 35 percent and as high as 70 or even 75 percent.

If you commit just 30 percent of your money (or less) to stocks, you might not be able to sustain an initial withdrawal rate of 4 percent (plus annual inflation adjustments) for 30 years. To be safe, the stock-shy should start by taking out only 3 percent or even 2.5 percent of their assets in the first year they retire.

Holding more than 75 percent in stocks can be equally counterproductive. The higher your stock allocation, the larger your dollar loss when prices plunge. If you have to make a withdrawal from your stock funds that year, you'll lock in a loss that will be hard to make up. Those who want to be mostly in stocks should be able to live without touching that money during bear market[6] cycles.

For the purpose of creating a lifetime retirement income, there's not much difference between holding 40 percent in stocks or raising your stake to 70 percent. A 4 or 4.5 percent withdrawal rule works with both. But you might have additional goals. To minimize the price swings in your portfolio, up and down, stay at the lower end of that range. If you can handle price swings and hope to leave a larger legacy for your kids or a younger spouse, go toward the higher end. Always knowing, of course, that there are never any guarantees.

Once you've settled on a stock allocation, what's left of your investment fund goes into bonds. For flexibility, choose bond mutual funds. For income security, choose bond funds invested in intermediate-term Treasuries. Never mind the low interest rate. Treasuries tend to rise in price when stock prices fall. They give your portfolio a cushion so that, in bad times, you can sustain your regular 4 or 4.5 percent withdrawal rate.

---

6   In the taxonomy of the market, "bear markets" go down and "bull markets" go up. A bear market rally, when stocks start to rise but then fall again, is a "dead cat bounce."

Like all bond funds, those holding intermediate-term Treasuries will fall in market price when interest rates rise (see page 247). To hedge against that risk, put part of your money into a high-quality short-term bond fund. It pays less interest but, when rates rise, it will lose very little in price. That makes it useful as a safety net. If you blow through your cash reserves and the general stock and bond markets are in a slump, you can tap your short-term bond fund to help pay your bills. A two-year cash reserve plus two years' worth of expenses in short-term bonds keeps you safe for four years—usually, time enough for a bad market to pass. Financial planner Harold Evensky, cofounder of Evensky & Katz/Foldes Financial Wealth Management (ek-ff.com) in Coral Gables, Florida, pushes his clients' short-term allocation up to enough for five years of expenses, including known future purchases such as a car or tuition aid for grandchildren.

For specifics on the stock and bond mutual funds you might choose, see Chapter 9. From the point of view of your asset allocation, the fewer funds the better. That's because rebalancing doesn't apply only to the split between stocks and bonds. It also applies to the funds you choose for each class of investment. For example, say that you're holding four funds invested in stocks and want to keep 25 percent of your stock allocation in each. Whenever you rebalance, you'll have to realign those four funds among themselves to get back to your original allocation. Only then do you proceed to rebalance between stocks and bonds.

The more funds you own, and the more individual stocks you keep, the more math you have to summon when you rebalance and take your annual withdrawals. Personally, that's not my cup of tea. You can create a regular retirement income using the 4 or 4.5 percent rule with as few as two mutual funds—a U.S. Total Market Fund and a Total Bond Fund. That's what Bill Bengen's research ultimately shows.

THE RETIREE'S ULTIMATE ASSET-ALLOCATION GOAL: NEVER BOOK A LOSS!

This strategy comes straight from the desks of some very smart financial planners. It assumes that—in any year—your savings and investment fund contains some assets that rise in value or whose value doesn't change. Those are the ones you tap for your annual cash withdrawal. You won't have to raise money by selling securities at a loss.

As an example, say that year-end is approaching and you need to take your regular 4 percent withdrawal to pay next year's bills. Your retirement investments are divided into four parts: an indexed stock-owning mutual fund, an intermediate-term Treasury bond fund, a short-term bond fund large enough to cover two years of planned withdrawals, and a two-year cash reserve (the cash reserve is this strategy's secret sauce). Here's how your no-loss approach might work, depending on how the markets performed in the past 12 months:

- If stocks and bonds have both risen in price—your withdrawal comes out of the stock fund and the intermediate-term bond fund.
- If stocks are up but the bonds are down—your withdrawal comes principally out of the stock fund. If the gain isn't strong enough to cover your entire withdrawal, you can top it up with money from your short-term bond fund or your cash reserve.
- If bonds are up and stocks are down—your withdrawal comes from the intermediate-term bond fund.
- If both stocks and bonds are down or flat—your withdrawal comes out of the cash reserve. If the cash reserve is insufficient, you'd tap the short-term bond fund. That fund will show a small loss but not enough to derail your plan.

By approaching your withdrawal choices this way, you have a good chance of preserving your capital. I'm not saying that a no-loss strategy works all the time. But if you follow it carefully, you have a high chance of success.

SHOULD YOUR ASSET ALLOCATION CHANGE AS THE YEARS GO BY?

There are three views on how you should handle the stock funds in your portfolio as you grow older: the traditional view and two better ones.

- **The traditional view calls for gradually reducing the percentage you hold in stocks.** Do it by taking extra money from your stock funds whenever you tap them for your annual withdrawal.

  The classic rule of thumb says that the percentage you hold in bonds should equal your age. For example, if you're 50, you'd hold 50 percent of your money in bonds with the rest in stocks. At 70, you'd hold 70 percent of your money in bonds. I think that advice is a little behind the times, given the increase in longevity. I prefer the rule of 110. It says that the percentage you hold in stocks should equal 110 minus your age. At 50, you'd be 60 percent in stocks with the rest in bonds. At 70, you'd be down to 40 percent in stocks.

  Gradually reducing your stock allocation feels pretty comfortable for people in midlife and later. It's also what most advisers recommend. Financially, however, it's generally not the best choice. You're slowing the rate at which your investment portfolio can grow. That adds to the chance that your money won't last for life or for the lifetime of a younger spouse. For protection, start with a 3.5 percent withdrawal instead of a 4 percent.

- **A better decision would be to maintain the same asset allocation throughout retirement.** If you start with, say, 50 percent in stocks and 50 percent in bonds, you'd rebalance to those same percentages, after taking your withdrawal every year. You'll get higher returns and your money should last longer than if you gradually reduce the percentage of stocks you hold. If you adopt this steady-state strategy and are a little bit stock-phobic, you might decide to maintain a more conservative allocation—say, 40 percent in stocks with the rest in bonds.

  Even if you're not stock-phobic, there's an argument for choosing a lower allocation for steady-state investing. The day you retire is also the day you face your maximum investment risk, says retirement expert Josh Cohen, head of the institutional defined contribution business at Russell Investments in Chicago. At this point, you have the largest amount of money in your retirement accounts (because you haven't started withdrawals yet), and the longest number of days ahead. Holding less in stocks gives you more protection from bad markets at that critical time.

- **The newest idea (here's a curveball) calls for *increasing* your stock allocation after you retire.** This strategy is gaining adherents among sophisticated financial planners. It combines safety in your early retirement years with growth in your later years. Here's how you'd handle your assets:

  First, gradually reduce your stock allocation in the four or five years before you plan to retire. When retirement day comes, you should be just 30 percent in stocks with the rest of the money in intermediate-term bond funds. That protects you from the risk of a stock market plunge in those first few critical years after your paycheck stops.

Second, take your annual withdrawals mostly (or entirely) from your bond investments for the first 10 years or so. When you rebalance, do so in a way that gradually increases the percentage you hold in stocks—say, by two percentage points a year. The percentage of your nest egg that you hold in bonds will shrink while the percentage in stocks will rise.

Third, when stocks reach 50 percent of your portfolio, switch strategies. Rebalance regularly to hold your allocation at 50/50, stocks and bonds.

By taking this approach you'll be using fixed-income investments to get you through the first part of your retirement while depending on long-term stock appreciation to fund the second part. If you're worried about rising interest rates, which would lower the market price of intermediate-term bond funds, Michael Kitces of Pinnacle suggests that you substitute Treasury bills or mutual funds invested in very short-term bonds.

It might go against the grain to hold a rising percentage of your savings in stocks as you grow older. We've been trained (me, too!) to think the reverse. But at age 60 or 65, we might have 30 years to live or even more. Stocks remain *the* investment for the long term.

TAXES AND YOUR WITHDRAWAL CHOICES

If all of your retirement savings are stashed in tax-deferred retirement accounts, taxes aren't an issue. You can rebalance your accounts, moving money from stock funds to bond funds and vice versa, with no tax consequences. When you take money out, it's all taxed at your ordinary income rate.

Your strategy changes, however, if you saved money outside a tax-deferred account in stocks, bonds, and mutual funds. Interest and dividends on these investments are taxed every year. So are any distributions from the funds. When you make your annual withdrawal, use this taxable money first. Sell shares in your stock or bond funds only if interest, dividends, and distributions weren't large enough to cover the withdrawal you need.

When you spend money from savings kept outside a retirement account, you're not taxed on the whole amount—only on the gain that your investment earned. You get a low rate on most dividends and long-term capital gains.

Don't rebalance by moving assets from one taxable account to another—that just adds to the tax. Instead, reestablish balance in the way you take your money out, by withdrawing dividends and mutual-fund distributions. If you can't rebalance in this way, come as close as you can and try again the following year.

If you're selling some shares at a gain, see if there are others that you can sell at a loss. When you offset gains with losses, you avoid the tax.

If you have investments in tax-deferred retirement accounts as well as in taxable accounts, your overall asset allocation should include them both. Take your interest, dividends, and distributions from the taxable account and do the rest of your rebalancing in your tax-deferred retirement account.

HELP! I NEED HELP!!

Don't faint, I've already called 911. Emergency financial medics, schooled in asset allocation, rebalancing, withdrawal plans, taxes, and portfolio resuscitations, are speeding your way. Jump to page 259.

WHY I LIKE THE 4 PERCENT RULE AND ITS KISSIN' COUSINS

There's no such thing as an ironclad *safe* withdrawal strategy. *Safe* means "as far as we can tell." Markets and investor behavior are nothing less than changeable.

Still, the withdrawal percentages discussed here aren't casual rules of thumb. They're backed by research that can give you some comfort as you start to tap your capital to pay your bills. Your mix of investments probably won't exactly match the ones that proved the rules. But as long as you have a well-diversified portfolio, 4 percent or one of the other rules discussed in this chapter gives you a useful place to start. As well, I encourage you to take a look at Appendix 2 (page 432) for tables that show you how many years your capital will last at varying rates of withdrawal.

WHAT ARE THE BEST INVESTMENTS FOR A RETIREMENT WITHDRAWAL PLAN?

Read on.

9

Investing for Income: Not What You Think

Nothing endangers your lifestyle more than to pile into "income investments."

I don't know about you, but I have a paycheck mentality. There's nothing I like better than a regular check deposited in my bank account. Or even an irregular check, as long as I'm sure that it will come.

In our 40s and early 50s, we live on our earnings and invest our savings primarily in stocks for long-term growth. Then one day we wake up, look in the mirror, and say, "Oops." Retirement beckons, the paychecks will stop, and a switch flips in our heads. Suddenly, we decide that we need conservative investments that pay a regular income. Usually, that means bonds, dividend-paying stocks,[1] and—if

---

1   I've said this before and want to say it again: Whenever I say "stocks" I always mean stock-owning mutual funds, not individual stocks. For the reasons why, see page 244. "Bonds" means intermediate- and short-term bond funds. "Mutual funds" includes exchange-traded funds (see page 241).

a salesperson gets his or her hands on us—variable annuities that pay lifetime benefits (ugh).

That belief stems from the ancient idea that we should spend only the interest and dividends from our savings. "Don't dip into principal" sounds like the polestar of retirement finance. But unless your expenses are low enough, your savings high enough, and you have enough income from other sources (Social Security, pension, rent, royalties, a trust fund, yes, please, a trust fund), interest and dividends won't be enough—especially when rates are low. They not only produce insufficient income, they won't grow by enough in value to pay our bills over the next 30-plus years.

It's time for an attitude adjustment. You still need to be an income investor. But for success you have to think about income in a different way. Here's what the professionals say.

Sticking with traditional income investments makes your retirement nest egg riskier, not safer. Say, for example, that you focus on dividend-paying stocks. You'll be concentrated in a small number of industry sectors (in 2007, the high payers were the financial stocks and you know what happened to them). You'll be ignoring the universe of growth stocks, smaller-company stocks, and international stocks, which leaves you even less diversified (and probably earning lower returns). You'll also lose income in years that dividends go down.

On the fixed-income side, you might lean toward high-yield (junk) bond mutual funds because they pay so much more interest than Treasuries do. But when stock prices drop, the share prices of these funds usually drop, too. They *add* risk to your portfolio, which isn't what bonds are supposed to do. Worse, the apparent high yields on junk funds invested in supposedly safe industries can be hugely misleading. As I write, I'm looking at a utilities fund that appears to be paying 14 percent. It's actually paying just 1 percent. The rest of the payout is simply a return of the investor's own capital. *Any interest-rate investment claiming to pay a fabulous annual return has a catch in it somewhere.*

Traditional investments might get you through the first half of your retirement but not through the second half. When you're reasonably healthy or have a chronic condition that's under control, it's easy to reach your 85th birthday (an unimaginable age when you're 55 or 60). You have a good shot at 90 or even 100, especially if you're female. Intermediate-term bonds provide some security during the first half of your retirement. But an initial 4 percent withdrawal rate[2] plus annual inflation adjustments would deplete them in 20 to 25 years, at 2 percent inflation, provided that you stuck to a strict lifetime schedule of withdrawing not a penny more. Your money would vanish faster if—as is likely—you have unexpected expenses or you put part of your money into short-term bonds and certificates of deposit.

When you were younger, you chose stocks for money you didn't expect to touch for a decade or more. That guideline doesn't change when you reach 60 or 65. Rising stock prices in a growing global economy are your best hope for funding the second half of your retirement starting 10 or 15 years from now. Stocks *reduce* long-term portfolio risk.

"Income" is the money that flows into your checking account on a regular or irregular basis, regardless of source. It might be Social

---

2   For simplicity, I'll refer to a 4 percent withdrawal rule throughout this chapter. It assumes that you withdraw 4 percent of your assets in the first year you retire plus an inflation adjustment in each subsequent year. The discussion applies equally to higher or lower withdrawal rates, as outlined in Chapter 8.

Security or a paycheck for part-time work. It might be interest and dividends. It might also be an annual withdrawal from an investment portfolio, as explained in Chapter 8. That portfolio will contain some stocks that don't pay dividends but do provide long-term capital growth. Capital gains are a source of income, too.

Your regular withdrawals from your investment account amount to a "homemade paycheck." Conceptually, the money is drawn from the portfolio's interest and dividends plus capital gains. If that's not enough to fill out your 4 percent, your withdrawal would include some of your principal, too. Don't worry about nibbling at your principal. As long as you stick to a well-thought-out asset-allocation plan, future increases in the market will replace part or all of any principal you used. That's why the 4 percent rule works.

Hold your homemade paycheck steady at the withdrawal rate you planned. It's just like the paycheck you might have gotten at work—a fixed amount plus an annual inflation raise. You might be tempted to take extra money whenever the value of your investment portfolio goes up. The withdrawal-rate research, however, assumes that you'll reinvest those gains in order to cushion future losses. Wait to recalibrate when you're 10 or 12 years down the retirement road, with several years of market experience behind you. If you want extra money to spend in your early retirement while you're still young, consider the 5.5 percent withdrawal rule (see page 201) or the discretionary fund (see page 229).

There's an exception to this Steady Eddie rule. It comes into play at a time when the values of your stock and bond mutual funds have both declined in price. In that year, you'd skip the withdrawal and pay your bills from your cash reserve (an account that holds enough money to help cover your bills for the next two years—see page 228). When the markets have at least partly recovered, start restoring your cash reserve by tapping your investments for more than your 4 percent scheduled amount. The extra money brings your cash reserve back to the two-year level.

For long retirements, a portfolio of well-diversified, short- and long-term investments is both sensible and safe

That's because markets, properly used, have been more reliable than you might think. Here's what we know:

- The major U.S. stock market falls and rises in cycles of varying length.[3] The time it takes for investors to recover their money—from the top of the market, to the bottom, and back up again—has averaged just 29 months, assuming that dividends were reinvested. The longest cycle lasted a little over five years (August 2000 to October 2006, after the tech-stock bust). The shortest one, starting in June 1998, took a mere five months.

  If you spent all the dividends instead of reinvesting them, the cycle averaged 39 months. In this case, the longest cycle lasted a little over eight years (December 1972 to July 1980 during the Great Stagflation). The shortest took five months, also starting in June 1998.

  The message is that average prices for the leading stock-market index have *always* recovered, and usually within a reasonable period of time. The mutual funds that follow this index have always recovered, too. But individual stocks in the market do *not* necessarily recover. Sometimes

---

3   For the following data, thanks to Towneley Capital Management of Laguna Hills, California.

they fly but sometimes they underperform or even go to zero. That's why it's so risky to buy them. You can't predict, reliably, which the brilliant or pooper stocks are going to be.

- Bond markets rise and fall in cycles, too. They have gone through shorter-term cycles, like stocks, but very long-term cycles, too. For 40 years, up to 1981, bond prices zigzagged down. From 1981 through 2015, bond prices zigzagged up. In both periods, the 4 percent withdrawal rule worked.

- No one knows when stocks or interest rates are going to rise or fall or by how much, no matter how professional or well informed your adviser sounds. The future is unknowable. Trying to follow "timing" advice is a loser's game.

- There is always turmoil and uncertainty somewhere in the country or the world. If you wait for "normalcy" to return before you invest you will never invest.

- Your margin of safety, against investment risk, is a cash account that will pay your bills for the next two years no matter what happens in the markets, plus short-term bonds as a safety net for the two or three years after that. You won't have to follow the news or daily stock prices to see if you're still okay.

- Your margin of safety against inflation risk and the risk of living a very long life is to hold a portion of your money in stocks.

To help you allocate your money among cash reserves, current income, and capital growth, consider the system of investing known as "bucketing." It suits the way we think as well as the way we behave.

BUCKET INVESTING AND HOW IT WORKS

The concept of bucket investing works especially well for investors who manage their money themselves. It's a process that's easy to understand and carry out. You put your money into different buckets, with each one reserved for a specific purpose. There's one for cash, one for fixed income (bond funds), and one for growth (stock funds). The buckets can be separate accounts or you can keep a single account divided into mental buckets.

Every bucket strategy starts with one for cash. You hold enough cash to help cover your living expenses for the next two or three years. That doesn't mean all your expenses—only those that won't be paid from your other sources of income. For example, say that it's costing you $55,000 a year to live and, between you and your spouse, you're getting $30,000 in Social Security. Your cash bucket has to cover the remaining $25,000. A two-year cash bucket would hold $50,000. You'd keep the money in bank or credit union savings accounts, money market mutual funds, a one-year certificate of deposit, or a very short-term (one- or two-year) bond mutual fund (see page 232). Think of it as a permanent reserve. You might tap it from time to time but you will always fill this bucket up again.

If you work with a professional money manager, you will probably follow a two-bucket strategy. One bucket holds your two-year cash reserve. The second one holds all your financial investments, both stocks and bonds. You and the manager will agree on a stock/bond allocation, which will appear on your quarterly statement. The account is rebalanced regularly. Once a year, the manager takes money out of your investment account, following the 4 percent rule, and deposits it into your cash reserve. You draw on that money every month to help pay your bills. Some managers will send you monthly checks if that's what your prefer.

When you're managing your own money, you'll probably use a three-bucket strategy. The first bucket is your cash account. The second bucket holds short- and intermediate-term bond mutual funds—effectively, your "income portfolio." The third bucket holds stock funds. Each fund should be reported separately on the statement you get from your mutual fund company. To rebalance your investments, you move shares from one account to another. You can accomplish that directly if you manage the money through an online account. Or ask the firm's telephone rep to make the changes for you. For simplicity, your money should be consolidated at a single financial institution.

Consider the value of a fourth bucket for a separate discretionary fund. That good advice comes from Jonathan Guyton of Cornerstone Wealth Advisors. Almost inevitably, you're going to "want" or "need" money for things your homemade paycheck doesn't cover. "People will rationalize extra withdrawals every which way till Sunday," he says, "and they put a chink in your armor." His solution: Put only 90 percent of your investments into the stock and bond buckets that support your inflation-adjusted withdrawal plan. The other 10 percent goes into a discretionary fund, invested conservatively in bank CDs and short-term bond funds. If you want or need more than your regular withdrawal allows, take it from this fund. When it's gone, it's gone. You might reconstitute it after 10 years or so if your long-term investments have done well.

This bucket might include any lump-sum expenses that you know will come up soon. For example, you might be planning to replace your car two years from now or help pay tuition for grandchildren. You'll need a specific amount of cash on hand. That's a job for a bank certificate of deposit.

Some planners advocate a two-bucket strategy known as "safety first." You hold the usual two- or three-year cash bucket in checking accounts or money market mutual funds. For your second bucket, you buy Treasury inflation-protected securities (see page 251), bank or credit union certificates of deposit, and short-term bond funds. Maybe some intermediate-term bond funds, too. You expect (hope!) that the earnings from your second bucket, plus Social Security and any other guaranteed income, will cover a bare-bones budget for the rest of your life. At this writing, the safety-first portfolio would pay only about 1 percent a year, so your budget would have to be bare indeed. To raise your safe income, you might add an inflation-adjusted immediate-pay fixed annuity (see page 129).

If it takes all your savings to fund the second bucket, so be it, the safety-firsters say. Your lifestyle will be modest but secure. You'd add stock funds only if you have money to spare, earmarking any gains for luxuries—travel, gifts, entertainment that you *could* do without.

If you've been a black belt saver all your life, a safety-first strategy might produce enough income to cover luxuries, too. In general, however, this approach works only for people who are willing to cut their spending significantly—and why would you do that if you don't have to? Better to include the bucket that owns stocks.

HOW MUCH RISK CAN YOU AFFORD?

Whether you're buying investments directly from a mutual fund company or dealing with a financial adviser, you'll probably fill in a risk-tolerance questionnaire. It's supposed to help guide your decision about how much money to keep in stocks and how aggressive or conservative your investments ought to be.

Sorry—risk-tolerance questionnaires are generally bunk. You'll lean toward more risk if stocks are going up, you've had a good day at the office, and your shoes don't pinch. If you've had a bad day because stocks went down and your unemployed child is moving in, you'll suddenly feel more conservative. In either case, the risk questionnaire will probably steer you toward "income and growth," which covers just about any investment option on the planet.

When choosing investments, don't start with your imagined tolerance for risk. Instead, consider your *capacity* for risk. Capacity measures whether you can afford the risks you take. A retiree with a pension, Social Security, a paid-up house, low expenses, and a multimillion-dollar IRA has a high capacity for risk. It won't cripple your lifestyle if you're suddenly hit with a large, unexpected expense or a temporary stock market loss. Conversely, if you're living on Social Security plus a small amount of savings your capacity for risk is zero no matter how willing you are to gamble. You might suddenly need some cash for home repairs or health-care expenses. You aren't in a position to risk a market loss.

If you have the capacity for risk, you can expand into stocks. If not, stay with safe investments and cut your spending to fit.

I don't mean to dismiss risk tolerance entirely. You might have the capacity to keep 90 percent of your money in stocks but wouldn't dream of doing so. Some retirees choose very low stock allocations because they can't stand the stress of watching the market rise and fall.

You don't need a questionnaire to tell you this. By the time you approach retirement you'll have been through several stock market cycles and should have a general idea of where your pain point lies.

Creep up on risk slowly, however, if you've never managed important money before. Maybe you just received an inheritance or took a large lump sum from a 401(k) whose investments were chosen for you. Invest just a modest amount at first, keeping the rest of the money safe. You need to discover how well you hold up in sunshine and in rain.

Consider your personal circumstances when picking a stock allocation. Anything from 40 percent to 65 percent is typical. But you might keep 90 percent in stocks if you won't need the money (because you're rich or your expenses are low) and you're managing it for the next generation. You might put zero in stocks if you're in poor health, your savings are modest, and you'll need cash to pay for care over the next 10 years. Even if you're healthy and comfortable with risk, you might stay with 35 or 40 percent in stocks if your future depends largely on a closely held business you intend to sell in the next couple of years. Wait until the sale goes through and you've cashed the check before stepping into the market any further.

Choose a bond allocation that minimizes risk. You do this by dividing your money between high-quality short-term and intermediate-term bond mutual funds.

Short-term funds pay less interest but are pretty stable in price. That makes them useful as a safety net. Say, for example, that you're keeping two years' worth of your cash needs in the bank or a money market fund. Say, further, that market conditions are poor, you skip your annual withdrawal for two years, and use your cash reserve to pay your bills. If conditions remain poor, you can start taking withdrawals from your short-term bond funds with little risk of a serious loss. Many planners advise that, between your cash reserve and your short-term bond funds, you hold enough money to protect yourself for four straight years, no matter what happens in the economy.

The remainder of your fixed-income money goes into high-quality intermediate-term bond funds. Intermediates pay higher rates of interest than short-term funds, which increases your income. They also rise and fall more in price when interest rates change. For more on bonds, see page 246.

When you're holding a cash reserve, your investment portfolio is more conservative than you think. Your reserve should be counted as part of your fixed-income allocation. So should your discretionary fund, if you have one. What looks like 40/60 in your investment account (40 percent stocks, 60 percent bonds) might actually be more like 35/65 or even 30/70, including the reserves. When you hold this much cash as a safety net, you should be putting more of your investment portfolio into stocks.

Repeat after me: After bear markets, the broad stock market has always recovered. Always. Individual stocks might not, which is why it's so risky to be a stock picker. But the price of a broad-based mutual fund will go back up. Selling the stock market when it falls is like feeding your money to the squirrels. It's gone for good. If you simply do nothing, and wait, the money will eventually return.

On this point, you had an object lesson in 2007 when the financial system almost collapsed. The average S&P stock lost 50 percent of its value over 24 months. Investors fled and some of you didn't return. Had you been in the market at its bottom in 2009, however, you'd have earned back all of your losses by 2012, then gained another 42 percent by mid-2015. Unfortunately, no one rings a bell when prices are starting up. You just gotta be there.

Sometimes markets zigzag for years without a net price advance. An example would be 1966 to 1982. During such periods you can still earn an average annual 5 percent or so by reinvesting dividends and rebalancing. You earn little or nothing, after inflation, by retreating and putting your money into a bank.

RISK AND THE OLDER INVESTOR

When you're pushing 80 or 85, should you still be in stocks? The answer depends on your temperament, financial resources, and when you're likely to need the money.

If you're sure that you have enough income and savings to cover your expenses for life (for healthy people that could be 95 to 100 or more), nothing requires you to take any risk at all. You can drop out of stocks, switch to short-term bond funds and certificates of deposit, and draw down your nest egg year by year. Taking some risk— with, say, 20 or 30 percent in stocks—becomes a matter of choice. It can also serve as a reasonable hedge against future inflation.

If you have more than enough to cover your lifetime needs and want to leave money for your kids, maintain a higher stock allocation—perhaps 40 to 80 percent. Growth becomes important when you're managing money for the next generation. You might also have to grow your assets to help support a longer-lived spouse.

If you aren't sure that you have enough money to cover your bills for life, consider switching part of the savings that you're holding in bond funds into an immediate-pay annuity. The annuity will provide a higher income than your bonds yield now and it's guaranteed for life. With that guarantee, you might feel better about keeping at least 30 percent of your money in stocks for growth.

If every stock market decline sends a shock to your heart, stick with short-term bonds and CDs. You're giving up the potential for growth but that's better than losing serious savings if you're likely to panic and sell when the next bear market strikes. If your super-safe savings aren't large enough to cover your expenses for life, you'll have to downsize in some way.

If you do commit to stocks, keep enough money in cash and short-term bond funds to ensure that you can pay your bills for at least the next four years (or even five). That protects your standard of living while you wait for a bad stock market to turn around.

CHOOSING THE RIGHT STOCK AND BOND INVESTMENTS FOR YOUR HOMEMADE PAYCHECK

Deciding how much to allocate to stocks and how much to bonds is just the start of your retirement investment decision. The next question is which of the thousands of stock funds and bond funds to choose. You need diversification within your buckets. The fewer and more streamlined your choices, the simpler and surer investment management will be.

What's in Your Stock Bucket?

You hold stocks for growth. Not growth next year (that's always a gamble), but growth over 10 or 15 years. You're betting that the U.S. and world economies will have expanded substantially by that time, with corporate profits and stock prices up. It's a good bet.

With dividends reinvested, Standard & Poor's 500 stock average has never lost money over 15-year periods and rarely over 10-year periods. Over the 15 years ending in March 2009, which covered the market collapses of 2000, 2008, and 2009, buy-and-hold investors still reaped 6.5 percent. And that's before the 2009–2015 stock market recovery.

If you own a stock index mutual fund that follows the market as a whole, the only way you can lose money—as a long-term investor—is to bail out when stocks prices drop. If you buy and hold, history says that your investment will succeed.

The case for buying stock-owning mutual funds. A mutual fund is a big pool of money contributed by thousands of people just like you and me. That money is invested in the stocks of many different companies. Your share in the fund gives you a tiny ownership interest in every one of them. You're spreading your money around, which is the right thing to do.

Fund shares can be purchased, cashed in, and switched around whenever you want. That makes it easy to construct an asset allocation, rebalance your investments, and take regular withdrawals. It's much harder to make a rebalancing and withdrawal plan work when you own a portfolio of individual stocks.

The case for owning index funds that track the performance of the stock market as a whole. The financial researchers who developed the 4 and 4.5 percent withdrawal rules based their findings on how the total market performed. They used specific indexes of stock and bond prices. You can't buy the index itself but you can buy a mutual fund that mimics the index. That's the only way of feeling reasonably sure that the withdrawal rules will work. Besides, index funds have a terrific track record for investment success.

What's an index? It's a way of measuring changes in price. For stocks, the media follow the Dow Jones Industrial Average, which tracks the price performance of 30 large American companies. When a talking head tells you that prices are up or down for the day, it's always the Dow. For investors, however, the most important index is Standard & Poor's 500, a composite of 500 leading American companies (S&P 500 for short). It's the measure tracked by professionals when they evaluate how well or poorly the general market performs. Dozens of other indexes cover narrower parts of the market, such as small companies, real estate, commodities, and international stocks. There are bond indexes, too.

An index mutual fund is designed to track the price performance of a particular index. For example, an S&P 500 fund owns all 500 of the index's stocks and in the same proportion. If the index rises by 5 percentage points, so does the mutual fund (plus dividends and minus fees).

There are index funds for every market you can think of. An international fund might follow the MSCI EAFE Index (that's Morgan Stanley Capital International, tracking the developed countries of Europe, Australasia, and the Far East) or one of the FTSE indexes (originally, the Financial Times Stock Exchange, now run by the London Stock Exchange). Funds invested in small U.S. companies might follow the Russell, MSCI, or CRSP indexes (CRSP is maintained by the Center for Research in Security Prices).

All the index funds following, say, the S&P 500 are essentially doing exactly the same thing. The only difference among them is cost. The lowest-cost fund will provide the best return—and, yes, it's that simple. As long as you buy low-fee funds and rebalance your investments, your annual withdrawals should last as long as the research says they will.

Vanguard, the granddaddy of the index-fund business (Vanguard .com), offers the longest list of low-cost funds. Fidelity Investments (Fidelity.com), its major competitor, offers just a handful of index funds, under its Spartan brand, but enough to make up a diversified portfolio. As a cost benchmark, Vanguard charges 0.05 percent a year[4] for its total market fund, covering both large and smaller U.S. stocks. Fidelity charges 0.1 percent. You buy directly from Vanguard or Fidelity. They're "no-load" funds, meaning that they don't charge sales commissions.

Financial advisers who earn commissions sneer at index funds and have a patented method for talking you out of them. "Why would you want *average* returns?" they ask with a superior smirk. "Average is for the ordinary schlub. You can do better than that!"

Before you nod and say, "Yes, please, please take my money now," think what a "market average" means. It has nothing to do with "the middle." It's more like par in golf. Only the best golfers can beat par. The average golfer never does. In the stock market, the index is "par." The miracle of index funds is that they let all investors, regardless of skill, score par all the time.

Which of the many index funds should you choose? Index funds come in many, many varieties. The most useful today are known as total market funds because they invest in smaller companies as well as large ones. They've mostly replaced the original S&P 500 funds, which owned only the 500 companies (mostly big ones) in the S&P index.

You can also find indexes for growth funds, containing stocks whose earnings are expected to grow faster than average; value funds, whose stocks are out of favor and down in price; small-stock funds, including small-stock value funds, a group with a good long-term performance record; international funds that cover the developed

---

4   For investments of $10,000 or more. At Vanguard, they're called Admiral shares. At Fidelity, they're Advantage shares. Expenses for accounts under $10,000 run a little bit higher.

world; emerging-market funds for the developing countries; total international funds, for large companies and small ones in every foreign market; funds that specialize in various industries such as energy, health care, precious metals, real estate, and commodities; and socially responsible funds for investors seeking companies that treat workers well, improve the environment, and avoid dangerous products such as tobacco and guns.[5]

A common piece of advice is to buy a total market fund, then add a couple of other funds that you imagine will beat the market. As an example, take energy stocks. Energy companies are included in a total market fund, along with companies from every other sector of the economy. If you add an energy fund, you have placed an extra bet on that part of the market. That's called "tilting" your portfolio. Some investors tilt to tech stocks or health-care stocks.

I don't tilt, myself. I'm not smart enough to know which industry will do the best (energy stocks were a flop last year). But if you like to gamble, tilting might make index investing a bit more fun.

It's less fun, however, when you start making regular withdrawals. Every year, you will have to decide how much of each specialized fund to sell and whether you ought to rebalance. If you own five stock funds, that's five rebalancing decisions before you even start thinking about your bonds. The diversification might or might not improve your performance. It will definitely test your skills in math.

Personally, my inclination is always to make things easier. I'd vote for holding one or two broadly diversified stock funds rather than a large collection. That's because your risks and returns are governed mainly by the total percentage you hold in stocks as compared with bonds. Beyond that, your allocation among different types of

---

5   Vanguard's FTSE Social Index Fund has held its own against the S&P 500 for the past 10 years. For information on social investing, see SocialFunds.com.

stocks—large, small, value, growth, foreign, domestic, and so forth—isn't of great importance, says William J. Bernstein, author of *The Four Pillars of Investing: Lessons for Building a Winning Portfolio* (EfficientFrontier.com).

Remember that it takes just *one* total market U.S. stock fund (for large and small stocks) and *one* total market U.S. bond fund to make Bill Bengen's 4.5 percent withdrawal rule work.

You might add an international stock fund. Vanguard's Total International Stock Index Fund includes both large and small stocks; Fidelity's focuses on large stocks.

That's three funds. Everything else is decoration.

What about all those stock funds run by brilliant/famous/rich professional managers who pick individual stocks? Supposedly, they can beat the market thanks to their technology and expertise. But study after study, year after year, shows that they don't beat the broad market index over time. I'll give you just one example, from Rick Ferri, founder of the investment management firm Portfolio Solutions, and Alex Benke, head of product development for Betterment .com, the online investment advisory firm. In "Whitepaper: A Case for Index Fund Portfolios"[6] they tested a three-index-fund portfolio against 5,000 simulations of similar and randomly chosen managed portfolios. They covered periods between 1997 and 2012. As benchmarks, they used three Vanguard funds: the Total Stock Market Index Fund for 40 percent of the money, the Total International Stock Index Fund for 20 percent, and the Total Bond Market Index Fund for the remaining 40 percent. The index-fund portfolio outperformed the stock pickers' portfolios more than 80 percent of the time.

In truth, there might be a manager who beats the market over the

---

6   Available for downloading from PortfolioSolutions.com.

length of time you'll be invested. My advice is to find out right away who that person is going to be. Famous stock picker Bill Miller, formerly head of the Legg Mason Capital Management Value Trust, beat the S&P 500 for 15 years straight—the longest streak that I'm aware of. Then his returns fell off the cliff. The only Value Trust investors who beat the market invested early, around 1982, before they had any idea of the returns they were going to get. Those who came late, after Miller became a star, would have been better off in the S&P.

At this writing, only one-quarter to one-third of managed stock funds have beaten the indexes over one-, three-, five-, and 10-year periods, according to the financial research firm Morningstar, *and they're almost never the same funds*. The three-year winners are not also the five-year winners. They rotate as their luck changes. This year's top funds will drop back to the middle of the pack or worse. Over periods of 20 years or so, the average managed fund has underperformed a comparable stock market index by about two percentage points a year.

One of the reasons for the lag is that managed funds carry higher expenses. To outperform, they not only have to beat the market, they have to do it by more than enough to cover their costs. The few managed funds with persistent good records have low costs, including some that Vanguard runs. Morningstar's research identifies cost as the only—repeat, *only*—dependable predictor of a mutual fund's future performance.

Another reason managed funds underperform is the complete unpredictability of stock prices. The market is far too surprising for any one manager to guess which combinations of stocks, out of the billions possible, will actually outshine.

Why do managed funds keep attracting buyers? Because they usually have one lucky market-beating period to brag about, which makes us imagine that they'll always be on top. Or because they're sold by brand-name firms that dazzle us with their famous-ness.

And, finally, because we the suckers hate to give up the dream that someone, somewhere, possesses secret stock market knowledge that will make us rich.

The only "secret" is index funds. You are paying your fancy fund manager to lose.

What about using exchange-traded funds instead of traditional mutual funds? Exchange-traded funds, or ETFs, are mutual funds in a different form. They almost always follow an index—a traditional one, such as the S&P 500, or a niche index for special situations. Their main difference lies in the way they're bought and sold.

Traditional funds are purchased from the fund company. They're priced at the end of each day. You pay the average net asset value[7] of all the securities in the fund. There are no sales charges if you buy from a no-load fund company.

ETFs, by contrast, are bought and sold on the stock exchange. They're priced like stocks. You can trade them whenever the exchange is open. The price of a broad-based ETF, such as one that follows the S&P 500, tracks the price of the index almost exactly. With more specialized ETFs that trade less, you might pay a little more than the fund's underlying net asset value, or you might pay less.

ETFs charge slightly lower management fees than similar, traditional index mutual funds, although the difference, for the broad-based funds, might be only a hair.[8] You'll need a brokerage account and will pay commissions to buy and sell unless you use the free ETF services of firms such as Charles Schwab, Fidelity, TD Ameritrade,

---

7   The fund's price per share. It's calculated by dividing the value of all the stocks in the portfolio into the number of shares outstanding.

8   Vanguard's index funds cost the same, whether you buy them in traditional form or as an ETF, if you have at least $10,000 invested.

and Vanguard. Even with free accounts there's a "spread" between a share's buying price and selling price—perhaps a small one but still a cost. An ETF's brokerage and trading costs might offset any savings on management fees.

There could be tax advantages to an ETF if you're investing with a taxable account. Both ETFs and traditional funds distribute your share of taxable interest and dividends every year. With traditional funds, any taxable capital gains are also passed along to you, even if you sell no shares. With ETFs, by contrast, you'll usually receive taxable gains only if you sell shares personally. This favorable tax treatment is immaterial, however, if you're investing with a tax-deferred retirement account. Even taxable accounts might not receive capital gains from large and well-diversified traditional funds that are managed for tax efficiency.

The leading ETFs follow the same broad indexes that many traditional index funds do. Under the iShares label, for example, you might choose iShares Total U.S. Stock Market or iShares Core MSCI EAFE (for the whole list, see ishares.com). The SPDRs label (spdrs .com) includes SPDR S&P 500 and SPDR Gold Shares. Charles Schwab offers Schwab U.S. Broad Market and Schwab International Equity. A popular ETF for smaller-company shares is the Russell 2000 Index Fund. At Vanguard, you can buy ETFs based on exactly the same portfolios offered by its traditional index mutual funds, such as Vanguard Total Stock Market and Vanguard Total International Stock.

ETFs come in hundreds of other flavors—value, growth, commodities, real estate, energy, health care, stocks in a single country or region, bear market stocks, and on and on. Some are run by active managers who don't follow an index. As with their traditional fund counterparts, they all complicate your retirement life. For easy rebalancing and withdrawal purposes, two or three broad-based ETFs are plenty.

So which should you use—ETFs or traditional index funds? You might as well choose what's most convenient. Traditional fund investors will stick with their fund companies. People who invest primarily through discount brokerage accounts or have taxable accounts will probably use ETFs. Just be sure that you aren't paying sales commissions when you rebalance your ETFs or take your annual withdrawal. The more you buy and sell, the more expensive ETFs become.

There's more than one type of index tracked by mutual funds. Traditional funds, like the ones above, use indexes that are "capitalization weighted." The more a stock is worth in the market, the greater its weight in the index. When you buy a cap-weighted fund, a larger portion of your money goes into its priciest or largest stocks and a smaller portion into smaller or undervalued stocks. The S&P 500 is a cap-weighted index, as are most of the other indexes followed by the leading funds.

Critics call that "wrong-way investing"—buying high instead of buying low. In a new approach, some exchange-traded funds track indexes that give more weight to the smaller or less popular stocks. *Fundamental index funds* follow stocks that meet specific tests of operating value, such as cash flow, dividends, sales, and book value. They tilt toward value stocks. *Equal-weight indexes* spread your money evenly over all the covered stocks, giving you a smaller-stock tilt. *Dividend index funds* collect stocks with a history of raising dividends. Some 24 other differently weighted indexes currently vie for investor attention, all of them claiming they'll beat the traditional S&P 500 because they're constructed in a smarter way.

When you adjust for risk, however, the evidence is against them, says Elisabeth Kashner, director of research for ETF.com, the go-to source for information about exchange-traded funds. They're generally less diversified than the broad market, rebalance more often (which raises costs), and rely on a stock picker's idea of what the best performing companies are likely to be. They might outperform the market in some years, then underperform it in others. When they outperform, they do so because they've taken more risk, not because of the magic of their special form of indexing. "There's still no free lunch," Kashner says. If you want to tilt your total market index fund toward smaller or value stocks, you can do it just as well by adding a small-stock or value mutual fund to a traditional fund.

What about diversifying with individual stocks? To be truly diversified, you have to own stock in at least 50 companies of different sizes and in different industries. That's not how individuals invest. What's more, if you owned all those stocks, how would you decide which ones to sell when taking your annual withdrawal, and once you sold them, how would you stay diversified? You'd almost certainly miss some of the meteor stocks that produce a decent chunk of an index fund's return.

You've probably owned some of these meteor stocks in your time. But you've owned a lot of losers, too, or sold good stocks too soon. If you averaged your winners with your losers and the stocks you'd call blah, you'd find—and I say this with confidence—that your personal performance has lagged the S&P 500. You've left a lot of money on the table over your investing life.

When you look in the mirror, you'll probably have to concede— unless you're a deeply experienced investment analyst—that you know very little about any of the individual stocks you own. Can you say how good the company's business is right now? What are the trends in profit margins, sales rates, and inventories? What earnings growth do you project and how much are you paying for it? What are the company's problems and how are they being handled? For each of its lines of business, is the market share rising or falling? What's the competition up to, at home and abroad? You probably can't answer these questions, so you have no idea whether holding the stock makes sense. Keeping it just for dividends isn't good enough. When the company faces headwinds, the dividends might be cut.

If you're investing with a taxable account, you might want to keep a stock that has risen substantially in value. If you sell, you'll owe a capital gains tax on the profits. If you don't, the tax vanishes when the stock passes to your heirs. But a lot can happen to a company over 20 years. If you're looking at a long life span, it generally makes more financial sense to sell, pay the tax, and diversify into mutual funds.

Stocks are amusing if that's what you'd like to play with during your retirement. You might put 5 percent of your investment portfolio into your entertainment budget. But do it as a single lump sum. If you lose it, don't throw good money after bad. Maintain a careful index fund allocation for the money you'll rely on for the rest of your life.

Some almost-great advice from Warren Buffett. Buffett, chair of Berkshire Hathaway, is best known for saying that you should buy good stocks and hold them forever. But in real life, he doubts very much that you and I know what a "good stock" is. He judges a company by whether he can estimate an earnings range for the next five years or more and whether those earnings can be bought today at a reasonable price. In his 2013 letter to shareholders, he wrote that people like you and me can't possibly do that. But he goes on to say that, luckily, we don't have to:

> The goal of the non-professional should not be to pick winners—neither he nor his "helpers" can do that—but should rather be to own a cross-section of businesses that in aggregate are bound to do well. A low-cost S&P 500 index fund will achieve this goal. . . .
>
> What I advise here is essentially identical to certain instructions I've laid out in my will. One bequest provides that cash will be delivered to a trustee for my wife's benefit. . . . My advice to the trustee could not be more simple: Put 10 percent of the cash in short-term government bonds and 90 percent in a very low-cost S&P 500 index fund. (I suggest Vanguard's.) I

believe the trust's long-term results from this policy will be superior to those attained by most investors—whether pension funds, institutions or individuals—who employ high-fee managers.

P.S. from me:

Dear Mrs. Buffett,

Your smart husband got it almost *right. His advice about indexing is right on. I'm guessing the trust is being managed for your children or grandchildren so 90 percent in stocks is fine. But, hey, why would you want all the money only in the S&P 500? How about all the rest of American stocks and then the world? You can be smarter than Warren. Tell the trustee that you want to own U.S. and international total market funds instead!*

Sincerely yours,
Jane

What's in Your Bond Bucket?

Everything in a retirement portfolio has a specific job to do. For stocks, it's growth. For bonds, it's ballast. All the safe withdrawal plans assume that you own high-quality bonds that hold steady or rise in price when the stock market falls. Bonds also contribute to your retirement income but their safety is more important than their interest rate. Even when quality bond markets fall, they never lose anywhere close to as much as you can lose in stocks.

Finally, you need bonds for liquidity in case stock prices decline for a couple of years and you have to come up with money for your annual 4 percent withdrawal. For this reason, you'd hold a generous helping of short-term bond funds along with intermediate-term funds.

Here's a very quick bond market primer:

- A bond is a loan. The issuer pays interest, usually quarterly, and promises to return your money after a certain number of years have passed. The safest bonds, in terms of default risk, are those issued by the U.S. Treasury. High-rated AAA or AA bonds issued by corporations and municipalities (see page 253) have a history of safety, too. If you're investing through a tax-deferred retirement account, you'd choose Treasuries or bond mutual funds that include both Treasuries and high-quality corporates. If your account is taxable and your income is high, you'd favor top-rated tax-exempt municipal bonds or funds. High-income investors might buy Treasuries, too. You owe federal income taxes on the interest that Treasuries pay but not state and local income tax.

- Bonds are issued in various maturities, from one year to 30 years. "Short-term" generally means one to three years; "intermediate-term," four to 10 years; long-term, more than 10 years. Their fixed interest rate is called a *coupon rate*. The *yield to maturity* tells you your annual percentage gain if you hold for the bond's full term and reinvest each interest payment at the same coupon rate that you're earning from the bond. If you spend the interest payments or put them into a bank account, your yield won't be as high.

- The main thing that you need to know about bond prices is that they move in the opposite direction from interest rates. When interest rates fall, bond prices rise. When interest rates rise, bond prices fall. You see this relationship clearly when you own bond mutual funds because their posted prices change every day. The prices of any individual bonds you own are changing, too, but you don't notice it—that is, unless you want to sell a bond before maturity. At that point, you'd get whatever price the market set.

- How much a bond's price rises or falls as interest rates change depends on the bond's *duration*. Duration is a calculation that includes such things as the bond's coupon rate, current yield, and final maturity.

    Bonds with longer durations rise and fall more sharply in price than bonds of shorter durations. For example, assume that interest rates change by one percentage point. Bonds with 15-year durations will rise or fall by about 15 percent. Those with six-year durations will rise or fall by about 6 percent. Those with two-year durations, by about 2 percent. It's important to understand duration because it helps you choose a bond mutual fund. Of two funds with the same average maturity (say, two intermediate-term funds), the one with the longer duration will rise and fall more in price when interest rates change. A shorter duration fund gives you a slightly smoother ride. No-load mutual funds show their durations on their websites. You can find this information for all fixed-income mutual funds, free, at Morningstar.com.

- Interest rates are also influenced by inflation expectations. Starting in 1980, inflation generally cycled down, lowering rates and lifting bond prices up. Holders of bonds and bond mutual funds received excellent returns. At this writing, the big institutions that drive the market foresee only moderate inflation over the next decade—the kind of cycle that bond investors have been through before and lived. For the effect of rising interest rates on bond mutual funds, see page 249.

- Yes, but . . . Government spending! National debt! Hyperinflation! Treacherous Federal Reserve! Destruction of our way of life! Not impossible, I suppose. But don't let the rowdy, freak-out forecasting crowd mess with your mind. The link between federal debt levels and long-term interest rates is, on average, exactly zero, a Vanguard study says. There's only a weak link between price inflation and deficits. During some quarters in 2015, average consumer prices declined. Wage inflation is nowhere in sight.

- You have two defenses in case the future brings us an inflation surprise. (1) Own short-term bond funds, whose prices normally fall only a small amount when interest rates go up. (You should own them anyway, as a backup to your cash reserve.) And (2) invest in some Treasury inflation-protected securities (TIPs). TIPS are merely inflation hedges not all-out investment bets because, well, you never know. It's okay to rant about debt and hyperinflation all you like but invest agnostically.

The Case for Buying Bond Mutual Funds

With a mutual fund, you're buying into a pool of bonds. The share value of your fund will rise or fall every day as interest rates change. If you sell your shares when rates are up, you might get less than you originally paid. You'll get more than you paid if rates are down. There's no guarantee.

But successful retirement withdrawal portfolios don't run on guarantees. They need *liquidity,* which means access to cash at any given time without having to take a discount from the current market price. And that's just what you get from mutual funds. These funds also make it easy to rebalance your investments. You simply move money from bond funds to stock funds and vice versa. Life isn't anywhere close to this easy if you hold individual bonds.

Investors worry about the share value of their bond funds at times when interest rates are going up. But during those periods, they do better than you think. The managers will invest the fund's cash flow in bonds that pay the higher rate. As a result, the income you receive from the fund goes up. If you're spending the interest, you'll have a little more in your pocket. If you're reinvesting it, you'll be purchasing shares in your fund at a lower price. When interest rates go down again and bond prices rise, those additional shares will provide you with an extra gain. You don't get these market advantages if you own individual bonds.

Funds have another edge over individual bonds in a period of rising rates. If you buy, say, a $10,000 individual bond paying 3.5 percent, you'll earn $350 this year. That's not enough to reinvest in a new bond. You'd probably put the money in the bank at almost zero percent. If you buy a bond mutual fund instead, that $350 can be reinvested in the fund at the same 3.5 percent (or whatever new rate the fund currently pays).

Bond funds are also diversified. That's not important if you're buying Treasuries. But for general bond funds that include corporates or tax-deferred municipals, safety lies in spreading your risk. You do have to pay the fund's management fees. That cost is at least partly offset by the fact that the managers can buy bonds at low institutional markups. If you buy individual bonds, you have to pay retail.

Treasury funds serve you better than funds primarily invested in investment-grade corporates when you're making regular withdrawals from your investment account. That's because Treasuries usually rise in price when the rest of the market is drowning in fear. The price of corporates usually goes down.

Speaking of fear, don't panic and switch your money into a bank when interest rates rise and the value of your bond fund falls. If you do this, three bad things will happen: (1) you'll lose current income because banks usually pay less than you earn from bonds; (2) the capital loss that you took on the sale of your bonds is permanent and (3) you'll lose the future capital gains that the funds will rack up when the cycle turns and interest rates decline again.

The Case for Buying Index Bond Mutual Funds

In general, all the funds that contain bonds of the same duration and type will perform about the same. The principal difference will be fees. Need I say that low-cost bond index funds almost always beat the pack? To do better than the index, a managed bond fund has to take higher risks, and why would you want that? This is the portion of your retirement portfolio that's supposed to be relatively safe.

In a tax-deferred account you could own a single fund—Vanguard's Total Bond Market Index Fund (costing 0.08 percent a year and primarily invested in government securities) or Fidelity's Spartan U.S. Bond Index Fund (0.1 percent and tilting toward corporates). They're both intermediate-term funds.

For price stability, you'd also want to own a short-term fund. All bonds fall in value when interest rates rise, but a high-quality short-term fund falls by only a small amount. You could use it for your annual withdrawal if stock and bond prices are down and you don't have enough money in your cash reserve. Short-term funds also recover quickly, as the bonds mature and are replaced with new ones paying higher rates. That makes them a good inflation hedge.

You can ignore long-term bond funds. Over time, they don't do much better than intermediate-term funds and are much more vulnerable to loss when interest rates rise.

International bond funds provide you with currency diversification against the dollar. But they cost more to own and complicate your investment plan. The simpler your bond bucket, the easier it is to rebalance.

What about Funds that Own Treasury Inflation-Protected Securities (TIPS)?

TIPS pay a fixed rate of interest plus an increase in principal value that matches the rise in the consumer price index. You buy them to hedge against unexpectedly high inflation. The "expected" inflation rate is already built into the price.[9] TIPS mutual funds distribute the interest and inflation adjustment monthly, which you can reinvest in additional shares.

TIPS funds don't protect you from normal market risks. Like other bond funds, they rise in price when interest rates fall and fall in price when interest rates rise—and by greater percentages than comparable Treasury funds. They perform especially badly when rates rise and inflation goes nowhere.

The TIPS market can be unstable, subject to sudden price hits whenever big institutional investors or hedge funds get alarmed. During the 2008 financial collapse, for example, intermediate-term TIPS funds shocked investors by dropping 12 percent in a month. (If you were a faithful rebalancer and bought TIPS during the panic, you were up 15 percent over the following year. But how many people actually did that?)

TIPS have just one purpose: to deliver inflation-adjusted income, which is what you'd want if inflation escapes to unexpectedly higher levels. As usual, the time to buy is when expected inflation lies low. Short-term TIPS funds carry less risk than intermediate-term funds, but they also provide inflation protection for a shorter period of time. Vanguard's short-term TIPS fund has an average duration of just 2.7 years.

Adding TIPS to your investment portfolio would give you a three-fund fixed-income bucket—a short-term fund for stability, an

---

9   To calculate the current expected inflation rate, compare the TIPS yield with the yield on a comparable Treasury bond that is not adjusted for inflation. For example, if a 10-year TIPS yields 1 percent and a 10-year Treasury yields 3 percent, the expected annual rate of inflation is 2 percent a year over the next 10 years. If inflation exceeds 2 percent under this scenario, TIPS will do better. If it's less than 2 percent, regular Treasuries will do better.

intermediate-term fund for more income, and a TIPS fund for inflation protection. That's three funds for bonds plus, perhaps, two funds for stocks—still not too hard to rebalance, but if you're a simplifier you're pushing the envelope.

Sometimes TIPS sell at negative yields. That means they'll pay you less than the expected inflation rate. This reversal occurs during periods of low interest rates and high demand for an inflation hedge. At such times, short-term Treasuries that are not inflation adjusted would generally sell at a negative real yield, too.

What about high-yield bond funds otherwise known as "junk"? Junk bonds are issued by low-quality companies and municipal entities. They're beloved by investors because they pay high interest rates. Unfortunately, their default risk rises when the economy turns down (see page 223). They often fall in price right along with stocks, so they can't provide you with safe withdrawals in bad times. Don't punch holes in your bond bucket. Stick with high quality.

What about tax-free municipal bond funds? If you're in the 25 percent federal tax bracket or higher and are investing with a taxable account, use part of your money for funds that own tax-exempt municipal bonds. They're issued by government entities for public purposes. As long as you buy a top-quality fund (not a high-yield "junk muni" fund) you should be okay. These are all managed funds, not index funds.

National muni funds own the bonds of many states. You pay no federal income tax on the interest income you receive. States tax only the portion of the income earned from out-of-state bonds. You can skip state income taxes entirely by buying a fund invested only in your state's bonds, but single-state funds charge higher fees. They're also not diversified. An apparently top-quality state could lose value in the next recession, as California and New York investors once learned the hard way.

By the way, muni funds are only *income* tax free. You can be taxed on any realized capital gains. For more about TK, refer to Appendix 1, page 430.

What about owning no intermediate-term bonds at all? During periods of low interest rates, some advisers suggest holding 60 percent in stock funds and balancing that higher risk by putting the other 40 percent into Treasury bills and short-term bond funds. High-quality, investment-grade short-term funds don't pay very much but they're solid protection against rising interest rates and inflation, if that's your worry. (Quality is critical. Some broker-sold short-term bond funds, peddled for their higher yields, have lost 10 to 15 percent during bond market meltdowns.)

Alternatively, you might also look into bank and credit union certificates of deposit for the safety portion of your portfolio. A five-year CD might yield more than a bond fund with a five-year duration. For high-yield CDs, insured by the Federal Deposit Insurance Corporation, check Bankrate.com.

Ginnie Mae funds invest in mortgages insured by the federal government. You earn higher returns than you would from other funds whose investments are government insured. Dividend income rises when mortgage interest rates go up and falls when rates go down. There's a complication. With each check, you receive part of your principal back as well as an interest payment. If you spend it all, you're spending principal, which should count toward your annual 4 percent withdrawal.

Bond "alternatives" are not bonds. When interest rates hang low, income investors reach for higher yields. These include real estate investment trusts (REITs), which invest in real estate companies and distribute rental income to shareholders; master limited partnerships (MLPs), which buy natural resource companies such as gas pipelines; preferred stocks that pay high dividends but carry more market risk; and mutual funds invested in floating-rate bank loans that rise and fall with interest rates and the economy. These investments provide diversification for investors willing to increase their risk and complicate their rebalancing strategies. But the extra income they provide in good times could be overrun by their loss of market value during bad times. They don't perform the proper function of bonds in a retirement portfolio—namely, as a source of cash in bad markets without having to sell stocks at a loss.

The case against buying individual bonds. At first blush, buying individual bonds sounds like a no-brainer. You know exactly what you're getting in advance. There's a fixed rate of interest. If you hold the bonds to maturity, you'll get all your money back. If you buy Treasuries, there's no default risk (and a vanishingly small default risk for top-quality five- to ten-year corporates and tax-exempt municipals). You don't have to worry about the bond market's ups and downs.

But you do have to worry if there's a risk that you might suddenly need extra cash.

Individual corporates and tax-exempts aren't liquid when owned in amounts of less than $100,000 or so. You can sell them but will take a haircut on the price. If you buy such bonds, you have to be very sure that you can afford to lock up that money until they mature.

Individual Treasuries can be bought, with no commission, from TreasuryDirect.gov. To sell before maturity, however, you'd have to transfer them to a brokerage firm.

Individual TIPS have a special disadvantage compared with TIPS mutual funds. The inflation adjustment[10] is taxable every year but not paid until the TIPS mature. You can defer the tax by keeping

---

10 In a deflation, your principal would be adjusted downward and interest paid on the reduced amount. At maturity, however, you'd get the bond's full face value back.

TIPS in your retirement fund but they don't produce current income. By contrast, TIPS mutual funds distribute the interest and inflation adjustment every month.

Newly issued individual municipal bonds can be bought from a broker with no commission. But brokers prefer to sell you older munis that already trade in the market. They mark up the price of those older bonds by two or three percentage points, which is close to what you'd earn in interest the first year. Some brokers hit you for even more. You're unlikely to know the size of the markup because the muni market is so opaque. Investment expert William Bernstein calls older munis a vehicle for transferring wealth from investors to brokers.

If individual bonds have a place at all, they're for wealthy people with large amounts of money to invest, not portfolios of small or medium size.

What about building ladders with individual bonds? A bond ladder is a series of bonds arranged so that one of them matures each year. A five-year ladder would start with bonds coming due in one, two, three, four, and five years. In theory, this answers the liquidity problem. On every due date, you'd have cash if you needed it for your annual withdrawal.

If you don't need the cash when the one-year bond comes due, you'd invest the money in a new five-year bond. If you always reinvest the principal, you'll soon own five five-year bonds with one coming due each year. Most bond ladders use Treasuries. You can do something similar with certificates of deposit. You need at least $100,000 (some say $500,000) for a well-diversified ladder of municipals.

But how does a ladder really help? If, in one of those years, you find that you need the cash for your annual withdrawal, you'll leave a hole in your ladder that you'll have to fill in some future year. Each time your broker sells you another muni, you pay another big markup in price. If interest rates rise, the payments from your ladder will lose value. And because of the inflexible maturities, it becomes difficult to rebalance your portfolio every year.

Wealth managers create million-dollar ladders for clients with a superhigh net worth at a minimal markup. For the rest of us, ladders waste our time and interfere with sensible withdrawal plans. Use mutual funds instead.

What about exchange-traded funds that own bonds? Bond ETFs work like stock ETFs. You need a brokerage account and might have to pay commissions when you rebalance or make withdrawals unless you choose a firm that provides free trades. Bond markets aren't as liquid as stock markets, which hurts the ETF price if a selling panic hits. If you use ETFs, stick entirely with funds that buy Treasuries or track the total U.S. investment-grade bond market. Low-cost possibilities include Vanguard ETF or iShares Core U.S. Aggregate Bond.

USING TARGET-DATE MUTUAL FUNDS

Target-date mutual funds are a terrific invention for people building wealth. All you have to do is pick a fund designed for the approximate date that you plan to retire (2020, 2025, 2030, 2035, and so on). After that, the fund solves the asset-allocation problem for you. If your target retirement date is far away, your fund will be invested primarily in U.S. and international stock funds with a small amount in bonds. As retirement draws closer, the managers will gradually reduce the stock allocation and raise the amount in bonds. Accounts are rebalanced automatically. If you're in a 401(k) plan, you can roll your target-date fund, intact, into the fund company's individual retirement account when you leave your job.

Target-date funds work well for people who agree with their investment philosophy. They usually hold roughly 50 to 55 percent of their assets in stocks on the day you retire with the rest in short- and intermediate-term bonds. As the years go by, the stock allocation will generally continue to decline. By the time you reach 70 or 80, the stocks in your fund will level out at roughly 30 to 20 percent with the rest in bonds. That's a pretty traditional progression for a retirement portfolio intended to last for 30 years or more. Vanguard's Target Retirement Funds, Fidelity's Freedom Funds, Charles Schwab's Target Funds, and T. Rowe Price's Retirement Funds all follow this general pattern. Declining stock allocations support an initial 3.5 percent withdrawal rate, plus annual inflation adjustments, but perhaps not 4 percent if the markets turn down when you first retire (see page 210).

Experience has shown that target-date investing is poorly understood, especially among savers who picked up these plans in their 401(k)s. They thought "target date 2020" meant "safe in 2020" and were shocked when stocks lost half their value during the 2008–2009 financial collapse. Savers who stayed in their funds recovered wonderfully. Their accounts were rebalanced, adding more stock at lower prices. At this writing, the market is up more than 142 percent from the 2009 low. But some people couldn't stand the stress. They sold their target-date funds and switched into fixed-income funds—a choice that permanently reduced the amount of monthly retirement income that their savings will support.

If 50 percent in stocks feels too risky when you retire but you like the automatic rebalancing that target funds provide, you have two choices.

In a 401(k) plan, choose a fund with a target date that's not far away. For example, say that you're 55 and will retire at 65 (in 2025). Ten years from now, the 2025 fund—apparently your predestined choice—will be 50 percent in stocks. If that's too much, you could choose the 2020 fund, which, 10 years from now, might be only 40 percent in stocks. (Remember that the date is just a title. These funds continue to be managed for many years past their target date.)

If you're not in a 401(k) plan, or you're rolling money out of a plan, consider a target-date fund that's set up specifically to reduce your retirement risk. The Russell LifePoints Fund, for example, holds 60 percent of your money in stocks and other growth assets 10 years before your target date, then gradually moves you down to a stock allocation of 37 percent when you retire. You stay at 37 percent for as long as you hold the fund. Russell believes that this approach increases the chance of sustaining lifetime withdrawals of 3 to 4 percent plus inflation adjustments.

A few target-date funds take your stock allocation down to around 10 percent at retirement, on the assumption that you will drop the fund and choose something else.

Funds with predetermined asset allocations aren't suitable for everyone. You might want a different balance entirely if your health is poor, or you have a substantial income, or you inherit a ton of money, or you expect to work until 85. The target-date world solves many problems but not all of them.

WHERE CAN I GET HELP?

You can manage a retirement account yourself if you keep it really simple—say, just two or three low-cost index funds. Rebalance at the end of the year, then take your annual withdrawals out of the funds on a pro rata basis. For example, if you're holding 40 percent in stocks and 60 percent in bonds, 40 percent of your withdrawal would come from your stock funds and 60 percent from your bond funds, after rebalancing. You might add some other investments if it's your hobby but you don't have to. The more funds you have, the more complicated your withdrawal math.

If you don't want to do it yourself, you have a few options:

- Put all your savings into an appropriate target-date fund. The manager does the rebalancing for you. At year's end, you simply take the total withdrawal (according to the 4 percent rule) in a single amount.

- Set up an automatic monthly withdrawal plan on each of your mutual funds. Part of your annual withdrawal should come from each fund. The fund company will send the money to your bank account. You'll have to do the annual rebalancing yourself.

- Use the computer program Quicken Financial Planner. It has a rebalancing program that tells you how to move your money around each year. Once you've rebalanced, it's up to you to take the proper percentage from each fund.

- Use a low-cost online adviser such as AssetBuilder.com, Betterment.com, PortfolioSolutions.com, Rebalance-IRA.com, or WealthFront.com. These firms create well-diversified asset allocations for you (mostly from indexed ETFs), manage the money, and rebalance when necessary. Annual fees run from 0.25 to 0.5 percent. So far, only Betterment will set you up with an automatic retirement withdrawal plan but others will probably follow. Whether these robo-advisers perform better than a total stock and total bond index fund remains to be seen. But the investment and rebalancing work is done for you, which is a big plus. They cost far less than the advice services of traditional brokerage firms and you don't run the risk of being sold dreadful investments.

- Some 401(k) plans offer personal services that advise new retirees on how much money to withdraw each year, taking into consideration their Social Security benefits and other investments.

- A fee-only financial planner will give you asset-allocation advice in addition to providing other personal financial services (see page 27). Some will manage your money and send you monthly checks. A wealth manager should be a registered investment adviser (RIA). Choose one who sells no financial products and charges under 1 percent.

- The big no-load mutual fund companies offer low-cost services to customers. Vanguard Personal Advisor Services provides money management, portfolio rebalancing, and ongoing personal finance advice to its customers for just 0.3 percent a year on portfolios of $50,000 or more. Fidelity Investments, T. Rowe Price, discount broker Charles Schwab, and others offer personal advice as well. Check their websites. These services, plus those of the online advisers, are terrific bargains.

FEES MATTER!

However you decide to invest, fees matter! The more you pay—for money management or for investments you choose yourself—the less cash you'll have in your pocket to spend. Traditional, broad-based index funds and exchange-traded funds cost the least and allow the 4 or 4.5 percent rule to work as planned. As cost benchmarks, use Vanguard's index funds, at 0.05 percent a year. Add 0.25 to 0.5 percentage points if you work with an online adviser or one of the advisory services offered by the big mutual fund groups. Add 0.5 to 1 percentage point if you choose to work with a fee-only financial planner or wealth manager.

You will not earn the net income you expect if you pay high sales commissions to a financial adviser, including the commissions hidden in high-cost variable annuities. The more famous the firm and the fancier the offices, the more they will extract from you in fees. They have no conscience. Trust me on this. A variable annuity with a guaranteed lifetime withdrawal benefit might cost 3.5 percent or more. A "wrap account" or "fee-based" account, where the broker or financial advisory firm oversees your money, might cost 2 to

3 percent. For each percentage point you pay in fees, the amount you can safely withdraw from your nest egg drops by about 0.4 percent.

So quit talking yourself into thinking that a high-cost adviser is doing you some sort of favor. Do the math. The lower your fees, the more money you will earn and the higher the income you can take from your retirement investments.

EARNING RETIREMENT INCOME FROM RENTAL REAL ESTATE

Real estate is a different world. If you buy rental properties, intending to add to your retirement income, you are starting a small business. You can't check your statement once a year and then go back to your favorite retirement pursuits. Running your rental real estate *is* your pursuit.

It's harder than you think to draw real personal income out of your property month after month. Your rents have to cover your costs with a decent amount left over. That's a reasonable expectation if you're renting an apartment carved out of your personal residence and the tenant pays on time. It's possible if you buy a rental property with cash so you have no mortgage payments. If you take a mortgage, however, your rental income will probably fall short. You might wind up dipping into savings to support the property every month. That's not what you had in mind. Your risk rises exponentially if you're carrying a mortgage after you retire.

Real estate investors get into trouble because they didn't accurately forecast their costs. Besides the mortgage payment, expenses include taxes, insurance, fix-up costs before the house can be rented, any utilities the renter doesn't cover, trash hauling, unexpected repairs, advertising for tenants, reserves for repainting and replacements, fix-up costs when you're in between tenants, loss of rent during those periods, legal advice when preparing a lease, and a dozen other things. You need reliable service people on call if you can't make emergency repairs yourself. A tenant without heat might not feel required to pay the rent this month. Or worse, sue.

Bad tenants can be your largest cost of all. They pay late, quit paying, resist eviction, and trash your property on the way out. They'll probably have an illegal cat that pees on the carpet. It's all the more painful if those tenants are in an apartment over your garage.

Before renting to anyone, do a credit check and call his or her previous employers and landlords. Get cash or money orders for the first month's rent and the security deposit (that gets rid of people whose checks bounce after they move in). Jack Reed (johntreed .myshopify.com), author of *How to Manage Residential Property for Maximum Cash Flow and Resale Value,* advises that you also spend an evening watching the movie *Pacific Heights,* a cautionary comedy about landlording gone wrong.

Not everyone has the temperament to be a landlord. You have to be cheerful about taking calls at any time of day or night, keep your temper with rude tenants, and handle problems right away. Know your local eviction laws and move to evict the first time the rent comes late. A good tenant will apologize and never miss the date again. A bad tenant will find excuses, not just once but again and again.

Ask yourself, honestly, do you have the guts to demand the rent on time? To demand rent at all if someone gives you a sob story? Can you throw out a single parent who has lost his or her job? Even if the child is small? And sick? If you can't answer all those questions with a hard-boiled yes, don't even try to be a landlord. In this game, nice guys get their clocks cleaned. You might set out to be the best landlord in history and discover, too late, that you were just incompetent. Buying any sad story, from any tenant, could cost you not only your income and profit but your principal and—if you have a mortgage— your credit rating, too. Grrrr.

Cash flow is the name of the rental real estate game. Selling the house at a profit, if that happens, won't cover your grocery bills today. You might be able to raise the rent as inflation rises but taxes and other costs will go up, too. Furthermore, real estate isn't liquid. Even highly desirable properties might not sell and close in less than six months. You'll need cash on the side, in the bank or in short-term bond funds, in case a tenant flees and you need ready money to pay your bills.

Fact: The days of easy profits on real estate investments are long gone. After counting the money you put into the house to fix it up, your compounded annual return might be minuscule compared with what you might have earned in stocks or even bonds. Nouveau landlords commonly overinvest in the houses they buy. They choose homes they might want to live in themselves and bring them up to their own high standards. It could be a long time before you recover those costs. The condition of rental properties needs to be adequate for the market and nothing more.

On rental properties that you plan to hold, focus on the *capitalization rate*—the rate of return on your invested capital. If your net operating income equals 10 percent of the price of the property, you have a 5 percent cap rate. (Net operating income is the rental income minus expenses but before mortgage payments.) Cap rates of 4 or 5 percent are mediocre investments, Reed says, considering your time commitment and the risks.

Rental income is taxable. But you can deduct expenses, including depreciation, which will offset part of the gain and possibly all of it. If your expenses exceed your rental income, the loss is deductible on your current tax return, up to certain limits. Assuming that you manage the rental house yourself and your modified adjusted gross income doesn't exceed $100,000, you can write off up to $25,000 in losses, which tax-shelters some of your other income, too. At higher incomes, the allowable deduction gradually phases out, terminating at $150,000.

A vacation home that you treat as a rental property is considered a personal residence if you use it more than 14 days a year or more than 10 percent of the time it is rented, whichever is less. It's also considered personal use if you rent to a relative or friend at less than the going rate. You'll have to prorate the expenses between days of business use (deductible) and personal use (not deductible).

Before getting into real estate investment, study up. It's not like buying index funds. Read books on real estate finance, learn about property values in various neighborhoods, analyze your local economy (have people been moving in or moving out?), and set rules for yourself, such as the cap rate you want. Successful real estate investors have to get their fingernails dirty. If your game plan relies mainly on prices going up, buy real estate mutual funds.

YES, THEY'RE OUT TO GET YOU!

Willie Sutton robbed banks because that's where the money was. For the same reason, greedy financial salespeople go after the retirement accounts of people in midlife and later. They're selling products that carry high commissions and conceal your annual costs and risks. Now fiduciary rules for 2017 are supposed to constrain them (see page 32) but we'll see. You're on their list if you're rolling over a 401(k) into new investments, choosing a lump sum pension payout instead of a monthly lifetime income, or looking for higher returns on your savings than you're getting from banks and bonds.

These modern-day Willies are especially eager to meet you if you haven't had much investment experience outside the protected world of 401(k)s and are looking for someone to help you make your money grow. You'll find them sooooo smart, sympathetic, and nice. They'll help you right out of the savings you worked so hard for. When you complain that you didn't understand what you were getting into, they'll say they disclosed the risks. Their firm will back them. Selling high-cost products is what their employers expect them to do.

The menu of sweet-sounding perilous products is long. Here are a few of the ones you might run into:

- **Nontraded real estate investment trusts.** These REITs invest in commercial properties such as shopping centers, apartments, and hotels. The danger word is "nontraded." Unlike other REITs, they're not bought and sold on a stock exchange, so you never know what they're really worth. They appear to pay high dividends, but part of that "dividend" might come from the capital you invested (you're just getting your own money back). Sometimes the managers borrow money to pay the dividend, which increases your costs and risks. To get your full investment out, you usually have to wait seven years or more. At that point, the REIT is supposed to sell the properties and distribute the proceeds or else go public so you can sell your shares. They might not be able to do either one, however, if market conditions are poor. If they do go public, the shares might trade for much less than you paid. If you have to sell before the seven years are up, you'll take a steep discount from what you thought was the market price. You'll probably never know what your nontraded REIT actually returned on your investment. In some cases, the answer has been zero.

  The sales commissions on nontraded REITs run as high as 15 percent, which explains why they're so popular among brokers and financial advisers. You're also paying high annual management fees to the sponsor of the REIT. Last year, the Securities and Exchange Commission started to require that nontraded REITs do a better job of disclosing costs. They're also supposed to provide you with periodic estimates of what your shares are worth. That estimate, however, will be far above the price you'll actually get if you want to sell early.

  In real life, nontraded REITs cannot do better than

publicly traded REITs. In fact, they are almost bound to do worse because they charge so much more in commissions and fees. If you want a REIT, buy one that's publicly traded and sold by a no-load mutual fund.

- **Private placements and business development companies.** You're buying into some sort of business—energy, cell phones, restaurant chain—which is supposed to pay high, periodic distributions with handsome profits at the end. The regulators pretty much ignore these placements because they're supposedly sold only to "sophisticated investors." The managers don't even have to provide you with financial statements, which makes them a hotbed for fraud. All too often, they come to naught. You'll discover that it's hard to bring suit because, in the offering document you signed, you agreed you were sophisticated and understood the risks. You might even find that the document prevents you from suing or requires you to pay the broker's legal costs.

- **Life settlements.** You're sold a share in a pool of life insurance policies, allegedly on people with short life spans. The premiums are paid from the policies' cash values. When someone dies, the investors share the proceeds, after costs. Naturally, you pay high commissions and fees. If a policy's cash value runs out before the insured person dies, the investors have to pay to keep the policy going. That's one of the many risks with these investments. The happy insured might live a lot longer than you expected.

- **Funds of hedge funds.** What are called hedge funds don't really hedge against anything. They're pools of sophisticated money that invest in different, complicated ways. They might take 20 percent of the profits plus fees in a year that the value of the fund goes up. If it goes down, all the losses are yours. Hedge funds have an undeserved reputation for making their investors rich. Some of them do, but those funds don't sell to the hoi polloi. Before you take the plunge, you might want to know that the average hedge fund underperformed the S&P 500 over the past 10 years. CalPERS of California, the country's largest public pension fund, announced last year that it was ditching its hedge funds and putting two-thirds of its stock allocation into low-cost index funds. With experience, even big institutions get smart.

- **A new category of "absolute return" funds.** These claim to make money whether the markets rise or fall. That's just what the hedge funds used to say. Same pitch, same likely result.

- **Early-retirement temptations.** A financial adviser might look at the size of your 401(k) or the potential lump sum payout from your pension plan and say, "Wow, you can afford to retire!" even if you're in your early 50s. If you jump at this dream, you'll be sold a variable annuity plus some risky, high-cost stock market investments on the side. The adviser might claim that you can withdraw as much as 8 or 9 percent a year from your investments and still have the money last for life. By the time you find out that's not true, you're halfway to broke and will have to go back to work. At 50, you could live for another 50 years. Unless you're a beneficiary of the Warren Buffett trust or can live on annual 2 percent withdrawals, it's much too early to retire. Did I mention that the sales commissions on variable annuities run in the range of 5 to 7 percent?

- **Inappropriate IRA investments.** Shares in nontraded REITS, private placements, and similar investments can't readily be sold. If you invest most of your IRA money there—as the greediest salespeople propose—you might be in trouble when you reach 70½. At that age you're required to start withdrawing a certain percentage of your IRA's value every year. To raise the money, you might have to sell these illiquid investments at steep discounts. If you can't sell them at all, the IRS will fine you 50 percent of the money you failed to withdraw on time.

- **Inappropriate rollovers from 401(k) plans.** When you retire, you might have the option of leaving your money in the company's 401(k). Costs will be low and you'll have enough mutual fund choices to create a well-diversified portfolio. Alternatively, you might switch to an IRA in a no-load mutual fund. Financial salespeople, however, want you to switch your money into an IRA with their firm. "Take control of your financial destiny," they'll croon. "Our IRAs give you more investment choice." Well, yes . . . you could choose the kinds of bad investments not allowed in company 401(k)s, including high-cost mutual funds. Unless you're leaving your 401(k) to buy low-cost index funds, consider keeping your money in the plan.

There's No Clean Way of Knowing Whom to Trust

Savers and investors have been duped by brokers recommended by close friends, members of their social group, advisers who come into corporations to give talks to preretirees, accountants who handle their taxes, and close relatives. Even experienced investors can be talked into terrible investments by persuasive salespeople.

You can check on a broker's conduct at the website of the Financial Industry Regulatory Authority (finra.org, click on "Broker Check"). You might find past settlements and complaints. Most complaints against brokers don't make it into the record, however, so you can't be sure. For the types of investments that the regulators worry about, go to FINRA's Investor Alerts and the similar alerts put out by the Securities and Exchange Commission (at SEC.gov, click on "Information for Investors," then "Investor Alerts and Bulletins").

I don't mean to scare you unduly. Many commissioned advisers have their clients' best interests at heart. But they also have to earn a living and keep their jobs, so they're always in conflict. I'd suggest an adviser whose firm does not accept sales commissions—a fee-only planner or the advisory services listed on page 260.

If you keep your investments simple and use low-cost index mutual funds, you will only have to trust yourself.

10

Home Sweet Income-Producing Home

Your house is a piggy bank. This might be the moment to break it open.

There's money in your house. Those friendly walls are packed with legal tender just waiting to be released. You can take the cash now or take it at some point in the future. The decision hinges on how you'll want to live in early or later retirement, and whether you'll need more income to maintain the style of life you want.

If you don't need more income, you can leave your home equity locked up for your heirs, in your current home or in an equal or fancier home that you buy somewhere else.

On the other hand, if your budget already looks tight, the equity in your home might fill the gaps perfectly. You can tap it while staying in place or release it by moving somewhere else.

If you move, you don't have to choose a new home for life. The right place for people in their mid-50s to mid-70s might be the wrong place when you reach 80. There could be two moves in your future, not just one.

Young retirees generally like to live among active, like-minded people. That might be a home in an adult community, with scheduled activities and near golf and tennis. Or a university town, where you can audit courses and attend football games. Or a city with plenty of theater, concerts, and access to jobs if you want part-time work. Or it could be a smaller house or apartment in the town where you live now, so that you can keep up with old friends.

Older retirees seek a lively social atmosphere, too, but their priorities lean toward health care, good public transportation, proximity to adult children, and easy-care apartments where someone else mows the lawn. A rising trend among boomers is the two-step retirement—first, downsizing to a smaller place, then, later, moving to a full-service retirement community.

WHATEVER YOU DO, TAKE THE LONG VIEW

Right now, my health is good. I hope yours is, too. But I wonder where I'll live when (and if) I start to need help with the daily business of living. I don't want to wait for my children to open "the conversation" in carefully casual tones of voice. ("Ahem, Mom, we were wondering . . .") I want to open that conversation myself. Their input will influence what I think but I want the decision to be mine.

Most of us want to "age in place"—whichever place we choose—with occasional side trips to other nice places. That works fine as long as we can take care of ourselves. If we slip, however, we'll have to depend on someone else. Who will be there to help and what can we do in advance to ease the transition? I don't want to be stubborn about aging in place if it's going to create caregiving problems for my children (not to mention medical risks for me).

Doing nothing is itself a decision. You're relying on someone else to step up and make the changes you failed to make yourself.

If you don't have children or children you can depend on, the question becomes even more important. Kindly neighbors running errands isn't a permanent solution.

People hoping to stay in their homes should look at the floor plan as if they were already on a walker. You might have to add a bedroom downstairs with a bathroom whose door can accommodate a wheelchair. Your pretty front porch will become a trap if there's nowhere to build a ramp to the sidewalk. Plan on renovating while you're still healthy, before an emergency crops up.

Besides renovation, consider your community access. What happens if it's no longer safe for you to drive? In car-centered suburbs, you'd have to depend on others to do your shopping or take you to doctor's appointments. Maybe it's impractical to age in place.

Eventually, you might need caregiving services if a spouse or child isn't constantly available. You'll also need someone you trust to supervise home care aides to be sure they're always doing right by you. Who is that likely to be? Do you want to lay that responsibility on your kids, and if so, how will they handle it? This shouldn't be a snap decision made under duress. The whole family should plan.

My own parents set an example for me. In their late 70s and in reasonably good health, they decided to sell their house and move to a lovely apartment in a continuing care retirement community (CCRC—see page 277). In a CCRC, you live independently among a group of like-minded people. If you start to fail physically, you can move to an assisted living or skilled care unit. These communities not only lift burdens from you, they relieve your adult children of the minutiae of parent care. The children will be especially grateful if they live far away.

For people who stay in their homes until they are frail, the best option—when you finally move—might be a residence for assisted living. There you live as independently as possible but can get help with basic physical needs such as dressing and bathing. Like CCRCs, they provide activities and a social life. There might be a nursing home wing attached. You can find reviews of local facilities at ALFA.org, the website of the Assisted Living Federation of America.

The key is to plan ahead. What can you afford—today and in the future? What's a reasonable way to live? Should you stay where you are or move?

THE GOVERNMENT PRACTICALLY PAYS YOU TO MOVE

A house is not only a piggy bank, it's a tax shelter, too. If you're married and sell it, you can take up to $500,000 in profits tax free.[1] By "profits," I mean any money you make on the house after subtracting the price you originally paid, the cost of all home improvements over the years, and fix-up costs and real estate commissions when you sell. If you're single, the first $250,000 in profits come tax free.

If you expect to sell, do it sooner rather than later. The older you get the harder it becomes, emotionally, to make a move, and the more you'll have spent on upkeep—furnace, roof, paint, repairs, and lawn work, along with real estate taxes and insurance. That money could have gone straight into a savings account instead. Why be house poor in retirement? Shake loose some of that cash.

You have several choices when you want to move and take equity out of your house.

1. **Buy a less expensive house or condo.** Add the money left over from the move to your savings and investments. That beefs up the current and future income you can afford to withdraw from your savings every year.

   Big question: Should you pay cash for the new place? I'd say yes, as long as you have enough money left over to provide yourself with a comfortable income for life. Owning a paid-up home confers great peace of mind. But if paying cash would squeeze

---

1   This tax break applies only to your principal residence, not a second home.

your budget, put 20 percent down and take a 30-year mortgage to cover the rest. Long-term mortgages make sense, even at older ages, because they hold down the size of your monthly payment. If you use a reverse mortgage to make the purchase, you won't owe monthly payments at all (see page 282).

If you buy another house, it will come with the same kinds of upkeep costs that your old one did. If you renovate and redecorate, the move might not save you any money at all. A modern, easy-to-care-for condominium or town house might be a better choice. If your children come to visit from far away, you can put them up in a motel for much less than the annual cost of maintaining a large home. (When I sold my four-bedroom house and moved to a co-op apartment, I solved short visits from family by buying pull-out sofas topped by feather beds.)

For an estimate of the dollars that downsizing can add to your income, use the calculator "Figure Out How Moving Changes Your Finances" under the heading "Tools" at Squared Away.bc.edu. It's one of a series of calculators backed by the Financial Security Project at Boston College.

If you owe more on your home than it's worth, you're stuck—for a while, at least. You can keep making payments and hope its market value goes up. The monthly cost might be less than you'd pay in rent somewhere else. Worst case: You let it go to foreclosure and move on.

2. **Rent instead of buying something new.** The cash you'll get from selling your home might appreciate faster in a diversified investment account than it will in a new house. You'll have more money to spend every month and the landlord will handle the property chores. Rent will go up, but if you buy another place, so will your property taxes, homeowner's insurance premiums, and upkeep costs. Any tax deductions might not even be worth very much to you anymore, thanks to the size of your personal and standard deductions.

You might resist renting because it's "money down a rat hole." But not if it frees up cash to keep you living well. Why own a house and build equity for your heirs if housing expenses crimp your income and limit what you can do during your freedom years? Renting is liberating. You can shut the door and leave. That's especially important if you moved to be closer to one of your adult children. What if the child gets a new job and moves away?

3. **Hit the road.** For younger retirees, these can be years of experimentation. You might buy an RV and tour the country, live on a boat, or find a warm nest in Costa Rica or Panama. Your new setup should cost only a small portion of the proceeds of your home sale, leaving you with extra income to live on. (But don't spend it all. Most likely, you'll come home again.)

4. **Move in with a willing adult child.** Use the proceeds from the sale of your house to put an addition on the child's house. Or renovate his or her existing house to create a separate bed/sitting room with bath, TV, microwave, and refrigerator. Or build your own cottage on the property, if the zoning allows.

   Co-living takes a lot of careful planning. Will you be expected to cook or take care of the grandchildren? Will your adult child be on tap to take you shopping or to the doctor if you can't drive? Will you go on family vacations? Which household expenses will you cover? What's an acceptable mix of privacy and family time? If you need daily assistance, who will help and who will pay? Do you need a home health aide? Can you have a separate social life—say, visits from friends? If you're single, what about sex (yes, grandparents do it!)? Will your children freak if you stay out overnight?

Check on medical coverage before moving to a new area. If you bought a policy through a broker or on one of the health-care exchanges, it won't cover you in a different city or state at in-network prices. It might not cover you at all except for emergency care. So shop for health insurance at the same time you're shopping for a new home. Apply for the new plan in the month you move. Your current insurance company will tell you how to make the transition without opening a gap in coverage.

There are no gaps in coverage when you're on traditional Medicare. That plan follows you wherever you go. By contrast, the Medicare Advantage plans generally limit you to local network doctors. If you expect to move, you might switch to traditional Medicare plus a Part D drug plan during the open enrollment period in the year before you move. Once you reach your new home, you might switch to a local Advantage plan again.

Consider a continuing care retirement community, if you can afford it. You'll live in your own townhouse or apartment and can take your main meals in a community dining room. There's usually a fitness center, along with movies and other social activities. As long as you're well (and you have to be in good health to move in), you carry on with your independent life. If your physical abilities start to fail, you'll move to a part of the campus that offers assisted living, such as help with bathing and dressing. Those who become seriously ill switch to the CCRC's nursing home or Alzheimer's unit. The community should be Medicare certified in case you need skilled nursing care.

Married couples often move to a CCRC to ensure that the survivor is in a safe place when one of them dies. The attraction for singles, besides the social life, is knowing that you've arranged for any long-term care that you might need. I count it a further plus that you've made your own decision rather than dragging your heels until your kids or other relatives have to choose for you.

Typically, you'd use the proceeds of the sale of your house to buy into a CCRC. There's an entrance fee (the median was $305,000 in 2015, meaning that half cost more and half cost less). You'll also pay a monthly maintenance fee (median: $3,150) that will rise a little every year. The contracts vary a lot but fall into three main types:

Type A— the most expensive choice. You buy lifetime housing, meals, amenities, and long-term care in a single package. Your fees won't rise if you transfer from independent to assisted living. You can generally remain at the CCRC even if you run out of money.

Type B— a moderate fee up front with the possibility of higher costs later. You buy housing, meals, amenities, and a limited number of days in the assisted living or nursing home wing. If you need more care, your monthly fee will rise. If it turns out that you can't pay, you will have to move.

Type C— a pay-as-you-go arrangement. You get the same housing-and-meals arrangement as the other contracts offer, but if you need comprehensive health care you pay at the market rate.

Consider Types B and C if you have long-term care insurance that will cover most of the CCRC's charges for assisted living or nursing care. (Check the details with your insurer before you sign.)

Visit more than one CCRC to get a sense of the spirit of each place. See the various types of living quarters, have some meals, talk to the residents, check the activities list, and visit the wings that provide assisted living or custodial care. How does the CCRC decide when a resident needs to move to one of those facilities, and if you have long-term care insurance, will it start to pay as soon as the move is made? What medical services are available to health residents on-site—perhaps weekly visits by an internist, podiatrist, hearing-aid specialist, or other health professional? Is there room service for meals if you're down with a cold? If the

CCRC doesn't have an Alzheimer's unit, will you be given priority to enter another home for care? Consult with family members as you go along.

There have been a handful of bankruptcies among CCRCs, but in almost all cases the facility was reorganized without affecting the residents' investment. To feel sure that you're buying into a financially strong community, have the contract evaluated by an accountant or real estate lawyer. One source: the National Academy of Elder Law Attorneys (NAELA.org). Among the things you need to check:

- The full list of services covered by the entry fee plus a list of the fees for extras.
- A five-year history of the community's monthly fees. Moderate annual increases are good. It's important that it has kept up with inflation. If it hasn't, large increases might have to be imposed in the future.
- The audited financial statement. Is the line labeled "fund balance" or "net assets" in the black?
- Cash on hand. The CCRC needs at least 150 days of cash on hand. The community probably carries bond financing, which might require much more. Is the facility meeting all its bond covenants?
- Operating costs. They should be covered entirely by the monthly fees that the existing residents pay. You don't want a community deeply dependent on new sales, which might not be forthcoming, or chewing into its cash reserves.
- Actuarial soundness. A CCRC that mainly sells Type A plans needs enough younger, healthier residents to ensure that the costs of the sicker residents can be covered. The facility should provide you with a letter from an actuary saying that, demographically, the community is on a sound financial footing.
- Any lawsuits against the CCRC.

- Accreditation. As a quality measure, the facility should be accredited by CARF International (formerly the Commission on Accreditation of Rehabilitation Facilities).
- Any plans for improvements that might require a financial assessment on the residents.
- Your financial protection if the community that you're buying into hasn't been completed yet. You'll want to be able to get your deposit back if construction is held up too long. To check the financial soundness of new CCRCs, ask for the track record and financials of the developer. Avoid a developer that never has built a CCRC before.
- Your financial options if you decide to leave. With some types of contracts, you simply move out. For those willing to pay higher monthly fees, the CCRC will give you part or all of your entry fee back. You might have to wait for your refund until your unit is resold.
- The quality rating of the community's nursing home section. Go to Medicare.gov/nhcompare/home.asp.

You will have to disclose some information, too. The CCRC will ask for your financials to be sure that you can afford the place, and you'll have to pass a health exam. You won't be accepted if you need assisted living right away or don't appear to have enough income to pay the fees for life.

For checklists on how to evaluate CCRCs, visit CARF.org and AARP.org. On the CARF site, type "Financial Performance" into the Search box to bring up a free booklet called "Consumer Guide to Understanding Financial Performance & Reporting in Continuing Care Retirement Communities." CARF.org and LeadingAge.org can help you find CCRCs in or near specific towns or cities.

If you're not ready for a full-service CCRC or it's beyond your budget, consider active adult communities for people 55 and up. At

55places.com, you'll find listings for communities around the country. They don't provide central dining or health care, as CCRCs do, but there might be a clubhouse and scheduled activities.

SQUEEZING YOUR HOME FOR INCOME IF YOU DON'T MOVE

You might take a loan against the equity you have in your home. The interest rate is low, although it will rise if general rates go up. For the first five years or so, you can pay only the interest. After that you have to start paying down principal.

You might refinance your current mortgage. At this writing you can get a low fixed rate for 30 years. The payments due might be lower than those on the loan you have now.

You might take in a boarder or roommate or add a rental apartment over the garage. This works best when the layout provides some privacy for you both. If you're splitting expenses with a roommate, the two of you should prepare a written agreement—who pays for what, how are chores divided, and what are the rules on splitting up your partnership?

Before becoming a landlord, check your legal position. Does your zoning law allow boarders? Are you subject to rent-control or eviction laws that might make it hard to move a bad boarder out? Is the boarder covered by your liability insurance? What are the tax implications of using part of your house as a rental property? Have you prepared a sound written lease? Do you have the temperament to deal with renters in your home? If you live in a popular tourist spot, you might operate like a motel, if local law allows. Airbnb.com will send you renters who need only a room and bath and will stay a night or three at a time.

Another option is selling your house to one or more of your children and leasing it back from them. This strategy is more talked about than consummated, but here's a quick peek at how it works: The children give you a down payment, which adds to your cash. You give them a mortgage for the rest of the money they owe. They send you a mortgage payment every month. You pay them rent, which is less than the amount of the mortgage payment you receive. This exchange increases your income and it's tax free. You pay utilities. The children pay the insurance and taxes and see to the maintenance and repairs. For them it's a rental property so they get deductions for their business expenses.

A sale/leaseback should be worked out with a lawyer. The house price, interest rate, and rent all have to be set at fair market value. Before getting into anything like this, however, consider the risks. What if one of your children loses his or her job and can't make mortgage payments or repairs? What if the children disagree? What if there's a divorce? What if you and your children have a fight? Remember *King Lear*. . . .

Another choice might be a reverse mortgage with regular payments that raise your retirement standard of living. These loans don't get good press but you should take another look.

NEW WAYS OF THINKING ABOUT REVERSE MORTGAGES

I've changed my mind about reverse mortgages. I used to see more risk than reward for most borrowers. But the risk has diminished. New federal regulations make reverse mortgages safer for people in their late 70s and 80s who need extra money to help them stay in their homes. New cash-flow strategies make them interesting for people in their early 60s and 70s who want to improve their monthly retirement income.

I'll have more to say about these strategies a little further on. First, here's a general explanation of reverse mortgages and how they work.

Reverse Mortgages Defined

A *reverse mortgage* is a loan against the equity you hold in your home. You don't have to repay it as long as you're living in the house. Instead the lender makes payments to you, entirely tax free. Your only obligation is to cover the cost of homeowner's insurance, property taxes, and general upkeep.

Eventually, the house will be sold—because you move, enter a nursing home permanently, or die. The proceeds of the sale will be used to repay the loan plus all the accumulated interest and fees. If the house sells for more than what's owed, the remaining money goes to you or your heirs. If it sells for less, you or your heirs walk away—you get nothing but you're also not responsible for any additional money owed.

You can get a reverse mortgage, individually, as early as age 62. If you borrow jointly with a spouse or domestic partner, only one of you has to be 62. The younger your partner, however, the less money you will get. If your spouse or partner isn't on the loan, he or she risks eviction if you die (see page 296).

Almost all reverse mortgages come in the form of a Home Equity Conversion Mortgage (HECM). It's issued by private lenders and insured by the Federal Housing Administration (FHA). You can borrow against a single-family house, a two- to four-unit home provided that you live in one of the units, an FHA-approved condominium, and most manufactured homes that sit on property you own. Mobile homes are out. So are vacation homes. Reverse mortgages can be used only for your principal residence. These loans work best when your home is completely (or substantially) mortgage free. But you can use them to help pay off an existing mortgage, too.

Reverse mortgages are *expensive* compared with traditional loans. Not only do you pay more in up-front and annual FHA fees but the total amount you owe goes up every month because the cost of the interest and fees compounds within the loan. Paying these fees makes sense only if the loan is part of a carefully thought-out plan.

How Reverse Mortgages Work, Step by Step

1. A lender agrees to make the loan. How much you can borrow depends on the appraised value of your home, current interest rates, the age of the youngest borrower, and how much (if anything) you still owe on the home.[2] The older you are and the less you still owe, the more money you can get. Appraised values are capped at $625,500, which limits the amount of money you can borrow on more expensive homes. For a quick estimate of the potential size of your loan, use the reverse mortgage calculator at mtgprofessor.com.

2. As part of the deal, you have to pay off any remaining mortgages on the house, including home equity loans. If you don't have the cash, you can use the proceeds of the reverse mortgage to help make the payoff. Any liens or court judgments secured by the house have to be repaid, as well. The loan is off the table, however, if you're delinquent on any federal debt, including student loans that you might have cosigned.

3. Before you can close the loan, you have to reveal the size of your income and savings. The lender must be satisfied that you can pay the ongoing costs of homeownership (insurance, property taxes, condominium fees, upkeep) and still have enough left to live on.

---

2   These loans work best for people who own their homes free and clear or who have small mortgages. If you have little or no equity, you won't qualify.

4. You're required to go through reverse mortgage counseling, by phone or face-to-face. The lender will give you some names.[3] Be warned that the counselors won't help you choose the best option for your circumstances. Their job is merely to ensure that you understand the terms of the loan and what it means, to you and your heirs, when you spend down home equity. They're also required to tell you about alternatives to the reverse mortgage, such as local programs that help low-income homeowners. A HECM counselor's advice is free or low cost (typically, $125).

5. You pay little or no cash up front. All closing and FHA insurance costs can be included in the loan.

6. You can receive the money from your reverse mortgage in one of several ways:

   ♦ **A credit line that you can borrow against at any time.** This is normally the best choice because it's not an ordinary credit line. The amount you can borrow rises every year at the same rate as the interest rate you're paying on the loan. If you use very little of the money during the first few years, you'll be able to access much more cash when you are older. That makes your HECM credit line an excellent hedge against future inflation or increased medical costs. If you borrow too much too fast, however, you might be entitled only to smaller amounts in your later years. For more on this magical credit line, see page 291.

   ♦ **A check a month, for a fixed amount, paid as long as you're in the house.** The lender will calculate the size of the check

---

3 You can also search for counselors online or call the counseling line of the U.S. Department of Housing and Urban Development at 800-569-4287.

based on the total sum you're allowed to borrow. The checks will keep coming even if they exceed your original borrowing limit.

- ♦ **A fixed number of checks.** Once you've received them all, the game ends. No more money will be paid. These checks can be for larger amounts than the check-a-month deal because the lender knows—in advance—when its obligation will end. You can't exceed your borrowing limit.

- ♦ **A lump sum.** This is the most tempting choice because it's nice to have so much cash in hand. But it also makes it more likely that you'll run through the money and still won't be able to keep your house. Lump-sum borrowers also have to pay higher fees.

- ♦ **A combination of the above.** For example, you might take $25,000 up front, $800 a month for as long as you live in the house, and a $60,000 credit line.

7. Each reverse mortgage check looks and feels like income. But it isn't income, it's a loan. You owe no taxes on the money. Also, you don't have to count it when figuring whether your Social Security is taxable or whether you owe a higher Medicare premium. It might affect your eligibility for Medicaid, however (Medicaid pays for nursing home care if you run out of money).

8. You don't have to repay a penny as long as you stay in the house. The loan normally comes due only if you sell the house and move somewhere else, enter a nursing home for a long stay (usually 12 months or more), or die. If you own the house with a spouse or partner and you're both on the HECM, these terms apply to you both. If one of you enters a nursing home, the other one can stay in the house and keep using the HECM credit line or receiving scheduled monthly payments.

9. You can be forced out of the house if you fail to pay real estate taxes or homeowners' insurance, or if you let the house run down. People run this risk when their income is too low to cover their projected living expenses. They take a HECM in a lump sum, spend all the money, then go broke. They default on their insurance and taxes and lose the home.

   A new regulation, first effective in 2015, is greatly reducing this default risk. If your income is marginal, the lender is no longer allowed to give you the whole loan amount. Part of it will be set aside in a special fund that's expected to cover your housing expenses (insurance, taxes, upkeep) over your lifetime. Sometimes these set-asides leave you with hardly any additional spendable income. In that case, skip the HECM. The lender is effectively telling you that you can't afford your home. Best to sell right away and downsize.

10. When the house is sold, the HECM is repaid out of the proceeds. If there's money left over, it goes to you or your heirs. If the proceeds of the sale aren't large enough to cover the loan, you or your heirs owe nothing but also get nothing. You'll have spent the entire value of your home. Anyone who strongly wants to leave a debt-free home to children is not a candidate for a Home Equity Conversion Mortgage.

Tell Your Heirs about the Loan!

Please, please involve your adult children in this decision if they're your heirs. In spending your home equity, you're using what could have been their inheritance. You're absolutely entitled to do so. You worked for that house and responsible children should agree that maintaining your standard of living comes first. But they shouldn't be taken by surprise after you die, learning suddenly that this piece of their expected inheritance is gone. What's more, your children can make a good sounding board while you consider your choices. One of them might have financial expertise.

If you borrow in the form of a lump sum, the odds are high that there will be no equity left when you die. When the loan is front-loaded, the costs build up fast. There's a better chance of getting some value out of the house if you borrow in the form of monthly payments or a credit line that you tap at a slow pace.

At your death, your legal heirs have an opportunity to buy the house themselves or sell it to a third party. The price to heirs is *either* the amount due on the loan *or* 95 percent of the appraised market value, whichever is less. For example, take a house worth $100,000. If the loan against it has grown to $150,000, an heir could buy it for $95,000. There's no equity left, after fees, but he or she could live there without having to repay the remaining loan. If the same house is worth $200,000, the heirs might want to put it up for sale. If they find a buyer, they could repay the $150,000 owed to the bank and pocket the rest. They generally have six months to sell. If they can't, the lender will foreclose or take a deed in lieu of foreclosure.

Some heirs have complained about the way that various lenders handle HECMs that come due. They might seize the home too quickly, or lose documents sent by heirs who are trying to buy the property, or give them the runaround when they're trying to find out the status of the loan. The more your heirs know about the loan in advance and during its term, the better prepared they will be to handle the sale or foreclosure process in the end.

What Does a Home Equity Conversion Mortgage Cost?

HECMs come with fixed interest rates or variable rates. You don't pay the interest monthly, as you do with regular mortgages. Instead, it's added to the amount of your loan. Both principal and interest fall due when the house is finally sold.

From a current income point of view, it makes no difference how much interest accumulates. You always get the amount of borrowing power that you signed up for—the lump sum, the monthly checks, or the credit line. The cost shows up in the amount of money you (or your heirs) realize from the proceeds of the sale. The more interest you owe and the less your house appreciated in value, the less money will be left over for the family. Here's how the two versions of the HECM work.

A fixed-rate HECM is of interest only to people for whom the fixed rate matters more than the cost or the amount of money they receive. The lender normally lets you borrow no more than 60 percent of the total allowable amount in the first year. That's all. You can't come back for the remaining 40 percent in the second year. You have to take the money in a lump sum; you can't get monthly payments or a credit line. The interest rate might be nearly double that of a new variable-rate HECM. At this writing, many lenders aren't even writing fixed-rate HECMs.

A variable-rate HECM also sets a normal borrowing limit of 60 percent of the allowable loan amount in the first year. But thanks to the lower interest rate, that might add up to more dollars than you'd get from a fixed-rate loan. Twelve months later, you can come back for the remaining 40 percent.

That is, assuming that you want to take as much as possible up front. You can also take the loan in the form of monthly payments or a credit line. The interest rate is usually linked to LIBOR (the London Interbank Offered Rate) plus an additional amount (the "margin") set by the lender. For example, if LIBOR is 0.2 percent and the margin is 2.5 percent, your opening rate would be 2.7 percent. The rate changes every week and can't increase by more than 10 percentage points above the starting rate. Some loans have lower caps. Remember that rising rates do not affect the income you receive from your loan. Instead, they reduce the amount of equity left in the house when it's finally sold.

You can pay the fees on HECMs out of pocket but usually they're added to the cost of the loan and accumulate over time. Here's a list of your costs:

- An up-front loan insurance fee, charged by the Federal Housing Administration. You pay 0.5 percent of the appraised value of your house, provided that you borrow no more than 60 percent of the allowable amount in the first year. For example, on a $300,000 house you'd pay $1,500. The value is capped at $625,500, so the most you'd pay is $3,125.

  You can take more than 60 percent of the loan in the first year if you need the money to pay off existing mortgages, tax liens, or other debt secured by your home. But in that case, your up-front FHA fee will jump to 2.5 percent of the value of the house. On a $300,000 home, that's $7,500—$6,000 more than you'd normally have to pay. On a more expensive house, you'd pay up to $15,625. A HECM that expensive might not be worth its price.

- The annual FHA mortgage insurance premium. You pay 1.25 percent a year on the outstanding balance of the loan.

- The loan origination fee. Some lenders charge this up front; others charge zero up front but raise your interest rate a little bit. Fees are capped at 2 percent of the first $200,000 of your home's appraised value and 1 percent of the remaining amount, up to a maximum fee of $6,000. On a $300,000 home, that's $5,000 up front.

- Repair costs. Before you can borrow, an appraiser has to certify that the house is sound. If the cost of repairs will amount to no more than 15 percent of the value of the house, you can take the reverse mortgage and use some of the proceeds to make the necessary fixes. If the cost will be higher, you have to make the repairs yourself before closing the loan.

- Closing costs. You pay many of the normal closing costs that you would for any other mortgage, such as document fees, courier fees, title insurance, recording fees, credit report fees, fees for sending your lender on a world cruise (well, maybe not that last one, but close).

- Annual service fees. These are usually included in the interest rate but some lenders charge them separately.

- Compounding costs. You pay interest on all the fees added to the loan. These costs build up fast, making it less and less likely that you'll have any equity left when the house is sold.

- TALC calculation. Reverse mortgage lenders are required to calculate a total annual loan cost, or TALC, based on all projected costs over specified holding periods. You can use TALC to compare two loans. But I wouldn't call it an effective form of disclosure. More customized cost estimates can be had from a reverse mortgage counselor (see page 285) working with specialized software. To make the best use of the software, you should talk with the counselor face-to-face, not just over the phone.

The HECM's Magical Credit Line

When you take a HECM in the form of a credit line, the only money you borrow—at first—is the amount of the settlement costs. That might run $12,000 to $15,000 or more. Beyond that, the lender has simply granted you a pot of money to use whenever you want. You will owe interest only on the amount that you actually borrow. For example, say that you take a $150,000 credit line and spend $12,000 of it every year. You pay interest only on the $12,000 annual increments. The 1.25 percent FHA fee is also assessed only on the borrowed amount.

Here's the magical part. The amount of credit available grows every year by the rate of interest you pay plus the FHA insurance fee. For example, say that in the first year your loan costs a total of 3.95 percent. Interest rates rise in the second year, bringing your borrowing cost to 4.25 percent. The amount of your credit line will also grow by 4.25 percent. By taking the line at age 62 *and not using it much*, it will grow and grow. You'll have much more borrowing and spending power by the time you're 70 or 75. That gives you a good inflation hedge.

The credit line grows even if you borrow against it heavily in the early years. But in that case, interest costs will be accumulating. If you're not careful, the credit line might run out.

Using a Home Equity Conversion Mortgage Strategically

A reverse mortgage puts extra money in your pocket right away. But always consider the endgame before signing up. What if you're unable to stay in your home for life? When you sell, you might net little or nothing after repaying the loan. That would be harmful if you needed cash to buy an apartment or enter an assisted living home. Ideally, you should manage the loan so that you'll always have home equity left or, alternatively, always have a pot of savings on the side.

Here's how to think about the most common reasons for taking a HECM:

Borrowing as part of a 20- or 30-year spending plan. This savvy use of a HECM is catching on with financial planners. It's what changed my mind about the potential value of HECMs for people in their early 60s and 70s.

Say that you're planning for a 30-year retirement. In Chapter 8, you saw that you should generally spend no more than 4 or 5 percent of your savings in the first year you retire, plus annual inflation adjustments, if you need the money to last for at least 30 years. For a 20-year retirement, you might take 5 or 6 percent. But what if that rate of withdrawal doesn't deliver the standard of living you want? A HECM can help you increase your annual income by combining your savings and home equity into a single spending pot.

To do that, take a reverse mortgage as early as age 62. Set it up as a standby line of credit and—at first—don't borrow against it. Instead, pay your bills by drawing, say, 6 percent out of your savings in the first year (for a 30-year retirement) and raising that amount by the inflation rate in each following year. When your savings run low, switch to taking the money you need from your reverse mortgage credit line. By now, the credit line will be much larger than it was when you started.

There are other ways of setting up your HECM-linked spending plan. You might pay bills from your savings in a year that your investments rise in value and pay them from the HECM credit line in a year the market falls. That saves you from having to sell stocks at a lower price. Or you might pay your bills entirely from the credit line for several years, leaving your investments alone to grow.

A well-planned rate of withdrawal from both pots of money raises your current income and can lengthen the number of years your money will last. The combo might even raise the amount of money you leave to heirs, if that's a concern.

The longer you wait to take the reverse mortgage, the less efficient it will be. You need 15 to 20 years to spread out the effects of the high up-front cost. Adopt this strategy only if you've determined that you're going to stay in your home and will need a higher income to keep you there.

Borrowing to pay the bulk of your living expenses. This is the classic—and riskiest—use of a reverse mortgage. You live on your savings for as long as you can. As a last resort, you take a reverse mortgage so that you can pay the bills and stay in your house. If you borrow in the form of a lump sum and run through the money, you're stuck. You might not be able to afford the taxes and insurance anymore. At that point, the HECM lender can call in the loan and force you to sell your house. The sale price might not be high enough to cover the loan repayment. You'd be on the street without enough cash to buy something else.

People with modest incomes do have some protection against eviction, thanks to a new regulation that took effect in 2015. The lender will now set aside part of the loan proceeds to help pay your future housing expenses if there's a risk that you might not be able to afford them.

If you find yourself facing set-asides, however, perhaps you shouldn't borrow at all. Consider selling the house and using the proceeds to settle in another, lower-cost form of housing—a condominium, a rental apartment, or an apartment attached to an adult child's home. If a reverse mortgage still appeals to you, choose monthly payments or the credit line to stretch out the loan for as many years as possible.

Borrowing to eliminate your traditional mortgage. Depending on how large your mortgage is, you might be able to use the proceeds of a reverse mortgage to wipe out everything you still owe. That ends the monthly payment and raises your spendable income. This use of a HECM, however, can also be risky business. Presumably, you're taking the loan because you're having trouble meeting the mortgage payments and other bills. The new loan will help you stay in your home only if you have enough cash flow to pay your expenses from now until the horizon, inflation included. If this is another form of last-resort borrowing, you should think about selling right away and finding less costly housing somewhere else. Always consider the endgame. What will you have left if you have to sell the house and enter a nursing home in your older age?

Borrowing to buy a new house. You can buy a new house or condo with the proceeds of a reverse mortgage plus some money of your own. Like the strategy above, this eliminates monthly mortgage payments. One potential problem is that you generally have to borrow in a lump sum. That increases your interest costs, which reduces your chance of maintaining any future equity in your home. The loan will be particularly expensive if you have to take more than 60 percent of the allowable amount.

Borrowing for major home improvements. These loans will be worthwhile if you remain in the home for 15 or 20 years. But think about the cost and effort of maintaining your house as you age. Five or 10 years from now, you might decide that your future lies in an easy-care condominium. Over short terms, the reverse mortgage isn't worth its cost.

Borrowing to get rid of large amounts of credit card debt. You'll wipe out burdensome monthly payments, but that won't help much if you run up consumer debt all over again. It's better to work with a credit counselor to cut your expenses than to spend your precious home equity on the cost of clothes, furniture, and meals that you bought in the distant past. If you take the HECM and sell the house in just a few years, the reverse mortgage will have cost you more than the credit cards did.

Borrowing for fun and grandchildren. I've seen celebrity TV ads aimed at the early 60s crowd, urging you to borrow a lump sum against your home and spend it while you're still young. Take a cruise! Buy an RV! Send your grandchildren to college! All worthy goals, but will you be blowing your home equity too fast? Can you pay your bills for the rest of your life when that form of savings is gone? Taking a reverse mortgage is an expensive way of paying for a vacation. Instead of the lump sum, consider taking a credit line and using modest amounts each year to give yourself a more comfortable life. (Note that lenders love you to take lump sums because they collect high interest on all the money from the first day. That's why they pay all those aging celebrities to shill.)

Borrowing to buy a variable annuity. It's illegal for a financial adviser to pitch you directly on buying a variable annuity with the proceeds of a reverse mortgage. But nothing stops you from taking the loan and then buying an annuity or other investment at a later date. To do so, you'll have to take your loan in the form of a lump sum. That's the most expensive way to borrow and leaves you with no flexibility. Proposals like these come very close to being scams (the "adviser" makes out like a bandit thanks to the high sales commission on the annuity). Anyway, why bother? The reverse mortgage itself can provide you with a monthly income and at a lower cost than the mortgage-plus-annuity deal.

When You Sell the House, What Then?

Don't leave yourself stranded with no cash on hand. If you decide to leave your house (or have to leave for reasons of health), you'll want enough savings or home equity on hand to set up new digs. If you'll need assisted living, you'll find better choices when you can pay the bill yourself for at least the first few months before going on Medicaid (see page 111).

So don't borrow every possible dime against your home. Take the reverse mortgage in the form of a credit line and monitor how much savings and equity you have on hand each year. Maybe your house will rise in value, adding a bit to your equity, but don't rely on that—especially after paying the reverse mortgage fees. If your total pot of savings looks threatened, downsize while you still can extract some cash from the sale.

Spouse Alert! What Are Your Rights If Your Partner Dies?

When couples decide on a HECM, each partner's financial security will depend on who owns the house.

If both your names are on the deed, you'll both sign the loan agreement. Its terms apply to you equally. If one of you dies or enters a nursing home, the other spouse (or co-owner) can continue to draw payments from the HECM, as before.

If only one of you is on the deed, however, things change. Only the homeowner will be granted the HECM. The other partner will be listed as a "nonborrowing spouse."

As a nonborrower, you run a potential risk if the borrowing spouse dies or enters a nursing home for more than 12 months. You can stay in the home, provided that you keep up with the taxes, insurance, any condominium fees, and repairs. But payouts from the HECM stop. A nonborrower cannot receive monthly checks or tap the credit line. You will have to pay all the household bills from whatever other money you have. If that's not possible, the loan will fall due. If you can't repay, the lender will foreclose and you'll have to move out.

The right to continued occupancy belongs only to spouses (or official domestic partners) who were in place when the HECM was made. A spouse who entered the picture later will have to buy the house, pay off the loan, or move out.

Please note! Nonborrowing spouses have the right to stay in the home only if the HECM was made on August 4, 2014, or later. If the loan was earlier, a nonborrowing spouse can usually stay in the home, under most of the terms listed above.[4] But he or she has no occupancy "right." It's up to the lender to decide. Generally, the lender shouldn't turn you out. But it could happen, especially if the nonborrowing spouse is much younger and the lender wants to get the loan off its books.

Alert to parents who have an adult child at home, perhaps a child who's impaired: The child can't be made part of the reverse mortgage contract. If you die or move to a nursing home permanently, the child will have to buy the house or move out. If the child inherits the house there might be no home equity left to assist with his or her support. For you, a HECM might not be the right way to go.

---

4   At this writing, the nonborrowing spouse can be turned out of the house if the borrower enters a nursing home for more than 12 months. But that inconsistent rule is likely to be dropped.

Where to Find Tons of Information and Advice on Reverse Mortgages

- Go to the website mtgprofessor.com. Jack Guttentag, real estate expert and professor of finance emeritus at the Wharton School of the University of Pennsylvania, has put together the best package of information and guidance I have found anywhere. You get a sophisticated calculator showing what you can borrow at different ages and with different options. At this writing, you can even get personal advice from Jack or one of his surrogates.

  You'll also find offers from loan advisers who agree to follow best practices when arranging a reverse mortgage. They'll suggest a package of up-front cash, fixed payments, and a credit line intended to meet your needs and hold down your costs over the period you'll keep the loan. The advisers might not serve all states.

- Go to AARP.org/revmort. AARP provides questions to ask yourself before taking a reverse mortgage, a guide to these loans, and warnings about what can happen if you borrow to cover your basic expenses and then run out of money.

- Go to ReverseMortgage.org, the website of the National Reverse Mortgage Lenders Association. You'll find more info on reverse mortgages and a glossary of terms. NRMLA also posts estimates of current reverse mortgage prices. But they're consistently higher—sometimes much higher—than the prices offered by lenders on mtgprofessor.com.

CONTEMPLATING THE PAID-UP HOUSE

If you have enough cash to pay off the mortgage, should you or shouldn't you? This is one of those questions that can only be answered, "It depends."

If you have spare cash, put it first toward paying off any high-rate consumer debts. If you're still working and have wiped out your credit card debt, use the money to raise your contributions to your tax-favored retirement account such as a 401(k), IRA, or Roth IRA. If you've maxed on these contributions, go ahead and reduce your mortgage by making extra monthly payments. It's bliss to own a paid-up house by the time you retire.

If you still hold a mortgage at retirement, the calculation changes. Should you take a lump sum from your savings to pay off the remaining mortgage debt? The answer is no, if you'd have to take the money out of an IRA or 401(k). It's best to defer withdrawals (and the taxes on those withdrawals) as long as possible. Also no, if repayment would seriously deplete your cash reserves. You need to maintain enough savings so that, at modest withdrawal rates (Chapter 8), you'll have enough money to pay your daily bills, including mortgage bills, for life.

If you have enough savings to live on comfortably, however, and have savings outside a retirement account, consider using them to eliminate the loan. A paid-up house reduces your living costs, saves you interest payments, and makes you feel secure.

Some financial advisers think that, instead of paying off the mortgage, you should invest that extra money in the hope of earning a higher return. That won't work if you primarily hold bonds or bank certificates of deposit. At this writing, repaying the mortgage yields more than you'd get from high-quality bonds and CDs. You might do better, however, by using the money to buy stock-owning mutual funds and holding them for 10 years or more. With that as an option, the prepayment question becomes a matter of temperament. Are you happier trying to make some extra money in the market? Or happier getting rid of those monthly mortgage bills?

Warning! If you have a variable-rate mortgage, prepayments don't automatically shorten the term of the loan. They generally reduce the size of your monthly payments but the number of years you have to pay remains the same.

As an example of how this works, say that you have a 30-year loan and the lender resets your variable interest rate once a year. You start paying an extra $500 a month, which is applied to reducing your principal. Next year, your schedule of payments will be based on that reduced principal, stretched over the loan's original 30-year term. The monthly amount that you have to pay will probably go down. But you'll still be in debt when retirement comes.

You *can* reduce the term of a variable-rate loan, but it takes some calculating. First step is to decide how soon you want to pay it off— say, in 12 years. Using an online mortgage calculator, find out how much that will cost per month and start paying it. Next year, when your interest rate changes, fire up the calculator again. Enter the new interest rate and the amount of principal owed, and say that you want to repay over 11 years. The calculator will give you a new monthly payment, perhaps higher than the last. Do the same in each subsequent year. Result: Your job and your mortgage should end at the same time.

If you have a fixed-rate mortgage, you don't have to go through these annual calculations. Any prepayment on a fixed-rate loan automatically shortens its term.

DOWNSIZED LIVING, RETIREMENT STYLE

Maintaining a home will probably be your largest retirement expense. The better you do at holding down these costs, the more money you'll have to spend to keep yourself happy and entertained. It's surprising how pleasant a stripped-down life can be. No boxes in the attic. Fewer rooms to clean. And passports at the ready, to see the world.

11

Living on Your Life Insurance

There's money in a life insurance policy and you don't have to die to get it.

What should you do about your life insurance policy when you retire? Keep it or use the money for something else?

When you were younger you bought insurance to protect your family. It would have replaced your paycheck if you died.

Motives change, however, when you retire. You don't have a paycheck anymore (or only a small part-time paycheck) and your children are grown and gone (with luck). There might be no point to owning life insurance. That's especially true for singles, including widows and widowers. Often it makes more sense to stop paying premiums so you can increase your spendable income. If your policy has cash value, maybe you should take that money out.

On the other hand, maybe you do need insurance for the rest of your life to meet your family obligations. In that case, you should find out immediately if your policy is secure. What does "secure" mean? Well some term insurance might not be renewable without a medical exam if you wait too long to act. Policies that include a savings element, known as "cash value," might lapse unless they're restructured in some way. Most owners of cash-value insurance have no idea that their policies might not last for life. You simply assume that your family is safe, then wake up one day to discover that your "safe" policy is about to blow up.

This chapter shows you how to extract more value—in cash or in coverage—from any life insurance you own. Just hop to the section that covers the type of insurance you have. If you're not sure about the type (which is pretty common in the confusing cash-value insurance world), your policy's cover sheet or annual report will usually tell you. It will be one of the following:

Term insurance—pure insurance with no cash value. It's designed to protect your family during the years you're working and end when you retire. (See page 306.)

Guaranteed universal life—designed for older people who want to buy coverage for life at the lowest cost. There's little or no cash in the policy. It's also called no-lapse universal life (see page 307).

Whole-life insurance—designed for people who decide, at an earlier age, that they will want coverage for life. The policy builds up cash value and is generally guaranteed, provided that you pay the premiums on time (see page 313).

Universal policies with cash values—these policies are not usually guaranteed and might not last for life. Whether they do or not depends on the amount of premium you pay and the investment return you receive on the savings element. If your cash values run out, your policy will lapse (see page 316). The universal group includes *universal life insurance,* whose cash values earn varying rates of interest; *variable universal life insurance,* whose cash values are invested in a variety of mutual funds; and *indexed universal life insurance,* whose cash values are loosely (very loosely) linked to stock market performance (see page 319).

WHO STILL NEEDS LIFE INSURANCE?

You don't need coverage anymore if you have no financial dependents or if your dependents are well provided for. You'd generally be better off using the premium money to add to your income, savings, and investments.

There are several circumstances, however, when you do need (or might want) insurance for life. Consider keeping or restructuring your policy if:

- You're married but the family assets aren't large enough to support your dependent spouse if you die first. Work out how much money each spouse is likely to have if left alone and compare it with his or her probable expenses. If the survivor's likely retirement budget looks tight, hang on to the insurance for now. You can reassess at a later date.

- You married or remarried late in life and still have young children to support.

- You're responsible for a child with special needs. The insurance should be payable into a special-needs trust that supplements the support the child will get from government programs. An organization that specializes in your child's type of disability can refer you to a lawyer who understands this important branch of trust law.

- You want to leave a special legacy to a nonprofit organization.

- You own a valuable business or some illiquid real estate and will owe an estate tax. You want your heirs to be able to pay the tax without selling out.

- Your health is so poor that your life span will probably be short. The insurance payoff will be well worth the remaining premiums paid.

- Your policy is an attractive tax-deferred investment (see page 329), paying enough to compete with bonds. If you die, that investment goes to your heirs income tax free.
- You have plenty of money to live on, can afford the policy's premiums, and want to leave even more money to your heirs.

If you plan to continue holding life insurance, take steps to ensure that the policy stays in force! There are three main reasons why it could lapse: (1) It's term insurance. You'll need to take timely steps to renew it. (2) It's universal insurance and your investments haven't done well enough to maintain the cash value. You'll have to put more money into the policy or else restructure it. (3) You grow forgetful and stop paying premiums. Consider having notifications sent to one of your beneficiaries, or your financial adviser or trustee if you have one, if you forget to pay. He or she should also be asked to check every annual policy statement you get (see page 325), to be sure all is well. The last thing you want is to lose a policy that you thought you were leaving to your heirs.

THE MISSING INGREDIENT IN MOST OF THE INSURANCE MARKET: GOOD ADVICE

Whether to keep a policy, ditch it, or restructure it is a huge decision, potentially worth tens of thousands of dollars to you today or your heirs tomorrow. Your choice will depend on your family and financial situation, your health, how the policy works, how much cash value you have, and whether you think life insurance is a good investment. It will also depend on the soundness of the advice you get.

There's the rub. You can handle the questions related to term insurance pretty easily (see page 306). But cash-value policies have multiple moving parts that can be impenetrable to laypeople. If you ask an insurance agent for advice, he or she will almost certainly try to earn a commission by selling you something new. The same will be true of commissioned financial planners. They don't earn any money by advising you not to make a change or by helping you re-structure your current coverage. At their urging, you might abandon a policy that it pays to keep and buy an expensive one that's not worth its price.

The sections below give you a feel for what you might do with an existing cash-value policy. But I strongly—*strongly!*—recommend that you get specific advice from a fee-only insurance adviser. These advisers don't sell policies or take commissions, so they have no con-flicts of interest. You pay them to evaluate your current coverage and help you decide how to manage any changes you want. If it pays to get a different policy, they'll work with an agent to design one that will meet your needs at the lowest possible cost.

For the names of fee-only advisers, start with the website of adviser Glenn Daily in New York City. Daily believes so strongly in spreading the word that he publicizes his fee-only competitors (go to GlennDaily.com and click on "Links"). A run through all their web-sites will tell you the type of service that each of them offers. Fee-only advisers usually charge by the hour (in the $350 range) with the maximum number of hours agreed to in advance. James Hunt (EvaluateLifeInsurance.org) of the Consumer Federation of Amer-ica charges a low fixed fee for calculating your cash-value policy's current rate of return on investment and suggesting whether to keep it or switch. These advisers work by phone and email, hold "face-to-face" meetings online, and have clients all over the country.

Another source of advice is a fee-only financial planner. His or her office might include a life insurance specialist or might work with one of the fee-only advisers.

It helps if your adviser also consults on annuities. One option for a cash-value policy that you don't need anymore is to convert it to a low-cost annuity, which earns you a tax advantage (see page 331).

To make decisions yourself, get what's called an "in-force policy illustration" from your insurance company. It shows you whether or not your policy is currently financially sound. For information on how to use this illustration, see page 326.

One easy piece of advice: If you can afford it, pay the premiums annually. If you pay monthly or quarterly, the hidden interest rate you're charged could run anywhere from 10 to 20 percent.

MANAGING TERM INSURANCE

Odds are, you're holding at least one large term insurance policy that you bought for family protection at a younger age. Term is pure insurance with no cash values. You're paying only to keep your spouse and kids financially safe. Most policies are sold with fixed premiums and for fixed terms, such as 5, 10, 15, 20, or 30 years. When the term is up, some policies lapse. Others continue, with premiums rising sharply each year. Whenever your need for insurance ends you just stop paying premiums.

But what if you're reaching the end of the term and find that you still need coverage? You have four options. Hint: The fourth is the worst.

1. If you're in good health and need coverage for just a few more years, you can shop the term insurance market for a new 5-, 10-, or 15-year policy. Prices are still reasonable in your 50s and early 60s, especially if you don't smoke. You might not need as much coverage as you had before. For a broad look at prices, go to the website Term4Sale.com. Most term policies are convertible into permanent insurance if you should ever need it.

2. If you're in good health and will need at least some coverage for the rest of your life, switch to permanent insurance—either cash-value or no-lapse (see page 307). A fee-only life insurance adviser or fee-only financial planner will help you get good value for your money.

3. If you aren't in good health and can't buy coverage on the open

market at a reasonable price, you can generally convert your existing term policy into permanent insurance. There's no medical exam. You'll be offered whatever types of conversion policies your insurer has on the shelf at the time (ask about "no-lapse" if you're sure you want coverage that lasts for life). The premiums will be higher than they were for term but you probably won't need as large a policy. Timing is important! You must convert within the time period that the policy requires, usually in the months or weeks just before it expires but sometimes earlier. If you miss that window, you've lost your chance.

4. If you're in poor health, can't pass a health exam, and miss your chance to convert your term policy to permanent insurance, you'll be really, really sorry. You can renew your expiring term insurance regardless of health but only at an incredibly high premium. Worse, the premium will jump every year by large amounts until you can't afford it anymore. You'd keep such a policy only if you're likely to die soon. Very soon.

GREAT NEWS!

If term policies are all you've ever had or will ever need, stop reading here. You're done! Skip to Chapter 12 for tips on getting started with your lifetime income plan.

Read on, however, if you own cash-value policies or need permanent insurance guaranteed for life. Your existing policies might or might not be working out. You need to know their status and what, if anything, to do about them.

NO-LAPSE UNIVERSAL LIFE: PERMANENT INSURANCE AT THE LOWEST COST

If you want to convert your term insurance to permanent lifetime coverage, see if your insurance company offers a type of policy called *guaranteed universal life* or *no-lapse universal life.*[1] To distinguish this form of coverage from other types of universal policies, I'll always refer to it as "no-lapse." It's designed to last for life and its death benefit is guaranteed. The policy's selling point is its low premium cost compared with the other forms of permanent insurance available.

As an example, take a man, 55, in excellent but not perfect health, needing $500,000 worth of coverage. His guaranteed premium for traditional whole-life coverage might run $16,000 a year. A blended policy combining whole life with term might cost $9,800 (blended policies are generally custom designs created by fee-only insurance advisers). Guaranteed no-lapse might be had for only $6,100 a year.

No-lapse coverage is cheaper than whole life because it offers fewer benefits. In most cases, you get almost nothing in the way of cash values. You can't borrow against the policy or make cash withdrawals. If you cancel, you'll probably get no money back. On the other hand, it's a low-cost way of buying lifetime insurance at an older age. Effectively, you're buying late-age term insurance with a lifetime guarantee.

No-lapse can also be helpful to people who hold universal policies that are underfunded and in danger of collapse (see page 311). You could switch their remaining cash values into a no-lapse policy using a tax-free exchange (known as a 1035 exchange). You might also switch if you want to reduce your premiums while maintaining the same amount of coverage.

The insurance agent or adviser will propose a premium structure for your no-lapse policy, depending on whether you want to roll over money from another policy, pay regular premiums, or mix the two.

---

1   These policies might also be called *universal life with secondary guarantees.*

Salespeople sometimes misuse no-lapse policies. They sell them as replacements for sound cash-value policies that are providing decent investment returns or could be restructured as "paid up" with no more premiums due. In most of these cases, you're probably better off with your existing coverage. Consider no-lapse as an emergency buy—for essential lifetime coverage when your term policy ends or you have universal policies that are likely to fail.

There's not much to say about managing no-lapse insurance. Buy it only if you intend to keep it for life. You lose most or all of the money you invested if you eventually drop it. The policy should be structured for lifetime coverage, beyond age 100 (current practice is for the coverage to last to age 121!). Pay the premiums on time to maintain your guarantee. Or buy a policy guaranteed to be paid up in a fixed number of years.

THE VARIETIES OF CASH-VALUE INSURANCE: WHOLE LIFE, UNIVERSAL LIFE, AND "CONFUSION LIFE"

I'm really sorry to have to put you through the following pages. Trying to make a good decision about existing—and *complicated*—cash-value policies can drive you nuts.[2] What's more, there aren't many people around who will give you objective advice.

For this chapter, I've asked some fee-only advisers what they might suggest for people in various personal and financial situations. Look for the heading that describes the type of insurance you have (it will say on your policy's cover sheet if you aren't sure). Then jump to the sections that describe how to use the money stored in the policy to achieve your particular goal.

---

2 Reporting, writing, and checking this chapter drove me nuts, too.

But first, here's what you have to know about all cash-value policies regardless of type:

Cash-value policies can cover you for life, no matter how long you live. They're sold as insurance combined with an investment. The "investment" develops because of the way the policy works. Essentially, you overpay for your coverage during the policy's early years. Your overpayment goes into the policy's cash reserve. The insurance company will draw from that cash reserve in your later years when your premiums alone aren't high enough to cover the rising cost of keeping you insured.

Your cash reserve or "cash value" earns an annual investment return, income tax deferred. You can withdraw some of that money or borrow against it, depending on the type of coverage you have. When you die, your heirs will collect the death benefit income tax free. If you cancel the policy and pocket the cash value, you'll usually pay taxes on any amount that exceeds the premiums you paid.

There's a difference between the policy's death benefit and its face amount. The "face" is the amount of insurance that you contracted to buy—say, $500,000. The death benefit is the amount the policy actually pays. It could be higher than the face amount if you used the policy's earnings or dividends to buy more insurance. It could be lower if you've borrowed against the policy or made cash withdrawals.

Cash-value policies come in two general types: *whole-life insurance,* which carries guarantees (see page 313), and a family of policies called *universal life insurance*[3] (see page 316), which depend for success on the size of the premium you pay and the policy's investment returns.

---

3   Excluding guaranteed universal (or no-lapse) life, which generally has no cash value.

You have to keep your policy's cash values up. Otherwise, your coverage might lapse. For many policyholders, this comes as a nasty surprise. You assume all is well as long as you pay the premiums on time. But the level of cash in your policy is critical, too. The insurance company taps that cash, year by year, to cover the policy's internal costs. If the cash value shrinks to a low enough level, the costs will be higher than the cash available. At that point, your policy will lapse.

The premiums for cash value policies are generally set at a high enough level to pay for the coverage as long as you live. But sometimes, things happen that undermine that grand design. Here are the three most common:

1. *You take a loan against the policy.* Often, insurance agents sell this as one of life insurance's virtues. Policy loans are supposedly cheap. On the surface, they might appear to cost just 1 or 2 percent. But insurers can raise the loan's internal cost in ways that you won't notice because you're not paying out of pocket. That loan is probably costing you 5 to 8 percent, compounded every year. The cost comes out of your cash value. After many years, the size of the loan (including interest) could endanger your coverage. You can reduce this risk by paying the loan interest out of pocket, but few people do. Loans also reduce the policy's death benefit.

2. *You make cash withdrawals.* With universal policies, you can take money directly out of the cash value without paying interest. If you take too much, however, your cash value might eventually drain away. Withdrawals also reduce the death benefit the policy will pay.

3. *The investment gains on your cash value are insufficient.* Universal policies depend on specific investment gains to maintain a high enough cash value to keep the coverage in force. If your investments do poorly, you'll have to add cash to the policy

yourself, either in a lump sum or by raising the amount you're paying in premiums.

If your cash value runs down, for whatever reason, you'll face a classic surrender squeeze. Either bulk up the cash in your policy again—by repaying the loan or replacing some of the withdrawals you took—or else let the policy lapse. If you can't afford to repay (the amounts might be large), you'll get even more bad news. If the size of your loan or withdrawals exceeds the amount you paid in premiums, you'll be taxed on the difference at ordinary income rates. The same is true if the lapse is due to insufficient investment gains. You'll wind up with no insurance, no death benefit, and a big potential income tax bill on your hands.

Insurance policies don't get into trouble right away. It might be 15 or 20 years before you reach the danger point. But by then, you might be 80 or 85 and counting on the coverage to support a dependent spouse. So keep track of your cash values (see page 325). There are creative ways of addressing the problem if you start early enough.

Don't buy a cash-value policy as a source of future tax-free retirement income. These policies should be purchased *solely* to provide yourself with insurance for life. Often, however, they're sold as a tax-avoidance scheme. On paper, it works in three steps: (1) Buy a large policy and let the cash build up. (2) When you retire, start taking loans or direct withdrawals against its cash value. That "income" will be tax deferred. (3) When you die, the remaining proceeds of the policy will pass to your family income tax free. The agent will give you a beautiful illustration showing how everything works. It looks like a perfect way to beat the IRS.

But is it? The risk in this retirement-income strategy, and it's a big one, is that you'll live longer than you expected or your policy's investment returns won't be as high as you hoped. You start out happy—taking regular loans or withdrawals and using the money to pay your retirement bills. A few years later, however, you might discover that the policy's cash isn't going to last. Unless you start repaying the loans or replacing the cash, you and your heirs could lose the life insurance that you carried all these years. You'll be pretty peeved at your insurance agent for not being clear about this possibility. But you're stuck, with no good way out and perhaps a large income-tax bill. (You can rescue the policy by dying, but that's not recommended.)

Don't underestimate your longevity! For healthy people, taking policies that end at age 90 or 95 isn't safe anymore. If you live to that age, the insurer might pay you the face amount of the policy in cash, net of any loans or withdrawals. If that happens, the proceeds become taxable to the extent that they exceed the premiums you paid.

MAKING DECISIONS ABOUT YOUR CASH-VALUE INSURANCE POLICY

What should you do with your cash-value policy after you retire? Drop it and reinvest the money somewhere else? Keep it? Restructure it? Switch to a different type of policy? Your decision will depend entirely on your personal financial needs. Look for the type of cash-value policy you own in the following pages, then read what you can do with it.

Whole-Life Insurance: How It Works

A whole-life insurance policy—the most conservative kind—guarantees you coverage for life provided that you pay the premiums on time and don't take unsustainable loans against the cash value. You pay a fixed premium every year. Alternatively, you can choose to pay higher premiums up front so the policy will be paid in full by a certain age, such as 65. The company usually pays bondlike interest on your cash values but only if you hold the insurance long enough. The interest rate isn't specifically disclosed.

The best whole-life policies, called "participating policies," pay dividends and are mostly sold by mutual life insurance companies. You can use those dividends to buy additional paid-up insurance, which raises the death benefit that will be paid to your survivors. Alternatively, dividends can be paid to you in cash or used to reduce your premiums.

Nonparticipating policies, sold by companies without "mutual" in their names, pay no dividends. Policyholders simply pay their premiums, earn interest on their cash values, and at death get the fixed payout that they contracted for. These are generally the types of policies sold by mail or on TV. Most agents stick with participating policies.

You *must* pay whole-life premiums regularly, with no interruption and on time. If you miss a month or more, the insurance company will usually collect the premiums through automatic loans against your cash values. The loan interest will compound. If that goes on long enough, the cash value will run out and the policy will lapse—even though you thought it was guaranteed. "We see this often," says Michael Kitces, director of wealth management and partner at the Pinnacle Advisory Group in Columbia, Maryland (kitces.com). "It's one of the ugliest insurance scenarios and the hardest to fix."

What You Can Do with Whole-Life Policies

If you decide that you don't need life insurance anymore: You can stop paying premiums on your whole-life policy, cancel it, and pocket the cash value. Ask the company whether any income taxes might be due. If the policy is worth less than the premiums you paid, you might convert the cash value, income tax free, into a variable annuity (see page 331).

If you don't need life insurance but your policy is paying an attractive rate of interest: A few whole-life mutual insurance companies are paying a tax-deferred 4 to 4.5 percent on your cash values after all expenses. That's an attractive addition to a fixed-income portfolio. You might keep the policy for a few more years with plans to harvest the gains at some point in the future. For a quick way of calculating the current gain, see page 329.

If you need some insurance coverage but don't want to pay premiums anymore: You can use your cash value to fund a smaller, paid-up policy from the same insurance company. Or see what you can do with dividends—if you've been using them to buy paid-up additions to the policy's face amount, start applying them toward lowering your premium costs instead. Some companies offer a partial surrender—reducing the face amount, premium, and cash value proportionately. If you're insurable, shop around. You could use the cash value in your whole-life policy to buy a lower-cost, paid-up no-lapse policy guaranteed for life (see page 307).

Large whole-life policies often are blends of whole life, term insurance, and paid-up additions bought with your annual dividend. With blends, you can lower the premiums and death benefit by dropping the term portion (some holders don't realize they own a blend). Be sure you keep track of your cash values in a blended policy. If the dividends aren't sufficient, your cash value could run down.

If you want to keep the coverage but need more income: You can collect the dividends in cash. Or cash out the value of the extra, paid-up insurance that you bought with previous dividends.

If you have policy loans: The interest is accruing inside the policy. If the loans are large or go on too long, your cash value could be reduced to zero. In that case, you'll lose your guarantee. Your whole-life policy will lapse. Anyone with a loan should immediately get an in-force policy illustration to see if you're headed for trouble (see page 325). It's often cost-effective to pay off the loan rather than let the policy lapse, especially if lapsing will create income tax problems.[4] To reduce the lapse risk, use your dividends to pay the loan interest or pay the interest out of pocket.

If you're in poor health: It pays to find a way to keep the full policy in force. If you live just a few more years, the return on your investment will be high—not for you but for your heirs, who will remember you fondly. If it's impossible to keep the full policy or even a reduced policy in force, consider putting it up for sale (see page 332).

Universal Life Insurance with Cash Values: How These Policies Work

Universal life policies are flexible—perhaps too flexible. There is usually no guarantee that your coverage will last for life—a point that the agent might have obscured. There's no fixed premium. You decide how much you want to pay, subject to certain minimums and maximums. Your cash values will earn varying rates of return depending on changes in the stock or bond markets. When setting your premium, you have to make an assumption about what those future returns are likely to be. Together—the premiums and the investment returns—have to add enough to the policy's cash value, year by year, to cover the rising cost of keeping you insured. If that doesn't happen, the coverage will eventually lapse.

Clearly, universal policies have to be monitored regularly to keep them on track, and most of them aren't. Your original agent is probably out of the monitoring business. Many such policies are failing even as we speak. One of them might be yours.

The good news is that you can keep your policy healthy or manage

---

4　When repaying any loan, including an insurance policy loan, your return on investment equals the loan interest rate. So repaying, say, a 6 percent policy loan gives you a 6 percent return, guaranteed.

it back to health once you know what to look for. It also helps to buy from a low-cost provider such as TIAA-CREF (TIAA-CREF.org).

Universal policies usually start on a firm financial footing. Your agent or adviser will suggest a premium that, hypothetically, could keep the policy in force until you reach some advanced age—say, at least 110. That premium level assumes that your cash values will earn a certain investment return (for example, 5 percent a year) and that there will be no unexpected rise in the policy's future costs.

You can choose to do one of two things with your policy's earnings. *Option 1:* Hold the death benefit level and use the earnings to create a larger cash value—good for your personal future. It's the choice that advisers generally recommend. *Option 2:* Use the policy's earnings to raise the death benefit over the years—good for your heirs. This choice will cost more as you grow older. At some point you'll probably want to switch to the level benefit, Option 1.

You don't have to accept the agent's suggested premium for either option. You might decide to pay more to protect your policy in the event of higher costs and poorer investment returns than your agent predicts. Or you might pay a lower premium because, at the moment, your budget is tight. Your insurance agent might even have advised you to choose lower premiums, based on a rosy assumption about how much your cash value is going to earn, such as 8 percent or 10 percent. You might stop paying premiums for a while and then start again (if you stop, you will probably have to pay higher premiums later, to catch up).

You're allowed to make cash withdrawals against universal policies. No interest is charged (there might be a $25 fee). Withdrawals are income tax free up to the amount of premium that you've paid into the policy. After that they're taxed as ordinary income in the current year (you'll get a 1099-R). Once you've reached the tax-free limit you could start taking loans. Both withdrawals and loans reduce your policy's death benefit and cash value.

However you decide to pay the premiums or make withdrawals,

one thing remains true: Your cash values need to keep going up. If they start declining, your policy could eventually lapse. To be sure that it lasts for your lifetime you might have to restructure it or put more money in.

It is easy to check on the status of your policy's cash value. Every year, the insurance company sends you an annual statement (see page 325). It tells you precisely how much longer your policy will last if everything continues as is. If you're healthy and the statement shows that the policy will fail before you reach at least 110, you should act right away. The sooner you focus on the problem the easier and less expensive the rescue will be.

You should pay particular attention if you bought your universal policy 10 or 20 years ago. Back then, insurance salespeople were illustrating higher rates of interest than have actually occurred and higher long-term returns on stocks. They also might have projected lower expenses than your insurance company is actually charging (expenses come out of your cash value). If you have raised the amount you're paying in premiums, your policy is probably still doing fine. If not, your coverage could be at risk.

There are three types of universal policies. They all follow the general rules explained on pages 316 and 317, but offer different ways of investing your cash values. Here are your choices:

Universal life insurance. Its yield depends on the interest rate, after expenses, that the insurance company pays each year. When you first bought the policy, the interest rate might have been projected at 6 or 7 percent. Now it's probably around its guaranteed minimum of 3 or 4 percent. Please note: The stated interest rate, including the guaranteed minimum, is not necessarily what your cash values actually earn. It's merely the credited rate before expenses are taken out. You're earning less than you think—perhaps not even enough to keep the policy alive.

Variable universal life insurance. This policy ties your cash value, and sometimes your death benefit, to the investment performance of stock and bond mutual funds. You decide how to invest the cash by picking from a menu of funds (called "subaccounts") that the insurance company provides. If the markets do well, after policy expenses, your cash value rises. Your cash value falls if your investments underperform.

There's a hidden catch to the returns you might be expecting on variable universal life. The salesperson will show you what the policy pays if it earns an average of, say, 8 percent over 30 years. But no market rises at a steady pace. How well your investment does in actual dollars depends not on averages but on how much the market rises or falls each day. Every time the market drops, your cash value goes down and—without your knowing it—the policy's internal cost of keeping you covered might go up. That extra cost leaves you with less cash in the policy when the market turns around, making it harder to get your cash value back on track.

That said, buyers of variable universal life should move most or all of their money into its stock-owning index fund options (if offered) or two or three stock funds that are similarly broadly based. Forget the bond funds. Their returns probably won't cover their share of the policy's costs. Going big on stocks is the most likely way of making variable universal insurance work. If you'd rather not hold stocks, you shouldn't be in this kind of policy at all. (One exception: You might want to switch into the fixed-interest account, despite its low return, if you're in late retirement. You'd want to avoid a large market loss that might require you, suddenly, to put up more money to keep the policy alive.)

Indexed universal life. Here your cash values are linked, indirectly, to the performance of a stock market index, not counting dividends. You're credited with a gain when stock prices go up over a certain period of time. When stock prices go down, you don't take a loss; instead, your cash values are credited with zero for that period. That's the sales pitch: all gain, no loss.

You don't necessarily get the whole gain. There's an annual cap on how much you can earn, which the insurance company can lower whenever it wants. Also, your credited gain, if any, might not resemble stock returns as you know them. They're often calculated over monthly or even daily periods and then averaged, producing returns that don't follow the market at all. The policy's costs are subtracted from your cash value and all the fees are not disclosed. To provide the "no loss" guarantee, the insurance company incurs hedging expenses and invests most of the remaining premium money in bonds. As a result, it's going to be hard for an indexed policy to produce anything better than a bondlike return, if that. If your cash values decline, you might have to pay more money—maybe a lot more money—to keep the coverage going. Of all the overblown and misleading sales pitches in the insurance world, those for indexed universal life might be the worst.

What You Can Do with Cash-Value Universal Policies

These policies vary tremendously in the personal choices they offer, depending on the insurance company and the particular contract. It's almost impossible for a consumer to figure out how to get the most from the money they're spending. I'll say it again: Get the advice of a fee-only insurance adviser or competent fee-only financial planner. For a modest cost you could save (or rescue) tens of thousands of dollars in cash value for yourself or insurance payouts for your heirs. At the very least, get an in-force policy illustration (see page 326) before meeting with an agent. You need to know how much cash you have in the policy and whether or not it's running down. Before making any decision about keeping or canceling universal life, compute the net investment return on your cash value (see page 329). If it's negative or low, chuck the policy with a smile on your face.

In general, here are your options if you own any sort of cash-value universal insurance:

If you're healthy and decide that you don't need life insurance anymore: You can stop paying premiums, cancel the policy, and pocket (or invest) the cash surrender value. This makes especially good sense if the cash values are shrinking or growing ve-e-ry slowly. If the cash amounts to less than you've paid in premiums, you can walk away clean. Alternatively, make use of the loss by transferring the money, temporarily, to a low-cost tax-deferred annuity (see page 331). Delay your cancellation until the surrender charge expires if you're close to that magic year. If you'll get back more than you paid in premiums, you'll owe ordinary income tax on the excess.[5]

If you don't need life insurance but your policy is financially sound and yielding an attractive return: Some (not many) universal policies might be paying a tax-deferred 4 percent or more after all expenses. That makes them a nice addition to your fixed-income investments. You might want to leave the policy in force and perhaps tap the cash at some future date. Before making this decision, however, scout out the true net investment return (after costs). Hint: It's less than the stated interest rate. If you've held the policy for a long time and have a large gain that's potentially taxable, the argument for keeping the coverage gets stronger, says fee-only insurance adviser Scott Witt of New Berlin, Wisconsin (wittactuarialservices .com). You might want to hold it until death and pass the entire proceeds to your heirs income tax free.

If you need some insurance for life but not as much as you have now: You can reduce the policy's death benefit. You might bring it

---

5 Depending on your income, a taxable payout from any type of insurance policy might bump you, temporarily, into a higher income tax bracket, a higher bracket for taxes on Social Security, or even into the lofty bracket for Medicare surcharges.

down to an amount that can be supported with a smaller annual premium, or use the current cash value to create a policy paid up for life. If you're insurable, consider using the current cash value to buy a smaller no-lapse universal policy from another company in a tax-free exchange. Always ask about the surrender charge. If it's still in force, you might want to delay the change until the surrender-charge period expires.

If you need full insurance coverage for a few more years but can't afford the premiums: You can stop paying premiums on any type of universal policy at any time. Depending on how the policy is structured, it might stay in force with no reduction in the death benefit until the cash value runs out. Ask the company for an in-force illustration showing what would happen if you stopped paying today. You'll see how many years you'd be covered and what the death benefit would be. If you've been using the policy's earnings to increase your death benefit, tell the company that you now want to use them to reduce the premiums. That would stretch out your coverage for a little longer.

If you plan to let the coverage lapse a few years from now, base your end date on your dependents' needs, not on the age you think you'll die. You cannot predict a likely life span based on family history or a health condition that's under control. Better to assume a long life and reduce your policy's death benefit than to keep a high death benefit for a shorter period and hope you die in time.

I've seen this choice up close and personal. Years ago, I had a friend who was seriously ill. His large universal policy was heading for lapse in a little over three years. Instead of reducing its face value to make it last longer, he gambled his wife's financial security on the guess that he'd die before the coverage ran out. He made it, just four months shy of the lapse date. But what if he hadn't? It's hard to describe that couple's pain and conflicted emotions as he went into a slower-than-expected decline.

If you want to keep at least some coverage for life but need more income now: You can take cash directly out of the policy. It's not a loan so you don't pay any interest. The withdrawals are income tax free up to the amount of the premiums you paid, which might be substantial. After that, you'll owe current taxes on any additional amounts you take. Be careful not to withdraw too much. You need to keep enough cash in the policy to keep it from falling apart.

Once you've exhausted the cash withdrawals, you could borrow against the policy, income tax free. That's generally not a good idea unless you plan to pay the money back (see page 311). Besides, there might not be much cash left to borrow against.

If you bought the policy as a way to save for retirement: Supposedly, you can start taking regular withdrawals from your cash value as a form of tax-free retirement income. This will work only if you put plenty of cash into the policy every year, its investments perform like a charm, and you die while there's still some cash value left. If you withdraw too much and live too long, the policy will lapse. You might be left with a big income-tax bill and no insurance for your heirs. Before executing this risky strategy, get an in-force policy illustration that shows the effect of your intended withdrawals on your policy's longevity. You might change your mind.

If you still have family obligations and don't want to reduce the size of your policy: Pony up whatever money is needed to keep the current policy going. Or, if you're insurable, consider using its cash value to buy a no-lapse universal policy from another company if it's a better deal. Two other options are the low-load universal life and variable universal life policies offered by TIAA-CREF (TIAA-CREF.org). You can avoid any taxes on the switch by using a 1035 exchange.

If you bought variable universal life as a "buy and hold" investment: Take another look at the policy's investment choices. Your helpful salesperson might have steered you into a "diversified portfolio" of 15 or 20 expensive funds, half in stocks and half in bonds. The bond funds probably aren't covering their share of the policy's costs. You'll save money and grow your cash values faster, over many years, by switching most or all of the money to lower-cost stock index funds, if the company offers them. Or choose no more than three broad-based, low-cost stock funds, focused on large and small U.S. stocks and international stocks. Note that there will be annual limits on how much you can switch out of your bond accounts, so reorienting your investments might take a while. (Owning some bond funds and fixed-interest accounts might be appropriate much later in your retirement if a big decline in stocks could wipe out your cash value.)

If you're someone who will switch out of stocks or quit paying premiums when the market falls, you should drop this type of policy. It absolutely will not work out for you.

If you've just discovered that your universal policy is close to collapse and you still need at least some life insurance: You'll hate this. You were sold the policy as something that would stay in force as long as you paid the recommended premium. You will yell at your insurance agent or financial adviser. After the yelling, you will have to decide what to do.

There are several ways of saving the policy, or at least part of it. You can put in more money to bring the cash value up to a level that will support the current or reduced death benefit. If you have an increasing death benefit you can switch to a level death benefit. If there's a loan against the policy, tell your insurer to use any payment you send to reduce the loan. Repaying the loan might cost you less than the tax you'd owe if the policy lapsed.

If you're in very, very poor health and your policy has a level death benefit: Quit paying premiums if it's clear that you'll die pretty soon.

Put that money into the bank instead. Your heirs will get the insurance and the bank account, too. Morbid, I guess, but good advice. A new policy illustration will show you what the death benefit is likely to be and whether you have enough cash to keep the policy in force.

If you've just discovered from your annual report or in-force illustration that your policy has enough cash value to last well beyond your likely life span: So here's yet another case where you should quit paying premiums. With universal insurance, the bills you get for premiums are optional, not required. Any unneeded money that you put into the policy helps the insurance company, not your survivors.

HOW TO FIND OUT IF A CASH-VALUE POLICY IS FAILING OR SUCCEEDING

You have two ways of checking on your policy's health: the annual statement, which comes to you by mail or email automatically, and the latest in-force policy illustration, which you have to ask for. The information in these free reports not only shows whether your policy needs repairs, it also helps you decide what to do about your coverage going forward.

The annual statement. Opening and reading this statement is the quickest and easiest way to check on how your universal policy is doing. It tells you specifically how much longer your coverage will stay in force if everything remains the same—meaning that you continue to pay the same premium, the insurer levies the same internal policy costs, you receive the same gross rate of interest or investment return that you're receiving now, and the status of any policy loans remains unchanged. For example, the statement might say, "If you continue to pay the planned premium under current charges, your policy will continue until November 2036." At this writing, that would be only 20 years away. If you're 65, you should read that date as a bright red light, flashing "Pay Attention! Fix This Now!" You don't want to reach 85 and discover an insurance fail. By then, your coverage would be *very* expensive to save. If you're in reasonably good health and need a policy that lasts for life, you want the annual statement to show that you're safely covered to age 110 or more.

The statement also discloses how much you paid in premiums this year, what charges were levied, how much your cash values grew (or shrank), how much you've borrowed (including interest owed), and the size of your death benefit. Some companies provide even more details.

Ignore any projections showing *guaranteed values*. They're misleading and often scary. The "guaranteed" numbers assume that, starting now, the insurer will levy the maximum insurance charge that the policy allows, making the lapse date look pretty close. That's certainly not going to happen right away and is highly unlikely to happen in the future. Concentrate only on the projection of *current* charges.

The annual statement for a whole-life policy contains much less information—generally, the cash value, the death benefit, the current dividend, and the gain in your cash value over the past year.

The in-force policy illustration. This is a multipage computer printout supplied by the agent or life insurance company. Like the annual statement, it shows how your policy will perform if nothing changes over the next 30 or 40 years. But here you'll see the potential change in your future cash values year by year. If there's any risk that your coverage will lapse, the in-force illustration will catch it first.

The illustration presents you with several columns of numbers. Some of them show guaranteed values. You should ignore them, as explained above. They overstate your likely costs, which makes the policy look riskier than it actually is.

The columns that matter show your current costs and returns and are known as *nonguaranteed values*.

Here's what to look at:

- **Premiums.** This is the sum the insurance company expects you to pay every year. Holders of universal policies can get illustrations based on lower or higher premiums.
- **Current cash value.** In general, your illustrated cash values should rise in every future year. If you're holding a universal policy and cash values are going down, you're not paying enough in premiums to keep the policy alive. A blank or a zero in the cash-value column shows the year that the policy is currently scheduled to lapse. If that zero comes too soon, you should think about raising your premium, restructuring your policy, or dropping it and investing your money somewhere else. If the cash value extends the policy well beyond any reasonable life span, get an illustration showing what happens if you stop paying premiums. You might have paid enough already.

  If you hold a universal life policy, the column showing future cash values is based on the rate of interest currently being credited by the insurer. In real life, your cash values will grow by a lesser amount because of the policy's costs (insurance companies generally don't adjust for costs in the cash-value columns). Don't believe an insurance agent or financial adviser who tells you that the rate you see is what you get.

  On a variable or indexed universal policy, the cash-value column reflects a future, hypothetical market return, projected—at the same rate—year after year. On many in-force illustrations, that return might be, well, *hopeful*. The agent might be projecting, say, a steady 8 percent. Get a second illustration at a lower rate of return to get a better feel for your risks. The illustration also shows the potential results if your investments earn zero over the years. (No

illustration shows the outcome if the value of your investments declines—a bit of a gap, I'd say.)

If you hold a whole-life policy, the illustrated cash value
will normally climb every year. These policies are guaranteed
not to run out. You might lose the guarantee, however, if you
borrow against the policy. A rising loan will send the cash value
down. If the illustration shows it going to zero in the future,
you should restructure the policy or start repaying the loan.

- **Current cash surrender value.** This is the amount of money
  you'll net if you want to cash out of your policy. It's also the
  amount you can use toward buying another policy or restructuring the policy you have. If you've held the policy for a sufficient number of years, the cash value and the cash surrender
  value should be the same.

- **Death benefit.** If you hold a universal policy, look down this
  column to see how the death benefit changes. If it's rising,
  you're using your policy's earnings to increase the payout to
  your beneficiaries. As you age, this strategy gets expensive.
  Consider using the earnings to build higher cash values while
  keeping the death benefit level. If you hold a whole-life policy,
  the death benefit rises if you're using your dividends to buy
  additional paid-up insurance. Again, you can level the death
  benefit by using your dividends to reduce your premiums.

- **Loans.** If you borrowed against the policy, there's a column
  showing how much you've borrowed and the projected annual increase as the loan interest compounds. Loans reduce
  your cash value and death benefit. You can get an illustration
  showing what would happen if you paid the loan interest out
  of pocket.

- **Cash withdrawals.** If, as a holder of a universal policy, you
  want to plan for cash withdrawals at some point in the future, you can have them illustrated. You'll see the effect on

your policy's cash value and how the withdrawals shorten your policy's life.

Get a new illustration every year! Small increases in policy expenses or decreases in credited rates of return can balloon into big reductions in cash values over many years. It's especially important to keep checking a variable or indexed policy. The illustrations don't show what happens to your policy if the stock market falls, let alone how fast or slowly the cash values might recover.

HOW TO CALCULATE YOUR POLICY'S INVESTMENT GAINS (OR LOSSES)

Here's a down-and-dirty way of checking whether an older policy is worth keeping for its investment value.

From the policy's annual statement or in-force illustration, take the cash surrender value at the end of last year. Add the premium you paid this year. Divide it into this year's final cash surrender value. Eliminate the "1" before the decimal point. The result is the latest annual percentage return on your investment.

For example, say that last year's cash surrender value was $135,000. You paid $3,700 in premiums this year, so you now have $138,700 into the policy. Your current surrender value is $145,000. Dividing $145,000 by $138,700 gives you 1.045. Eliminate the "1" and you get a cash-on-cash investment return of .045, which is 4.5 percent. Tax deferred. Compared with the rates on Treasuries and corporate bonds, that's an investment worth keeping for at least another year.

The numbers above come from an actual Northwestern Mutual whole-life policy held for 21 years. In that case, there was no surrender charge. You might get a higher rate of return from a universal policy in a year when the surrender charge declines rapidly.

If you apply this calculation to your own policy and don't get a "1" in front of the result, it's yielding a negative return. You are paying more to the insurance company than you are getting back. That's common in a policy's early years but it shouldn't persist. Note that you can be earning negative returns even if the policy's cash value is going up. If you're losing money on your investment and don't need life insurance, you'd be better off cashing the policy in and investing in mutual funds.

USING YOUR POLICY FOR LONG-TERM CARE EXPENSES

Many whole-life and universal insurance policies let you use part or most of the face amount, income tax free, to cover long-term care expenses. It's called an *accelerated benefit rider* and is usually provided at no extra cost. If you have the rider, you might consider keeping your policy as a health insurance backup.

Alternatively, you might be offered a hybrid policy: long-term care insurance packaged with either cash-value life insurance or a lifetime annuity. The pitch for both of these products is "dual use." If you become ill, these hybrids provide money for long-term care. If you don't need care, you can use the cash in the form of a policy loan or a lifetime annuity.

There's a catch, natch. If you take a policy loan or some income from the annuity, you lose the guarantee that the hybrid will cover your long-term care for life. If you use it for long-term care expenses, you'll reduce the size of the annuity or your family's future insurance payout (put another way, you'll be paying your LTC bills with your own or your family's money). So much for "dual use."

Hybrids cost more than traditional long-term care insurance because of all the extra insurance or annuity fees. Your premiums are generally fixed but insurers can short-change you, secretly, by holding down the internal interest rate that's paid on your investment.

If you're interested in a hybrid, you should buy it with money that you never otherwise intend to touch. If you need long-term care, the product will pay. If you never need care, your heirs will receive the proceeds of the insurance policy or the money in the annuity.

A TAX-SMART WAY OF HANDLING A CASH-VALUE POLICY THAT YOU DON'T NEED ANYMORE

If you no longer need life insurance, there's no point paying for it. But instead of pocketing the cash, think about switching it into an annuity for a short period of time, using a tax-free 1035 exchange. It has some valuable tax advantages.

If you'll get more money out of the insurance policy than you paid in premiums: You'll owe ordinary income taxes on the amount of the payout that exceeds the premiums you paid. A large enough payout might bump you into a higher tax bracket. To avoid that cost, don't take the insurance payout all at once. Instead, roll it into, say, a five-year immediate-pay annuity, using a tax-free exchange. You'll get regular monthly payments that are partly taxable and partly tax free. If you're in your 60s, the annuity payments might help you put off taking Social Security until you reach 70.

If you'll get less money out of the policy than you paid in: You have a financial loss that can't be deducted on your tax return. But you can transfer the loss to a variable annuity in a tax-free 1035 exchange. Choose a low-cost annuity and put your money into one of its broad-based stock-owning mutual funds. Any investment gains that you make in the future will be income tax free up to the amount of the loss you transferred. Once you've used up the loss, you can cash in the annuity and invest the money in regular mutual funds. Outside the annuity, long-term gains will be taxed at the low capital gains rate.

I have many reservations about variable annuities (see page 138). But for this purpose, they're ideal. Go for the low-cost annuities offered by Vanguard or TIAA-CREF. They have no early surrender charge.

SHOULD YOU SELL YOUR POLICY?

Are you 68 to 70 or older? Got a universal life policy? Got no bene-ficiary who could use your policy's payout? Want to pocket its cash? Not feeling too well these days? You might be able to sell the policy to an investor for substantially more than its current cash value. The investor will pay any required premiums while you live and collect the payout when you die. Younger people with short life spans can also apply.

Investors are primarily interested in universal life policies with face values of at least $250,000 to $500,000. They might also consider a term policy that's convertible into paid-up cash-value insurance.

The amount of money you'll be offered will depend on your health (investors like sellers with life expectancies of no more than 10 years who are doddering a bit) as well as such things as the premium amount, the cash value, and how old the policy is. The investors will want your medical records and access to your doctors. They'll keep checking for your name on Social Security's death index and might even contact you or your representative from time to time.

Don't sell your policy if you still have heirs who need protection. If you can't afford the current premiums, pay them out of the policy's cash values. When you die, your beneficiaries will get the payout. If you outlive them, you can sell the policy at a later date and for more money because you'll be that much older. Many insurance compa-nies let you use part of your policy's face amount to cover the costs of a dread disease or long-term care. That's generally better than a desperation sale.

If you want to explore a sale, you can find a life settlement bro-ker through life insurance agents, financial planners, and insurance consultants. The Life Insurance Settlement Association (LISA.org) lists the names of its members on the Web. If the policy's sale price exceeds the amount you paid in premiums, the excess is taxed as ordinary income. Money you receive in excess of the cash value can be taxed as a capital gain. If you sell within two years of death, the proceeds might be income tax free.

KEEP TRACK OF YOUR LIFE INSURANCE!

Keep your policies (or the records of them) in a special file for your heirs. Some people lose track of their policies, especially if they're paid up and the company is no longer sending bills. No surprise—insurance companies can be, well, let's say, "careless" about finding out whether you're still alive. It's easy to check. All they have to do is scan Social Security's death records. Instead, they might sit on the money and wait to see if a beneficiary makes a claim. That can happen even when the company knows you're dead.

Some state regulators have started requiring insurance companies to check death records and make serious efforts to locate beneficiaries. New York passed this rule in 2011. Since then, almost 8,000 beneficiaries have received $52.6 million—money they were entitled to but that the insurance companies didn't bother paying. Matches have been found on another 28,900 policies, which are currently being processed.

In most states, however, it's primarily up to you to see that your family gets the insurance proceeds you paid for. That might surprise you, but it's a fact.

Insurance companies can't hang on to unpaid policies forever. After a certain number of years—typically seven—the money is supposed to be sent to the unclaimed property bureau of the state where the policy was purchased. Every few years, potential heirs should check the appropriate state bureaus to see if they're holding any money in the name of the person who bought the policy. Find the bureau through the National Association of Unclaimed Property Administrators at unclaimed.org. You'll be asked for the Social Security number. While you're at it, enter your own name, too. I did that two years ago and found two royalty payments that had never reached me. Claiming was simple; the check came right away.

In another situation, you might simply neglect to pay the premiums because you're losing track of your financial life. It's awful but it happens. These policies could eventually expire unless someone is watching. You might consider having payment notification sent to a responsible child who will see that the coverage doesn't lapse. Adult children who step in to help with parents' finances should be sure to find out if any life insurance premiums are due. Ask the agent or insurance company for a copy of the most recent annual statement and an in-force policy illustration. The company will send you a copy of the policy and the beneficiary form, too.

READ YOUR MAIL!

Many of you—I'm sorry to have to say this—simply aren't opening the mail from your insurance company. If you're reading the annual statement, you aren't necessarily focusing on what it says. Your policy might be programmed to expire. The sooner you repair it, the cheaper and easier the fix will be.

Forget what you thought you knew when you bought your cash-value policy. Life insurance isn't forever anymore.

12

Just Tell Me What to Do

Whew! At last!

Sit back. Relax. Take your shoes off and reflect. Millions of others have passed through these same emotional and financial stages, from "worker" to "retiree," and emerged into a different life. Maybe they prepared for retirement and walked toward it gladly. Maybe not. Either way, time is ticking. Once you get over the surprise of your age (I've been surprised ever since I turned 50), a second surprise comes barreling along behind. You have 20, 30, or even 40 years ahead. What are you going to make of them?

During your journey, your friends and colleagues are your support group and vital source of information. If you're in the preretirement stage, talk to people who have already jumped. If your paycheck has just stopped, talk to fellow retirees about how they found, or are finding, their path. We need our children for love and visits but at this stage not so much for advice. We learn the most from people like us who share our challenges and hopes.

START WITH A PLAN (YOU KNEW I WAS GOING TO SAY THAT, RIGHT?)

Three numbers matter when you sketch a retirement plan. Which ones matter most depend on where you stand on the retirement spectrum.

Preretirement. Your number is the gap between the annual income you can count on after you retire and the amount of money you think you'll need to pay your bills. Chapter 2 helps you figure this out. If the gap is wide and your savings small, keep working (if you can). There's no better preretirement plan than to maintain your paycheck, add to your retirement savings, and put off taking Social Security for a few more years. You might also practice living on a retirement budget to see what might have to change.

Retirement. Your number is the amount of cash you decide to hold in your cash reserve (Chapter 9). It should cover any gap between your expected income and expenses for the next two years. That's your financial safety net, so you won't have to worry about what your retirement investments are doing every minute.

Postretirement. Your number is the size of the first withdrawal you take from your invested savings to help pay your bills. If you're 60 to 70, with investments reasonably balanced between stocks and bonds, a typical target is 4 to 5.5 percent. After that, you take annual inflation adjustments (Chapter 8). Revisit your withdrawals every few years. You might want to raise or lower your take, depending on changes in your spending and how your investments performed.

Throughout retirement. Write your numbers down, noting any changes in plan as you go along. It's all too easy to lose track of what you "meant" to do. Are you really taking the same amount of money you took last year plus an increment for inflation or are you taking more? What are your investments currently worth? It's especially important to note your target asset allocation along with a reminder—in CAPITAL LETTERS—that you intend to rebalance, not sell, when stock or bond prices fall.

YOUR RETIREMENT CHECKLIST

1. If you're still working, jack up your contributions to your company retirement plan or individual retirement account (IRA). The potential for saving more money is exactly what a paycheck is for.

2. If you're married and eligible for a pension, lean toward "joint and survivor" payments that will cover your spouse after your death. It's tempting to take a pension that covers your life only, because you get a larger check. Before making that decision, however, figure out what your spouse's income would be if you were hit by a truck the day after you retire. How well would he or she live on the savings and Social Security you left behind? There has to be a very good reason to choose a pension that ends when you die—for example, your spouse already has a good pension or you married a multimillionaire.

3. Put off taking Social Security. Age 62 is too young unless you absolutely have no other choice. Your benefit would be chopped by 25 to 30 percent, reducing your Social Security income now and for the rest of your life. At the very least, hold off until you reach full retirement age—probably 66—when your full benefit will be paid. If you're in good health, or your spouse is, wait until 70. You earn an additional 8 percent of your full benefit for every year of delay (see Chapter 3). It's even worth taking money out of savings to live on while you wait. The interest your savings earns is small compared with the delayed retirement credits that Social Security pays.

4. Nail down your health insurance. If you bought a plan through your state's health exchange, revisit it every year. New plans are coming into the system all the time and prices change. You can switch plans once a year during Open Enrollment, November 15 to February 15. You can switch or enroll at any time if you meet certain criteria—for example, marriage, losing employer

coverage, or moving to a new area. To find your state's plan, go to HealthCare.gov.

You have annual Medicare choices, too. Studies show that older people don't do much cost comparison when they sign up for the drug plan, Medicare Part D. Once they've chosen they rarely switch. That could be an expensive mistake. There are always new plans, many of which will cost you less. Read about your choices in Chapter 4 and then go to Medicare.gov.

5. If you need a major spending cut, look at housing first. That's where the big bucks are and the sooner you harvest them, the better. You might sell your house and buy something smaller, sell and rent, or take a reverse mortgage (Chapter 10). Once you've reduced your housing costs, including upkeep, taxes, and insurance, the rest of your budget might fall into place.

6. Take lifetime annuities seriously if you find that your retirement savings are "just enough" or "a little short" (Chapter 6). Consider an ordinary or inflation-adjusted immediate-pay annuity. Odds are the monthly payment you receive will be at least comparable to what you'd get by applying the 4 percent withdrawal rule to your savings and investments and you won't have to manage the money. Alternatively, look at a deferred-payout annuity. For a modest investment up front, you can provide yourself and your spouse with a lifetime income starting 10 or 15 years from now. Do not—*not*—fall for the variable annuity with lifetime withdrawal benefits. All the reasons start on page 137.

7. Check every one of the beneficiary forms you ever signed, to be sure the right person will get the money when you die. Individual retirement accounts are usually paid to the named beneficiary, no matter what it says in your will. Your ex-spouse might inherit if you forgot to take him or her off the form. Also check the forms at your mutual fund company and brokerage

firm and the beneficiaries named on your life insurance. If you get married or divorced, do the forms all over again. Immediately.

8. Keep a large enough cash reserve—in a bank, credit union, or money market mutual fund—to be sure that your bills will be paid for the next two years. That saves you from worry in a year that the value of your investments drops.

9. For retirement investments, buy index mutual funds. Low-cost index mutual funds. *Only* low-cost index mutual funds, such as those at Fidelity and Vanguard. The high-cost index funds sold by commissioned financial advisers waste your money, reduce your returns, and make it harder to stretch your savings over your lifetime.

10. Buy stock-owning index funds with at least 35 percent of your retirement savings if you or your spouse is likely to live 30 years or more. Choosing 40 to 60 percent would be better. Divide your bond allocation between high-quality short-term and intermediate-term funds. The bond portion of your investments supports your annual withdrawals in years when stock prices decline. Chapter 9 has the details.

11. Choose a withdrawal rule that fits with your stock allocation. If you hold just 30 percent of your money in stock-owning index funds, a reasonable starting place is 3.5 percent in the first year plus annual inflation adjustments. With 40 to 60 percent in stocks, you can start your withdrawals at 4.5 percent. If you can be flexible about your spending, start with 5.5 percent, plus annual inflation adjustments—intending to cut back in a year that stocks turn bad.

12. Remember that it takes just one total market U.S. stock fund and one total market U.S. bond fund to make the 4.5 percent withdrawal rule work.

13. Resist temptation. You *know* there's something wrong with

"income investments" promising safe and superhigh yields (they're all Venus flytraps in the financial jungle).

14. Don't watch your investments every day. Please. It's stressful and a waste of time. Walk the dog, read a book, jump out of a plane—anything but watch the numbers change. You thought carefully about putting your plan in place. Now let it run.

15. If you're holding a life-insurance policy, make sure that it isn't going to lapse (see Chapter 11).

16. Simplify your financial life. Assemble all your IRAs and 401(k)s in the same place. Invest in the fewest possible low-cost index stock and bond mutual funds to make rebalancing easy. Consolidate any stray bank accounts. Gather all your financial records together where your spouse or other heirs can find them (if they're on your computer, tell them where your passwords are). If you're managing rental properties, consider setting up a plan to sell them, over time. They'll become a burden in your older age. Slim down your living quarters and possessions. Clear your mind.

17. Have "the talk" with your spouse. If you've been making most of the family financial decisions, retirement is the time to share. If you're a spouse who's been ducking the money side of life, it's time to wake up. Ditto if you've been spending and saving on separate tracks without knowing what your mate has been doing. Both of you should know what's happening with the bills, the debts, the bank accounts, the retirement savings and investments, the pension, the insurance, the mortgage— everything that affects your welfare if your spouse dies first. How much income will you have as a widow or widower? Will it be enough? What investment decisions, if any, will you have to make?

Sometimes a spouse (usually the wife, I'm sorry to say) doesn't bother learning or imagines that she can't. She trusts that everything will be okay. And maybe it will. Then again, maybe not. I've seen widows shocked by the mess their husbands left behind. The day after the funeral is no time to be starting a crash course in personal finance.

Sometimes a spouse (usually the husband, I'm also sorry to say) holds all the financial cards to his chest. He might be playing with stocks, buying underwater real estate, or running up debts and doesn't want his wife to know. Or maybe he's just naturally bossy.

These are bad situations for both of you. Talking about money can be challenging, emotionally, but once you get it all on the table you can make better plans. Take it one subject at a time. Monday, income. Tuesday, bills. Wednesday, insurance. Yum, yum.

18. Update your will (you have one, of course). This isn't a book about estate planning. I'm just checking to make sure you have a will, a living will that explains the extent of the medical treatment you'd want if you can't decide for yourself, a health-care agent to be sure that your wishes are carried out, and a durable power of attorney (POA). The power gives someone the right to manage your money if (dread thought) your mind turns dim.

THE LAST AND HARDEST PLAN

Readers of this book have their wits about them. You're assessing your options and making decisions. But once you've set up your well-thought-out retirement plan, what happens if you lose your grip?

You might think that you'll need financial protection only if you develop dementia or have a stroke. But you can be perfectly healthy and yet lose the good judgment you had 10 or 20 years ago. You become more suggestible, as all the research on aging shows.

That's when a financial adviser might persuade you to buy

unsuitable annuities, trade high-risk stocks, or plunge into risky business ventures. I'm not talking about shady brokers in bucket shops. I'm pointing a finger at the nation's finest. In a 2014 audio recording, secretly made at one of America's largest and most prestigious investment banks, a senior executive is heard to say, "[Our] view was that once clients were wealthy enough, certain consumer laws didn't apply to them." He was talking about you, if you have even a halfway decent net worth. Brokers and "advisers" think it's up to you to figure out if a product they sell carries high hidden risks or isn't worth its price.

So you have one more financial plan to make. You need a defense for your income and assets in case your mental edge gets seriously dulled. Do it now while you're still sharp. The tighter you can draw a circle around yourself the safer you will be.

Primarily, you need to give someone your financial power of attorney. It needs to be a *durable* power, which stays in effect if you become incapable. You can give your agent (or "attorney-in-fact") limited powers—say, to manage your investments—or general powers to handle all your financial matters, including paying your bills.

You might hand the reins to your agent if you yourself start feeling uncertain about the decisions you have to make. I know that I'd be happy to be relieved of the burden. Otherwise, your agent steps in only if your family and doctor conclude that you're incompetent. Your family might start this persuasion process if they see your bills piling up unpaid or learn that you're sending money to vultures who cold-call with cheating investment pitches. If you resist, they might have to go to court. It's better to have named your own agent than have a court name someone for you.

You're always free to do something dumb with your money as long as you're competent. It's your money, after all. But it's smart to have someone standing by for a second opinion. If you have a living trust, your trustee can serve in that role.

There are no rules of thumb for naming an agent. You have to find someone you trust—your spouse, a responsible child or other relative, a business partner, a close and reliable friend. If the friendship fails, you can name someone else as long as you're sound of mind. Or name co-trustees, as a check on each other.

Have a full discussion with your agent about your financial needs and goals. That person has to agree with the program and have the persistence to carry it through. Tell your whole family what your wishes are. If your agent is someone outside the family, they should meet and talk with that person. If one of your children is the agent, your other children should be told why you made that choice.

The potential need for financial protection is yet another good reason to have a written investment plan. You can set your asset allocations and suggest that the agent buy only low-cost index funds, as Warren Buffett did when he instructed his wife's trustee (see page 245). Your future stand-in should also have a general overview of your finances. If you decide to go radically off plan, explain it to your agent first. If you start sneaking around on the person you've chosen to protect you, you're already off the rails.

You can get a durable POA from the attorney who did your will. There are also forms on the Web. Do-it-yourselfers have to be very sure that they execute them correctly, including your agent's name exactly as it appears on the document he or she will use to prove identity. Your signature has to be notarized and you might need two witnesses. Financial institutions are suspicious of DIY forms. They will refuse to accept your agent if the slightest thing is out of order.

They might even refuse to accept your power of attorney when everything *is* in order. Many institutions worry so much about doing something wrong that they make your agent fight for access to your financial affairs. Some (especially brokerage firms) will say that the POA should have been on their own institutional form (no; they're required to accept your document if it was properly prepared). Some will stonewall an agent who merely asks for information— for example, a question about what your health insurance covers.

(Tip: Call your health insurer now, to add the name of your spouse or agent to the list of people it's allowed to talk to.)

Your agent can't expect to get anything done, financially, with just a phone call. The institution will want to see a copy of the POA. If the customer rep won't help, a supervisor should. Worst case, your agent can ask your lawyer to handle it, but there's no reason to have to pay to assert the right that the POA grants.

Theoretically, your agent can act at any time, but financial institutions will normally check on what happened to you before accepting an agent's word. In some states you have to execute new powers every five years to prove that your intention holds. You should review them regularly in any event. Maybe you've had a dispute with your agent and need somebody else.

With luck, you'll be able to manage your money right up to the end, in which case the power of attorney will molder in your files, unused. But just as you protect yourself against investment risk, you need to protect against disease or judgment risk. As poet Robert Frost wrote, "Provide, provide!"

YOUR NEW LIFE

Putting together your financial plan will take some time. So will finding your new path. Freedom is daunting when you first encounter it, after a lifetime of being scheduled every day. The common second stage of retirement—disenchantment—might set in. But that's only a way station. Once you start poking around, you'll encounter a world of interesting people like you, engaged in new projects and adventures. There's a vibrancy to life after work, at its slower pace. We let go of who we were and discover who we've become.

Appendices

Appendix 1
Sound Advice at Any Age

Where you stand in the money cycle

**The finest of all human achievements—
and the most difficult—is merely being reasonable.**

All of our deepest beliefs about money are formed in the years when we grow up. We learn the great lessons of our era and set out to put them all to work.

But time is a trickster. Just when you think that you've learned all the rules, some hidden umpire changes the game.

Think about the Depression Kids. Those woeful years left a legacy of fear. Forever after, the generations marked by the 1930s saved compulsively. A loan made them feel sick to their stomachs. They took no risks. When the Great Prosperity swelled around them, they mistrusted it. They knew in their hearts it wouldn't last.

Now think about the Inflation Kids, raised in the 1960s and 1970s. They saw in a flash that a dollar saved was a dollar lost because inflation ate it up. A dollar borrowed was a dollar saved. You could use it to buy a car or a stereo before the price went up. They learned to love debt and couldn't change.

Then came the Bubble Kids of the 1980s and 1990s—years when stock and bond values soared, real estate boomed, and everyone thought it was going to be easy to get rich. Even after the bust, they didn't save much, because they still trusted "the market" or "home equity" to rebuild their wealth automatically. Can they change their approach to money any better than earlier generations could?

The new turn of the wheel—the 2008 financial bust—is bringing us the Struggle Kids. They endured the Great Recession, with jobs hard to get, layoffs and wage-cuts common, foreclosures and bankruptcies wiping families out, investments unreliable, and global interconnections that no generation has grown up with before. They're saving more, spending less, and coping with large student loans. What will their orthodoxies be? Can we all find a better place to stand? On the answer to those questions, everything depends.

A CYCLE OF SPENDING AND SAVING

Money comes and goes in your life at different times. Mostly goes, when you're young. Those are the spent years. Maybe the misspent years. But never mind. As you grow older, the urge to save creeps up on you. Here's the typical cycle of wealth:

Ages 20 to 30. You establish credit, wrestle with your first budget, buy your first furniture and appliances, take out your first auto loan or lease, learn about insurance and taxes. Maybe (here I'm dreaming) you save a little money, in the bank or in company retirement accounts. Retirement accounts are money machines for young people because you have so many years to let them grow untaxed. By the end of the decade, you cohabit or get married, maybe have a baby, buy a house. (You save for a house the old-fashioned way: by borrowing some of the down payment from your parents.) Entrepreneurs start a business.

Ages 31 to 45. You don't know where your money goes. Bills, bills, bills. College for the kids is a freight train headed your way. Maybe (here I'm dreaming again) you start a tuition savings account. Money still dribbles into retirement savings, but only if your company does it for you—by taking it out of your paycheck before you get it to spend. Saving for yourself is hard. When pressed, you open a home equity line of credit and borrow money against your house. If you haven't started a business, you think about it now. This is also a good time to get more education. Invest in yourself and hope for a payoff.

Ages 46 to 55. You *do* know where your money goes: to good old State U. At the same time, you get the creepy feeling that maybe you won't live forever. You thrash around. You buy books about financial planning. You have an affair. When all else fails, you start to save.

Ages 56 to 65. These are typically the fat years. You're at the top of your earning power, the kids are gone, the dogs are dead. Twenty percent of your salary can be socked away—which is lucky because you will need extra money for your children's down payments when they buy a house (kids never really go away). Consider long-term care insurance.

Ages 66 to 75. How golden are these years? As rich as your pension (if you're lucky to have one), Social Security, and the income from the money you saved. Start out by living on the first two, if you can. Let the income from savings and investments compound for a while, to build a fund for later life.

Ages 76 and up. Quit saving. Spend, spend, spend! Forget leaving money to your kids—they should have put away more for themselves. Dip into principal to live as comfortably as you deserve. This is what all those years of saving were *for*.

WHEN YOU FALL OFF THE CYCLE

You say you can't find your place on the cycle? That's no surprise. Almost no one lives exactly to order anymore. There are a million ways of getting from birth to death, and they all work. If you fall behind financially during any decade, you'll need a plan for catching up.

You have your children in your 30s. It seemed like a smart idea at the time: diapers tomorrow but never today. No one told you that, in your 50s, you'd be paying for college just when you were trying to save for your own retirement. (And even if they'd told you, you'd never have believed that you would ever be that old.) You might have to choose between sending your children to a low-cost college and shortchanging your own future. Maybe your children will have to pay for their education themselves. The moral, for those who can think ahead: save more in your 20s, using the discipline of tax-deferred retirement plans. These plans penalize you for drawing money out, so you're more likely to leave it in.

You get divorced and start over. Divorce costs you assets and income, with the greater loss usually falling on the woman. She can rarely earn as much money as her ex-husband takes away. For the man, a new wife and new babies might mean that college tuition bills will arrive in the same mail as the Social Security checks. Unless you're rich or remarry rich, divorce is a decision to cut your standard of living, sometimes permanently.

You don't marry. You lack the safety net that a second paycheck and an in-home caregiver provide. On the other hand, there's usually no other mouth to feed. You can start saving and investing earlier than most.

You're married, with no children. You've got nothing but money and plenty of it. You are one of the few who really can retire early, not just dream about it.

Life deals you an accident. A crippling illness. Early widowhood. A child with anguishing medical problems. A family that has always saved can scrape through these tragedies. A family in debt to the hilt cannot.

You're downsized. That's today's euphemism for getting fired. The money in your retirement plan goes for current bills. Your next job pays 30 percent less, with no retirement plan. But you can still secure your future by downscaling your life to match your income.

There's honor at every monetary level of life. For more on downsizing—which I call "rightsizing"—see Chapter 2.

You get the golden boot. A forced early retirement. Sometimes you see it coming, sometimes it blindsides you. You get a consolation prize in a lump sum payout or a higher pension for a retiree of your age. But you lose 5 to 10 years of earnings and savings. This risk is the single strongest argument for starting a retirement savings program young. At your age, a new job will be hard to come by, but you can't afford to retire for real. So you do project work, part-time work, and unexpected work such as clerking, to pad out your early-retirement check.

Memo to all workers: Employers don't care that you've worked hard and late, that you haven't been sick in a dozen years, or that every supervisor you've had thinks you're hot stuff. They ask only: What have you done for me lately? Is your job essential to business today? Are your skills the right ones for business tomorrow?

Few people "hold a job" anymore. Instead we have talents that we sell to employers for various projects, some longer term than others. In this kind of world, nothing is more important than continuing education and upgrading skills.

WHO NEEDS WHAT WHEN

The number of financial products on the market today—bank accounts, insurance policies, annuities, mutual funds—I estimate conservatively at two zillion point three (2.3Z). Most of them nobody needs but buys anyway because some salesperson convinces you to. In fact, you need only a few simple things, matched to your age, your bank balance, and your responsibilities. To find out how to choose them, check out my comprehensive personal finance guide called *Making the Most of Your Money NOW*. Here I offer a general framework for your thinking.

Young and Single

Admit it: you are living your life on hold. Cinderella, waiting for Prince Charming. Peter Pan, not wanting to grow up. You are serious only about your work (or finding work!). Everything else is temporary. There is nothing in your refrigerator and nothing in your bank account. "Wait until I'm married," you say. But what if you don't marry? Or you marry late? Looking back, you'll see that you lost ten good years. Your future starts now. As a young person you should:

- *Establish credit with a low-cost bank card.* Practice on one card before getting two. Debt tends to rise to the highest allowable limit. If you're in college, apply for a bank card before you leave. Banks give credit faster to students than to job-seeking young adults. (They count on the parents to save their kids' credit rating by paying off their debts.) Pay your student loans on time! Defaults are a killer on a credit report.

- *Get disability insurance coverage if your employer offers it.* It pays you an income if you're sick or injured and can't work. How will you afford the premiums? By not buying life insurance. You don't need life insurance when you have no dependents to support.

- *Get health insurance if you don't have a company plan.* It's the law. You'll pay a tax penalty if you go bare. To find the plans available in your area, go to HealthCare.gov. If you're healthy, consider the lowest cost plan. It will have a high deductible, which means that you'll pay a lot out of pocket if you have a bad accident or get seriously ill. But the odds are that your medical bills won't amount to much. If your income is low, the government will help you pay the premiums. For more on health insurance, see page 85.

- *Invest in your own education and training* even if it means more student debt. Your earning power is your single greatest asset.

- *Start saving money.* Put away 10 percent of your earnings. I hear you saying "I can't do it." So sneak up on it: start with 5 percent, then move up to 7 percent. You can get to 10 percent within the year. Where should the money go? For starters, part to a bank account and part to a retirement plan.

■ *Start a tax-deferred retirement plan:* an individual retirement account (IRA) or a savings plan through your employer. Put the money into stock-owning index mutual funds and leave it there. (See page 235.)

■ *Rent, don't buy an apartment.* You don't yet know whether you're ready to put down roots. Except in unusual boom years, like the ones at the turn of the twenty-first century, it's hard to make money on real estate that you'll hold for only a short time—say, less than four years. Resale prices for condominiums and cooperative apartments typically lag behind those for single-family homes. At this point in your life, the money you'd spend on a down payment is better invested somewhere else. Buy only when you have a place you expect to live in for many years.

■ *Buy property insurance if you have valuable possessions.* You especially need it for business property if you work out of your home. But you don't need it for furniture if your apartment's style is Modern Attic.

■ *Make a will* unless it's okay for your parents to inherit everything. If you die will-less, that's where your property will probably go.

■ *Create a power of attorney, a living will, and a health care proxy.* That's basic protection in case you meet with a horrible accident that leaves you alive but not alert. Someone has to act for you, both financially and medically, and you should pick those people yourself. You can find your state's forms online.

Older Singles

You might be your own sole support for life, but don't let that scare you into playing your hand too conservatively. Stocks do better than bank accounts or bonds over long periods of time. For financial self-defense, you need:

- *A good credit record*—good enough to be approved for a mortgage or a business loan.

- *Enough education and job training* to keep your income moving up.

- *Good health and disability insurance.* The older you get, the greater your risk of illness or injury. When you pass 60, consider long-term care insurance. (See page 109.) You don't need any life insurance unless someone depends on your income for support.

- *A home of your own.* Living will be cheaper and expenses more predictable if you own a house or apartment free and clear when you retire. Keep your homeowners insurance up to date.

- *A habit of saving.* Try for 15 to 20 percent of your income. No, that's not too much.

- *A retirement plan:* pension, company tax-deferred savings plan, traditional or Roth individual retirement account, Solo 401(k), or simplified employee pension (SEP) for the self-employed. Get more than one plan if you qualify. Fund everything to the max.

- *A mix of investments in your retirement plans:* U.S. and foreign stock-owning index mutual funds; some Treasury or other tax-exempt municipal bonds. See Chapter 9.

- *An interest beyond your regular job*—a pastime or charity. It may open the door to a second career.

- *A will, a living will, a health care proxy, and a durable power of attorney.*

- *A surrogate you trust who will manage your money if you can't do it yourself.*

Married Couples

You have a lot of responsibilities. Your mate needs security if you die. Children have to be set up too. After that, the big question is how to handle the family money. You need:

- *A cost-sharing system.* If you are a two-paycheck couple, will you split the bills or pool your money in one account? If you are a one-paycheck couple, will you start a savings account for the nonearning spouse? Financially speaking, there is no best way, only your way.

- *Credit cards in the names of both spouses,* or separate cards—at least one in each of your names. A wife without joint responsibility for the debt, or a card of her own, could have her cards yanked if her husband dies or leaves. And vice versa, of course.

- *Disability insurance.* Every income-earning person should consider it, to cover lost paychecks (and maybe home health care bills) if you become too sick or disabled to work. Unfortunately, it's expensive. If you're lucky, you'll be able to buy it through an employee group plan at a lower cost.

- *Health insurance.* Don't let it slip away from you, even for a moment. If you're covered by a company plan and lose it (say, because of job loss or divorce), arrange to transfer, immediately, to something else. There's COBRA, which continues your current group plan for up to 36 months at your expense (your company is required to send you COBRA information). Or switch to a cheaper family policy on your state's health insurance exchange (check what policies are available at HealthCare.gov). Take the deadlines seriously! You'll pay more for COBRA if you sign up late. There's a tax penalty if you let a gap arise between company coverage and a plan bought on the health exchange. If you lose your own plan but can get coverage on your working spouse's plan, sign up immediately.

- *Life insurance.* If your family depends on your income for support, you need life insurance. If your family can get along without your income, you don't. Working couples with no kids may do fine with whatever group term insurance they get from their companies or perhaps no insurance at all. But you'll need a ton of coverage if children arrive. You can afford it by buying low-cost term insurance (for premium costs, see Term4sale.com). Buying insurance on a nonearning spouse is a luxury purchase. Buying it on a child is a waste.

- *A will,* so that beneficiaries will inherit exactly as much as you intend.

- *A power of attorney,* so that someone can manage your finances if you can't.

- *A living will and health-care power of attorney,* in case you fall into a permanent or temporary coma and can't make your own health care decisions. You need a surrogate to speak for you, or your living will might be ignored.

- *A premarital agreement,* if you want to limit what your spouse will collect at divorce or inherit at your death. These agreements are used mostly by people of unequal wealth, the previously divorced who swear that they won't be "burned again," and older people with children from previous marriages to protect. There are postmarital agreements too, for arrangements you wish you had made earlier.

- *Your own home.* It should be an acceptable investment if you own it long enough. It's also a form of forced saving and a cheap way to live in retirement, once you own it free and clear. Keep the dollar value of your homeowners insurance up to date. Homes gradually get more expensive to repair or replace even if their market value isn't going up.

- *Regular savings.* Sprinkle 10 to 15 percent of every check among ready savings, his-and-hers tax-deferred retirement plans, and college savings. Come to think of it, sprinkle more. Be sure to fund both spouses' retirement plans. Some couples waste a tax deduction by forgetting to fund a plan for a spouse who has only modest earnings. For power saving, see Chapter 7.

- *Job skills.* A spouse without them is asking for trouble, even if he or she is home with the kids. Life is not fair. Death or disability occurs. Breadwinners lose their jobs. Not all spouses love each other until the end of time. As the poet said, "Provide, provide."

- *Long-term care insurance* once you pass 60. (See page 109.)

Blended Families

Life gets expensive when both bride and groom come with children attached. You need everything that any other married couple does, plus extra protection for stepchildren. Check:

- Whether all the kids are covered by health insurance.
- Whether you want to change your will to include the stepchildren.
- Whether you need trusts to ensure that the children of your former marriages inherit the property they're due.
- Whether all the kids will have enough money for college.

Younger Widows and Widowers, and the Divorced

Maybe you're just plain single again. More likely, there are children to support. It's harder alone. You'll need a substantial safety net:

- *Buy as much disability insurance as you can get.* If you can't work and can't support your children, the family might break up. It's affordable if you can buy through a company group plan.
- *Don't be without a family health policy for a moment.*
- *Buy a lot of life insurance* if your children's future depends on you. Stick with low-cost term insurance and cancel it when the kids grow up. For premium costs, see Term4sale.com.
- *Write a will,* especially to name a guardian for your children. Add a living will, a health care proxy, and a power of attorney.
- *Call Social Security.* An unmarried child under 18 or 19, or a child disabled before age 22, whose mother or father is dead, can get a monthly Social Security payment on that parent's account. So can a widowed person (including a divorced spouse whose ex-spouse dies) if his or her child is disabled or under 16.
- *If you're divorced, report your new status*—in writing—to everyone who gave you credit and cancel all joint credit cards. You don't want your ex-spouse's new charges to show up on your personal credit history. (You'll still be responsible for the past debts that you contracted together.)

- *If you're widowed and have a joint credit card,* maybe you want to report your new status to credit granters. Then again, maybe you don't. If the card was based on two incomes or on the income of the spouse who died, you may not be able to keep the card unless you can prove that you're creditworthy. If the family credit history is good and you have an income, the card would doubtless be reissued. But if you have only a small income, it might not be reissued or its terms might change. In that case, nothing in federal law stops you from keeping your old card and keeping mum. Eventually, the credit card company will find you. You can deal with the issue then.

- *Find work.* Or find better work. Train for a higher-paying job. You can't afford to coast.

- *If you collect child support,* take out a term insurance policy on your ex-spouse (this should be part of your divorce agreement). The insurance proceeds will make up for your lost child support if he or she dies.

- *Save money even at the cost of your standard of living.* Maybe you will remarry, but you can't count on it.

- *Consider trading down to a smaller house.* Keep your homeowners insurance up to date.

- *Own a home*—your current house or a smaller one—if you're rooted in place. Otherwise hang loose and rent on a short-term lease. Who knows? Your next life may lie somewhere else. Get renters insurance to protect good furniture from fire and small, expensive objects from theft.

- *Take no quick advice about money.* Not from your brother. Not from your friends. Above all, not from anyone selling financial products. Salespeople love widows for their ready cash and their presumed dependence on a sympathetic (male) ear. Keep your money in the bank until you've learned something about managing it and know exactly what you want to do.

- *Don't automatically turn your life insurance proceeds into an annuity,* which the broker might propose. Inflation will gradually wipe out the value of a fixed monthly income. You might want to take a lump sum instead and invest it conservatively.

Older Widows, Widowers, and the Divorced

You have great freedom if your children are grown. Your life can be reconstructed from the ground up. Your checklist includes "cancels" as well as "buys":

■ *Cancel your life insurance.* Use the money to add to your savings and investments.

■ *Cancel your disability insurance* if you have retired and no longer get a paycheck.

■ *Keep your health insurance.* At age 65, you can go for Medicare. For the Medicare rules, see page 97.

■ *Call Social Security.* If you worked at least 10 years, you're owed a retirement benefit on your own account, starting as early as age 62. Alternatively, you're entitled to benefits based on your spouse's account. You can collect whichever is higher. The widowed are entitled to benefits on their late spouse's account as early as 60 (50 if you're disabled) unless their current earnings are too high. But don't collect early unless, financially, you must. The longer you wait, the higher your lifetime benefit will be (see Chapter 3).

■ *Study up on money management.* If you've never handled investments before, this is the moment that nature has chosen for you to learn. In the meantime, keep your money in the bank. Don't give it to anyone else to manage until you've learned a lot about money yourself. You have to be able to follow what your "expert" is doing. Otherwise your money might be expertly "managed" away. For help, see Chapter 9.

■ *Write a will or change your old one.* A living will and a health care power of attorney grow even more urgent as you age. You need someone to speak for you if you become incapable.

■ *Write to your late spouse's (or ex-spouse's) company immediately after the death or legal separation.* Better yet, write in advance. You may be due some employee benefits, including up to three years of health insurance at group rates. The employer is supposed to notify you about the health insurance but doesn't always do so. If you don't apply for the policy immediately after losing your coverage as a spouse, you won't be able to get it at all.

- *Find work if you need it,* perhaps through a temporary help agency.

Sort of Married

More than single but less than married, you have only to change the locks to "divorce." You need:

- *Separate bank accounts.* Contribute to common bills in proportion to your earnings. If one of you earns only 30 percent of the total, that person should pay only 30 percent of the expenses. It's not fair to hit him or her for 50 percent.

- *Separate property.* One buys the lamps, one buys the couch. Put a note in your file, showing who owns what.

- *Written agreements for property bought together.* What happens to it if you split up? If one of you dies?

- *A will, to be sure that the other gets—or doesn't get—what you intend.* If you have no will, everything will go to your family, not to your partner.

- *The same health, disability, and living will protection that you'd give yourself as a single person.* If you both work and can support yourselves, you need no life insurance unless there are children. If you decide that one of you won't work, buy a policy to protect the partner at home. If you're in a registered civil union, your partner might be covered by your employee benefits plan.

Appendix 2
The Ultimate Wish List

What you've got and where you're going

Need rises with income. What was out of the question when you made $30,000 becomes urgent at $60,000 and indispensable at $100,000.

Your own financial plan starts with a wish list. Write it all down, every single thing. A speedboat. A week in Barbados. State U. for two children. Enough money to retire early. Forget that you can't afford it. Maybe you only think you can't. The whole reason to have a financial plan is to focus on what matters most and work out a strategy for getting it.

So get out a yellow pad and a pencil, or set up a "Life Goals" file on your computer, and start dreaming. On the left side of the pad or screen, write "What I want." On the right side, write "When I want it"—next summer? In three years? In the middle, write "How I get there from here." That middle column is you terra incognita. You need to develop some real numbers and a real timetable so you won't still be dreaming five years from now. If you're married, your spouse should create a wish list and Life Goals file, too.

Once you've listed all your material wants, stare off into space and think. Even if you can have it all, the cost of getting it might be an extra job, working nights and weekends, working to a later age than you'd intended, or hanging on to a job you hate. Is it worth it? Or would you rather take that speedboat off your wish list?

When reflecting on this question, take another piece of paper (or open a new file) and write down your personal goals. Don't kid yourself. If money and status are important, say so. Do you want to write a book by the time you're 30? Start a business? Spend more time with the kids? Move to the country? Become a top officer of your corporation? Change careers? Give more time to charity? All the things you care about most are likely to affect how much money you'll have, which in turn will shape your financial plan. The planning process asks you to set priorities and make trade-offs. Include your spouses priorities, too.

The plan you finally develop may not work—at least, not exactly. Some things may go better than expected, others may go worse. You may fall behind schedule. You may filch money for a new car that should have gone into the education fund.

But the point is, you'll know it. You'll see the hole in your kids' tuition account and figure out how to make it up. The reason financial plans succeed is almost stupidly simple. It's their specificity. Instead of vague hopes, you have hard targets—something concrete that you're working toward every year. Once you see it, you can get it.

YOUR BASIC SECURITY PACKAGE

Back to your dreamy goals. I know you've remembered to list "Barbados vacation." But one or two other things might have slipped your mind, without which your prettier plans might be undone. Here is the basic security package that also has to be on your list:

1. Life insurance. Do you have enough? If you die, will your spouse or mate be self-supporting or will he or she need you to leave a pot of money behind? Your children need support and education. Part of that money will probably come from the surviving spouse's earnings. You need enough insurance to cover the rest.

2. Disability insurance. Most people are covered by insurance if they die. But what if you fall off a ladder, break your back, and live? That's the risk nobody thinks about (or wants to). You need two levels of disability coverage: (1) for a short illness of 6 to 12 months, during which you'd try to keep your way of life intact, and (2) for a permanent disability, usually requiring a drop in your standard of living. It's the most affordable when purchased in an employee group plan.

3. Health insurance. Most people get it from the companies they work for. If not, choose a policy on your state's health care exchange (HealthCare.gov). Either way, insurance premiums are going up. Employers are not only charging you more for coverage, they require higher deductibles and co-pays. In the individual market, policy premiums are rising every year, sometimes by a lot. These expenses are squeezing family budgets. But if you don't have comprehensive health care coverage you don't have a financial plan.

4. Repaying debt. It's pointless to save money at 1 percent interest while you're still supporting a Visa card habit at 18 or 26 percent. Pay off the Visa first. Often, the best use of savings is to pay off the debts that are costing you more than your savings earn. For ways of saving more money, see Chapter 7.

5. Owning a home. How much do you need for a down payment, and how will you raise it? The lucky ducks go to the Daddy Bank. Failing that, you will have to throw every resource you have at the problem. Meet with a banker to learn about loans with low downpayments.

6. College. How much will college cost when your children reach 18, and how long do you have to accumulate the money? Four years at the average public college, for a student living in the state, might cost as much as $84,000, starting in 2016 (assuming annual increases of 4 percent). For the average private college, it might be $186,500 (before tuition discounts). The most selective and expensive schools top $50,100 *a year*.

7. Fun and games. Put some luxuries on your list. A new kitchen. An RV. A trip to Europe. August at the racetrack. Estimate what they will cost (except for the racetrack, where you'll make money, right?) and when you will want them.

8. Retirement savings. How much will you need to retire on? A younger person hasn't a clue. Too many incalculables exist in the economy and your personal life. Still, you ought to make a start. By your late 40s, the picture should be coming clear.

For your pains, you'll wind up with a daunting list of expenses:

1. The price of more life insurance.

2. The price of a disability policy.

3. The price of health insurance.

4. The extra monthly payments needed to zero out your consumer debts.

5. How much you'll have to save each month for a down payment on a home.

6. The net cost of your children's college (after any student aid) and the length of time you have to raise the money.

7. The price of anything special you want for yourself and how long you have to save for it.

8. The amount of savings you'll need for a decent retirement.

Some of you are starting out at the top of this list; others are already partway down. In either case, the total may look unattainable, but I promise you it's not. It's like running a marathon: you do one mile at a time until you finish.

FINDING THE MONEY

Winning a lottery would be nice. Maybe you could marry rich. An inheritance is dandy, the drawback being how you get it.

Windfalls aside, there are only three ways of getting the money you need to underwrite a financial plan: culling current income, taking loans, and using the gains from your savings and investments. But everything ultimately springs from income, which sets up your savings and pays off your debts.

No plan will succeed if you live to the brink of your income and beyond. You must hold back something for savings and investments. "No way," you say? It takes $50,000 just to pay the grocer? Sure, but only if you build your life that way. Every single one of us can look down the street and see someone living as well as we do on $5,000 less a year than we make. That's $5,000 we could be saving every year and still hold up our heads in the neighborhood. Only by living on less than you make will you ever be able to live on more than you make.

KEEPING SCORE

Start your plan by figuring your present net worth. Recalculate it once a year. These figures, and the changes in them, will show you a lot of interesting things:

Whether your debts are under control. Is your indebtedness growing faster than the money you're saving?

How well you're investing the money you save. Does your investment account keep up with the market? Or does it fall behind?

How much money you could lay your hands on in an emergency. Do you have enough readily salable assets to help you through a bad patch, or are too many of your assets tied up?

Whether you need more life and disability insurance. What income could you get from your assets compared with how much you need to live on?

To find your net worth, add up the value of everything you own (your assets), figured at what you could reasonably sell each item for. Then subtract everything you owe (your liabilities). The remainder is your net worth. It's the money you'd have if you converted all of your salable property into cash and paid off your debts. If you owe more

YOUR NET WORTH

Date _____

WHAT YOU OWN (ASSETS)	AMOUNT
Quick Assets	
Cash in checking, ready savings, and money market mutual funds	$ _____
Other mutual funds	_____
Stocks, bonds, government securities, mutual funds	_____
Publicly traded partnerships	_____
Other easily salable investments	_____
Money due you soon for work you've done	_____
Life insurance cash values	_____
Precious metals	_____
Easily salable personal property: jewelry, silver, cars	_____
Restricted Assets	
Certificates of deposit if they have early-withdrawal penalties	_____
Retirement accounts: IRAs, tax-deferred annuities, company investment plans, deferred salary	_____
Current worth of your vested pension if payable in a lump sum	_____
Stock options	_____
Slow Assets	
Your home	_____
Other real estate	_____
Art and antiques	_____
Other valuable personal property: furs, boats, tools, coins	_____
Restricted stock, not readily salable	_____
Limited partnerships, not readily salable	_____
Money owed you in the future	_____
Equity value of a business	_____
Total Assets	_____

WHAT YOU OWE (LIABILITIES)	AMOUNT	INTEREST RATE
Current bills outstanding: this month's rent, medical bills, insurance premiums, utilities, and so on	$ _____	_____
Credit card debt	_____	_____
Installment and auto loans	_____	_____
Money borrowed from family members	_____	_____
Home mortgage	_____	_____
Home equity loan	_____	_____
Other mortgages	_____	_____
Student loans	_____	_____
Loans against investments, including your margin loans	_____	_____
Other loans	_____	_____
Income and real estate taxes due	_____	_____
Taxes due on your investments if you cash them in	_____	
Taxes and penalties due on your retirement accounts if you cash them in	_____	
Total Liabilities	_____	
Net Worth (assets minus liabilities)	_____	

than you own, you have a negative net worth, and maybe an ulcer. ("I'm going to be a millionaire," a gambler friend of mine used to say. "I'll die owing a million dollars." He came close.)

Your aim is to raise your net worth over time, through a combination of new savings, sound investments that recover after market setbacks, and fewer loans.

Just as important, you need a good balance between assets that are tied up, such as your house, and assets that can quickly be turned into cash.

The parts of your net worth that are always on tap are your *quick assets*, such as cash, mutual funds, stocks, bonds, and life insurance cash values. You fall back on your quick assets in an emergency.

The parts that might take a long time to sell are the *slow assets*, such as most real estate. Don't load up on slow assets until you have plenty of quick assets on tap.

Some of your slow assets are effectively frozen. That would include your home, if no buyer wants it right now, an interest in a limited partnership or other investment that can't be sold easily, money owed to you at some point in the future, and a lump sum due from your pension plan. Mentally, you might also add a pending inheritance, although it doesn't belong on your personal balance sheet until it's actually yours.

Yet another part of your net worth is restricted in that it can be reached only by paying a penalty. This includes most unmatured certificates of deposit, tax-deferred retirement plans, and tax-deferred annuities if you're younger than 59½.

When figuring your net worth: (1) You don't have to know the exact value of everything. A ballpark estimate will do. (2) To find out what your individual bonds are currently worth, ask your financial adviser to price them for you. They will bring more or less than face value, depending on market conditions today. To price bonds yourself, check Investinginbonds.com. (3) Sherlock Holmes couldn't ferret out the value of limited-partnership shares unless they're traded publicly. Ask your adviser whether he can sell them and for how much. If no one is biting, list the shares at zero. When the partnership dissolves, thank the gods for every dollar you get back. (4) In a pinch, you could sell your cars and jewelry. But you won't, so they're not truly part of your usable net worth. You need to know their current value only to keep them well insured.

PATCHING YOUR SAFETY NET

Optimist: "This is the best of all possible worlds."
Pessimist: "That's right."

So far, you've been thinking like an optimist. You're worth more than you thought! Your pencil is flying! Your stock options will pay off your loans, and then you'll be on easy street! All it will take is a few more years.

But what if you don't have a few more years?

Here's where the average plan comes a cropper. How would your family manage if you died? How would you live if you had an accident and couldn't work anymore? There would be some income from your spouse's earnings, Social Security, disability insurance (if you were clever enough to have bought it), and so on. But probably not enough. You'd also have to live on your savings.

To measure the real strength of your position, you have to look at your net worth in another way. How much cash would be available to you or your family if you had to marshal all of your assets to live on?

Start with the figures you just reached and assume three things: (1) you (or your survivor) would not sell your house, one car, and personal property; (2) all other slow assets would be converted to cash; (3) your restricted assets would be freed up for use.

You need a large enough nest egg so that when your savings are combined with other sources of income, your dependents will have enough to meet their expenses. If your savings fall short, fill the gap with more life insurance. If your household depends on two paychecks, do these calculations twice—first assuming that the husband dies, then assuming the death of the wife.

If you think that your family would move to a smaller house at your death, they would net some money from the sale of the house you own now. Add those funds to their assets.

Disability is another story. There's no life insurance payoff, so your usable assets are much smaller. I've shown few liabilities in the table shown on page 370 because you can't predict your lump sum expenses. Even the size of your uninsured medical bills is a question. You have three ways to prepare for a disability: get a better disability insurance policy, save more money, or invest better.

Use this same calculation for early retirement.

There is one more way of measuring your personal security: Do you have enough quick assets to cover all the bills coming due this year? That would give you a 12-month breathing space if you lost your job. Figure it this way:

1. How much has to be paid on your debts over the upcoming 12 months? Call this your current debt: $_____.

2. What are your rock-bottom living expenses: food, shelter, transportation? Call this your current costs $_____.

3. How large are your quick assets, not counting personal property and life insurance cash values? Call this your ready money: $_____.

4. Your ready money should be greater than your current costs and debt. If not, you are living with a lot of risk. As time passes,

---

YOUR SURVIVOR'S USABLE CASH

Date _____

	AMOUNT
Assets	
Quick assets (not counting life insurance cash values, one of two cars, and personal property)	$ _____
Restricted assets	_____
Slow assets (not counting your house and personal property that your spouse would want to keep)	_____
Proceeds from life insurance	_____
Total Usable Assets Left for Survivor	_____
Liabilities	
Loans against insurance policies	_____
Death costs, including funeral and estate administration, up to 5 percent of assets	_____
Taxes, including final income tax return and estate taxes if you're wealthy enough to owe them	_____
Total	_____
Money Left for Survivor (usable assets minus liabilities)	_____

your ready money should grow larger and larger than your current costs and debt.

ROUNDUP DAY

Once a year, sit down with your spouse or mate (if you're single, sit down with yourself) and see where you stand. Go over everything. Are you spending too much? Did you save enough money? Should you change your investments? Did your net worth improve? Do you need more insurance? What financial goal will you shoot for in the next 12 months? What personal purchases would you like to make?

I call this annual accounting Roundup Day. A good time for it is the week after New Year's, when things are usually slow. Another good time is the week you do your income taxes, when every money nerve is tingling. Working couples need this day to tally their separate savings and investments, and show their spouses what's happening

---

YOUR USABLE CASH IF YOU'RE DISABLED

Date _____

	AMOUNT
Assets	
Quick assets (except for one car and personal property)	$ _____
Restricted assets	_____
Slow assets (not counting your house and any personal property you want to keep)	_____
Total Usable Assets	_____
Liabilities	
Taxes on funds you withdraw from retirement accounts	_____
Uninsured medical bills (make a guess)	_____
Total	_____
Money on Tap (usable assets minus liabilities)	_____

---

with their 401(k)s. Spouses who don't handle the family money need this day to keep in touch. Everyone needs this day to gloat over triumphs, fix mistakes, and start the next year fresh.

HOW MUCH IS ENOUGH?

You don't have to get richer every year. At some level of personal security, all you need is enough growth to keep your after-tax assets even with inflation. Knowing when to quit and go fishing is just as important as knowing when to keep your shoulder to the wheel.

My job is to help you grow wealthier and more secure. But not everyone is so lucky. Accidents happen. Investments fail. Companies fold. So here's a heretical thought: If your income dropped, would that be so bad? Would it be so terrible to live in a cheaper place with fewer clothes and luxuries? People who earn $5,000 less than you live happy lives, and so do people who earn $5,000 less than *they* do.

I wish you every increase, but if the gods frown, there are worse things in life than having to step down.

Appendix 3
I Have It Right Here Somewhere

The right way to keep records

(Don't go away. I'm still looking.)

Okay, I confess.

Sitting here, right now, I can't remember the name of my life insurance company. The keys to my safe-deposit box are in my office, but I'm not sure where. In the pile of papers on the floor to the left, I think there's the booklet explaining the changes in my group health insurance. In short, I am often a slob about my own financial records.

But I am reforming. Writing this chapter has embarrassed me into reorganizing the scattered Quinn financial files. And take my word for it: when you finish this kind of job, you feel new, as if you had shined all your shoes and cleaned up the cellar.

With good records:

You can find things. I estimate 84 hours saved per year, right there.

You can remember what you have. Did you sign that power of attorney? Did you fill in the beneficiary form that says who should get your retirement accounts if you die. Now you'll know.

You can remember what you don't have. No, you didn't sign that power of attorney, because you kept misplacing it. Now that you're putting your records together, you'll get it done.

You can save money for your heirs. They will be able to find things too, without paying a lawyer to do detective work for them. They won't shake their heads and mutter "What a mess."

You can feel terrifically smart and well organized. You will know that if a ceiling fell on your head this very moment, your heirs would get every dime that was coming to them. Sometimes a deed, contract, or bank account is hidden away and never found. Ditto for old stock certificates, records of small brokerage accounts, and retirement savings accounts left with a former employer. After several years, unclaimed money passes to the state (page 378). Lawyers tell story after story about stumbling across a stray piece of paper that entitled a widow to money that she didn't know anything about. Think of the number of widows who throw those pieces of paper out.

WHERE TO KEEP RECORDS

Invest in a file cabinet. It doesn't have to be steel; cardboard works fine. You can tuck a two-drawer cabinet under a table. Or use it as a table (put a piece of plywood on top and cover it with a cloth). Don't put it in the attic or behind the ice skates in the closet under the stairs. Unless your cabinet is so handy that you practically trip over it, you'll put off filing your records, which means that your system will fall apart.

Eventually back tax returns and old bank records will overflow your file drawers. Don't compulsively save everything with your name and a dollar sign on it. Some records can be thrown away (See "What to Keep, Where to Keep It, What to Toss," page 380). Put beloved old statements that you can't part with into labeled boxes. Keep them in the attic or on a closet shelf.

What? You had a fire? I forgot to tell you: invest in a fireproof home safe or bank safe-deposit box for records that are a pain in the neck to replace. Or buy a service that keeps online records in a server off-premises.

A home safe should be rated for fire resistance by the Underwriters Laboratories. You need a class 350 safe, which protects paper documents against high heat for at least a half hour and perhaps up to four. If you keep computer records on CDs, you'll need a class 125 safe. An unrated metal box with a lock won't do anything except keep curious children out; in a fire, the heat would scorch to ashes any documents inside.

These safes, incidentally, won't stop a jewel thief for a moment; they're only for papers. You might as well write the combination on the top to save the burglar the trouble of whacking off the lock. To protect valuables at home, you need a much more expensive vault. For items that you consider irreplaceable, rent a safe-deposit box.

Safe-deposit boxes are normally rented from a bank, although you might find one at a credit union. Small boxes, for holding papers, photographs, and a little jewelry cost around $25 to $100 a year. For a lot of valuables or your magnificent hubcap collection, the bank has larger boxes at a higher price.

Sometimes there's a waiting list, especially for the bigger boxes. As an alternative, you might look at a private vault company. It charges more than banks but is supposed to follow bank security procedures and may even offer 24-hour access—handy for dropping off your diamonds after the ball. If you have something to hide, it will interest you to know that most private vaults let you open an account under a false name (banks require identification). On the downside, private vaults may not provide all the security that customers were promised. Many have gone bankrupt.

When you rent a safe-deposit box, you sign a card. The bank or vault will also need the signatures of anyone who you think should have access to the box: your spouse, your executor, the person who holds your power of attorney, a business colleague, a friend. Every time you visit your diamonds or hubcaps, you sign again so that your signature can be checked. It takes two keys to open the box, yours and the bank's. You get two copies of your own key. If you lose one, no problem; it costs maybe $10 to $20 to replace. But it might cost $150 if you lose both. The bank doesn't keep a copy of your key, so it has to drill into your box and start you out with a brand-new lock. Give your cosigners a key only if you want them to be able to enter the box at any time. If you want them to enter it only in an emergency, keep the second key yourself but tell them where it is. (Note that the person who holds your power of attorney does not have access to your box unless he or she is on the signature card.)

What to keep in your safe-deposit box depends mainly on how hard the item is to replace. Most financial documents, such as insurance policies and cemetery deeds, can be replaced pretty quickly; you might put a copy in your box, for reference in case of fire, while keeping the original at home. But reverse that procedure—copy at home, original in the box—for documents that take a long time to procure or will cost you a fee. This category might include birth and marriage certificates, divorce papers, military records, the deed to your house, and citizenship papers. Few people have stock certificates or paper bonds anymore, but those that exist should be kept from harm. So should signed notes for any money you're owed. Safe-deposit boxes are also good repositories for personal treasures such as old family photos, lists of the contents of your house (to prove what you owned, in case of fire or theft; digital photos can be stored online), the Master List of your financial documents (page 398), and heirloom jewelry you don't wear. Keep your own list of what's in your box in a file at home, so you won't forget.

Unfortunately, nothing in this world is 100 percent secure, not even safe-deposit boxes. If a thief breaks in, the bank or vault company is not responsible for your losses unless you can prove negligence. Federal deposit insurance isn't responsible either. It covers only your deposit accounts. But your homeowners or tenants insurance should pay up to the limits of your policy. After a theft, you have to prove what you kept in the box, which is not always an easy job. Keep receipts, appraisals, and photos, including a photo of your box with the valuables in it. Put items that could be damaged by water (a flood or a burst municipal pipe) into ziptop bags or plastic containers.

When you rent the box, ask the bank who will have access to it after your death. Almost all the states give ready entry to anyone on the signature card who also has a key. If the cosigner has no key, the bank will drill the box. Anyone not on the card needs proof—for example, a *letter of testamentary*—that he or she is an heir who's allowed to remove property. If your will is missing and your representative wants to search the box for it, he or she will need a search order. Ideally, someone with signature authority should also be present. To simplify life for your heirs, keep your will at home and give the executor a signed copy (the executor is the person who makes sure that your will's provisions are carried out). If you have a cemetery deed, keep that on hand too.

If you and your spouse or mate keep separate boxes, give each other access, just in case something happens. Important! Tell your heirs and executor where the box is and where you keep the keys! Lots of property is lost because relatives haven't a clue where to look for a box in your name. If you keep a home safe, note the combination to the lock on your Master List (see page 398).

The extra careful might consider a waterproof emergency flight bag, kept on a bedroom shelf. Ask yourself what you'd need if you had to evacuate your house in a hurry because of a hurricane, flood, or fire. Pack that bag with your critical records and mementos: a copy of your homeowners insurance policy, your birth certificate, some wedding pictures. That way, you won't have to stop and think if you smell smoke in the middle of the night. Just pick up the bag and run. Include photos of what's in your home. Hurricane victims, for example, have received thousands of dollars extra from their insurers when they were able to prove exactly what they owned.

Do you really need a safe-deposit box? Few of us have documents that are truly irreplaceable. If you don't need your box for other items—heirloom jewelry, gold coins—you might decide that the annual fee isn't worth it. If the worst happens, you'll face the nuisance of replacing your birth certificate, citizenship papers, and so on, but many people consider that a risk worth taking. As an alternative to a safe-deposit box, consider scanning your important documents, filing them in your computer, and backing them up.

KEEPING RECORDS ONLINE

Set up folders on your computer for your bank statements, credit card statements, bill-pay accounts, scanned documents, and other records you keep online. File them faithfully and *back them up*! Without a backup, those records will fry when your hard drive fails (as it inevitably will). You can use a second hard drive or a service that backs up your records at another location or in the cloud. Personally, I use both. Some banks market online storage as a "virtual safe-deposit box." Make paper copies of documents you need to keep for tax purposes and file them with your tax records.

Pay your servicer's bills on time! Otherwise, you risk being locked out of your own financial records. On your Master List, include the password to this account so that your heirs, or anyone acting for you, will have access.

YOU DIDN'T LOSE IT, YOU FORGOT IT. NOW WHAT?

Money—billions of dollars of it—is mislaid in America every year. People move and don't leave a forwarding address. They forget to give their new address to every institution holding money due them. Sometimes they don't know they're owed money. Sometimes they get dotty. Maybe they die without leaving the well-organized records that you're about to create, and their heirs can't find all the property.

The federal government is holding an estimated $42 billion worth of uncashed Treasury securities and savings bonds; unclaimed Social Security benefits, civil service retirement checks, tax refunds, veterans' benefits, and refunds for mortgage insurance premiums owed to many homeowners who prepay Federal Housing Administration (FHA) loans; and property left on federal land.

The states hold perhaps $10 billion in unclaimed bank and brokerage accounts; individual retirement accounts and other pension savings; paychecks and dividend checks; funds left in unused prepaid tuition plans; refunds from telephone and electric companies that people failed to collect when they moved; uncashed money orders and cashier's checks; unused gift certificates; contents of unclaimed safe-deposit boxes; and life insurance policies that the heirs never knew about.

Every state's unclaimed-property law is a little different. But in general, a bank or other private company, including nonprofits, can't hold dormant funds for more than three to five years.

Your bank account or mutual fund is considered dormant if you've made no transactions for several years and don't answer mail about the account. Untended savings accounts are especially vulnerable. So are safe-deposit boxes that your family doesn't know about.

Dormant funds held in private hands are eventually transferred (escheated) to the states. The states list the missing owners in newspaper ads, usually in obscure publications. They may also try to find you through telephone directories, online searches, credit bureaus, and motor vehicle records. Some states try harder than others.

You can reclaim the value of your eschewed property no matter how many years have passed (except in New Hampshire, which confiscates money after three years). When stocks, bonds, and mutual funds go to the state, they're usually sold after three years and the proceeds retained, waiting for owners to show up.

To see if you're due any money held by a state, go online to the National Association of Unclaimed Property Administrators (NAUPA) (unclaimed.org or missingmoney.com), where you can link to all the state unclaimed-property offices. If you're not online, you can get online help at your local library. Most of the states list the names of everyone they're holding money for. Check for your own name in every state where you've ever lived. While you're at it, check for your parents (including those who have died) and your adult children. Recheck every couple of years to see if anything new has been added to the list. If you find your name, follow the instructions on how to claim the property. States often pay interest on reclaimed interest-bearing accounts, such as bank deposits, but not on other funds.

Unfortunately, there's no central unclaimed-property office for money held by the federal government, nor do the feds try to track down missing owners. But you can find links for specific types of unclaimed funds—such as taxes or lost pensions—at USA.gov/unclaimed -money. If you're lucky, you'll get a letter from a private tracing service saying it knows where some federal money is stashed that probably belongs to you. The price of retrieving it runs around 30 percent of the recovered funds (the service might ask for 50 percent, but when you call, you can usually talk it down). People sometimes get sore at these services because they think they charge too much. But if it weren't for their efforts, you wouldn't get any money at all. Never pay up front; that's not a legitimate request. Pay only when money is produced.

WHAT TO KEEP, WHERE TO KEEP IT, WHAT TO TOSS

Clarity, clarity. A filing system should be so logical that anyone who opens the drawers can find exactly what he or she wants. Label every folder, choosing titles that are sensible, not cute. If a financial document doesn't fit exactly into one of the categories you have already, start a new file for it. Keep weeding out documents that don't matter anymore. No sense sending your heirs on wild-goose chases. Most of these documents can be kept at home in a simple filing cabinet. There's an outside risk of losing documents to a fire or flood, so for supersafety, choose a fireproof home safe or safe-deposit box.

Your Will

You have one, of course. A good-looking, clever, glowing social success like you wouldn't be so dumb as to go without.

It is simple and safe to leave the will with your lawyer, keeping a copy for yourself. Or vice versa. On your copy, put the lawyer's name, address, and phone number. One drawback—if you see it that way—is that your family might feel forced to use that particular lawyer to handle your estate. They don't have to. They can retrieve the will and pick a different lawyer. If you think that would embarrass them, keep the will yourself. Another drawback is that your lawyer might die. Be sure there's someone in the firm who will inherit his or her files.

If you keep the will yourself, a safe-deposit box is okay, provided that you know it won't be sealed at death and your cosigner can get into it without any trouble (see page 382). If your only cosigner is your spouse, however, you run the risk of dying together. It might take some time for your remaining heirs to get the will, which is needed to confirm the executor and start settling the estate. You also might put your will into a fireproof safe, giving the executor a copy.

If you don't keep your will at home, put a note in your file telling your heirs where to find it. Whenever you make a new will, destroy the old one along with all copies.

Your Durable Power of Attorney

This is a piece of paper that says, "The named person can act for me, in all financial matters or in certain matters that I have specified here." The empowered person might be able to manage your money, sign checks to pay your bills, or sell your real estate.

Keep the power of attorney at home, in a filing cabinet or a fireproof home safe, as long as the person you named knows the combination. Give that person a signed copy for safekeeping. (I assume that you trust your deputy; otherwise you wouldn't have given him or her the power.) Don't put this important document into your safe-deposit box. Your deputy might not be able to get into it if you become mentally incapable, which is just when the power of attorney might have to be used.

Your Living Will, Health Care Proxy, and Uniform Donor Card

Your living will is a piece of paper that says, "If I'm in a permanent coma, pull the plug," or "don't pull the plug," depending on how you feel about it. The health care proxy names the person who will make sure that your wishes are carried out. This deputy can also make other medical choices if you're temporarily incapable of deciding for yourself. You should give your deputy written permission to see your medical records. If you want other friends or family members to see your records, put that in writing too.

A lawyer can draw up these documents for you. Alternatively, you might fill in the free forms you'll find at CaringInfo (caringinfo.org) or Legaldocs (legaldocs.com). Be sure you get them witnessed, as required by the laws of your state. The forms you find on the Web will explain what to do.

Keep these papers in your filing cabinet or fireproof home safe where people can find them. Give signed copies to the people who will make these ultimate choices in accordance with your wishes: your spouse or partner, your child, a friend, your doctor.

If you want to donate any of your organs after your death (please say yes; they're of no use to you and may save another person's life), fill in a Uniform Donor Card and keep it in your wallet. Tell your family of your intent. If that dreadful day should ever come, you'll have made the decision for them.

Life Insurance Policies

Keep them in your safe-deposit box only if the bank assures you that, under state law, your beneficiary can get to them immediately. Include all correspondence affecting the policy, such as change-of-beneficiary notices or proof that ownership of the policy has been transferred to someone else. The insurance company should have those records too, but there's a risk that it might lose track. Add the name, address, and phone number of your insurance agent. If you keep the policies and correspondence at home, put copies in your box or scan them into your computerized records, just in case.

In the same file, include a note about any life insurance you have through your employer and how to claim it. Also, file your receipts for mortgage-life and credit-life insurance if you've bought any. These policies pay off your loans if you die. If your executor doesn't know about them, he or she will waste money by paying the debts out of your estate.

You may have some other forms of coverage that your executor should know about. For example, if you charge a travel ticket to a credit card, it might generate $100,000 or more of life insurance if you die during the trip. You might also be covered for accidental death and dismemberment, whether you travel by plane, train, bus, or ship. Ditto if your accident occurs in an airline terminal or while traveling on public transportation to or from the terminal.

The government will cancel your guaranteed student loans or PLUS loans (Parent Loans for Undergraduate Students) if you die or become permanently disabled.

There may be government benefits if you ever served in the armed forces. Your surviving spouse or minor children should also get a $255 death benefit from Social Security.

Credit union members sometimes have small life insurance policies linked to their savings accounts.

If you belong to the American Automobile Association (AAA), you might be covered if you die in an auto accident. Not all clubs offer this protection, however, and coverage varies according to the type of accident.

Other clubs and organizations may also offer small policies as part of your membership package.

Clues to any payments of this sort should be kept in your life insurance file.

Health, Disability, and Long-Term Care Insurance Policies

Keep the insurance policy or the booklet explaining it in your file cabinet, so you can check it whenever you want. As backup, put the names of your health insurer, the policy numbers, the phone number of your company's employee-benefits office, or the name of your insurance agent on your Master List. Also, keep the booklets explaining your benefits under Medicare or Medicaid.

If you're arguing with your HMO or insurance company about what should be treated or which bills should be covered, put everything in writing and keep copies. You'll need these records for an appeal or a lawsuit.

A disability policy or long-term care insurance can also be kept on file. Add the name of the insurer and the policy numbers to your Master List.

Homeowners, Tenants, and Auto Insurance

You usually get a new policy every 6 or 12 months, but don't throw the old ones out right away. If someone was injured on your property or in your car 18 months ago and develops back pains from a previously undiscovered crack in a spinal disk, you'll want to be able to prove that you were insured at the time (especially if you've changed companies). Your insurer should have all the records, but you need backup, just in case. Furthermore, the language of insurance policies changes over the years. It could be important to know exactly what you were covered for when an injury occurred.

Keep current policies on file and old policies in a box somewhere. State statutes of limitations normally run for two or three years from the time the medical problem is discovered, so you could be sued for an injury three years after it happened. When your liability has expired, you can throw the policies out.

As usual, put the names of these insurance companies, the policy numbers, and the name of your insurance agent on your Master List. File information on how to make a claim. If you bought special riders for valuables such as furs, art, jewelry, and silver, include appraisals of their current value or sales slips showing what you paid for them.

Monroney Labels

A *what*? Who's Monroney? He's an otherwise obscure U.S. senator who, in 1958, helped create the label you get on a new car listing all its features, serial number, and other important data. These labels come in handy when you need information for insurance claims, recalls, and resales. Drop them into your auto insurance file.

Household Inventory

I'm not your mother. I don't care that your room is messy and you don't write, but you still haven't done your household inventory, and how many times do I have to tell you? I know it's boring. I know that you started out in the living room, put down your pencil while you made some coffee, and never got any further. That's because you were using a pencil. The simple way is to use a camera. Take pictures of every room, every open closet, every open drawer. If you're using a video camera, comment on anything especially valuable. Keep sales slips for expensive purchases. Otherwise you'll have to compile an inventory of all your possessions from memory if your house burns down. Get appraisals on your antiques, art, rare books, furs, good jewelry, silver, and special collections. Some will need special insurance riders.

Put the appraisals, pictures, and sales slips in your safe-deposit box or scan them into your computer records. If you use a home safe instead, stash copies at a friend's house in case your safe isn't quite as fireproof as promised.

Personal Papers

Anything that you need to prove who you are, how long you've been around, and what you're entitled to needs to be carefully filed—some items in a file cabinet, others in a home safe or safe-deposit box or scanned into your computerized records. The important papers would include your birth certificate, marriage certificate, all documents relating to separation and divorce, military service records, proofs of citizenship, adoption papers, diplomas, licenses, passports, permits, union cards, Social Security card, and family health records such as vaccinations and dates of operations. Keeping an expired passport makes it easier to get a new one. Don't stash your military records before checking with the service to be sure that its dates agree with yours. If the service has them wrong and your survivors don't realize it, they might not get all the benefits they're due. Military service organizations send out newsletters about benefit changes; save those, too.

As a general strategy, keep at home anything you'll need to produce for employment, insurance, or government benefits. Choose safer storage for records that are rarely used or hard to replace. You might consider a safe-deposit box for originals, while keeping copies at home.

Tax Records

Yes, I know. You accidentally added the veterinarian's bill to your deductible medical expenses. How long does the Internal Revenue Service (IRS) have to catch and fine you? Three years, during which time you'd better keep not only your tax return but all supporting data. After that, you're in the clear and can toss the return, unless the vet is the least of it. The government has six years to audit you if you underreported your income by more than 25 percent. If it pursues you for fraud, or if you filed no tax return at all, there is no statute of limitations; you can be hit for back taxes anytime.

If you lose your federal returns, you can get copies covering the past 10 years. You pay nothing for an IRS transcript (a computer print-out showing what was on the original return). For actual copies of the returns, or returns for earlier years, you're charged $50 each. Request Form 4506 for copies and Form 4506T for transcripts. For state returns, ask the state what's available. These are just the returns themselves, of course, not the data proving your right to the deductions.

In many cases, you should keep returns longer than the typical four years (the year you filed plus three more). For example:

Keep the returns and supporting documents that show any investment losses you're carrying forward and tax deductions taken on limited partnerships.

Keep the returns that show any contributions you made to a traditional individual retirement account that were not tax deductible. When you start withdrawing money, you'll need these records to establish how much of each IRA withdrawal is tax exempt. Leave a note for your heirs telling them to watch out for this. If they don't know you made those contributions, they may inadvertently pay taxes on the whole amount.

If you qualify for a company pension, consider keeping every single return you file, together with your W-2 forms. Companies don't always keep accurate records of how long you worked and how much you contributed to your retirement plan, especially companies that merge or are sold. You may need your tax returns and W-2s to prove what you're due when you leave your job.

In fact, it's worth keeping all your returns if you have the room. You can ditch the supporting documents (except for the W-2s and 1099s). But it's nice to have the full returns on hand if one of your employers didn't report your earnings to Social Security, reported an incorrect amount, or reported it under the wrong Social Security number. The returns also protect you from claims that, in some past year, you never filed returns at all.

Paycheck Stubs

If you trust your employer to add up your annual earnings correctly (as I do), you can throw your pay stubs or receipts away. But sometimes they contain important information that isn't included on your year-end W-2, such as the number of hours worked. If your union or employer keeps poor records, you may need your pay stubs to prove your eligibility for pension and welfare benefits. The stubs also make it simple to claim unemployment pay. Freelancers should keep all payment receipts for the year. Compare them with the 1099 forms you get, to make sure that your clients reported the payments correctly. Then you can throw the receipts away.

Employee Benefits

They've gotten so complicated that companies often publish them in loose-leaf notebooks. File everything. Keep the annual statements on the status of your pension, profit-sharing, salary deferral, or retirement savings plans so you can follow their progress. Keep employment contracts in your home file, with a copy in your safe-deposit box or the office of the lawyer who negotiated them.

Retirement Plans

Add to your Master List the numbers and locations of all your retirement accounts: individual retirement accounts, simplified employee pensions, 403(b)s, 457s, Solo 401(k)s, company plans. Keep the plan documents in your file cabinet along with the annual reports showing how your investments are doing. Keep records of any loans you took against your plans and loans repaid. An unpaid loan may cost you a tax penalty if you leave the job, and you'll want to be sure that your employer's records are right. Finally, keep withdrawal records. Throw them out when the withdrawals show up on the annual statement of your account.

Bank Records

Canceled checks come in many forms these days. You might get the actual checks with your monthly statement; miniature pictures of the checks; or lists of the checks, delivered with a statement online. The miniatures and online statements are easy to file. If you get the checks themselves, keep the ones you might need for tax or insurance purposes. You might keep other checks too, for three years or so. You never know when they'll come in handy. Here are seven good reasons to have them on hand:

If you want to make a budget, old checks are a road map to what you've been spending.

The IRS might disagree with your version of life and ask for proof. Canceled checks can sometimes stand in for receipts in substantiating tax deductions (although usually the IRS wants receipts).

Old checks show the names of the people you've done business with and might want to find again.

It's easier to collect in full on a property insurance claim if you can show the company what you paid for your rugs, furniture, and other damaged items.

Your ex-spouse might claim that you missed some child support payments. If you didn't, your canceled checks will prove it.

You might have to prove to one of your creditors that a bill was paid. For this purpose, keeping checks for six months should be enough.

If you're one half of an unmarried couple and own property jointly, the checks prove what you paid for, which could be important if you split or your mate dies.

If you also have loans or certificates of deposit, keep the most recent statements showing their status. Old ones can be tossed. (I do cleanup once a year.) When you make new deposits, keep the receipts until the monthly statement comes in, so that you can check that they were entered correctly. Keep loan agreements; when the loan is repaid, throw out the agreements but keep the final closing statement. File any records for open savings accounts. Keep copies of letters that confirm the instructions you gave about your accounts or CDs, including beneficiary forms. Keep all disclosures you receive from the bank about its fees and interest rates so that you can check any changes you question. Note your PIN (personal identification number), lest you forget.

Receipts for Paid Bills

In your file cabinet. Keep receipts for every expense that is tax deductible, along with the checks or credit card statements showing that you paid. The IRS prefers both if you're ever audited.

In your fireproof safe or safe-deposit box. Keep receipts for high-cost purchases such as furs and antiques. They'll prove your claim if you have to dicker with the insurance company after a fire or theft. Also, keep statements that show you no longer owe money on past debts such as mortgages, closed credit card accounts, old cell phone contracts, and private loans. That protects you if the company ever claims that you never paid.

In a box on your bureau or desk. Keep receipts for gifts until you know that you won't have to take them back (if asked, many stores now put "gift receipts" in the box, so that recipients can return things themselves). If you pay in cash, keep the receipt long enough to be sure that the item is in good working order. Throw other receipts out. Your canceled check, debit-card entry, or credit card bill is normally proof enough of payment.

Medical and Drug Bills

Submit them all to your insurer. They'll be rejected until you have met the annual deductible, but unless you submit them, your insurer won't know when reimbursement should start.

File copies of all unreimbursed bills for the year. Expenses exceeding 10 percent of your adjusted gross income are deductible on your tax return. You might qualify for this write-off if you've been very sick, are poorly insured, or if you're paying premiums on long-term care insurance. If you get no tax deduction, throw the bills away.

Keep any bills that you and your insurer are arguing about, along with copies of all the letters you write and receive and notes of telephone calls.

Monthly Credit Card Statements

Check every one as soon as it comes, to be sure that every bill is actually yours. A thief needs only your credit card number, not the card itself, to buy goods and charge them to your account. Paper bills are easy to check; get in the habit of reading through the purchases when you open the envelope. If you're billed online, however, it's all too easy to pay without checking the statement, especially if you've arranged for automatic payments. Put a recurring alert in your computer's calendar, telling you to read the bill.

Add to your file on homeowners insurance any statements that show the price of something particularly expensive. Keeping the rest of your statements is optional. Personally, I hang on to them for two years. Who knows when an item charged and paid for will erroneously pop up on my bill again? Who knows what will break and need returning—and how else will I remember the store? Who knows when I'll want to look up the name of that great Cajun restaurant in Biloxi? Back bills also help you track your spending and draw up a budget. But if you never use these records, toss them. For tax purposes, you need to keep records only of business purchases.

When you take something back to a store, you'll get a return receipt. Keep it right where you open your mail, to remind you to check that the money was actually credited to your account. When it is, throw the receipt away.

Deeds, Titles, Title Insurance, Surveys

Records of purchase, property descriptions, and proofs of ownership, including the title to your car, belong in your fireproof home safe or safe-deposit box or scanned into your computer. Copies are available if you lose the originals, but it's simpler to protect the records you have.

If you inherit property, keep any evidence of what it was worth when you got it. You'll need it to figure the gain when you sell.

File any records of legal proceedings, current tax assessments, and—if you're in a condominium or planned community—rules of the property owners' association. If you rent, file a copy of your lease.

Debts

In the file cabinet: your mortgage, bank loan records, contracts for installment purchases. No problem if a fire burns them up. Your creditors will remember. They'll even have copies.

But paid-off debts are another story. Get a receipt for the canceled note and keep it in your safe-deposit box. Proof of payment is especially important when you borrow money from an individual. He or she may note the debt in his or her records and forget to erase it. The heirs might ask you (or your survivors) for payment. The receipt shows that you're clean.

Instructions and Warranties

File the operating instructions for any equipment you buy. File warranty information. File maintenance contracts.

Money Owed to You

Keep the note in your home safe or safe-deposit box. Keep the repayment records in your file cabinet. When you get all your money back, formally cancel the note.

Note any refundable deposits, to the electric company, the phone company, your landlord. When you move, you're entitled to get them back.

Household Help

If you have an employee, keep proof that you paid all applicable taxes: Social Security, unemployment, disability, and any other tax your state requires. Keep a copy of the W-2 form you give your employee each January.

Your Phone File

If you keep track of your friends' names, addresses, and phone numbers in your computer, be sure the list is backed up. Your appointments too. If you keep these records in a book, photocopy it every few months.

Your Computer

Back up your files! If your computer is password protected, note the password in a separate file in your filing cabinet. Email critical information to another computer—say, in your office—in case a virus destroys both your computer and your hard drive backup. You also can use an Internet storage service that keeps your data in a remote location. This applies to phones and tablets as well as laptops. Beware free storage services. In the past, they've tended to go out of business, taking your backups with them. A service you pay for will be more dependable.

Investments

Your safe-deposit box, fireproof home safe, or files of scanned documents are the right place for the following items:

Paper stock certificates. They're rarely issued anymore, but you may have inherited some. At home, keep a list of their names, denominations, certificate numbers, and CUSIP (Committee on Uniform Securities Identification Procedures) numbers, so you can remember—and refer to—what you have. Take great care with your paper securities: It's costly and time consuming to replace them.

Records of new purchases are almost always held by your brokerage firm, which is simpler and safer.

Your right to stock options or deferred compensation. These are payments that your heirs might overlook.

Paper bonds. All new U.S. Treasury securities exist only as blips in the mind of a computer, so you have no actual certificates to store. Most corporate bonds and municipals are also issued this way, but store any certificates you have. Also, store any paper U.S. Savings Bonds. In your home file, keep all your purchase records, including a list of the bonds' denominations, serial numbers, and issue dates. You may need them to prove your ownership if an interest or principal payment goes astray.

Gold, silver, or platinum bars or coins.

The names and account numbers of your mutual funds and on your Master List).

Your home file is the right place for:

Informational material you get from your mutual funds. Keep the original prospectus and sales literature. They tell you what you bought, how to redeem shares, and the services offered to investors. Keep any letters that say the fund has changed its rules. Keep the fund's annual reports. They show its performance compared with the market in general—a valuable history when you're deciding whether to hold or sell. Keep your year-end statements, showing purchases and sales. You needn't keep all the interim statements and reports.

Your brokerage house agreement and annual statements. Keep all confirmations of trades. You have to know exactly when each security was bought and sold, the price, and the commission you paid in order to figure out your income tax. Add up your commissions once a year to see what you're paying for the account. (Commissions usually appear only on your "confirms," not on your annual statement. Some packaged investments, such as certain types of annuities, don't disclose commissions at all, which is why they get away with charging 5 to 7 percent!)

The original prospectus and sales material for any initial public offering you own. If a deal goes bad and was misrepresented, your prospectus could help establish grounds for a lawsuit. Also keep the annual reports that chart the investment's progress.

Take notes of all conversations you have with your financial adviser. Put all your instructions in writing, including follow-up letters after a phone conversation. Keep copies. If you get into an argument about how the broker handled your account, these records can support your case.

Rental Properties

For reference, keep a couple years' worth of income and expense records in your current files. Older receipts belong on the shelf with your back tax records.

Business at Home

There you are, in the spare-bedroom-turned-office, trading currency futures for all the parents at your day care center. You know that you can write off your telephone expenses (a separate phone line is best) against the potloads of profits you're making. But what else? For a home-based business, take a lesson from an accountant on how to keep track of income and expenses and what your tax deductions are. For example, you may be able to depreciate that part of the house that serves as your office. You might also be able to write off a portion of what you pay to heat, light, clean, and insure your house.

So you'll need to keep all those bills and canceled checks. Keep current bills in the filing cabinet and old bills with the tax records. Carry a business diary or personal device to record tax-deductible expenses for travel, entertainment, supplies, and so on. The IRS gets dark under the eyes when your diary reads as if you composed it just in time to make the audit.

Trust Documents

Keep the originals with your lawyer or in a safe-deposit box. Put copies in your files.

Charities and Gifts

Keep copies of pledges to charities and the letters that acknowledge your contribution. Keep canceled checks showing how much you gave. Keep the appraisals on donated property. If you do volunteer work, keep track of the miles you drive on the charity's business. They're tax deductible.

Put notes about important gifts to friends and family members in your safe-deposit box if the gifts will affect the size of your estate tax or keep the peace in a squabbling family.

Bankruptcy Records

I hope you never find yourself in bankruptcy court. But if you do, keep careful records of all the debts that were discharged. Creditors have a nasty habit of trying to collect debts you no longer owe.

In Case of Death

Keep a last-wishes file. Include the cemetery deed if you have one, material for your obituary (relatives often get things wrong), final instructions about your funeral if it matters to you, and a copy of your living will if you don't want to be kept alive by extraordinary means. Tell your relatives and executor about this file and where to find it. President Franklin D. Roosevelt made detailed notes about how his funeral was to be conducted and put them in the White House safe. They weren't found until after he was buried.

Safe Deposit Box Key

Drop it into a toolbox. Keep it with the handkerchiefs. For obscurity—the usual fate of a key to a safe-deposit box—those places are as good as any. In my dreams, however, I see the key resting in your top desk or bureau drawer, labeled, with the bank's name attached (what's the good of a key if your survivors don't know which bank to take it to?). I see a note on your Master List telling everybody where it is. Ditto for the combination to the lock on your home safe.

The Master List of Where Everything Is

Record the results of your masterful filing system in your computer or on a couple sheets of paper and leave this Master List in your home file for your executor and heirs. Put a copy in your safe deposit box. List:

- Your insurance policies and insurance agents
- Employee benefits and the phone number of the office that handles them
- Bank accounts and any particular banker that you deal with
- Where to find your safe-deposit box and keys
- Where you keep your will or living trust and the name of the lawyer who drew it up
- Your executor or trustee
- Where other trust documents are
- Where all your personal papers are

- Your brokers or investment advisers—names, addresses, and phone numbers
- Your accountant
- Where to find your securities and retirement accounts
- Where your tax records are
- What properties you own and where the deeds are
- Your debts and any money owed you
- Your Social Security number and that of every family member
- Your important computer passwords
- Where you've hidden your home safe and what the combination is
- Where you keep your emergency flight bag, if you have one
- A list of all your credit cards—account numbers and emergency telephone numbers—in case your wallet is stolen and you have to cancel them
- Where your last-wishes file is

Finally, photocopy everything in your wallet: ID cards, driver's license, health insurance card, and other items you carry for reference. That makes them easier to replace.

Appendix 4
Be Your Own Planner . . .
Or Find One You Trust

The secret, revealed

**You've been waiting for the secret to handling
money well. Here it is: Use common sense.
The simplest choices are the best ones.
Impulse is your enemy, time your friend.**

Most families don't need professional investment advisers, especially
if your assets are principally in retirement plans. Sensible management isn't hard! To be your own guru, you need only a list of
objectives, a few simple financial products, realistic investment expectations, a time frame that gives your investments time to work,
and a well-tempered humbug detector to keep you from falling for
rascally sales pitches. Don't put off decisions for fear you're not making the best choice in every circumstance. Often, there isn't a "best"
choice. Any one of several will work.

On the other hand, almost everyone can profit from a two-hour
conversation with a *true* financial planner (see what I mean by "true"
on page 405). The planner can help you set priorities, align your
spending and saving with your lifetime goals, spot things you've
overlooked, and make other valuable suggestions.

I can think of some circumstances where a planner is a must.
For example:

You earn good wages but cannot manage to save a dime.
You need a reality check. Someone has to show you—in dollars and

cents—how little you'll have when you retire unless you shape up. Most of us shape ourselves up. If you can't, get help.

You face a question that can be answered only by someone with technical expertise. For example, your company might have made you an early-retirement buyout offer and you want to examine your alternatives. Or, you're retiring and have several choices about how to handle the money in your retirement plan. That's a one-time decision with many tax and personal ramifications, and you want to get it right.

You're following your own plan—for savings, investments, and insurance—and wonder if an expert can improve it. Arrange for a meeting at an hourly fee. Make it clear that you want to talk about strategies and concepts, not sit through a sales pitch for financial products. (You shouldn't be with a planner who sells products in the first place.) Make no decisions until you've gone home and thought about it.

You have a substantial amount of money and lack the time, interest, and knowledge to manage it yourself.

You're not interested in planning, won't do it yourself, or are uncomfortable making decisions on your own. You start with a plan but don't have the discipline to keep it up. Find a planner and off-load the job.

You're pretending everything is fine even though you have only $5,000 in retirement savings and $25,000 in credit card debt. A planner can yank you out of denial and ease you onto a more productive path.

A talk with a planner will have one of three results: (1) You'll find a wonderful adviser who makes suggestions you're grateful for and whom you'll decide to work with on a continuing basis. These will almost certainly be fee-only planners—see page 408. (2) You'll feel more confident that your personal decisions have generally been good ones and will continue managing your affairs yourself. You'll incorporate some of the planner's new ideas. (3) You'll run into a planner who makes you doubt your competence while urging you to rely on his or her advice. Or a planner who says that you'll do even better by buying the products (especially annuities) that he or she sells. In this last case, turn up the volume on your humbug detector. These planners earn commissions and plan to earn them from you.

Don't go near a broker or commissioned planner if you've just come into a lot of money (an inheritance, an insurance settlement, a lump sum retirement payout) and don't know what to do with it. Clients with loose cash and weak convictions are fresh meat, ready for roasting. A self-interested planner may urge you to buy high-commission investments that serve his or her objectives better than yours. Because you don't know much about investing, you won't know what's going on.

Before you set foot in the office of a stockbroker, insurance agent, or financial planner, learn the basics yourself. Sock your money into bank certificates of deposit or a money market fund, then study up. Read books. Work out your priorities. Take all the time you need to understand the tried-and-true principles of successful investing. Six months, one year, the wait doesn't matter. During that time, your money will quietly earn interest with no risk of loss and no risk of slipping into bad hands. The only expert that a novice can safely visit is a certified public accountant, for tax advice. That is, provided that the accountant doesn't sell financial products.

When you're ready to launch, you have two possible directions: (1) Try investing yourself, a little in this mutual fund, a little in that one (Chapter 9). Give it a year, see how it feels, then invest some more. Don't worry about "missing the market." There's a new market every day. Once you've had some experience, you might discover you like it and keep going. Or you might decide that you want professional advice. (2) Turn to an investment adviser. You now know the language. You should be able to tell the difference between good and poor advice. That's what this long apprenticeship was for: to develop your ability to judge.

THE BEST THING A TRUE PLANNER CAN DO FOR YOU

Help you set goals, prepare for life's potential shocks, then align your spending, saving, and investing to get you through. Picking investments is incidental compared with the importance of creating a framework for long-term success.

WHICH KIND OF PROFESSIONAL TO SEE

See a certified public accountant (CPA)—for tax planning, tax form preparation, and small-business planning advice. Enrolled agents, who are licensed to represent you before the IRS, and public accountants, also have tax practices. Some CPAs have expanded their practice into personal financial planning, earning a personal financial specialist (PFS) designation. It's a weaker designation than a CFP (page 405), but the accounting profession intends to strengthen it.

See a tax attorney—for wills and estate planning. Any lawyer can provide an "I love you" will. That means "Everything to my spouse; if my spouse dies first, everything to the children (in trust, if they're minors); with my spouse's name on all beneficiary forms, such as 401(k)s and IRAs." For anything more complicated, see an attorney who specializes in estate planning.

See a life insurance agent—*Term life insurance* is right for young families and for workers past midlife who want to leave additional money to a spouse. Premiums are low. The policies don't accumulate cash values; they simply pay off if you die. You can shop for term insurance yourself at Term4sale.com. Cash value policies, by contrast, accumulate money that you can borrow against or cash in at a later age. For that privilege, you pay much higher premiums. *Whole-life policies* guarantee the size of their cash values. The types of insurance called *variable life* and *universal life* make no such guarantees. Instead, the amount of your cash value will depend, in part, on the performance of the bond and stock markets. For highly competitive variable or universal life, go to TIAA-CREF.org or AmeritasDirect.com.

A chartered life underwriter (CLU) knows more about insurance than the average agent. Your attorney and insurance planner should work together if you want a policy to help pay estate taxes or buy your share of a closely held business.

See a health insurance agent—for health insurance, disability insurance, and long-term care policies.

See a stockbroker—for help with buying stock, bonds, and mutual funds, although there are better ways. See page 235. Note that most brokers nowadays call themselves financial consultants, financial advisers, financial analysts, or vice presidents. They're all still stockbrokers, and their business is selling. They're not true planners or investment advisers.

See a Registered Investment Adviser (RIA)—for managing a large sum of money. Independent advisers set minimums in the $150,000 to $1 million range. They're *fiduciaries,* meaning that they have to put the interests of their clients ahead of their own. They also have to be registered with the state or the Securities and Exchange Commission and make a variety of disclosures about their backgrounds, the products they sell, and the fees they charge.

Titles such as "investment consultant" or "wealth manager" are self-awarded. Anyone can use them, whether they have expertise or not. I'd assume *not.* For personal money management, stick with RIAs. Anyone who charges you for investment advice and isn't an RIA could be breaking the law.

For an excellent explanation of the difference between brokers, advisers, and financial planners, including their services and differing legal obligations to customers, get the free brochure "Cutting through the Confusion" on the website run by the North American

Securities Administrators Association (nasaa.org). Click on Investor Education, then on Library.

See a "planner"? *No.* Anyone can claim to be a financial planner. There are no rules. When scouting for a true planner, you're seeking specific professional and educational credentials. Plain old financial planners, without those credentials, are imposters.

See a Certified Financial Planner (CFP)—for advice on how your finances fit together: budgeting, saving, taxes, insurance, investing, college accounts, and retirement planning. There are two types of CFPs:

1. CFPs who sell financial products and charge commissions. They're qualified planners. But because they have to sell to make a living, their advice is inevitably biased, even if they don't mean it to be. They don't have a lot of time to spend on issues such as budgeting, getting out of debt, and retirement savings such as 401(k)s, which don't require you to buy something from them.

2. CFPs who sell no products and charge only fees. To my mind, these are the true planners. They engage you in personal discussions that help you sort out your priorities, align your budget with your goals, and arrive at a financial plan that works. Many fee-only planners are also Registered Investment Advisers and will manage your money, if that's what you want. Usually they invest it in low-cost, no-load mutual funds or exchange-traded funds. To qualify for money management services, you'll probably need an investment account in the $50,000 to $200,000 range, although some planners accept less. In a full-service shop, you'll also find accountants and tax attorneys, and will be given leads to insurance professionals.

See a bank trust department—for handling a large trust for dependents after your death. Some trust departments have stellar investment records; others are mediocre and with customer service

I'd call languid at best. Look for a bank that provides full reports of its investment performance (many of them don't), and examine at a sample before signing up. You want to see your trust's percentage gain or loss compared with standard stock and bond indexes. Minimum trust: in the $200,000 to $500,000 range, depending on the institution. Big brokerage firms handle trust business too.

See the websites of the major no-load (no sales commission) mutual fund groups—for useful consumer advice about allocating assets and making long-term investment decisions. They often have online newsletters explaining different kinds of investments and helping do-it-yourselfers with college or retirement planning. You'll also find excellent materials at morningstar.com.

I have mixed feelings about the retirement-planning calculators available on the Web. You enter certain financial data and the calculators purport to tell you how much more you ought to be saving for your retirement. Their weaknesses are obvious. Some ask for data that are hard to get (if you have a pension, do you know how much it will pay when you retire?). Some ask for too little data to give you a meaningful result. You have to make loads of assumptions (What's the likely future inflation rate? How fast will your salary increase? What will you spend in retirement?)—as if you knew. A 1 percent change in your forecasted investment returns could add or subtract $200,000 from your projected retirement assets. What good is that? A couple of years ago, *Kiplinger's Personal Finance* magazine put a simple case through five prominent online calculators: a married couple, with a simple savings plan, wondered how much retirement income they could expect their growing nest egg to deliver. The answers differed wildly.

On the other hand, using an online calculator shows a commitment to finding out what you're going to need to retire on. The answers may be different, but they give you a general sense of whether or not you have enough. Usually you don't, and the numbers you see are a wake-up call. Research has shown that people who use these calculators save more money than people who don't.

Should I See a "Senior Specialist"?

No, no, no! State regulators warn that "senior specialists," "senior advisers," or "retirement advisers" have little expertise beyond marketing and selling. They probably earned their so-called credentials by taking a weekend course. They're trained to appeal to older people who might be susceptible to pitches for fixed- or equity-indexed annuities, variable annuities, living trusts, and other products that pay high commissions. Typically, they'll advertise an "educational" seminar, with a name such as Senior Financial Survival Seminar or Senior Financial Safety Workshop. You'll get a free lunch and lectures from "experts" who claim to have nothing to sell. But of course they do. They'll offer to review your investments or estate plan "free," then advise you to switch into the products they offer. Don't do it! Throw away almost every business card that suggests you're dealing with someone especially trained to understand the kinds of investments older people need. For warnings from regulators on free-lunch seminars and the typical investments sold there, see the pages for individual investors at nasaa.org and sec.gov.

I said throw away *almost* every business card. There are three legitimate designations, based on rigorous curriculum. For details, see page 30.

Other Financial Designations

There are hundreds of letters that financial advisers can put next to their names, many of them worthless. If you wonder about what stands behind a particular designation, go to finra.org and under "For Investors," click on "Products & Professionals," then on

"Understanding Professional Designations." You'll see who awards the title and how much study it takes. If you can't find it at **FINRA**, look it up on the Web. If the adviser can get a designation with just a few days of study—say, 30 hours—what does it say for his or her expertise? Not much. All it does is create apparently credible business cards for a hustler with something to sell.

WHAT ABOUT "THE PLAN"?

Among most financial planners, The Plan is out of style. In theory, it's your starting point: a comprehensive tome—part customized, part boilerplate—that analyzes everything you've done so far and points to additions and changes that you ought to make. In professional hands, true plans cost a lot of money—typically $2,000 to $6,000. Clients haven't wanted to pay.

So most plans today amount to sales tools, promoted by stockbrokers, insurance agents, and planners who primarily sell products. The cost: anywhere from $250 to $2,500. You fill in a questionnaire about your finances. Back comes a computer-generated program, in hard covers, telling you what you lack. The analysis may well produce some good ideas. On the other hand, GIGO often rules: garbage in, garbage out. The program is designed to sell, not to explore alternatives. The questionnaire might not even consider your best investment options—for example, adding more money to your tax-deferred 401(k). The planner would rather you spent the money on products he or she has for sale.

As an experiment, I once purchased three of these commercial plans. My question to each salesperson was "Can I afford to retire?" The plans came up with radically different answers and were short of true planning ideas except for investments I should add. Those investments would have led me wrong.

What if you pay $1,500 for what turns out to be an unsuitable plan? Some clients execute it anyway because they don't want to "waste" the money they've already spent. That attitude plays into the planner's hands, who's ready to sell you products on the spot. I say: *walk away.* You're lucky that you've lost only the fee you paid up front and not all the rest of the money that might have followed.

When you work with a genuine planner, not a salesperson in disguise, a plan will evolve. Initially, you might get a miniplan addressing the question you came to ask—for example, "Am I saving enough for retirement?" or "What should I do with the money I've inherited?" If you keep working with that planner, you'll gradually address other issues, and a full-fledged blueprint will emerge. It won't be a plan in hard covers, it will be a comprehensive strategy for reaching your personal goals.

GOALS-BASED PLANNING

All planning should be based on what you want out of life. Start with your goals: a sufficient retirement income, college for your children, getting out of debt, a nice vacation every year, leaving a legacy for your heirs. A good planner will look at your current and projected income and assets, apply it to your goals, and see if your current savings are enough. If not, the discussions begin. What matters most? What could you downgrade? How much more could you save? Note that nothing involves buying financial products! This is entirely a mind game. You have to understand, deep in your soul, how your spending and saving affect what you'll be able to do. You might even call this *budget-based planning.* Having money tomorrow depends on what you spend today.

If you're doing your own planning, get out your trusty yellow pad. You'll find plenty of guidelines in the earlier chapters of this book. Define your financial objectives and estimate how much money you'll need for each. Set out a strategy for debt repayment and how you're going to raise your retirement savings. Implement your investment program with suitable mutual funds. It's important to write everything down. In your head, a plan is only a vague hope that things will turn out well. On paper, it's an action project that can be tested against your progress every year.

To help you with retirement saving, you'll find plenty of calculators on the Web. They'll give you a general idea of how much you should save to reach the retirement income you want or at what age your savings will run out if you don't improve. None will give you exactly the same answer; some are wide of the mark. Nevertheless, if they all say that you'll be flat broke somewhere between ages 71 and 76, you'll know what to do: work longer (if you can), save more, *and* plan to spend less after you retire.

WHAT MATTERS MOST WHEN YOU'RE LOOKING FOR A FINANCIAL PLANNER?

You might expect me to say empathy, expertise, clear thinking, ability to explain, patience, delicacy in dealing with family issues, understanding your particular goals and financial position, investment smarts, honesty, responsiveness, and fidelity to the Boy Scout and Girl Scout oaths. Yes, you want every one of those things. But first and foremost, you want a planner who charges no sales commissions, only fees—that is, a *fee-only* planner. You pay for advice and perhaps money management, not for financial products.

Planners who charge commissions can make their living only if they sell you products. No matter how nice, no matter how smart, no matter that he or she is your friend, neighbor, or cousin, commissioned planners have to put their own interests first. They think, sincerely, that the stuff they sell is exactly what you need. How else would you expect them to think? But what you need is unbiased advice, and commissioned planners can't give it. Nor do they have the time to help you sort out your priorities and think your way through family issues. They have to sell.

So when you're shopping for a planner, ask how he or she is paid. If the answer is "I'm paid by fees" (because that's what people want), you have to unwind the answer. There's a big difference between *fee* and *fee only*. Here are the five ways advisers are generally paid.

Commission only. These planners don't make a cent unless they sell you something that carries a sales commission. They lean toward high-commission products, which presents a tremendous conflict of interest. You might not be able to see the commission because it's hidden in the product's fees (for example, inside your annual cost of a variable annuity). But trust me, the fees are there. If the planners say, "You pay nothing, I'm paid by the annuity company," laugh. *Of course* you pay.

Fee and commission, also called fee *based*. This is probably the most common arrangement. The planner charges a fee for certain services—for example, for drawing a simple plan or overseeing your investments—and also earns commissions on any products you buy. If commissions are deducted from the fee, the arrangement is called *fee offset*.

But make no mistake about it: sales commissions are the driving force and produce the same biases you see in commission-only planners. About half the planners disclose their commissions to clients, according to a study by the Securities and Exchange Commission. The rest leave you in the dark unless you press for information.

You can get good advice from a competent fee-and-commission planner, but it always comes with something to buy. In judging any proposed investment, keep in mind that it serves the planner's needs, probably ahead of yours. A bias toward high-commission products, such as variable annuities, is easy to spot. So is the bias away from investments that don't yield commissions, such as putting more money into your 401(k). More subtle is the bias to sell you something, anything, in cases where nothing but good advice would have served.

Some fee-based planners are in transition to a fee-only practice. They work in independent shops, not big brokerage houses. You can spot them by their interest in genuine planning—paying attention to your spending, saving, employee benefits, and personal goals. Even so, you're better off waiting until they finally cut the cord to sales commissions.

Fee-based managed accounts. I list these separately because they masquerade as fee only. A stockbroker (oops, I mean "financial adviser") oversees your account and makes recommendations while separate investment advisers manage your money. You pay a fixed percentage of assets. The total cost typically comes to 2 to 3 percent, and you get no additional financial planning services. What stops this arrangement from being fee only is that the broker can sell you commissioned products on the side—for example, variable annuities and non-traded real estate investment trusts. Pass this arrangement by.

Salary and bonus (or commission). This is typical for planners who work at banks. They may also act as agents for insurance companies. In either case, they generally sell commissionable mutual funds and tax-deferred annuities and have the same biases as any other planners whose income depends on how much they sell.

Fee only. These planners charge only for their advice, accepting no other form of remuneration. Their fee structures vary—hourly charges, monthly or quarterly retainers, fees per job, or a percentage of the money they have under management. If all they do is manage money, you should pay less than 1 percent. One percent is a fair price, however, if they also provide other forms of financial advice. Some planners combine retainers with money management fees in the 0.3 percent range. Either way, the products that fee-only planners sell are entirely no-load—meaning that no sales commissions are attached. Of all the financial consulting arrangements, this is the cleanest.

Fee-only planners have conflicts of interest too. Say, for example, that you're leaving your job and have money invested in the company's 401(k). You can leave it there or roll it into an individual retirement account. Often, it's best to leave the money where it is. But if the planner can persuade you to switch to the IRA, he or she will probably get the money to manage, at a fee of perhaps 1 percent a year. Or say that you're thinking of using a chunk of cash to pay down your mortgage. The planner might advise you to leave the money in your managed investment account, where, again, it will throw off a 1 percent fee. The planner's advice might be right, financially, if the numbers show that your investments are doing well. A true planner, however, should consider whether you'd be happier owning your home free and clear. You have to be on your toes when evaluating any planner's advice.

Some fee-only planners, especially certified public accountants, provide no ongoing help. They give you advice, then turn you loose. That's not too helpful unless you can implement the plan yourself. Otherwise you'll pay double: once for the plan and again for the services of a stockbroker or insurance agent (who might change the plan and charge you commissions of their own).

Incidentally, fees charged for tax and investment advice, on taxable accounts, can be written off on your income tax return. They're part of that bagful of miscellaneous expenses that are deductible to the extent that they exceed 2 percent of your adjusted gross income. Sales commissions, however, are not deductible up front; they're used to reduce your taxable profits when you sell.

WHICH TYPE OF PLANNER IS MORE EXPENSIVE: ONE WHO CHARGES SALES COMMISSIONS OR ONE WHO CHARGES FEES?

On the surface, fee-only planners seem more expensive. You pay more for The Plan, if you want one. You pay hourly fees for analysis and advice (usually in the $75 to $200 range) or maybe quarterly retainers. You're charged a fixed percentage of any money the planner manages for you. So you're always getting bills. What you don't pay, however, is sales commissions. Any products that the planner buys will be no-load (no sales charge).

By contrast, fee-and-commission planners might charge as little as $250 for The Plan. That's often the only payment you will make out-of-pocket. The rest of the planner's compensation is indirect, from up-front sales charges or annual charges subtracted from your investments. Because you don't write separate checks to pay the commissions, you may not realize how large they are or how much you pay. Usually it's a lot; 5 to 10 percent of the money you invest in the more complicated products.

ASK ANY PLANNER YOU WORK WITH HOW MUCH HIS OR HER SERVICES WILL COST.

Fee-only planners will have brochures listing their prices. If the planner will manage your money, add the cost of the types of investments he or she recommends—for example, the annual fees charged by the mutual funds the planner chooses. The planner's fee plus the fees embedded in your investments are your total cost.

It's harder to suss out what a commissioned planner costs. There's the gross commission, of course—the total commission, shared by the planner and his or her firm. If you're buying stocks, the commission will show on your confirmation form. Next, you pay any listed fees. There are also the annual fees embedded in the financial products you buy—for example, in your mutual funds, non-traded real estate investment trusts, or variable annuities. The planner's commission might come out of your investment up front or might be paid out of those product fees. It's not easy to excavate those fees. Your planner should give you a written list, including the commissions earned. Some planners try to put you off by saying, "I don't ask how much money you earn." That's totally irrelevant. You're asking for the price you're paying for products and services. You should know what you're being charged, including commissions, just as you'd expect to know the cost of anything else you buy. When you add up the price of dealing with commissioned planners, you may well find that they're more expensive than planners who charge only fees. They're especially expensive if they sell you products you don't need.

Don't let a commission- or fee-based planner tell you that his or her services are free or that there's no commission on a particular product. *Nothing* is free, even services that look free. If you want financial advice, you'll have to pay for it. Different systems of payment carry different incentives. Commissions encourage planners to sell whether you need the product or not. Fees, by contrast, encourage planners to be good enough to persuade you that their advice has value.

When making investments, always work with an adviser who is a fiduciary! Fiduciaries are legally bound to put your financial interests ahead of theirs. That means recommending investments based entirely on their long-term value to you, the client, as opposed to the upfront commissions the adviser can earn. They have to disclose the cost of the investments and all ongoing fees. When working with a fiduciary, you should *never* have to pay a 5 to 7 percent upfront commission, high fees for exiting an investment early, ongoing fees of 3 or 4 percent on complicated products, or anything more than a tiny ongoing fee (maybe 0.5 or less) for a mutual fund.

Any investment advice is considered protected by the fiduciary rule, including the advice to roll your 401(k) money out of your company plan and into the adviser's investment firm (see page 410). Stockbrokers don't have to act as fiduciaries if all they do is take orders to buy or sell stocks that you've researched. They *are* fiduciaries, however, if they recommend the stocks and other investments that you buy. The fiduciary rules—when followed—should protect you from financial abuse.

FOUR PLACES TO LOOK WHEN SHOPPING FOR A FEE-ONLY PLANNER

- *National Association of Personal Financial Advisors* (napfa.org), more than 2,400 planners in all states. To see if there are any near you, go to its website and type in your zip code or address. When names pop up, click on their profiles, where they announce their specialties. Some look for clients of high net worth. Others say they serve "middle income client needs." If you don't see the "middle in-come" phrase, email local planners, explain the services you want, and ask if they offer advice by the hour or by the job. Some take hourly clients without advertising it. You can also get names of fee-only planners by mail. Call NAPFA at 888-333-6659.

- *Garrett Planning Network,* a group of about 300 planners in 41 states. Look for their names at garrettplanningnetwork.com. They work on an hourly basis, with no minimum required. Fees range widely—at this writing, the majority charge $180 to $210 an hour. Middle-class clients are their specialty.

- *Certified Financial Planner Board of Standards (cfp.net).* Click on "Search for a Certified Financial Planner" to find CFPs in your area. Some will be "fee based" or "fee offset," others are "fee only." Go to their websites to find the true, fee-only planners.

- *Financial Planning Association.* The majority of these planners charge commissions, but the group includes fee-only planners too. Go to plannersearch.org and enter your zip code. Then narrow your search to fee-only planners in your local area.

Most fee-only planners offer a get-acquainted session free. If you engage one, you'll sign a contract specifying what services the fee covers and how long the contract will last. If the planner is an invest-ment adviser and will manage your money, decide whether it's to be on a discretionary basis. *Discretionary* means that the adviser makes the investment decisions, keeping you informed. *Nondiscretionary* means that you have to approve every transaction before it's made.

There aren't enough fee-only planners to help everyone who wants one, especially people with incomes and assets in the middle range. As a result, many middle earners wind up, by default, with stockbrokers or with fee-based planners who can charge commis-sions. Before taking this step, however, consider managing your in-vestments yourself, following the principles in this book on mutual funds. It's easier than you think.

ALTERNATIVELY, CONSIDER THE RETIREMENT INVESTMENT SERVICES OFFERED BY THE MAJOR NO-LOAD MUTUAL FUNDS.

They look at your assets and savings rate and give you a retirement investment plan. Here are two: T. Rowe Price (troweprice.com), an advisory planning service for $250, with regular checkups. You need at least $100,000, and it doesn't have to be in T. Rowe Price mutual funds. The Vanguard Group (vanguard.com) offers Vanguard Personal Advisor Services. Cost: Just 0.3 percent a year for people with investable assets of $50,000 or more. You also might consider a low-cost online adviser, such as Betterment.com and WealthFront.com. For these and other options, see page 260.

If you decide that you want to work with a fee-based adviser, be armed against the sales pitches. Stick with mutual funds, not individual stocks (page 244); avoid variable annuities (page 137) and non-traded real estate investment trusts (page 266); maximize your 401(k) investments before putting money into products that the planner sells (even though the planner claims that his or her products are better); and keep your investments simple. Be sure that the adviser takes you through the full planning checklist: setting goals, budgeting for debt reduction, maximizing your employee benefits, deciding how much term life insurance to buy, considering long-term care insurance, and reminding you to sign a will and a health care proxy. If your planner doesn't want to spend much time on anything other than investments, you're in the wrong place. Find someone else.

WHOMEVER YOU WORK WITH, ACCEPT ONLY ADVICE THAT MAKES SENSE TO YOU.

If you're not sure about any of the investments or ideas the planner presents, you have only to mumble and hesitate until the session is over. Don't say yes when you're undecided. Never say yes under pressure, even of the most jovial sort. If you think you'd like to work with a particular planner but are a cautious type, start small. Add to your investment as you gain confidence in the planner's MO. If you don't gain confidence, quit.

EIGHTEEN WAYS OF LOOKING FOR A PLANNER

There's no easy way to find a good planner. As in any other field, competence ranges from brilliant to dim. You can probably spot the dim, but working with mediocrities is risky too. They may steer you wrong because they don't see all the angles of the questions you pose or understand the risks in some of the products they sell so enthusiastically.

I gave you some quick advice on finding a planner on page 410. Here's more detailed information, to help with your research:

Gather recommendations from associates who investment objectives are similar to yours. Also, go to the fee-only websites recommended above. Pull together a list of possibles.

Call or email the people on your list, telling them why you're seeking help and what services you need. For money management, ask about the minimum account requirement. If there seems to be a fit, ask for written material about the firm, including the state or federal ADV (that's the background check for investment advisers). You might be able to download this material from the adviser's website. Read it before deciding to set up an interview. You might be able to download this material from the adviser's website.

In the written material, check out the planner's educational background. Here's what you want to see:

• *Higher education.* A college degree is a reasonable proxy for a mind that can tackle complex issues.

• *Evidence of planning expertise.* Look for the Certified Financial Planner designation (CFP), awarded by the Certified Financial Planner Board of Standards to planners who have met its requirements and passed its test. A number of colleges and universities, such as Texas Tech University in Lubbock, Texas, give financial planning degrees. The American College in Bryn Mawr, Pennsylvania, gives a chartered financial consultant designation, or ChFC. It identifies insurance agents who have studied financial planning with an emphasis on using life insurance products.

All these diplomas attest that the planner has passed a number of exams in areas such as goal setting, taxes, insurance, investments, and estate planning. But degrees and certificates are only a starting point. They don't say whether a particular planner is any good.

• *No kidding around.* If the business card says "Financial Planner," look for the CFP designation. If it's not there, you could be dealing with anyone: a stockbroker in hiding, an insurance agent with pretensions. You can tell who they are by the products they advise you to buy. People calling themselves "retirement planners" are often insurance agents. "Financial consultant," "financial adviser," and "registered representative" mean stockbroker. None of these salespeople is a planner in the sense you seek. Dump a "senior specialist" (page 407) fast.

Decide on two or three planners to speak with in person. The opening interview should be free. Take a financial statement with you, showing your assets and liabilities, to give the planner a general idea of what he or she will have to do.

Ask about the planner's professional background. The basics should have been in the written material, but ask about previous employers and occupations. You want someone who has been practicing financial planning for 10 years or more, preferably at the same firm. Skip any new kids on the block, including career switchers who have been practicing for only a couple of years. They may turn out to be wonderful, but you want them to practice their new profession on someone else. Also skip any planner who has hopped around from firm to firm.

Ask what kinds of clients the planner has. Firms often specialize: in doctors, entrepreneurs, entertainers, teachers, or young, upper-middle-income families. The more experience the planner has with people like you, the better.

What are the planner's special areas of expertise? Which lawyers, accountants, or other specialists are on tap?

Does the planner sell financial products? (You trolled for fee-only planners, but check.) Does he earn referral fees for recommending you to particular specialists, such as insurance agents (fee-only planners shouldn't). Is she involved in any other financial businesses, such as real estate, that she might recommend to you? Avoid planners with conflicts of interest.

Think about what the planner asks you. He or she should inquire not only into your finances but also your family, feelings about money, general knowledge of investments, personal goals, and way of life. If you're married, your spouse should attend at least the initial meeting, and the planner should elicit his or her feelings too. Planners who don't seem interested in you won't give you the best advice. You might take a list of objectives to the initial meeting and ask how the planner would approach them, one by one.

Think about how the planner answers the questions you pose. Does he or she seem open, straightforward, comfortable with issues, friendly, willing to explain? If the chemistry isn't right, the relationship won't work, no matter how bright the planner is. If you have any reservations, raise them on the spot, to see what the planner has to say.

Ask for professional references: lawyers, bankers, accountants. If you're refused, take your business elsewhere. Call each reference, ask what the relationship is, how long they've worked with the planner, and whether they can recommend him or her. Professionals don't put their names on the line for bad guys (unless, of course, the professionals are bad guys too).

Ask for the names of three clients you can speak with who have been with the planner for at least three years. Don't take no for an answer. When offered the names, don't fail to call. Ask how the planner is to work with, any problems they see, and how much better off they are thanks to what the planner did. In my experience, calls like these are incredibly useful. The clients are usually very fair in assessing the service they've been getting. (That is, unless you're with a sleazy operator, in which case the "clients" will be relatives. Your gut will probably tell you that something's wrong.)

If the planner will manage your money, discuss investment philosophy and approach. What kinds of investments does he like, and what might be his strategy for you? Also look at the performance reports that clients get. They should show the period's total, annualized return, net of all fees and expenses, compared with several standard indexes: Standard & Poor's 500 stock index, the Russell 2000 index of smaller stocks, the EAFE index of international stocks, Barclays Capital U.S. Aggregate Bond Index, 90-day Treasury bills, and consumer price inflation. That helps you keep track of your progress relative to the rest of the world. It also tells you how well the planner is performing relative to your goals.

Ask if the planner will acknowledge, in writing, if his or her relationship with you is one of a fiduciary. A fiduciary is an adviser required by law to put your interests first. Requiring this in writing will eliminate most questionable planners.

Ask the planner, "How are you paid?" This question is critical. The planner should hand over a schedule that discloses his or her compensation in full.

Find out how you can terminate the relationship. You should be free to quit at any time, with nothing owed beyond the end of the current month.

Don't pick a planner just because he or she is quoted in the newspapers. Reporters look for colorful quotes and comments and rarely check on whether the planners are any good. Courting the press is one way that planners advertise.

Don't pick a planner just because he or she gives investment seminars. That's advertising too. A San Francisco planner, Lawrence Krause, once told his trade secrets to the magazine *CALUnderwriter:*

"You don't have to know as much as you think you have to know in running a seminar. All you have to know is more than your audience, and your audience doesn't know your subject. . . . You also have to remember that you're not there to educate. You're there to sell. The purpose of a seminar is twofold: one, to confuse your audience; and two, to create dependence. . . . As long as you are going to confuse them, do a good job of it. Then you ask for the order, so that they'll come to see you afterward."

Now you know.

THE BACKGROUND CHECK

Financial planners who handle investments have to register with the law as investment advisers. Here are the rules and what you can find out:

■ *Investment advisory firms that handle $25 million or more in assets* have to register with the Securities and Exchange Commission (SEC).

■ *Firms that handle less than $25 million* register with the states.

■ *Individual advisers (investment adviser representatives, or IARs) are regulated by the states,* including those working for the larger firms.

■ *The investment advisory firm has to make various disclosures.* Firms filing with the SEC fill in Form ADV (for "adviser"), parts 1 and 2.

Part 1 is for the regulators. It includes various disciplinary actions taken against the firm or its individual investment advisers.

Part 2 is for the public. It lists the firm's services and investment methods, the education and business backgrounds of the principals, whether the adviser conducts other types of financial businesses, and the way customers are charged. (Here's where you'll see if an adviser claiming to be fee only actually sells products on commission.) New customers have to be given a copy of the ADV part 2 or a brochure containing the same information. Ongoing clients have to be offered an updated copy every year.

The firms also file a Schedule D for each individual adviser, giving the details of his or her disciplinary history, if any: criminal charges, civil actions, and regulatory proceedings. The firm doesn't have to give you the Schedule D. By law, it has to tell you only about any disciplinary actions taken against your adviser. But I wouldn't do business with a firm that didn't release its Schedule Ds.

The states have an equivalent ADV form with similar disclosures for the firms and advisers they regulate. They require advisers to demonstrate some minimal knowledge, such as an acquaintance with state and federal securities laws. The states may also have some operating requirements, such as bonding, minimum amounts of net capital, and rules on maintaining books and records. Their disclosures include arbitration claims against advisers in excess of $2,500.

You don't have to wait for an adviser to give you his or her ADV. You can find it yourself at the Investment Adviser Public Disclosure website. Go to adviserinfo.sec.gov. Click on "Investment Adviser Search" and enter the adviser's name. You'll get the full ADV, including part 1, with the disciplinary infractions, and Schedule D. The site covers advisers registered with the states as well as with the SEC.

Check what's checkable on the ADV (education, prior employment), to see if the planner is on the square. The regulators have no idea whether these documents tell the truth.

If the adviser has no ADV and is giving you investment advice, he or she may be breaking the law. That's not someone you should be working with.

- *The ADVs let you look up the firm but not the background of the individual adviser, who is known as an Investment Adviser Representative.* If it's a small shop where the adviser *is* the firm, the ADV covers what you want to know. If you want to check the background of an adviser in a larger firm, check the CRD (page 424) or ask your state securities commission for a report. To find the commission, call the North American Securities Administrators Association (202-737-0900), or go to nasaa.org and click on "Contact Your Regulator." Some states are responsive, others slo-o-o-o-w.

■ *If your adviser is an employee of a brokerage firm, he or she should have a record at the Central Registration Depository.* (Find it at brokercheck.finra.org). It will show the planner's past employment, where he or she is registered to sell securities, certain customer complaints, and infractions of various sorts. One hitch: firms don't always forward customer complaints to the CRD, as the rules require. If you make a complaint, send a copy to your state securities commission and to the Financial Industry Regulatory Authority (finra.org). They'll see that it's filed properly.

■ *The black holes.* There are three: (1) States may not have the budget or the will to enforce their own securities laws. (2) When a state licenses an adviser, it may not check to see if he or she has a disciplinary record in another state. (3) A state may not respond to your request for background information on a particular adviser.

WHEN A PLANNER DOES YOU WRONG

In the largely unregulated industry of financial planning, no formal body sets the rules and punishes rule breakers. You can file a complaint about CFPs at the Certified Financial Planner Board of Standards (cfp.net or 800-487-1497) or complain to the Financial Planning Association in Denver (plannersearch.org or 800-322-4237). But all they can do is yank the offender's professional certification or membership—hardly an onerous penalty, since he or she can go on practicing without it. If your planner is a member of an exchange, you can go to arbitration. Here's a sampling of the complaints typically brought against financial planners:

- Putting clients into investments unsuitable for someone of their age and circumstances
- Churning your account (that means buying and selling more often than necessary) to earn extra commissions
- Failing to tell the truth about how large a fee the planner earned

- Failing to diversify a client's investments to minimize risk
- Exaggerating an investment's likely yield while failing to disclose the risks
- Roping clients into outright frauds: nonexistent investments, ponzi schemes, misrepresentations of every sort
- Misrepresenting the tax benefits and investment outlook for tax-sheltered investments
- Giving bad tax advice
- Failing to disclose that the planner had a financial interest in the investment being sold
- Failing to process a client's investments or insurance properly, leading to financial loss
- Ignoring a client's specific investment instructions and goals

If you think you have grounds for a legal complaint against your planner, start by trying to work out a settlement. Sometimes a letter from a lawyer helps. If you're stonewalled, complain to the appropriate state regulator. For recalcitrant investment advisers, stockbrokers, or insurance agents who sell variable annuities or variable life, call your state's securities commission (find it at nasaa.org, 202-737-0900). For other insurance agents, call the state insurance commission (find it through naic.org). Occasionally they can help.

If your loss is large, you might be able to bring a lawsuit. More likely, your planner will have required you to sign an arbitration agreement, which generally requires your case to be heard in a forum dictated by the securities industry. To find a lawyer, contact the Public Investors Arbitration Bar Association (piaba.org or 886-621-7484, in Norman, Oklahoma) or the National Association of Consumer Advocates (consumeradvocates.org or 202-452-1989, in Washington, D.C.).

DO YOU NEED AN INDEPENDENT INVESTMENT ADVISER?

A few sessions with a fee-only financial planner will benefit almost anyone. The planner can steer you toward mutual funds and asset allocations that are appropriate for your age and circumstances. With that advice, plus the explanations in this book's investment and retirement plan chapters, you can probably manage your IRA or 401(k) yourself. There's no need to pay extra for continuing investment advice.

There are some circumstances, however, when having a personal investment adviser makes sense. For example:

▪ You have a truly large pot of money—say, $3 million and up—and want someone to think continuously about how it should be deployed.

▪ You have only a modest pot of money but don't have the time to think about it yourself. Or you're all thumbs with money and not interested in learning.

▪ You face a lot of family complications, such as stepchildren, mixed inheritances, and some unfriendly family dynamics. You need a good planning mind to lead you through the minefields.

When looking for an investment adviser, consider fee-only financial planners with substantial amounts of money under management, or bank or brokerage house wealth management departments. As always, compare costs. Banks and brokers are likely to hit you with fees at every turn, including fees for investing in their own high-cost mutual funds (or pooled trust funds, which amount to the same thing). Keep a close watch on how the account is handled. A bank trust officer can churn an account just as easily as a stockbroker can—perhaps more easily, if the account belongs to an orphan or to someone who's old and no longer paying a lot of attention.

TO PROTECT YOURSELF

When doing business with a planner or investment adviser, proceed in an orderly way, with written goals, notes of conversations, and so on. In a confrontation, you might find that the planner kept his or her own notes, which a court or arbitration board might consider more credible than your memory.

If the planner tells you that a specific investment carries little risk, ask for a letter confirming it. This sort of paper trail supports a winning claim. It may also encourage your planner to proceed with caution and exactitude. If your planner makes a move that differs from what you thought you'd agreed on, telephone immediately. If you don't like the explanation, send a letter reiterating how you want your money handled.

YES, BUT . . . HOW DO YOU AVOID A CROOK LIKE BERNIE MADOFF?

Madoff fooled the experts based on his sterling reputation, haughty self-confidence, trappings of wealth, and apparent ability to magic money out of the market year after year. The story of his $65 billion fraud is especially scary for individuals who understand how easily they, too, could have been taken in. They ask, "Who is it possible to trust?"

The answer is, "Trust no one." Instead, set up your account so that the manager can't get his or her hands on it.

Here's the single best question to ask any would-be financial adviser: "When I send you money to invest, whose name do I put on the check?" If the manager answers, "Make out the check to my firm" or a firm that the manager controls, walk away. The manager should not—repeat, *not*—hold the money that he or she is investing for you. Your account should be held by an independent custodian, such as State Street, TD Ameritrade, or some other third party. That's the name you should put on the check.

Why? Because it's the custodian's job to know where your money is at all times. Independent custodians hold your securities, collect interest and dividends, process trades, send you the confirmations of trades, receive any money you send into the account, disburse money at your direction, and compute your quarterly reports. They don't make any investment decisions. Your money manager tells the custodian what to buy and sell. But thanks to this separate relationship, your cash never passes through the manager's hands.

If you allow the manager to hold custody of the accounts, he or she has free rein. No one is there to check whether transactions actually went through or what the prices were. The manager might hire a respectable accounting firm to handle the annual audit, but the accountant will work with the data the manager produces. Auditors normally don't dig into whether the data were created honestly.

Some legitimate money managers insist on taking custody of your funds themselves because it simplifies reporting. An example might be a fund of hedge funds. But frankly, you don't need those kinds of expensive investments anyway. Plenty of dependable managers work only with independent custodians. That's the pool to fish in when you're trolling for investment help.

One warning: In the Madoff case, some banks signed on as custodians and then hired Bernie's firm as subcustodian. As a result, investors got their reports from Madoff rather than from the bank itself. If you see that happening with a custodian you hired, pull out immediately. Something smells.

The second best way of avoiding fraud is to disbelieve any manager who claims to earn steady or high market returns in good years and bad. No one does that. Even if God had been investing, he'd have lost money in the Flood!

Finally, be careful of someone who sells investments within your specific religious or ethnic group. Mormons have fallen for schemes pressed by fellow church members in the belief that a coreligionist wouldn't lie. Bernie Madoff looted the Jewish community. In my old hometown, a smart, preppy hedge fund guy hoodwinked college pension fund managers, maybe because they all wore bow ties. Never assume that a money manager must be okay because he or she is just like you.

I'll say it again—ensure that your account resides in the hands of an independent custodian. That's foolproof protection against a Bernie clone.

AUNT JANE'S LAST RECIPE: A DO-IT-YOURSELF FINANCIAL PLAN

Over the next eight weeks, take the following nine steps to success:

1. Make a List of Specific Objectives

The list might read: "A college education for Julia and Joe, a down payment on a house, graduate school for Peter, hockey camp for Kai next year, Juno's wedding, two weeks in France year after next, a retirement income worth $60,000 a year in today's dollars, pretax." Put down exactly what you want. Your objectives will change as your life does, but you should always know what you're working toward.

2. Draw Up a Spending Plan

This isn't a big deal. You've known about budgets all your life, and, if you've forgotten, refer to Chapter 2.

3. Calculate What You Need to Save

This isn't a big deal either, once you've specified what you're aiming for. Ask yourself, "How much will each objective cost?" and "When am I going to need the money?" Then point your savings toward those goals. Plot short-term savings in your head. You want to go to France year after next? Take this year's price, divide by 24, and put away that much per month. Nothing complicated about it. Use Web calculators to estimate what you need to save for longer-term goals.

You'll have to coordinate your savings with your spending plan, which is the hard part. But if you didn't intend to try, you never would have bought this book. (You say your mother bought this book for you? Oh, well. Try anyway.)

4. Secure What You Have

This is your safety net: life, health, disability, homeowners insurance, and auto insurance. I've steered you toward inexpensive coverage, where it exists. Do-it-yourselfers can buy some policies on the Web.

5. Develop a Risk Plan

Decide on a prudent level of investment risk for someone of your age, goals, and circumstances. On this point, Chapter 9 will help.

6. Follow Through with an Investment Plan

You will do splendidly with a few no-load mutual funds, chosen yourself and held long term, plus some Treasury securities, tax-exempts, or certificates of deposit.

7. Minimize Your Taxes

For savings, use a tax-deferred retirement plan (Chapter 7) and, if you're in a high bracket, municipal bonds. What could be easier? If you have a high net worth, however, you'll have to deal with estate taxes, trusts, executive compensation contracts, and all the other tax entanglements that wealth is heir to. That's when you need professional help—and only the most experienced planners will do. Your outriders will include a clutch of specialized professionals: tax lawyer, accountant, actuary, investment adviser.

8. Maximize Your Retirement Plan

For how much to save, see Chapter 7, again. When you actually retire, ask a fee-only planner about the best way to take withdrawals from your retirement plan. You can't afford to make mistakes. Chapter 8 gives you a look at the landscape. The planner can spell out the tax and investment implications of your various choices, and project a spending and investment plan to carry you through the rest of your life.

9. Get a Financial Checkup

Ask a fee-only planner to take a look at what you're doing and make suggestions.

That's it! The planning process from first sharpened pencil to final phone call. A project that you can handle, step by step, just by applying some basic, down-home common sense.

For generations, most Americans have managed their own money and done a pretty good job of it. You still can. The trick is to turn your back on today's insanely complex financial marketplace and buy the simple things that you can handle yourself. Trust me on this one. In the world of money, one or two clear and strong ideas, persisted in, will make you richer in the end.

Appendix 5

How Long Will Your Capital Last?

The following tables show how many years your capital will last at varying rates of withdrawal. For annual withdrawals of equal size, use the first table. The remaining tables assume that you'll take enough extra money each year to keep up with the inflation rate. At 2 percent inflation, for example, a first-year withdrawal of $5,000 grows to $5,100 the second year, $5,202 the third year, and so on.

To use these tables, choose a likely inflation rate, up to 7 percent. In the left-hand column, find the percentage of your capital that you will withdraw in the first year. If you withdraw $5,000 from a $250,000 nest egg, for example, you have taken 2 percent. Read across to the pretax rate of return that you're expecting to earn on your money. Where those lines intersect, you will find the number of years your capital can last. I've assumed that the money is taken at the start of each year. The # symbol means that, at that rate of withdrawal, your capital will never be exhausted.

The source for all the tables in Appendix 5 is the accounting firm RSM McGladrey, New York City.

Table A-1.

ANNUAL WITHDRAWALS OF EQUAL SIZE

% of Original Capital Withdrawal Annually

WILL LAST THIS MANY YEARS IF INVESTED AT THE FOLLOWING AVERAGE RATES OF RETURN

	3%	4%	5%	6%	7%	8%	9%	10%	11%	12%
2%	#	#	#	#	#	#	#	#	#	#
3%	119	#	#	#	#	#	#	#	#	#
4%	53	83	#	#	#	#	#	#	#	#
5%	29	37	62	#	#	#	#	#	#	#
6%	22	26	32	49	#	#	#	#	#	#
7%	18	20	23	28	40	#	#	#	#	#
8%	15	16	18	21	25	33	#	#	#	#
9%	13	14	15	17	19	22	28	#	#	#
10%	11	12	13	14	15	17	20	25	45	#
11%	10	10	11	12	13	14	16	17	22	32
12%	9	9	10	10	11	12	13	14	16	19
13%	8	8	9	9	10	10	11	12	13	15
14%	7	8	8	8	9	9	10	10	11	12
15%	7	7	7	8	8	8	9	9	10	11

Table A-2.

ASSUMING 1 PERCENT INFLATION

Percentage of Capital Withdrawal In the First Year	WILL LAST THIS MANY YEARS, IF THE ORIGINAL WITHDRAWAL RISES BY 1% ANNUALLY AND YOUR MONEY IS INVESTED AT THE FOLLOWING AVERAGE RATES OF RETURN									
	3%	4%	5%	6%	7%	8%	9%	10%	11%	12%
2%	180	#	#	#	#	#	#	#	#	#
3%	53	111	#	#	#	#	#	#	#	#
4%	33	43	78	#	#	#	#	#	#	#
5%	25	29	36	59	#	#	#	#	#	#
6%	19	22	25	31	47	#	#	#	#	#
7%	16	18	20	23	27	38	#	#	#	#
8%	14	15	16	18	20	24	32	#	#	#
9%	12	13	14	15	16	19	22	28	#	#
10%	11	11	12	13	14	15	17	19	24	38
11%	9	10	10	11	12	13	14	15	18	21
12%	9	9	9	10	10	11	12	13	14	16
13%	8	8	8	9	9	10	10	11	12	13
14%	7	7	7	8	8	9	9	10	10	11
15%	7	7	7	7	8	8	8	9	9	10

Table A-3.

ASSUMING 2 PERCENT INFLATION

Percentage of Capital Withdrawal In the First Year	WILL LAST THIS MANY YEARS, IF THE ORIGINAL WITH-DRAWAL RISES BY 2% ANNUALLY AND YOUR MONEY IS INVESTED AT THE FOLLOWING AVERAGE RATES OF RETURN									
	3%	4%	5%	6%	7%	8%	9%	10%	11%	12%
2%	68	167	#	#	#	#	#	#	#	#
3%	40	52	105	#	#	#	#	#	#	#
4%	28	33	43	75	#	#	#	#	#	#
5%	22	25	29	36	56	#	#	#	#	#
6%	18	19	22	25	31	45	#	#	#	#
7%	15	16	18	20	23	27	37	#	#	#
8%	13	14	15	16	18	20	24	31	#	#
9%	11	12	13	14	15	16	18	21	27	51
10%	10	10	12	12	13	14	15	17	19	23
11%	9	9	10	10	11	12	13	14	15	17
12%	8	8	9	9	10	10	11	12	13	14
13%	7	8	8	8	9	9	10	11	11	12
14%	7	7	7	8	8	8	9	9	10	10
15%	6	7	7	7	7	8	8	8	9	9

Table A-4.

THE 3 PERCENT SOLUTION

Percentage of Capital Withdrawn In the First Year	WILL LAST THIS MANY YEARS, IF THE ORIGINAL WITH-DRAWAL RISES BY 3% ANNUALLY AND YOUR MONEY IS INVESTED AT THE FOLLOWING AVERAGE RATES OF RETURN									
	3%	4%	5%	6%	7%	8%	9%	10%	11%	12%
2%	50	67	158	#	#	#	#	#	#	#
3%	33	40	52	100	#	#	#	#	#	#
4%	25	28	33	42	71	#	#	#	#	#
5%	20	22	24	29	36	54	#	#	#	#
6%	16	18	19	22	25	31	44	#	#	#
7%	14	16	18	20	22	27	36	#	#	#
8%	13	13	14	15	16	18	20	24	30	#
9%	11	11	12	13	14	15	16	18	21	#
10%	10	10	10	11	12	13	14	15	17	19
11%	9	9	9	10	10	11	12	13	14	15
12%	8	9	9	9	9	10	10	11	12	13
13%	7	7	8	8	8	9	9	10	10	11
14%	7	7	7	7	8	8	8	9	9	10
15%	6	6	7	7	7	7	8	8	8	9

* Assumes a single withdrawal at the start of the year. All the numbers are rounded.

Table A-5.

ASSUMING 4 PERCENT INFLATION

Percentage of Capital Withdrawal In the First Year	WILL LAST THIS MANY YEARS, IF THE ORIGINAL WITH-DRAWAL RISES BY 4% ANNUALLY AND YOUR MONEY IS INVESTED AT THE FOLLOWING AVERAGE RATES OF RETURN									
	3%	4%	5%	6%	7%	8%	9%	10%	11%	12%
2%	40	50	67	150	#	#	#	#	#	#
3%	29	33	39	52	95	#	#	#	#	#
4%	22	25	28	33	42	68	#	#	#	#
5%	18	20	22	24	28	35	53	#	#	#
6%	15	16	18	19	22	25	30	42	#	#
7%	13	14	15	16	17	19	22	26	35	#
8%	11	12	13	14	15	16	18	20	23	30
9%	10	11	11	12	13	14	15	16	18	21
10%	9	10	10	10	11	12	13	14	15	16
11%	8	9	9	9	10	10	11	12	13	14
12%	8	8	8	8	9	9	10	10	11	12
13%	7	7	7	8	8	8	9	9	10	10
14%	6	7	7	7	7	8	8	8	9	9
15%	6	6	6	7	7	7	8	8	8	8

Table A-6.

ASSUMING 5 PERCENT INFLATION

Percentage of Capital Withdrawal In the First Year	WILL LAST THIS MANY YEARS, IF THE ORIGINAL WITH-DRAWAL RISES BY 5% ANNUALLY AND YOUR MONEY IS INVESTED AT THE FOLLOWING AVERAGE RATES OF RETURN									
	3%	**4%**	**5%**	**6%**	**7%**	**8%**	**9%**	**10%**	**11%**	**12%**
2%	35	41	50	67	145	#	#	#	#	#
3%	25	29	33	39	51	92	#	#	#	#
4%	20	22	25	28	33	42	66	#	#	#
5%	17	18	20	22	24	28	35	51	#	#
6%	14	15	16	18	19	22	25	30	41	#
7%	12	13	14	15	16	17	19	22	26	34
8%	11	11	12	13	14	15	16	18	20	23
9%	10	10	11	11	12	13	14	15	16	18
10%	9	9	10	10	10	11	12	13	13	15
11%	8	8	9	9	9	10	10	11	12	13
12%	7	8	8	8	8	9	9	10	10	11
13%	7	7	7	7	8	8	8	9	9	10
14%	6	6	7	7	7	7	8	8	9	9
15%	6	6	6	6	7	7	7	8	8	8

Table A-7.

ASSUMING 6 PERCENT INFLATION

Percentage of Capital Withdrawal In the First Year	WILL LAST THIS MANY YEARS, IF THE ORIGINAL WITH-DRAWAL RISES BY 6% ANNUALLY AND YOUR MONEY IS INVESTED AT THE FOLLOWING AVERAGE RATES OF RETURN									
	3%	4%	5%	6%	7%	8%	9%	10%	11%	12%
2%	31	35	41	50	67	139	#	#	#	#
3%	23	26	29	33	39	51	89	#	#	#
4%	19	20	22	25	28	33	41	64	#	#
5%	15	17	18	20	22	24	28	35	50	#
6%	13	14	15	16	18	19	21	25	30	40
7%	12	12	13	14	15	16	17	19	22	26
8%	10	11	11	12	13	14	15	16	17	20
9%	9	10	10	11	11	12	13	13	15	16
10%	8	9	9	10	10	10	11	12	12	13
11%	8	8	8	9	9	9	10	10	11	12
12%	7	7	8	8	8	8	9	9	10	10
13%	7	7	7	7	7	8	8	8	9	9
14%	6	6	6	6	7	7	7	8	8	8
15%	6	6	6	6	6	7	7	7	7	8

Table A-8.

ASSUMING 7 PERCENT INFLATION

Percentage of Capital Withdrawal In the First Year	WILL LAST THIS MANY YEARS, IF THE ORIGINAL WITH-DRAWAL RISES BY 7% ANNUALLY AND YOUR MONEY IS INVESTED AT THE FOLLOWING AVERAGE RATES OF RETURN									
	3%	4%	5%	6%	7%	8%	9%	10%	11%	12%
2%	28	31	35	41	50	66	134	#	#	#
3%	21	23	26	29	33	39	51	86	#	#
4%	17	19	20	22	25	28	33	41	62	#
5%	15	16	17	18	20	22	24	28	34	48
6%	12	13	14	15	16	18	19	21	25	29
7%	11	12	12	13	14	15	16	17	19	22
8%	10	11	11	11	12	13	14	15	16	17
9%	9	9	10	10	11	11	12	13	13	15
10%	8	8	9	9	10	10	10	11	12	13
11%	7	8	8	8	9	9	9	10	10	11
12%	7	7	7	8	8	8	8	9	9	10
13%	6	7	7	7	7	7	8	8	8	9
14%	6	6	6	6	7	7	7	7	8	8
15%	6	6	6	6	6	6	7	7	7	7

Appendix 6

Pension Maximization: Will It Work for You?

At retirement, you have two ways of taking your pension: (1) *Lifetime only:* you get a higher monthly income, but it stops when you die. (2) *Joint-and-survivor:* you get a lower income, but it lasts for the lifetimes of you and your spouse.

A pension max salesperson will propose that you take the lifetime-only pension. To protect your spouse, you buy a life insurance policy. At your death, the proceeds of that policy can provide your spouse with a lifetime income.

This plan is potentially workable if: (1) your net lifetime pension, after paying the insurance premium, is greater than you would have received had you chosen the joint-and-survivor pension; *and* (2) after your death, the insurance proceeds are sufficient to buy your spouse a lifetime income at least equal to what the joint-and-survivor pension would have paid for life. Most proposals fail one or both of these tests.

The following worksheet will tell you whether a proposed plan will work or whether it puts your spouse at risk of running out of money. It was prepared by the late John Allen, J.D., of Allen-Warren in Arvada, Colorado. You and the salesperson should fill in the following blanks:

STEP ONE: *To see if a pension max scheme will improve your income as a couple, while you're both alive.*

1. Your monthly pension, if paid for your life only. $_____
2. Your monthly pension after all taxes.* $_____

(continues)

3. Your monthly pension as a couple if you take a
   joint-and-survivor option. $_____

4. The joint-and-survivor monthly pension after all taxes.* $_____

5. Your spouse's monthly pension after your death if you take
   the joint-and-survivor option. (This may or may not be the
   amount you reported on line 3.) $_____

6. Your surviving spouse's monthly pension after all taxes.* $_____

7. The midpoint between lines 5 and 6. Use this as a rough target for the
   monthly lifetime annuity payment your spouse ought to get if you
   choose pension maximization.† $_____

8. The size of the insurance policy needed to buy your spouse the
   appropriate annuity after your death. To calculate it, visit Immediate
   Annuities (ImmediateAnnuities.com). Enter your spouse's
   age in the year you'll retire‡ and the monthly income from
   Line 7. The calculator will tell you how much such an
   income will cost. $_____

9. The monthly life insurance premium required to buy the size policy
   shown on line 8. $_____

10. Subtract the monthly premium (line 9) from the after-tax income you'd
    get from a single-life pension (line 2). This gives you the disposable
    income that you, as a couple, would have left to live on. $_____

11. Compare this with the income you'd get from a joint-and-survivor
    pension, after tax (line 4). $_____

If your income after pension max is less than you'd get from a joint-and-survivor pension, stop here. It usually makes no sense to use the insurance scheme.

---

* Federal, state, and local. Don't estimate from a tax bracket. Calculate the actual tax.

† The midpoint includes a tax adjustment. A professional planner will be able to target the amounts in lines 6 and 7 exactly.

‡ Your plan should protect your spouse in the worst case—namely, if you die immediately after retiring.

STEP TWO: *If pension max provides you with more income as a couple, continue the calculation to see if it protects your spouse after your death.*

12. Your spouse's life expectancy, based on his or her age when you retire.*
    The number comes from the Life Expectancy Table on page 446. _____

13. The portion of the spouse's annuity income that will be
    excluded from income taxes. This is called the
    Exclusion Ratio.† Carry it to three decimal places. _____

14. Subtract the Exclusion Ratio from 1.000. _____

15. Enter the monthly annuity income you targeted from line 7. $_____

16. Multiply line 14 by line 13. This tells you how much
    of the spouse's annuity income is subject to tax. $_____

17. Subtract income taxes‡ from the spouse's annuity
    income (line 13) and enter that income after tax. $_____

18. Enter the actual amount of net spousal income
    you need to protect (line 6). $_____

* For safety, refigure for 5, 10, and 20 years ahead. Each year the spouse lives, his or her life expectancy improves.
† To get the Exclusion Ratio: Multiply the spouse's monthly annuity income by 12. Multiply the result by the life expectancy (line 12). Divide the result into the size of the life insurance policy (line 8).
‡ Federal, state, and local. Don't just estimate from a tax bracket. Calculate the actual tax.

If line 17 is larger than line 16, you need more life insurance to protect your spouse. Redo the worksheet using a larger policy. If the cost of the larger policy reduces your income as a couple to less than you'd get from the joint pension, pension max doesn't work. *This is the usual case!*

If you start pension maximization earlier than retirement, you'll need a "present value" analysis. This recognizes that $1,000 spent on insurance today is worth much more than $1,000 received in higher pension benefits in the future. A present value analysis tells you whether those extra pension benefits are worth their cost. Don't buy from an insurance agent or planner who won't (or can't) do that calculation for you.

This worksheet does not consider the value of pensions with cost-of-living adjustments. You can simulate the analysis by estimating what your pension will be in 5, 10, and 20 years and using this sheet to see if the life insurance will indeed supply a comparable pension for the spouse.

THE RISKS OF CHOOSING PENSION MAXIMIZATION

If your pension has a cost-of-living benefit, you will need to purchase a much larger amount of insurance in order to provide your spouse with a similar amount of income. And even that might not be enough if inflation explodes.

If you buy a universal life policy or an interest-sensitive whole-life policy and interest rates decline, your plan may not work out. You might have to pay a higher insurance premium or accept a lower death benefit. Ask the agent to show you what happens to the pension max plan if interest rates drop to the policy's minimum guaranteed rate.

At your death, annuity rates may have dropped. Your spouse may not be able to buy as high an income as you expected.

Inflation or unexpected expenses may eat away at your income. At some point in the future, you may not be able to afford the life insurance premiums. If you have to cancel the policy, and die, your spouse will lose that part of his or her income.

If you become forgetful, your insurance might lapse accidentally, leaving your spouse to do without. If the marriage goes bad and the husband owns the policy, he might cancel it or change the beneficiary.

Your spouse may get health benefits from your pension plan, which could be lost when you die and your pension stops. It is particularly unwise to sever all connection with a public-sector plan.

THE ADVANTAGE OF PENSION MAXIMIZATION

If your spouse dies first, the insurance can be canceled, leaving you with more disposable income.

If you want to continue paying for the insurance after your spouse dies, you'll have a larger estate to leave to your heirs (although, if leaving a larger estate is important to you, you can carry extra life insurance without using pension max).

If there's a divorce, the pension holder could cancel the policy (although the divorce settlement might require that the policy be kept in force).

If you and your spouse live for many years, you can—at some point—withdraw some cash from the policy. You will shrink the death benefit left for your spouse. But at later ages, less money is needed to provide the spouse with a lifetime income.

These advantages are speculative and don't begin to compensate for the disadvantages. You are gambling with your spouse's future security. Not a good idea.

Appendix 7

Life Expectancy
(Group Annuity Table)

These average life expectancies are determined by pension actuaries. They reflect how long people with pensions live, projected into the future. They're slightly higher than the life expectancies published by Social Security. That's because people with long-term attachments to the workforce (and, probably, continuous health insurance) live longer than workers on average. When applying the numbers to yourself, consider your family history and state of health. Half the time people live longer than these statistical averages show—and half die earlier. If you're a married couple (opposite sex), there's a 17 percent chance that one of you will live to at least 100!

AGE OF RETIREES		LIFE EXPECTANCIES	
MALE	FEMALE	MALE	FEMALE
55	55	84.5	87.6
60	60	85.0	87.9
65	65	85.8	88.3
70	70	86.8	88.9
75	75	88.0	89.9
80	80	89.7	91.3
85	85	92.0	93.2
90	90	94.9	95.8
95	95	98.4	99.0
100	100	102.4	102.8

IF YOU'RE THIS OLD:	INSURERS THAT SELL ANNUITIES ASSUME THAT YOU WILL LIVE UNTIL THE FOLLOWING AGE:	
	MALE	FEMALE
57	83.8	86.3
58	83.8	86.3
59	83.8	86.4
60	83.9	86.4
61	84.0	86.5
62	84.1	86.6
63	84.2	86.7
64	84.3	86.8
65	84.4	86.9
66	84.6	87.1
67	84.8	87.3
68	85.0	87.4
69	85.2	87.6
70	85.4	87.8
71	85.7	88.0
72	85.9	88.2
73	86.2	88.4
74	86.5	88.7
75	86.8	88.9
76	87.1	89.2
77	87.5	89.5
78	87.9	89.8
79	88.3	90.1
80	88.7	90.4
81	89.2	90.8
82	89.7	91.2
83	90.2	91.7
84	90.7	92.1
85	91.2	92.5

IF YOU'RE THIS OLD:	INSURERS THAT SELL ANNUITIES ASSUME THAT YOU WILL LIVE UNTIL THE FOLLOWING AGE:	
86	91.9	93.0
87	92.5	93.6
88	93.1	94.1
89	93.7	94.7
90	94.3	95.2
91	95.1	95.9
92	95.8	96.6
93	96.5	97.2
94	97.3	97.9
95	98.0	98.6
96	98.9	99.4
97	99.7	100.2
98	100.5	100.9
99	101.4	101.7
100	102.2	102.5

Source: The 2009 UP94 Pensioner Mortality Table with full projection, Ron Gebhardtsbauer, FSA, MAAA, Penn State University–Smeal College of Business.

Acknowledgments

I owe so much to so many. This book never could have been written without the patient help of a small army of experts in their fields. They generously sat for interviews and reinterviews, corrected and recorrected my drafts, helped me sort through ideas, and gently (or not so gently!) corrected me when I got things wrong. I never cried on the phone to them but sometimes I came close. Any remaining errors of fact or judgment are my own.

For the chapter on Social Security, I'm indebted to Bill Reichenstein, professor of investments at the Hankamer School of Business, Baylor University, in Waco, Texas. He's coauthor, with William Meyer, of the slim and skillful book *Social Security Strategies: How to Optimize Retirement Benefits*. Together they're principals in the firm SocialSecuritySolutions.com, a service that helps you choose your best strategy for taking benefits. A special shout-out to the firm's Robin Brewton, vice president of client services and master of answers to technical questions. Thank you, Robin!

Thanks, too, to economist Russell Settle, now retired from a professorship at the University of Delaware. Russ is a founder of SocialSecurityChoices.com, also a service that helps you collect the maximum from your Social Security account. And yet more thanks to economist Larry Kotlikoff, founder of MaximizeMySocialSecurity

.com. His service helps people optimize not only their Social Security claims but their disability claims, too. Larry is a professor at Boston University and coauthor, with Philip Moeller and Paul Solman, of *Get What's Yours: The Secrets to Maxing Out Your Social Security*. You'll find his online financial planning service at ESPlanner.com.

For health-care policy information, there is no better source than the Henry J. Kaiser Family Foundation (KFF.org). The health insurance chapter was read by Karen Pollitz, senior fellow for health reform and private insurance, and Patricia Neuman, senior vice president and director of the foundation's Program on Medicare Policy. They both greatly improved my understanding of how these programs work. KaiserHealthNews.org is the top source on the Web for what's going on with Medicare, Medicaid, medical costs, state health policies, and the Affordable Care Act. I check it every day.

Many eyes scoured the chapter on annuities. My thanks to Moshe Milevsky, associate professor of finance at York University's Schulich School of Business in Toronto and widely recognized as a leader in the field. Mark Cortazzo of the MACRO Consulting Group in Parsippany, New Jersey, has extensive on-the-ground experience with evaluating annuities and helping people make decisions. Jack Marrion of Advantage Compendium Ltd. read the section on index annuities (confession: We didn't always agree but I'm grateful for his help in my getting the facts straight). Hersh Stern, founder of ImmediateAnnuities.com, was my expert reader on immediate-pay annuities.

For life insurance, I had the help of three distinguished fee-only insurance advisers: Glenn Daily (glenndaily.com), based in New York City; Scott Witt (WittActuarialServices.com) in New Berlin, Wisconsin; and James Hunt (EvaluateLifeInsurance.org) in Concord, New Hampshire. They guided me through the pages that provide readers with advice for specific personal situations.

The chapter on retirement plans was vetted by Ed Slott (IRAHelp .com), author of *Ed Slott's Retirement Decisions Guide*, and James

Lange (PayTaxesLater.com), author of *Retire Secure!: A Guide to Getting the Most Out of What You've Got.*

For advice on tapping home equity, my thanks to Peter Bell, president and CEO of the National Reverse Mortgage Lenders Association, and Jack Guttentag, professor of finance emeritus at the Wharton School of the University of Pennsylvania. Jack's website, mtgprofessor.com, is the most comprehensive source I know for good consumer information about mortgages of all types.

The investment chapters passed through the hands of the reigning gurus of withdrawal rate research: Michael Kitces, director of wealth management of the Pinnacle Advisory Group in Columbia, Maryland (kitces.com); Wade Pfau, a professor of retirement income at American College in Bryn Mawr, Pennsylvania (RetirementResearcher.com); Jonathan Guyton of Cornerstone Wealth Advisors in Edina, Minnesota (cornerstonewealthadvisors.com); and financial planner Bill Bengen of El Cajon, California, author of the original 4 percent withdrawal rule (now retired). I highly recommend Mike's and Wade's websites for all the newest information related to retirement income research.

These chapters also benefited from the wisdom of retirement researcher and financial planner Joe Tomlinson (josephtomlinson .com); financial planner Harold Evensky, cofounder of Evensky & Katz/Foldes Financial (ek-ff.com) in Coral Gables, Florida; Wesley McCain, founder and chair of Towneley Capital Management, based in Laguna Hills, California; Elisabeth Kashner, senior vice president of analytics for ETF.com; investment manager William Bernstein for EfficientFrontier.com, author of several thoughtful investment books; and Rick Ferri (PortfolioSolutions.com), founder of the investment management firm Portfolio Solutions and expert on low-cost index fund investing, and Jack Reed (johntreed.myshopify.com), whose books are bibles for people investing in rental real estate.

To help me make technical issues clear, I had a test audience—readers who aren't financial professionals: my longtime friend, Judy

Hole, who spent her career as an exceptional TV producer for CBS News; my sister, Laurie Young, an expert editor, who, among her many other talents, murders extra commas; and my brother, Bob Bryant, who loves to investigate investment theories. They're all at the stage of life where the issues raised in this book matter to them personally. They read the chapters when I thought they were in finished form. Whenever a sentence or paragraph confused them, I hurried to set it right.

And thanks, extravagantly, to my husband, Carll Tucker, founder and chair of the online local news company DailyVoice.com and author of *The Bear Went Over the Mountain*, about America's presidents and vice presidents. Carll is a splendid reader and editor. This is the third book he has suffered through with me, for which he has earned a Top Husband medal from this author and wife.

Index

Underscored page references indicate tables.

M